DESPATCHES FROM THE GULF WAR

DESPATCHES FROM THE GULF WAR

EDITED BY

BRIAN MacARTHUR

BLOOMSBURY

First published in Great Britain 1991
This anthology copyright © 1991 by Brian MacArthur

This paperback edition published 1991

The moral right of the author has been asserted

Bloomsbury Publishing Ltd, 2 Soho Square, London W1V 5DE

A CIP catalogue record for this book
is available from the British Library

ISBN 0 7475 1 0539

Typeset by Hewer Text Composition Services, Edinburgh
Printed in England by Clays Ltd, St Ives plc

CONTENTS

THE AFTERMATH

CARTOONS AND ILLUSTRATIONS

ACKNOWLEDGEMENTS

The editor gratefully acknowledges the help and co-operation of the following in compiling *Despatches from the Gulf War*: Andrew Neil and James Adams of the *Sunday Times*; Max Hastings, editor in chief of the *Daily Telegraph* and the *Sunday Telegraph*; Simon Jenkins, Peter Roberts and Ralph Nodder of *The Times*; Charles Burgess and Diana Pepper of the *Independent* and the *Independent on Sunday*; Peter Preston and Gerald Knight of the *Guardian*; Donald Trelford and David Randall of the *Observer*; Don Short of Solo Syndication (the *Daily Mail* and the *Mail on Sunday*); Kelvin MacKenzie and William Newman of the *Sun*; Simon Courtauld and Simon Heffer of the *Spectator*; Peter Brooks, Nicholas Garland, Michael Heath, Gerald Scarfe, Colin Wheeler, Steve Bell, Trouw Kwartet and Wally Fawkes (Trog); Graham Cross of Colorific; Susannah Clapp of the *London Review of Books*; Anita Covert and Lynda Arnold of the *Wall Street Journal*; Elizabeth Newnham of Intercontinental Features; the Cartoonists and Writers Syndicate; Pat Vaughan; Sir Anthony Parsons, Stephen Sackur and Edward Said; Edward Luttwak; John Pilger, Phillip Knightley, Norman Stone, Paul Foot, Denis Healey, Roy Hattersley, Bernard Levin and Lynn Moorlen.

INTRODUCTION

'Something's happening out there,' said Bernard Shaw. 'We see the sky lightening up to the south with anti-aircraft fire. It looks like a million fireflies, sparklers on the Fourth of July. There's a huge red rose explosion lighting up the sky. Holy Cow, that was a huge outburst.'

When the bombing started, the news was broken to the world by the excited voices of Bernard Shaw, John Holliman and Peter Arnett, the Cable News Network team on the ninth floor of the Rashid Hotel in Baghdad.

More than five months after Saddam Hussein's invasion of Kuwait, the air war had begun and a million allied troops were ready and waiting in Saudi Arabia to liberate Kuwait when the bombers' work of destroying the Iraqis' will to fight was done. The allies' strategy for dealing with the Iraqi Army was put with memorable succinctness by General Colin Powell: 'First we're going to cut it off, then we're going to kill it.'

The months of negotiation and United Nations diplomacy were suddenly and abruptly over. Muddling through with sanctions – the strategy urged by, among others, Edward Heath, Denis Healey, Gerald Kaufman and the *Guardian* – wasn't working fast enough. Every overture for peace had been rejected by Saddam. So we were on our way to the new world order set out by President Bush with enthusiastic support from Margaret Thatcher and John Major as well as most of the House of Commons, where, as Roy Hattersley reports, MPs opposing the war were shouted down. There was going to be no Munich in 1991.

Apart from a *Sunday Times* editorial of August 1990 setting out the case for war against Saddam in the terms that became official policy, this anthology starts with the debate about the justness of the war that arose within Britain even as its inevitability was becoming obvious in January. Against the denunciations of John Pilger and Paul Foot from the left, the war was sanctioned as just not only by Dr Robert Runcie, Archbishop of Canterbury, but also by almost the entire British press

– exemplified by *The Times* or such liberal commentators as Hugo Young of the *Guardian*.

The war proceeded in distinct phases. At first, the nation revelled in the heroic demeanour of the RAF pilots – at their bravery as well as their frank confessions of fear. Then Saddam's Scuds were launched on Israel and Saudi Arabia – and the West prayed that Israel would not respond. After the overkill of reporting in newspapers and on television, a period followed when the story moved off the front pages, the soldiers waited and the airmen carried on their thousands of missions over Iraq. There was the foray at Khafji and then, the moment when Saddam scored a propaganda coup and started worrying Western public opinion, the bombing of the Baghdad bunker. The land war itself was over almost before the reporters on the frontline could get their despatches back to Britain.

After the war was over there were scores to be settled with the doubters; the discovery of the horrors of Saddam's torture chambers in Kuwait as well as the Kuwaitis' revenge on the Palestinians; the first reports of the devastation wrought on the retreating Iraqi Army at Mutla Ridge; and then Saddam's revenge on the Kurds. The long aftermath of the war still goes on – and the new world order seems even farther away.

Yet that vivid report from CNN at midnight on January 16, which was captured so well by Nancy Banks-Smith, was a singularly appropriate start to the first major war fought in the electronic global village created by satellite television news stations whose broadcasts are watched simultaneously throughout the world. As the war – often potently and controversially – demonstrated, we are also living in a village whose global purveyors of news acknowledge no concept of national interest and who broadcast from behind 'enemy' lines.

Whose 'side' is CNN on when it was being watched simultaneously that night by President Bush in the White House and Saddam Hussein in his Baghdad bunker, as well as John Major in 10 Downing Street, President Gorbachev in the Kremlin and the exiled Emir of Kuwait in Saudi Arabia? The debate about the power and the responsibility of television stations during a war is reflected throughout the following pages. That power was often condemned as the war was fought – but when the war was over its power in arousing world opinion to the plight of the Kurds, forcing Bush and Major into action to set up safe havens, was applauded.

This was the first war in which television was constantly used as a diplomatic weapon. As the diplomatic manoeuvrings went on after the invasion of Kuwait on August 2, George Bush at one time became so worried that he was losing the 'CNN War' against Baghdad that he called in Roger Ailes, his presidential campaign media guru, to help his propaganda battle against Saddam.

The CNN war worked both ways. Every move by Bush was broadcast simultaneously to Baghdad and Kuwait; every Iraqi statement was broadcast instantly to the United States. The Pentagon used CNN to send messages to Saddam. A CNN reporter was even allowed to fly in a F-15 and photograph the weapons and radar system in action. The message was loud and clear: Watch out, Saddam. When Saddam wanted to frighten Bush, he gave CNN two hours warning so that CNN could clear its schedule and carry the broadcast live to the White House. As the Iraqis took their Western hostages, the message back was equally loud and clear: We've got a human shield.

A war in which television plays so powerful a role raises profoundly difficult issues for the military and the politicians as well as the civilian spectators. On the part of the military, they undoubtedly make the case for censorship and strict control of reporters' movements more persuasive than ever. Why, by meeting the demand for open information from journalists – and, it should be said, the citizens for whom they write and broadcast – should they betray their plans to the enemy and risk defeat for which they will then be roundly condemned?

Censorship, however, was an issue that was muffled during this war, mainly because, unlike the situation during the Suez crisis of 1956, there was virtual unanimity in the House of Commons and Fleet Street about the justness of the war. Opinion polls showing that eight out of ten Britons supported the war suggested that MPs and editors were in tune with public opinion. Only a few lonely voices, such as those of Pilger, Foot and Edward Pearce, were raised against Andrew Neil, editor of the *Sunday Times*, or Max Hastings, editor of the *Daily Telegraph*, the most committed supporters of the allied cause (apart from the jingoistic *Sun* and *Daily Star*). Liberal commentators such as Hugo Young, Neal Ascherson of the *Independent on Sunday* or Michael Ignatieff of the *Observer* each became reluctant supporters.

All editors were obviously aware, as Max Hastings argued in a speech to the Royal Television Society, that for every Pilger or Foot, there were ten thousand readers or viewers bitterly critical of any perceived disloyalty to the allied cause or any apparently helpful gesture to the enemy. 'Collective conceit' was the journalists' greatest peril, Hastings declared. 'If we seem to walk with arrogance and matter-of-factness when others are dying and taking life and death decisions, we shall command no respect from soldiers or political leaders or the public. We must earn their respect by sharing the humility most of them feel, in the face of the greatest challenge for any journalist, the reporting of human conflict.'

So the strict ground rules that governed what was reported were observed with only a few exceptions and the war was reported on the terms dictated by the military. The land war was also so brief that the system of censorship was never put under any real strain. 'There is an obvious danger that publication of authoritative information about the operations, current and/or future, of British or allied forces could unwittingly jeopardise their success,' said the guidelines issued by the British Ministry of Defence.

'Similarly, information about other preparations relevant to operations – for example, the location and movement of units; logistic activity; command appointments – could give the enemy vital clues. It will often be desirable to give as much information as the operational situation permits, as early as possible to counter rumour and speculation which might portray a situation far worse than it is. Nevertheless there is a danger that specific information about ship or aircraft movements, or about the extent of damage to fighting units, could be of advantage to an enemy, either by disclosing weaknesses that might otherwise be unrealised or by confirming what was otherwise uncertain.'

As the television channels devoted hours a day to reporting and analysis, especially when there was a scarcity of hard news, a reaction quickly set in against the notion of war as armchair theatre, particularly since it was a theatre where the viewers rarely got a seat in the front row, could discern the plot or see any live action from the real actors. Unlike the Falklands, however, journalists did eventually get to the front line in combat teams and several reports from the battlefield are included in this anthology.

Given the power of television, the military's power to censor was undoubtedly abused, whether by the allies whose briefings emphasised the deadly power of their bombing but not its failure rate, and by Saddam to weaken the allies' will to fight by emphasising civilian casualties and trying to push Western public opinion against the war. There was also, as Phillip Knightley pointed out, a new attempt to offer a sanitised version of war without death, to persuade the public that all the new smart technological weapons removed a lot of the horror of war. Yet what else should we expect from the military? It is naive to expect freedom of information during the conduct of a war in the age of global television – and the outcry after the bombing of the Baghdad bunker demonstrated all too powerfully for the military the volatility of public opinion.

Steve Anderson, a BBC Newsnight producer who worked with correspondents in the Gulf, wrote later in the *British Journalism Review* that the basic lesson that the military existed to win wars, not win awards for journalists, had still not been fully absorbed. 'Flexibility is the key to any military success, regardless of whether this renders a lot of journalistic effort useless. If it happens to smother the publication of important and potentially controversial news in the process, then so much the better. Perhaps after the Gulf war, journalists and their bosses will exercise a proper scepticism when they are offered a special level of access by the military. Let's hope that is the case. I remain to be convinced.'

The result was that throughout the war we saw only fragments of the truth from both sides – and almost continuous television only added to the fog of war as a seemingly endless stream of commentators wrestled to interpret the progress of a war about which they knew next to nothing because of military censorship. We still do not know the success rate of all those thousands of allied bombing raids on Iraq. Yet they were clearly less successful than was suggested by what was carefully shown on televised news briefings. Nor do we yet know the true role of the bombed Baghdad bunker.

The bombing of that bunker and the pictures of sobbing mothers round the corpses visibly shook experienced reporters such as Brent Sadler and Jeremy Bowen and created the most passionate media controversy of the war, accentuated by the issue of whether British reporters should be behind enemy lines. What would have happened to the British bulldog in 1944, asked the critics, if Richard Dimbleby had been reporting from Dresden and Cologne? Neutrality favoured the dictator.

The answer is that it is the job of journalists to tell the truth, even when it hurts. Lies do much more damage. It is also an insult to the innate commonsense of the people to suggest that they cannot cope with the truth or recognise that there are always civilian casualties in war. Still more persuasive in the global village, especially in democracies, is the question why one combatant nation should alone be singled out and isolated from the truth when it is being broadcast throughout the world? As for the argument from the Second World War, that was well seen off by Robert Harris in the *Sunday Times*,

SATURATION BOMBING

who pointed out not only that British bombers would have switched from civilian to military targets but also that the war would have been over sooner.

The British turned to television as their main source of news during the war. Even a war could not topple soap operas such as *Eastenders*, *Coronation Street* and *Neighbours* from the top of the television ratings but news bulletins were watched on several evenings by more than 20 million viewers compared with the 15 million who were buying national daily newspapers. Twelve of the top 30 BBC programmes in Week One were news broadcasts. Yet television brought more heat than light from the Gulf, as Christopher Dunkley, its television critic, noted in the *Financial Times*. 'When you think about it carefully, you realise that television has offered only the sketchiest idea of what is happening in Iraq or anywhere else.' Television's mission to explain was taken to its outer limit and at times scored an own goal by developing a bias against understanding. Newspapers therefore remained a more satisfactory medium for trying to understand what was going on in the theatre of war than the armchair voyeurism of television.

So at a time when the reputation of Fleet Street has rarely been lower, what is remarkable about the journalism in this anthology is its sheer quality. That quality is shown in the power and the passion of the debate between the left and right of Fleet Street – a debate that was more potently argued in the press than in the Commons.

That debate provoked some settling of scores after the war was over, particularly in the *Sunday Times* and the *Daily Telegraph*, where John Keegan accused such television opinion-makers as Jeremy Paxman and the Dimbleby brothers of chipping away at sober military experts in a condescending and incredulous tone and of a petulant demonstration not to learn. Strategy, Keegan argued, was not a matter of opinion. The settling of scores is reflected towards the end of the book.

The quality of British journalism was also demonstrated in the vivid reporting from the battlefields by the men and women who were catching history on the hoof. Just tell the story, a news editor once said when I was wrestling with a complex news report. The reporters with the soldiers and airmen in the Gulf just told their stories. How well they still read – and this book is dedicated to them.

WAR AIMS

WAR AIMS

Sunday Times, August 26, 1990

War in the Gulf is imminent. So it is important that the United States and its allies formulate their war aims and articulate them clearly. There is no mystery about what they should be. First, the defence and long-term security of Saudi Arabia and the Gulf states. Second, the liberation of Kuwait. Third, the toppling of Saddam Hussein and the destruction of Iraq's ability to develop and deploy chemical and nuclear weapons. If the military might being assembled in the Gulf fails to realise all three of these war aims, then America and its allies will have lost the war, no matter the short-term victories it may score.

The immediate threat to Saudi Arabia and the Gulf states has largely been thwarted thanks to President George Bush's speedy mobilisation of the international resistance to Saddam. Though the American forces on the ground are still somewhat vulnerable, because of their lack of tanks and anti-tank weapons, to a mass onslaught of Iraqi tanks, the United States probably has enough air firepower in the region to deter any Iraqi attack. The priority is no longer to contain Saddam but to roll him back, then secure his demise. The long-term security of Saudi Arabia, the rest of the Gulf, and much else, depends on that.

The next step, therefore, is to retake Kuwait. It makes both political and military sense to do this first, before moving on to Saddam. Kuwait is the clearly aggrieved party in the Gulf crisis, an essentially defenceless small country stolen in the middle of the night by the local bully. Its liberation will command widespread international support, and it can be done without a full-frontal assault on the substantial Iraqi forces dug in along the Kuwait-Saudi border. The likely American tactic is an amphibious and air invasion of Kuwait City, which would also cut off the supply lines of the Iraqi forces on the border; these would then be pummelled into submission by American airpower.

It is a military venture fraught with danger both for the American forces and the Western residents still left in Kuwait. But with luck and good planning it could succeed with the minimum of casualties. President Bush has said that the American aim is to restore the Emir of Kuwait to power. But that should only happen if that is what the Kuwaitis want. The proper American aim is self-determination for Kuwait, and a prerequisite of that is obviously the removal of Saddam's forces. Once that is done it should be up to the Kuwaitis to decide what sort of government they want.

The Pentagon estimates that it will have the men and materials in position to do the Kuwaiti job by the first week in September. But it is ready to act if Iraqi troops move to harm Western diplomats or residents in Kuwait. The American hope is that the loss of Kuwait, coupled with the recent surrender of all Saddam's gains in the Iran-Iraq war, will so discredit him in his generals' eyes that they will rise up and depose him. Fine if it happens, though his demise would have to be coupled with the destruction of his worst weapons of war and the reduction of the Iraqi army to a less threatening size. But if Saddam survives the loss of Kuwait, the Americans are ready to move on Iraq to ensure his downfall. The taking of Kuwait may involve such a conflagration that an attack on Iraq may become inevitable anyway.

This is the most controversial war aim, but it is also the most significant for the future peace of the Gulf and the security of the West. All the usual voices in the West will oppose it, so it is important to realise now why they will be wrong. Saddam must go not because he is a tyrant, though anybody who reads Republic of Fear, which starts on the front of this section, can be left in no doubt that, thanks largely to him, Iraq is a hellhole of repression, savagery and brutality, and that the world will be a much better place when he no longer holds sway over anybody. But Saddam is not the only despot left in the world (though on any list he would be in the front rank), and the United States is not proposing to use force to topple the others.

Saddam must be removed because he is a tyrant with expansionist ambitions to spread his tyranny across the Middle East – a goal which would clearly be against the interests of the West and its Gulf allies. He must be removed now, because if he survives the current crisis he will steal again, and again, until he has realised his ambitions, and next time nobody will be able to stop him.

Saddam is close to realising his dream of a nuclear arsenal. Just as important, he is developing the missile technology to deliver both chemical and nuclear weapons over great distances. Those who

4

would wish to negotiate with him, either before or after Kuwait has been liberated, need to explain how, after some sort of negotiated settlement, the West would handle his next rape of an innocent nation, say in two or three years' time, when he will have intimidated the rest of the Gulf into raising oil prices so that he will have more money to pour into his chemical and nuclear weapons programmes. It must be clear to any but the most muddle-headed that Saddam has to be removed now, and that any resolution of the Gulf crisis which leaves him in power and his military machine intact would leave the Gulf at his mercy.

Of course, to achieve all three war aims could be costly. But not to do so could prove priceless. Casualties will be kept down if America pursues its war aims with all the military force that it takes, applied decisively. To settle for some lesser route would only prolong the crisis and ensure many more casualties later. President Bush seems to realise this (though not all his allies do), which is why he has provided the resolute leadership the West and its friends in the Gulf require. When the shooting starts there will be plenty of voices on both sides of the Atlantic calling for an early cease-fire so that more limited war aims can be negotiated. Western public opinion needs to keep in mind that, vital as it is to defend Saudi Arabia and important as it is to liberate Kuwait, if the Gulf crisis of 1990 ends with Saddam still in power in Baghdad and Iraq's nascent nuclear and existing chemical weapon capabilities intact, America and its allies will have made a mistake of historic proportions that will haunt them well into the next century.

STILL TIME TO ESCAPE ARMAGEDDON

Denis Healey

Observer, January 6, 1991

In just over a week the United Nations deadline for Iraq's withdrawal from Kuwait expires. Even if Saddam Hussein orders his troops out today, it will be physically impossible for him to meet that deadline. Then what?

President Bush has indicated that he will immediately start a war to force Iraq out of Kuwait, although his generals have told him they will not be ready for at least another month. This is not what the Security Council prescribes. In fact, it is directly contrary to the words of Resolution 678, which he invokes to justify such action.

The Resolution authorises member states 'to use all necessary means to uphold and implement Resolution 660' – which calls for Iraq's withdrawal from Kuwait – 'and to restore international peace and security in the area'. The sort of war the president plans to fight is not only unnecessary; it is totally incompatible with the restoration of peace and security in the area.

There are now a million armed men on both sides, with nearly 8,000 tanks and 3,000 aircraft between them. The war would start with Western bombing raids on military installations all over Iraq, from Basra to Mosul. Washington estimates there could be 100,000 Iraqi casualties, mainly civilian. The land attack on Kuwait which is planned to follow could not guarantee success. The British colonel of the Engineers on the spot has said that the Iraqi obstacles could 'almost certainly stop a Western advance'. An attack from the sea would require a devastating bombardment of Kuwait City which would leave few of its remaining inhabitants alive. A war could indeed, as the US General Schwarzkopf admitted, 'last a long time and kill a lot of people'.

And if, in the end, Iraq was defeated, would that 'restore peace and security in the area'? On the contrary. At best the Gulf would once again be dominated by Iran – to prevent which the West supported Saddam Hussein with arms for eight years. At worst Syria, Turkey and Iran would fight over the corpse of Iraq, while the Kurdish people tried to establish their own state in the ruins.

The political and economic consequences of such a war would spread far beyond the Middle East. Those Arab regimes which had supported the war would be swept away by their own peoples; their successors would turn their arms against the West, like Khomeini after the fall of the Shah. We might see a holy war uniting the whole of the Muslim world from Morocco to Indonesia.

At best a war would push the price of oil up to $50 a barrel for about a year – producing a world recession, crippling the hope of recovery in Eastern Europe, and plunging the Third World into catastrophe just as 15 million Africans are threatened with death by famine. At worst, if Iraq burns out the 100 Kuwaiti oilwells an contaminates Saudi oil facilities with mustard gas and anthrax, there would be a global ecological disaster and a great slump worse than the 1930s.

Even to contemplate a war which might have such consequences points to a stupefying lack of proportion, at a time when the world is wrestling with new and formidable problems on every continent after the end of the Cold War. Yet no one has demonstrated that such a war is 'necessary', as is required by the Security Council resolution.

Indeed, the hearings held recently by the US Congress – which, to its shame, the British Parliament has failed to emulate – produced an array of experienced witnesses who not only argued that a war would be disastrous but also that sanctions should be given a chance to work. Besides men who had earlier been defence secretaries and national security advisers, such as McNamara, Schlesinger, Bundy and Brzezinski, the same line was taken by both of General Powell's predecessors as chairmen of the Joint Chiefs of Staff, Admiral Crowe and General Jones.

How can President Bush escape from the corner into which he has painted himself?

First, he must give sanctions time to work. James Schlesinger said that Washington started sanctions in August knowing they would take a year to have a decisive effect. Even the leading hawk, Secretary of Defence Richard Cheney, admits that by Easter the Iraqi forces will be running out of spares; they are already short of the chemical additives needed to convert crude oil into fuel and lubricants for tanks and aircraft. William Webster, as head of the CIA, has predicted that Iraq's aircraft will be in severe difficulties in three to six months, and the rest of Iraq's equipment within nine. The British Air Commander, Air Chief Marshal Sir Patrick Hine, has therefore argued that 'sanctions should be given several months or longer to take effect'.

That would mean waiting until next autumn before considering military action, when, if it is necessary, its chance of rapid success would be far greater. As General Schwarzkopf said: 'If the alternative to dying is sitting out in the sun another summer, that's not a bad alternative.'

Meanwhile, we should use the time thus gained for far more active diplomacy to spell out how we hope to 'restore peace and security to the area'. The allies spelt out the post-war settlement at Yalta and Potsdam even while they were demanding unconditional surrender of Germany and Japan. Politically, we must undertake to implement Resolution 242 on the Palestine problem. A long-term solution of the Iraq-Kuwaiti dispute, involving the islands and the tip of the Rumaila oilfield, has already been proposed by Defence Minister Sultan of Saudi Arabia.

There must be discussion among all concerned – except Iraq at this stage – of a new security framework in the Gulf area, perhaps modelled on the European security conference as Douglas Hurd has proposed, perhaps through the Arab League with UN guarantees as suggested by William Waldegrave. Iran, however, must have a place.

Most important, there must be a serious attempt to deal with the arms race in the Middle East. Iraq already has chemical and biological weapons and is developing nuclear weapons; according to the Pentagon, Saudi Arabia is trying to acquire nuclear weapons from China. The sale of conventional arms should also be strictly controlled.

Given the political fragility of many Middle Eastern regimes and the lessons the West has been taught by Iran and Iraq, it seems incredible that the United States, Britain and France still regard the Middle East as a sound market for their arms. If there are to be controls on Arab weapons, however, there must also be control on Israeli weapons, however unwelcome this may be for Congress.

Simply to list the agenda for Middle East diplomacy is to illustrate its difficulties. All the more reason to get down to it immediately and to forswear a war which would make everything infinitely more intractable. President Mitterrand's proposal for a new Security Council meeting gives us the chance to make a start this week.

THE SELF-IMPORTANCE
OF SADDAM

Edward N. Luttwak

Times Literary Supplement, January 18, 1991

As I write, Iraqi troops are still in occupation of Kuwait and war is imminent. His perceived power hugely inflated by the very magnitude of the coalition assembled against him, and even more by the absurdly disproportionate war preparations made by the United States (a further *million* reservists have just been listed for possible mobilisation), the sometime village ruffian, would-be murderer of dictators and dictatorial murderer Saddam Hussein is still alive, and still pretending to be both the residual legatee of the inherently secular Ba'ath movement and a fiery Islamic activist; both the greatest exponent of an exclusively Arab nationalism and the caring father of Iraq's Kurds; both the aspiring Arab-Israeli peacemaker and the leading advocate of immediate war against Israel; both the protector of all Arab interests and the advocate of a redistribution of Arab oil revenues throughout the Third World.

It was undoubtedly Saddam Hussein alone who abruptly decided to invade Kuwait. Having pursued extortion by public threats, once the Kuwaitis failed to tremble he probably felt compelled to punish them by invasion – just as any Mafia boss must remedy by murder any failure of intimidation, lest he be murdered himself by his *sottocapi* exposed to evidence of successful defiance.

Yet Saddam Hussein's conduct also embodied the confluence of two long-established agencies of disorder; and the crisis moreover was magnified by an accident of timing. For matters could well have been resolved more quickly and more cleanly if Iraq had not collided with a United States and a president just unbalanced by complete victory in the Cold War – a victory that as always yielded its own paradoxical punishment, i.e., the obsolescence of the very attributes and instruments that allowed the outcome to be so completely successful.

The first of these agencies is the cruel joke of geology that during the present stage of the world's economic development places large and totally disposable oil revenues in the hands of grotesque tyrannies that might otherwise be prevented from projecting their foibles and misdeeds beyond municipal boundaries. It is not that oil revenues are all that vast. Austria has roughly twice the gross national product of Iraq, while the Swiss GNP is more than twice as great as Saudi Arabia's, even after the vast increase in the price of oil abruptly induced by the crisis itself. But oil revenues are different. They do not have to be extracted by taxes levied on populations whose consent is likely to be the more necessary in the degree that there is more to extract. However imperfectly earned prosperity and political participation may be correlated, great divergence is rare. Oil revenues by contrast are simply telexed into government bank accounts.

Where democratic governance is feeble or absent, as in some of the oil-exporting countries of Latin America, Black Africa and Asia but seemingly always and everywhere in the Middle East, oil monies can be spent by tyrannical rulers as they desire – and what rulers, with what desires! Saddam Hussein is uniquely evil, we are told, an Adolf Hitler *redivivus*, presumably entirely different from the other Arab oil rulers now deemed not merely respectable but actually worthy of the world's protection. But in his desires at least, Saddam Hussein is not different at all.

He has reportedly built inordinately opulent palaces for himself filled with the costliest furnishings, but so have the rulers of Saudi Arabia, Oman, Qatar, the United Arab Emirates and Kuwait itself – and Saddam Hussein can at least protest his singularity, while in Saudi Arabia alone there are some 2,000 princes who each claim their palace, with a great many having more than one. Washington's own Saudi prince, Bandar bin Sultan, a reputed intimate of President Bush and, in pre-crisis times, eloquent on the plight of the Palestinians 'living in tents', averted a similar fate for himself by acquiring the largest private mansion in the capital, and also had another house built in Aspen, Colorado, whose hugeness was only granted permission after a multi-million donation to that uniquely affluent municipality, a donation that might have come in handy in, say, Gaza. Palaces aside, there have been the yachts, the villas on the Riviera, the Mayfair apartments, the jewels, whores and assorted other fripperies of the Gulf-Arab carnival of consumption.

Other people's unearned high living easily arouses a pseudo-egalitarian indignation but is hardly criminal. Indeed luxury may be deemed virtuous in so far as it denies money to worse uses. For Saddam Hussein has also been far from exceptional in devoting enormous amounts of money to the purchase of weapons and the upkeep of military forces. For years now, not only Saudi Arabia and Libya but also small fry such as Oman have been purchasing the most elaborate and costly of all weapons of their respective categories – weapons happily and most irresponsibly sold to them by the United States and Britain as well as France and of course the Soviet Union, and indeed all others who could do so. Iraq's weapons are more dangerous to be sure, in the sense that the Iraqis can actually use them, and even maintain them in large degree. In fact when Western governments sell devastatingly powerful modern weapons to the equally lawless dictators and tribal rulers who command oil revenues, they proffer the incapacity of the recipients as their excuse, even while arguing that they have genuine defensive needs. It is the sort of thing that gives a bad name to cynicism.

That is how the US government justified the sale of the very latest F-18 fighter-bombers to Kuwait last year, and the British government still justifies the sale of Tornado strike-bombers to Saudi Arabia – whose absolutist rulers constantly profess their intention of using them against Israel, and who certainly violate every species of human rights every day, having just expelled and dispossessed more innocent Yemenis than there are Kuwaitis for Iraq to expel. There may be something in the incapacity argument and perhaps a great deal in some cases, but arms too *habent fata sua*. As I write, US pilots are in danger of being shot down by US Hawk missiles once sold to Kuwait.

Nor is Saddam Hussein unique in using oil revenues to promote terrorism – indeed that too is almost *de rigueur* in the region. Aside from the all too notorious Gadaffi, every murderous band has been able to raise funds in the Gulf, obviously with the consent of the rulers – with Kuwait being exceptionally generous. As for Saudi Arabia, its funds are more decisive than many realise in promoting the spread of an increasingly murderous religious extremism. When half-educated youths, disappointed by their failure to cope with modern life, revert to religion, all too often they find not the old village mosque and its benign customs but a new Saudi-financed urban structure, controlled by Saudi-financed preachers of Saudi-style Islam, rigidly puritanical, rigidly intolerant of any local, usually long-established *modus vivendi* with infidels. When the Christian Copts of Egypt, traditionalist Afghans, the Chinese and Hindus of Malaysia and Indonesia, and the animists and Christians of the Sudan come under attack, it is often the Saudi influence that is at work. Its revolting nature is more nakedly revealed at home by the arrogant denial of religious freedom, by the corporal punishment of beer drinkers on behalf of whisky-drinking princes, and by the intrusions of Saudi Arabia's 'religious police', whose members now reportedly break into houses of Westerners suspected of hosting parties in which drinks are served, and women are allowed to chat with men not their fathers and husbands. Such are the official practices now directly protected by more than 300,000 Americans in uniform, both male and female – as well as by the soldiers and airmen of Britain, France and other Western countries.

It is thus not only Iraq's violence that is magnified by all too disposable oil revenues, now an agency of disorder in the Middle East simply because they allow the otherwise incapable to inflict harm far and wide – often enough with Western assistance, always with a shameful Western connivance.

True enough, Saddam Hussein's regime is nevertheless different in being responsible for overt military aggression as well, and that owes much to the second agency of disorder, which adds the worst of ideological motives to dangerous means. Instant books as up to date as last week's headlines are now offered to explain Saddam Hussein's seizure of Kuwait (an example is John Bulloch and Harvey Morris's *Saddam's War*, an informative if shallow scissors-and-paste account which contains some useful minor observations and an interesting

11

intercept of an exchange between Saudi Arabian and Kuwaiti leaders). But the reader might gain a far deeper understanding from a brief essay first published almost two decades ago in which Saddam's name does not appear. The eponymous essay in Elie Kedourie's *Arab Political Memoirs* – a work of profound wisdom and surpassing elegance, not only in its style but also in the scientific sense of proving much with no more evidence than is needed – explains all that one needs to know of Saddam Hussein. For his mentality is that of the Ba'ath (renaissance) movement, neither new nor original to the man – and certainly not an 'Arab' mentality, that creation of Western Arabophiles (the most indulgent of friends, the worst of enemies) – which knows not ease or moderation but only strident militancy, not feasible hope but only reckless ambition, not a decent regard for self, family, neighbourhood or country but only an unlimited devotion to the glory of an imaginary entity (the Arab 'world') composed of all who speak any dialect philologically classified as Arabic.

Professor Kedourie recounts in the tragic voices of its disenchanted adherents how the ideology of the Ba'ath was born as an amalgam of now wholly discredited Western ideas – the more unbalanced fragments of Nietzsche, the racism of H.S. Chamberlain and Alfred Rosenberg, statalist socialism before its downfall, and exclusive nationalism in the rabid style of Eastern Europe. While far gentler nationalisms were sufficient to evoke the cohesion of most other Arab and non-Arab peoples seeking independence from colonial power and colonial influences, in Syria as well as Iraq with their varied ethnicities and religions, the virulent Ba'ath prescription offered a deceptive remedy for the lack of any organic solidarity. The creation of Alawite, Christian and Muslim schoolmasters during the 1930s, it attracted the thinly educated among journalists, aspiring writers, pharmacists, dentists, doctors and lawyers. After the Second World War it enrolled barely literate army officers and full-time party activists, who exiled, murdered or subjugated their party predecessors in both Syria and Iraq as soon as they seized power.

The Ba'ath is a fit ideology for Saddam Hussein, as it is for Hafez Assad of Syria, for it rationalises oppression as justice (justice for the Arabs only being obtainable by a very 'strong' government), tyranny as freedom (freedom for the Arabs only being obtainable by the unity of autocracy), and indeed death as the most valid expression of life – given that the highest purpose of life is to advance, by death if necessary, the cause of the Ba'ath: the renaissance of a mighty Arab power, indeed a superpower able to match the United States. Any reader of Kedourie's essay would have known that the travails of eight years of war with Iran would not suffice to induce Saddam Hussein to accord a decent interval of tranquillity to the long-suffering peoples of Iraq: neither the twenty years normally required to grow a new crop of young men ready to follow NCOs in battle, nor half that span. And he would have known too that when the United States intervened, Saddam Hussein would not retreat pleading *force majeure* as enough of a face-saving excuse, for a struggle with the United States is the most appropriate of confrontations for the mighty Arab power envisaged by the Ba'ath.

It is a pity that we have no Kedourie to instruct us in the mentality of George Bush. He too is still here, and still what he has been since Margaret Thatcher firmly instructed him in his responsibilities while both were in conference at Aspen, Colorado, on August 3, 1990 – not recognisably the President of the United States (an office with a great variety of duties both foreign and domestic), but rather a very able, very hard-working and totally concentrated full-time Persian Gulf 'crisis manager', with no president to report to.

A president would have avoided demeaning the office and himself by exchanging insults with Saddam Hussein; he would have avoided the wild hyperbole of the Hitler comparison – Iraq has not the capacity of the meanest province of Germany – and he would have kept matters in proportion by delegating diplomacy to the diplomats instead of doing it all himself on the telephone, for hours on end every day, for weeks on end. More substantively, a president mindful of the balance between his responsibilities would have concluded on, say, August 6, 1990, that the dominant priority was to end the crisis quickly, by bombing or by negotiations, or both – lest a prolonged crisis disturb the fragile economic equilibrium of the greatly indebted United States, precipitating a serious recession.

For by then it had been discovered that it was not only the Federal government that was on the edge of insolvency but also many state governments and almost all large municipalities; not only the notoriously mismanaged Savings and Loan companies but also a great many commercial banks, including several of the very largest; not only small-time issuers of 'junk bonds' but also famous airlines, celebrated department stores, most holders of commercial real property, leading industrial corporations and millions of home-owners with mortgages greater than their equity.

Instead, very much in the manner of the aristocrat still disdainful of the tradesmen pleading bills at his door as he sells yet more of the family's broad acres, Bush insisted in 'optimising' the management of the crisis, careless of time and cost, only mindful of diplomatic priorities, Arab sensibilities, and the fine coordination of UN and bilateral proceedings. Happily leaving behind all serious concern for the economy, and even more happily content to see photographs of Saddam Hussein replacing those of Neil Bush on the front pages, George Bush threw himself into crisis management on a full-time basis with boyish enthusiasm, barely turning aside to explain, most unconvincingly, the reason for it all.

Not that there was anything much to explain about the need to stop further aggression by Iraq, or indeed to punish its aggression by the prompt use of air-power. A vast majority of Americans readily agreed that 'a line in the sand' had to be drawn. Any post-war president would have done that, including Jimmy Carter. But ever since 1945 such lines have always been protected in numerous crises by deterrence from afar, albeit non-nuclear, not actively defended by troops on the ground except in Europe and Korea (there was no 'line' in Vietnam, nor an intervention decision as such, but only a gradual involvement). Had Bush resorted to deterrence he would have had nothing to explain. Had he then quickly proceeded to issue a withdrawal ultimatum, beginning to bomb Iraq as soon as it expired, that too would have been accepted by most Americans. Instead of deterrence and bombing, he chose defence by an expeditionary force, followed by waiting, and followed much later, from November 8, by the assembly of an army of reconquest.

Well before then, Bush was insistently pressed to explain why American 'boys' – and women, and reservist fathers and reservist mothers, had to be sent to Arabia of all places. After trying and failing to evoke support for the imperative of restoring the Al Sabah family over its enterprise of Kuwait, and keeping the Al Saud family in ownership of its own larger enterprise ('Americans do not die for princes', remarked the impeccably conservative Congressman Dornan), the Bush Administration tried the 'oil needs of the industrialised world' argument.

That collapsed very quickly, as two things soon became clear. First, that in what I have called the 'geo-economic' era, the earlier geopolitical imperative of providing cheap energy for the Western coalition in its struggle with the Soviet Union no longer applied. On the contrary, it was possible that the United States might gain in the new geo-economic era if its chief competitors, notably Germany and Japan, were burdened by higher energy costs. After all, the United

States would have to retool with capital and economic skills – in lieu of military power and diplomatic skills – to wage the struggle that will determine who will make the aircraft, computers, advanced materials and other high-added-value products of the next generation. Second, it soon became clear that the supposed beneficiaries of the American effort to secure their oil supplies, Germany, Japan and the rest of them, were (correctly) persuaded that the price of oil would continue to depend on the substitution cost (roughly $25 per barrel right now), and not on who or what controlled the oil of the Persian Gulf. Hence they flatly refused to contribute seriously to the effort, offering only pennies and uselessly symbolic frigates. It was indicative that only ever-faithful Britain, not a beneficiary of cheap oil at all, was willing to join the expedition in earnest, fundamentally for reasons neither economic nor geoeconomic. Operation 'Tin Cup', the begging visitation of Treasury Secretary Brady to Japan last September, has so far yielded a mere fraction of the $6.6 billion Matsushita has paid to purchase the entertainment company MCA (the second law of geo-economics: if you cannot make a better product, in this case than Hollywood film and US pop music, purchase the producers).

The Bush Administration did finally come up with a new, fully original justification for taking on Saddam Hussein ever so slowly, with troops on the ground, under the mantle of the UN: the (post-Cold War) 'New World Order'. When public opinion reacted very negatively, foolish television pundits explained that the idea was much too abstract for the untaught masses, which could not be expected to understand. Actually the public at large understood that most un-American notion all too well. The American people has never supported any kind of 'world order', old or new, but rather human rights, pluralism and democratic expression, all often subversive of 'order' in much of the world, and notably in the countries of Arabia being immediately defended. Had Americans supported world order, they could have had that commodity for the asking from the 1970s if not before, when the Soviet Union – then no mean hand at the game – offered a beautifully ordered condominium, with the noisome Chinese well isolated, and all others shared out between Washington and Moscow.

Furthermore, the particular world order being offered by the Bush Administration was that of the permanent members of the UN Security Council, namely a disintegrating Soviet dictatorship, the world's largest non-democracy of China, conniving, declining France, unconniving but declining Britain, and the United States itself, *sans* India, or Germany, or Japan. The notion was further discredited when the associations and obligations that the 'New World Order' entailed came to light. The United States in the person of George Bush had to sit on a divan if not get into bed with murderous Assad of Syria in its name and – much more important – it would have to prop up an increasingly weak, increasingly sinister Gorbachev and his crumbling USSR edifice, against Yeltsin and the other leaders of other organic nations emerging from under the rubble. It would also have to appease and humour the grim butchers of Tiananmen, thus assisting them in preserving their oppressive monopoly of power.

Such are the dissatisfactions that moderated the support of American public opinion and of the US Congress for the Bush Administration, much more than any partisan sentiment in House or Senate. And such is the conditionality of its *de facto* declaration of war against Iraq that any fighting beyond the use of air-power – certainly any serious ground fighting – would certainly exceed its stringent limits. Many in Congress have noted that ground fighting would not only kill Americans but would also end with the destruction of the Iraqi army, leaving the regime of Iran free to pursue Islamic policies of expansion, in lieu of having to defend its Farsi empire, and the regime of Syria also free to do its worst. In other words, as of now the only war that the Bush Administration can fight is an *inherently limited* war of air bombardment, which could have been fought as from the middle of last August, without need of all those tearfully separated reservists, or the vast deployment of army and Marines as a whole, nor the agonising prolongation of the crisis that has, as already said, hugely inflated the apparent importance, and self-importance, of Saddam Hussein.

NO CHOICE BUT WAR

The Times, January 16, 1991

Nothing on earth is so obscene as the prospect before the armies massed in the Gulf. Days are long past when nations gloried in war. Vast expenditure and constant effort are expended to avoid it. Rarely do they fail, but in the matter of Iraq's occupation of Kuwait, they have done so. Not since 1939 has an aggression left so clear a choice to those seeking a just international order. Blame for the failure of diplomacy since August 2 lies squarely with Iraq. Now, the only choice lies between capitulation to evil or a fight.

During most of yesterday only France's implausible and unilateral proposal to set aside United Nations resolutions if Iraq merely declared a vague intention to withdraw appeared to stand between President Saddam Hussein and the unleashing of an attack. But last night even that had collapsed. The alliance against Saddam consists of 28 Arab, Asian and Western nations, supported by a United Nations mandate. Of those nations, Britain has committed 34,000 troops, the largest force dispatched overseas since the Second World War. The most optimistic projections of a swift victory rely on the intensity with which battle is joined. That is the obscenity of war. That is why any nation, not least a democratic one, must know with great clarity to what end it is fighting.

Hobbes wrote that war is a condition, not necessarily of fighting, but of the absence of a 'common power to keep men in awe'. There has been no such common power in the Middle East since the end of colonialism. Hostilities began on August 2 last year, when Iraq invaded Kuwait. The outside world thus had a choice. It could have decided to treat the invasion as a local outrage, to be accepted like other unprovoked aggressions since 1945. Or it could decide to reassert Hobbes's common power through the medium that has since 1945 held that power uncertainly in its grasp, the United Nations. It could counter Saddam's crushing of an independent state, restore Kuwaiti independence and deter similar acts in future.

The decision to compel Iraq to leave Kuwait was near unanimous, in the Arab world and beyond. Even those with an aversion to foreign involvement in the Middle East, with an aversion to any alliance with Israel, wished Saddam out of Kuwait. The legal framework was meticulously laid in no fewer than 12 UN security council resolutions. These demanded Iraq's unconditional withdrawal and the restoration of Kuwait's legal government; they imposed sanctions, declared Iraq liable to compensate states and individuals, and in November set a seven-week deadline after which a 28-nation military coalition was authorised to use force.

Saddam has ignored all such external pressure, not only since August last year but since seizing absolute power in 1979. Iran was the victim of his aggression before Kuwait. The path to war today leads directly from the security council's failure to condemn that invasion in 1980 or to penalise Iraq for its illegal use of chemical

17

weapons against Iranian troops and Iraqi Kurds. Saddam has nothing but contempt for words and, as indicated in his treatment of Javier Pérez de Cuéllar on Sunday, for the UN as well.

Saddam's contempt for diplomacy has embraced every attempt to reason with him and even attempts at compromise which ran perilously close to rewarding him for his aggression. After six hours of talks with the American secretary of state in Geneva, Iraq's emissary disdained the word withdrawal, let alone the name of Kuwait, which Saddam has erased from the map while his troops and secret police convert the country into a wasteland of terror.

Señor Pérez de Cuéllar reportedly took to Baghdad proposals which, if not rewarding Saddam, would at least have offered him a modicum of dignity in climbing down. Without offering the notorious linkage of Kuwait with the Palestinians, he was in a position as UN secretary-general to point out that Middle East 'peace conferences' have been on the international agenda for years. They are fraught with difficulties of representation and substance, but forms of words might yet be found to enable progress to take place on such a conference, after a complete Iraqi withdrawal. Long-term regional security was a matter on which the UN also had constructive ideas. In none of this did Saddam or his emissaries show the slightest interest. They simply said they would not withdraw from Kuwait.

Having demanded Iraq's withdrawal, the UN security council had no other choice but to capitulate or to seek the means to enforce its will. These means embraced economic and military sanctions. That economic sanctions might have led Saddam to put his entire strategy into reverse has been moonshine from the start, though 'giving sanctions time to work' has become a depressing leitmotif of anti-war protests in recent weeks. The most that could be achieved by such sanctions was a weakening of Iraq's war effort, but since sanctions are seen by their proponents as an alternative to war, this was hardly a harsh stick. Economic sanctions do not achieve political goals. Against Cuba, Rhodesia, South Africa and Panama, they have tended to strengthen regimes in power and discipline their economies. The sanctions against Iraq may be the tightest ever, but nations enduring acute economic distress merely close ranks behind strong leaders.

Worse, the mere suggestion that months, possibly years, of sanctions might be 'needed' would have led Saddam to become ever more sure of his invincibility, and thus to a crumbling of the alliance and of the will to enforce compliance with UN resolutions. Some observers believe that sanctions were indeed 'working', largely on the evidence that there were shortages of consumer goods. Only those deluded by middle-class comforts could maintain that such shortages would induce the political trauma of a voluntary withdrawal by Saddam from Kuwait. Giving sanctions 'time to work' is an excuse for no war, excuse for surrender to Saddam's aggression and for the encouragement of the international anarchy of which he is so stark a symbol.

Even this argument does not exonerate those advocating war from justifying such an horrendeous course. The UN has authorised, not ordered, military action after 05.00 GMT today. Unless Iraq precipitates action by first striking Israel, as Saddam has threatened, the final decision to counter-attack rests with the allies. Each nation must ask itself whether the cause for which they will be fighting truly requires the ultimate sacrifice from its armies. The answer must begin with a clear understanding of what this war is not about.

British troops would not be fighting to defend British territory or British lives. Kuwait is a small and distant country of which, until it was overrun, most Britons knew little. The emirate was a peaceable country which never sought the headlines and whose conduct, unlike that of some of its Arab neighbours, was never so reprehensible as to invite them.

Nor would this be a war for democracy. The goal of the alliance is to restore the legitimate government of Kuwait, a non-constitutional monarchy. Kuwait has experimented with elect parliamentary democracy, albeit on a tightly limited all-male franchise, but at the moment of invasion its parliament had been dissolved by the emir and the press was censored. The West may hope that once restored to his throne, the emir will heed demands for political reform. Such reform cannot be imposed on him.

A by-product of an allied victory in Kuwait could be to overthrow one of the world's most unscrupulous and savage tyrants. So much the better, if so, but the objectives in this war are more limited. As laid down by international law, they are the reversal of Iraq's aggression and restoration of Kuwait's integrity, though conflict would be difficult to contain geographically and attacks on targets inside Iraq would be militarily inevitable. Only if Iraq resorts to chemical or biological warfare would Saddam have put his conduct so beyond the pale as to invite outright defeat on his own territory.

19

Iraq may have laid waste Kuwait, robbing, torturing and murdering its citizens. Retribution is for civilian, not military, justice.

To be sure, the war would be about wealth, notably the wealth and the power represented by oil. Iraq invaded because Kuwait was wealthy, and in that wealth lay the key to satisfying Saddam's ambition to dominate the 'Arab nation'. But what is really at stake in the Gulf is not oil supplies – useless to Iraq unless put on the market – but the manner in which disputes between states are to be resolved. In almost all cases, they are settled by diplomacy. Kuwait offers no such remedy.

Even before August 2, Saddam posed a threat to the balance of power in the Middle East with such formidable military capacity that Western governments had already begun to think him too powerful to quarantine. If Iraq is not stopped now, no Arab government would dare resist its aggrandisement. Iraq's neighbours are no match for its army. Blackmail backed by such power – paid for with oil – would suffice to establish Iraq's imperium through the Middle East, always threatening the security of the region, good countries and bad alike.

Saddam could exert his blackmail in many directions, some plausibly, some perhaps less so. He could compel the West to abandon Israel, for example, or demand deliveries of sensitive nuclear and military technology. The almost certain consequence of a failure to stop him would be another war later, possibly against more formidable odds. The unscrupulousness of the international arms business knows no ethics. In a few years, London as well as Tel Aviv and Riyadh could come within range of Iraqi missile attack, conventional, chemical or nuclear.

Both international morality and self-interest thus justify a counter-offensive against Iraq, in the words of the United Nations pledge 'to save succeeding generations from the scourge of war'. For once, the UN's most senior members clearly possess both the means and the will collectively to enforce international order against a threat, precisely the objective so long espoused by the 'peace movement'.

The Cold War has ended with the collapse of communism in Eastern Europe and the relative decline in Soviet power. This does not guarantee a more stable world. In East Europe, where Soviet-imposed certainties have disappeared and democratic institutions have yet to take root, there is danger enough. Further afield, the superpower balance may soon be seen to have restrained more conflict than it inflamed. Governments may be more tempted to attack their neighbours if free of the threat of superpower intervention.

The coalition ranged against Iraq represents a step towards the collective enforcement of international law. This experiment must be made to work in the Gulf or countries must arm and ally themselves as best they can against the law of the jungle. This is a war about peace, not just in the Middle East, not just in our time, but in tomorrow's world. That is why British soldiers are rightly asked to risk their lives.

THE LANGUAGE
OF PEACE

THE LANGUAGE OF PEACE

Guardian, January 16, 1991

The language of war is tough. The language of peace and diplomacy, by contrast, can seem witteringly tender. Language has been a terrible confusion through the first third of the Gulf crisis. As, barring miracles, that phase draws to a close, it is necessary to rescue meaning and purpose from a pile of verbiage.

The allies have pursued two policies since Saddam Hussein – misreading indolent signals from the American State Department – invaded Kuwait. The first policy was to bolster a fearful Saudi Arabia against attack and to impose the most draconian of trade embargoes upon Iraq. Two months on, that policy was a success. The Saudis were safe; and the lifelines of trade for Baghdad were severed. Then the policy – for reasons which remain obscure – changed. There was a White House decision to give the defensive allied troops along the Kuwait border an offensive capability. Millions of tons of hardware poured in; troop levels doubled. The long-term costs became gargantuan. A deadline for possible military action – January 15 – was set.

Well, it is now January 15; the clock stands at midnight. How does that second policy look? By its own espoused ends – 'the last, best chance for peace', as George Bush told Congress only three days ago – the policy stares bleak failure in the face. The combination of sanctions and offensive military build-up has not worked as the politicians who designed it hoped. It leaves, now, armed attack as the last, best chance for peace. That is a bloody nonsense.

Let us explain, one more time, why the first allied policy – sanctions and a defensive ring – seemed the right one to this paper. Saddam Hussein, on his record, is a murderous thug. He ran Iraq, through the eight-year debacle of the Iranian war, with three shots in his locker. Terror against opponents. Military back-up from what is laughingly called the world community. And money from the same source. The reaction to Kuwait stripped him of the last two of those comforts. His military machine is grinding to a stop for want of spares and outside expertise. And, absolutely crucially, the cash he depends on

25

to oil the wheels of Iraqi society dried up the moment his pipelines were cut. Take the CIA's own figures. Ninety-seven per cent of Iraqi exports have stopped. Saddam's life support system is cut. It is only a matter of time before sanctions bring him down.

Ah – the immediate counter cry – but how long could you give that first, more peaceful policy? Three months? A year? Three years? It is a facile debating point, easily turned upon the proponents of war. How many casualties are they prepared to endure? Three thousand? Thirty thousand? How long are they prepared to fight for? Three days, or months, or years? How much of Kuwait City are they prepared to flatten in the exercise, the liberators of Dresden?

The advantages of the sanctions and defence route were twofold. In the precise circumstances of Iraq – forget Rhodesia or South Africa or Libya, because the parallels are meaningless – they offered a certain way of bringing a change of regime in Baghdad. And, crucially, they meant that that transition might be moderately coherent: in short, that there would be an Iraqi government left to build again upon the ashes of Saddam's folly.

How, then, did we stumble into Policy Two? What wind of change blew us, and the initial UN stance, off course in October and November? Historians and archives, much later on, can get the balances right, but the simple answer is: political frailty. George Bush, struggling with his own public opinion and a pretty unconvinced world community, sought to still the doubters by building up troops on the ground. The UN wrote in January 15 to keep the Soviet Union on board – because it was a deadline that seemed to give plenty of time. American reservists in their tens of thousands were called up to fill the diplomatic vacuum with an appearance of decisiveness. As the forces were decanted in the desert, the rhetoric against diplomacy hardened. No linkage. No partial withdrawals. And the inevitable, infinitely predictable result is what we see today. Great armies massed in the desert. Diplomacy seemingly ended. The political imperatives all set for war. Yet remember: this was the policy for *peace*. It is an awful flop. It does not betoken strength. Any weakling can call in the generals and then turn ashen as the options drain away. It betokens feebleness: a political inability to lead rather than drift with the tide of events. There has been too much feebleness in the first phase of this crisis. Take one current example. The early rhetoric warning Saddam against partial withdrawal – compared and contrasted with present rhetoric, which would fall gratefully on his neck if he moved a few tanks. If some movement would help now, why on earth did our leaders pretend that it would be anathema in December? If sanctions were working in October – and that is what the White House solemnly told Congress – why on earth did the tune change in November? It was nothing Saddam Hussein did: it was what our politicians did to themselves. They built the box they now wriggle in.

Two things can happen now. One is that, even after the passing of a purely permissive deadline, there may be a continuance of diplomacy and sanctions. That would see, to repeat, Kuwait liberated – if we had the will and the money to see it through. But nothing in the last five months hints at such will. So we must prepare for imminent war.

The *Guardian* doesn't shrink from that. War is what we've been left by those who claimed to be fighting for peace. No one can tell how it will go. The odds, for what they are worth, are on allied success. The allies have trillions of dollars of shiny new kit for the testing. They have air and sea dominance. They face, immediately, a conscript army. It may all (the dream scenario) be over in a week. The hawks may have their chortling day. The Iraqi generals may swiftly revolt against pending slaughter. Let us fervently hope that it goes that way.

But there are also no guarantees. The Israeli dimension, the scope for Arab chaos in the allied ranks, is manifest. The Storming Normans of the Sixties thought Vietnam could be bombed into submission. The problems of leading a multi-national force are huge. Much of the technology is untested in battle. That goes for 90 per cent of the foot soldiers, too. The language of the operating theatre – as in surgical strike – is curiously inapposite. War is mayhem. This war may be mayhem too. Perhaps the operation will be a success: apart from the possibility that the patient, what is left of Kuwait, will die.

The Gulf crisis, for historians, will fall – as we say – into three phases. The efforts to punish Saddam and persuade him to retreat. The conflict, if it comes. And then the problems of victory. It is not to soon to anticipate those. We are belatedly told that, without linkage of course, there must now be a final Middle East peace settlement. James Baker and Douglas Hurd affirm it with all the vehemence of Francois Mitterrand. Yet nobody, at midnight, can foresee what can be built on the rubble of war. Smash the Iraqi Army as well as Saddam, and Iraq breaks – like a gigantic Lebanon – into warring fiefdoms. Create another supposed Arab martyr and the fault lines open instantly. Posit a situation where American troops must permanently remain to defend feudal kingdoms against their own citizens and the endless ordeal becomes evident. If the genuine third phase of the exercise

27

is a lasting Middle East peace it is a genuine hole in the heart: because no one involved has any plan for turning battlefield victory into diplomatic settlement.

For a while, of course, it may all seem much simpler. The politicians will fade as the generals take over. Saddam has chosen to fight, for a short span at least. The course of that battle will shape what comes next. But it is worth, one more time, pausing to take stock. Within a few days, barring those ephemeral miracles, the 'new world order' will manifest itself in a single decision from the White House to order half-a-million troops into a firestorm. The UN goes, cold-bloodedly, to war. That may be where the logic of five, febrile months has got us. But it is a perversion of the original logic. It remains, whilst there is any chance, worth striving to avoid. And, if it happens, it will require a level of leadership from our leaders that they have so far given scant hint of. The slide to conflict has been a tender stumbling: emerging from it, with lasting peace, will truly be the toughest challenge.

ONE MAN AND WORLD TRAGEDY

Hugo Young

Guardian, January 3, 1991

Before the war it is important to get the pre-war pinned into focus. War is what each participant now prepares for with an ever more unrelenting eye as January 15 approaches. When, or just possibly if, it happens, what led to it may be forgotten in the maelstrom. As the horrors mount, they will obliterate what came before. It will become very easy to misperceive the past, as a way of allocating blame for the present. Before that present arrives, let us reckon up its antecedents.

This pre-war has been different from almost any other in the slow calculating build-up it has allowed all sides. The war will not happen by accident (the First World War), nor grow from small to large by negligence and indecision (Vietnam), nor consist of sudden swift attack (Grenada, Panama). Its scale can be quite accurately prejudged. For the US and British military, it offers an unprecedented opportunity to work out their war games and then make them real. Already one seems to have the opportunity to watch a Gulf war that has not happened with something of the same detachment we customarily direct towards wars and battles in history.

But the space of five months has not just been taken up with military arrangement. There has also been a debate. It was slow to start, and has been of variable quality. It was less impassioned in Britain than in the US, even allowing for the Labour Party's unwillingness to lead it and the media's one-sided reporting. But in the end, the issues were delineated. Would the war be just? Would it be winnable? Did it have a legal basis? Were there alternatives for securing the same objective? Only in a few quarters have venomous war-mongers, convinced from the start that war would be necessary and good, sought to stigmatise and silence those who asked these questions. One can say that they have all been exhaustively addressed.

What has this debate revealed? It has been especially serious in Washington, where congressional hearings have ventilated many issues and called presidential executives to account. A struggle looms, not for the first time, over the President's right to make war without formal congressional approval. But what I believe this enormous and unusual lapse of time has most importantly done is to deprive anti-war opinion, especially in Europe, of several of their usual dialectical props.

Of course, there is still a strong anti-war case to be made. But it needs to be done without forensic cop-outs. It needs to say, if it is honest, that what happened to Kuwait does not in any circumstances justify the kind of reprisals which the UN has authorised its members to take in the interest of collective security. Kuwait is simply too small an issue for so large a response, this school says. But by extension there is a strong whiff of a further argument: that no circumstance in this day and age would justify the kind of war that now looks imminent. This is close to pacifism. Maybe that is a proper doctrine, but it would be better if it were argued with fewer weasel words.

What have disappeared are some of the easy explanations that survived so many wars which the European left did not like. These can mostly be included under the heading of anti-Americanism.

It is not credible, for example, to explain a Gulf war as another attempt by Washington to dominate the world. The idea that it is all about cheap oil, as if that were an exclusively American preoccupation, can also be thrown out of the window. There is nothing President Bush would rather have, I guess, than an excuse not to go to war. He is taking an appalling political risk, with public opinion going off the boil just about coincidentally with the

29

time it takes for the war machine finally to declare itself ready for action.

An extension of the American *imperium* is no longer on the popular agenda. Anyone who doubts this might consider why the articulate right have been from the start among the most prominent members of the anti-war lobby. Equally, it is notable that Washington has throughout permitted the UN to set the narrow objective of the exercise: freeing Kuwait, not removing Saddam. It will be a pity if, as part of this objective, Iraq's nuclear potential is not bombed out of existence. But the predominance of UN agenda-setting, if not military control, further complicates the picture of an aggrandising Uncle Sam.

Nor is it credible, secondly, to argue that the US, Britain or anyone else is blundering on regardless of the consequences. This is not a drift to war, but a war that will happen after all due consideration. Again time has made that an inescapable reality. All the consequences cannot be known, and most of us live outside the secret world where the war machine is readied for combat. But the war-gamers have not spent five months doing nothing, and the politicians have not been hustled into unalterable commitments before consulting them about what might happen. By no stretch of language can any of those most crucially involved be said not to know the enormity of what they may soon do.

Thirdly, it will be necessary, in the aftermath I'm envisaging, to recall with utter clarity who was to blame. Once again, the useful demon of Uncle Sam simply won't stand up. Surprisingly, most of the anti-war left go halfway to admitting this even now. Almost everyone has said that Saddam Hussein's iniquity must not stand. No Ho Chi Minh he. But between their resounding denunciations of him and their resounding refusal to countenance decisive measures against him, a well-meaning but obvious unreality echoes off the walls of silence.

Sanctions alone are supposed to get him out. But vastly the biggest sanction is the threat of his army's destruction and his own fall, and this hasn't shifted him. Again the sheer lapse of time carries its message. The conditions where mere economic destitution, brought about by economic sanctions, might change history do not seem to be present. Equally, direct diplomacy is urged between Washington and Baghdad, not least by Ted Heath. But who has been the prevaricator since Bush made his sensational offer to negotiate, which came close to cracking the UN alliance?

The hope to which any sane person will be devoting their prayers is that diplomacy still has a chance. Once January 15 was set, it was probable that the test of nerve would go down to the wire, and that if Saddam shifted it would be at the last moment. No doubt such an outcome was always likely, too, to be preceded by the kind of bloodthirsty rhetoric heard from both sides between Christmas and New Year.

But if there is no movement and if that is followed, as a high British official predicted to me in mid-December, by the beginning of war, it will be necessary to see it plain for what it is: a tragedy for the world, brought about by one man, which nobody else wanted and everybody else strove by every means to prevent: a disaster on many counts, from which reasonable statesmen acting in good faith could find no escape. It will be Hussein's war not Bush's, as five months have given us every chance to understand.

THE HOME OF TOLERANCE?

Roy Hattersley

Guardian, January 19, 1991

Three years ago, I travelled between Grosvenor and Parliament Squares in the company of Senator Sam Nunn of Georgia. Exceeding peace having made me bold, I asked the chairman of the Armed Services Committee why he was not running for the Presidency of the United States.

I must have worded my question in a way which suggested that he was my favourite son. For when he had disappeared into the Distinguished Strangers Gallery of the House of Commons, the diplomat who was his chaperon expressed humorous surprise that I should admire the highest flying hawk in Congress.

In those chilly days before glasnost and perestroika, Senator Nunn was regarded as the patriot's patriot. He is still believed to be the hardest headed Democrat – a man who would not disband an armoured brigade without the reciprocal demolition of a missile silo. Yet, last week, he made a speech which, had it been delivered in the House of Commons, would have provoked cries of treachery and treason.

'I believe', he said without the accompaniment of a single Senate hiss or boo, 'that before this nation is committed to what may be a large-scale war, each of us should ask ourselves a fundamental question. Will we be able to look the wives, the husbands and the children in the eye and say that their loved ones sacrificed their lives for interests vital to the US and that there was no reasonable alternative? Mr President, at this time, I cannot.'

Congress accepted that sentiment as an expression of acceptable opinion which damned neither the senator nor the party of which he was a member. It could not happen here.

There are all sorts of explanations for our political intolerance – the iron hand of party politics which makes every disagreement an opportunity to score points and win votes, the traditional Tory confusion between Conservative prejudices and the national interest, and, most worrying of all, the psychology of the British establishment.

A senior cabinet minister was quoted last Monday as describing the British as a warlike people. If that is so, it may be that intolerance of dissent about foreign policy aims is another deadly legacy of empire – a liability to put alongside the belief that all exports are invisible, that Britain is not part of Europe, and that the purpose of the education system is the preparation of colonial civil servants.

The warlike people thesis was developed by William Deedes – ex-Tory cabinet minister and sometime editor of the *Daily Telegraph*. He predicted that 'for every *Guardian* reader who can write a well-turned letter giving four good reasons why war in the Gulf – or anywhere else – would be a denial of all that we hold most dear, a score will find their pulses quicken when, as Kipling put it in his poem, The drums begin to roll.'

It is not a very well-turned sentence. So I am not clear if Mr Deedes writes of 20 jingoistic *Guardian* readers or a score of chauvinists who obtain their news and opinions from the *Sun* and the *Daily Star*.

One thing, however, is certain. Mr Deedes has not made a close study of the poem from which he quotes. It begins with a bitter couplet. 'I went into a public-'ouse to get a pint o' beer. The publican 'e up an' sez, We serve no red-coats here.' The poem is a complaint about the British habit of only treating soldiers with respect when there is dangerous work to be done. That is not the characteristic of a warlike people and Rudyard Kipling was not a warlike poet.

The most trivial of his verse – lines, for example, to commemorate the foundation of the Irish Guard, which were bad enough for a poet laureate – certainly glorify war. But the real poems are written in praise of soldiers not soldiering.

Often heroism is demonstrated by description of the horror that soldiers face. Danny Deever – the account of a military hanging – is unlikely to encourage young men to enlist. And the Widow of

Windsor, the poem which denied Kipling his place in the Honours list, continually complains about 'poor beggars' who pay the price for keeping the empire safe. It ends with the admirably pacific wish that the beggars in red get 'all they desire, an' if they require, a speedy return to their 'ome'. It is not only Senator Nunn who would be shouted down in the modern House of Commons.

The cliché describes bone-headed intolerance as saloon bar behaviour. But many bars of my acquaintance would be ashamed to behave as Tory backbenchers often behave these days. Sometimes they dress up their hooligan conduct as respect for the rules of the House of Commons.

When Denis Healey, limited by standing orders to a speech of 10 minutes, overran his allotted time by a second or two, they began to chant and point at the clock. Mrs Maria Fyfe was howled down on the pretext that her question lasted too long. There would have been no howls if she had been demanding total war.

I was brought up to believe that the House of Commons existed to examine rival interpretations of the country's best interests. Perhaps I was wrong. Last Thursday, Mrs Edwina Currie invited the Prime Minister to note 'the unanimous vote in the Iraq National Assembly backing Saddam Hussein and his efforts in war'. She then asked the Prime Minister to agree that a similar vote in the House of Commons would demonstrate the British people's parallel, but conflicting, determination. And you thought that we were against all that Saddam Hussein did and stood for. The idea that Parliament is the home of tolerance, like the notion that we are a warlike people and the libel that Rudyard Kipling was a jingoist, would well do with re-examination.

THE MYTH-MAKERS
John Pilger
Guardian, January 7, 1991

At the height of the First World War, Lloyd George, the prime minister, confided to C. P. Scott, the editor of the Manchester *Guardian*: 'If people really knew, the war would be stopped tomorrow. But of course they don't know, and they can't know.'

His words may soon apply to a modern equivalent of that slaughter. Like events in the Gulf, current and beckoning, the First World War was distinguished by a 'drift to war' – a specious notion that allowed for war preparation – and by an inferno of which there was little public comprehension or warning, and by the theatrical distortions and lies of the warlords and their mouthpieces in the press.

'There is no need of censorship,' wrote Philip Gibbs, a leading journalist of the time, later knighted for his services. 'We were our own censors . . . some of us wrote the truth . . . apart from the naked realism of horrors and losses, and criticism of the facts which did not come within the liberty of our pen.'

Max Hastings, a former Falklands war correspondent and now editor-in-chief of the *Daily* and *Sunday Telegraph*, said something strikingly similar on BBC Radio the other day: that it was the duty of a journalist in effect to gloss over during wartime because 'one should recognise the national interests of the nation of which one is a part . . .'

That 'national interests' include going to war when one's nation is not in any way threatened is rarely mentioned these days. Hastings's view is widely shared: if not openly, then subliminally. My own experience of war reporting is that journalists – bar the few 'mavericks' – seldom question the assumptions behind 'our wars'. The myth about Vietnam is that the media were against the war. This was not so; most were against the fact that the war was fought inefficiently, and that the Americans were losing it. Equally, some of the journalists in the Falklands who had previously defended their objectivity were unabashed in praising their own *subjectivity* in the cause of Queen and country. Their main complaint was about access, being denied the facility to be on 'our side' and help win the propaganda war.

If war breaks out in the Gulf the British media – which, unlike Iraq's, is said to be 'free' – will bear much of the responsibility for a 'patriotic' and culpable silence that has ensured that people don't know and can't know.

It is as if the very notion of the journalist as a teller of truths unpalatable to ruling elites, as whistle-blower in the *public* interest, has been fatally eroded in recent years. This is in great part the result of the 'communications revolution' (to quote Rupert Murdoch) that has produced not an information society but a media society in which vast amounts of repetitive information are confined to a narrow spectrum of 'thinkable thought', and the vocabulary of state and vested-interest manipulation is increasingly elevated above that of free journalism. In the Gulf coverage, the effect is that many people are overwhelmed and immobilised, their misgivings not reflected in the opinion polls, only their compliance.

From tabloids to television, radio to 'qualities', the war drums are heard, their beat perhaps made all the more acceptable by the work of honourable sceptics, humanitarians and professionals, journalists like John Simpson and Robert Fisk. Otherwise we have the 'ugly momentum that is driving Bush steadily towards war' (the *Observer*); a war that is 'necessary to protect civilised values' (*The Times*); a war for which 'no price is too heavy to pay' (Bush reported uncritically almost everywhere). And anyone who gets in the way is a 'yellowbelly' (the *Sun*); or 'an eccentric with a lust for publicity . . . a very British kind of nut' (*The Times* on Tam Dalyell); or using 'weasel words' (the *Guardian*).

And of course war is fun! Every night there is Peter Snow's bloodless sandpit to play in, and the sexy shots of Hornets and Tornadoes, with a camel left of frame and the sun rising over the cockpit. Cue the bagpipes; cue the British major who wants to 'get in there now!'.

Military minders attached to the Joint Information Bureau manipulate most of what you see from the Gulf. A well-known broadcaster, who does not wish to be named, says: 'The cocoon is such that you end up being gung-ho and unquestioning. It's a bit much when you know things that you can't say: for instance, that many of our lads will almost certainly be killed by friendly fire, from the allied side.'

The military's ability to distort and the media's malleability were demonstrated in August when television showed images of what appeared to be a highly efficient US military machine moving into the desert. In fact, this was a bluff: many aircraft arrived half full, the 'machine' was unprepared. Most of the media accepted what they were told.

We are told the use of nuclear weapons has 'not been ruled out'. Yet a study on the effects of a nuclear war in the Gulf has been virtually ignored. Nik Gowing, diplomatic editor of Channel 4 News, describes the narrowness of the debate thus: 'It's quite shocking. I am thunderstruck that the British public know so little about the potential nightmare of this war. Naively, people are unaware that even if Iraq is defeated, the war may come to them: in acts of reprisal and terrorism in the centre of London, as the director of the CIA has warned.'

Stewart Purvis, editor of ITN, gives an especially interesting reply on this issue: 'The role of the opposition party in Parliament is important to our news coverage. Labour is synchronised with government policy, so that the level of debate on television matches the level of debate in Parliament.'

Few other broadcasters and senior press reporters will go on the record. 'My access to the MoD and the Foreign Office is a lifeline,' one of them says. 'I can't jeopardise it.'

The *Independent*'s correspondent in the Gulf has written: 'Second-guessing President Saddam's intentions have not proved a precise science. Who predicted that he would invade Kuwait on August 2?' The answer is almost certainly that the United States predicted it; and it is in the area of America's war aims and strategic purpose that distortion by omission has been most evident.

Minimal coverage has been given in Britain to a meeting that the US ambassador in Baghdad, April Glaspie, had with Saddam Hussein on July 25, a week before the invasion. According to the Iraqi transcript – which the State Department has not disputed – the ambassador asked what the Iraqi dictator's intentions were and was told that Iraq could not 'accept death' in the face of Kuwait's 'economic war and military action against us'.

Saddam could not have made his plans clearer. In return, the ambassador gave no warning that the US would oppose an Iraqi takeover of Kuwait. On the contrary, she said she had 'direct instructions from the president to seek better relations with Iraq'.

Two days before the invasion, Assistant Secretary of State John Kelly told a congressional hearing that the US was not committed to defend Kuwait. Four days before the invasion, according to the chairman of the Senate Intelligence Committee, the CIA had predicted that the invasion would happen when it did. Channel 4 News was one that did cover the warning but, Gowing says, 'it quickly became history, overtaken by more current events'.

Journalism is nothing if it is not a process of weaving together the strands of contemporary history. Put these events together, add the absence of any US effort to create an international opposition while there was time, and urgent questions are raised which, at the very least, mock Bush's nonsense (as expounded to David Frost) that the Gulf raises 'the greatest moral issue since the Second World War'. Such a statement takes hypocrisy to the limit; forget the invasion of Panama in which perhaps as many as 7,000 civilians were killed.

In a genuinely free society, there needs to be unrestricted debate, drawing on a diversity of sources that reflect the complexion of a society that is not one nation. As the *Daily Mirror* has pointed out, it will be the sick and old who will pay the bill for this war. So whose 'national interest' is at stake?

Are we heading for a war that is in American interests? Is the build-up a demonstration of America's world 'leadership' at a time of deepening recession and diminishing sources of raw materials and opportunities for 'free trade'? Why have sanctions not been allowed time to succeed?

We all, it seems, live by the January 15 deadline. Saddam must leave Kuwait by that date. But the facts are not as they have been represented in much of the media. At his news conference on November 30, Bush actually hoped Saddam would meet James Baker 'at a mutually convenient time' between December 15 and January 15. He did not name a specific date. The Iraqis may be awkward about the date, but so is Bush; and why should life and death for thousands of innocent people, who do not appreciate the 'values' of High Noon, hang upon it?

The *Observer* on December 30 illustrated an article about the British Army in the Gulf with a picture of a Colonel Denaro blowing a hunting horn to summon his driver. The colonel was described as 'an extravagant character with an attractive swashbuckling manner'. His regiment, the Hussars, 'are sometimes to be found wearing their big Browning automatics in shoulder holsters over tank crew's overalls, which gives them a rakish appearance'. Some of the officers come from 'the same stock as Wellington', and are heirs to the Light Brigade, 'the same gallant six hundred . . .'

Perhaps this was meant to be ironic. The Charge of the Light Brigade was one of the most pointless imperial disasters in history.

The editors being called to discuss war coverage at the Ministry of Defence today should read the Crimea diaries of perhaps the greatest of all British war reporters, William Howard Russell, of *The Times*. Not for him propaganda in the 'national interest'. He wrote about the sacrificial battles, the waste, the blunders.

'Am I to tell these things?' he wrote to his editor, John Delane, 'or am I to hold my tongue?' To which Delane replied: 'Continue as you have done, to tell the truth, or as much of it as you can'.

Both incurred the wrath of the Establishment which, of course, ought to be no more than an occupational hazard.

BYE, BYE BAGHDAD

Paul Foot

London Review of Books, February 7, 1991

The *Sun* (January 15) announces on its front page: THE *SUN* SPEAKS FOR EVERY MAN, WOMAN AND CHILD IN BRITAIN. This would normally be a joke, a fantastic flight of fancy to prove that editor Kelvin Mackenzie had at last gone mad. But when, the next morning, the *Sun* devotes its entire front page to the Union Jack with a good old British Tommy in its centre, and the rubric up above SUPPORT OUR BOYS AND PUT THIS FLAG IN YOUR WINDOW, thousands of people do so! The *Sun* has its best morning for years. The *Star*, the ailing tabloid from the Express group, has a good time too, starting with its headline (January 16): GO GET HIM BOYS over a picture of a Tornado jet skimming across the desert 'to blast the evil dictator Saddam Hussein out of his bunker'. 'War is seldom bad for business,' says a leader in *The Times* Business and Finance Section, which goes on to hope that a war in the Gulf will 'pull Britain out of the recession'. Such optimism seems deranged. But as the circulation figures rise, and as the 'key targets' in Baghdad fall victim to allied air power, so caution is thrown to the winds and the papers stoke up the war fever they helped to create in the first place.

What is most remarkable about the press coverage of the Gulf crisis is its unanimity. Those who run the *Sun* and the *Star* will always support a fight, especially if it can be waged under a Union Jack. The *Sun*'s obsession with nuclear weapons (LET'S NUKE 'EM. GET READY TO PUSH THE BUTTON, BUSH TOLD – headline, January 8) is of long standing. No doubt the *Daily Telegraph*'s enthusiastic support for the war was predictable. The paper's former editor, William Deedes, an archetypal buffer who once dealt expertly with press relations for the Tory government under Sir Alec Douglas Home, tells his readers on deadline day that for every yellow-bellied *Guardian* reader 'a score will find their pulses quicken when, as Kipling put it in his poem, "the drums begin to roll".' The drums of death and mass destruction do something for the pulses of such people, and always have. Yet if the enthusiasm for the war were confined to

the *Sun*, *Star*, *Telegraph*, *Mail* and *Express*, there might at least be an argument. It is the spread of that enthusiasm into the 'middle ground' – the *Independent*, the *Observer*, *The Times* and *Sunday Times*, the *Mirror* and its associate papers – which gives to the war party its precious unanimity. Even the *Guardian*, which appeared to be against the war before it started, threw up its hands at the first sound of gunfire, and declared that the 'cause' of the war party was 'just'. Like the politicians against the war, the writers against the war – Edward Pearce in the *Guardian*, John Diamond in the *Mirror*, John Pilger wherever anyone prints what he writes – have to be winkled out from the chauvinist mass.

How to explain the mood which swept otherwise independent-minded journalists and editors into the stampede for war? The answer is that the intervention in the Gulf appears to many in the centre as an example of the world order for which they have craved since 1945. Here at last is the United Nations in action, bringing together, under the umbrella of internationally agreed resolutions, all the forces of the world to defeat the aggressor and the bully. People who hated the Cold War now hail a new era when Russian, Chinese and Americans can fight together against a common enemy who, everyone agrees, has broken the rules. If the allied forces in the Gulf successfully discipline Iraq, so the argument goes, the world can look forward to an age of peace and order which, at long last, can be enforced.

To such people the standard arguments against the war are worse than useless. It is argued, for instance, that the post-war world has been full of dictators, some of them worse than Saddam Hussein, and many of them put in power or sustained there by the very forces which are now calling down death and destruction on the Butcher of Baghdad. Who put Pinochet in power? Who made it possible for Pol Pot to set about mass murder in Kampuchea? Who organised armed resistance to overthrow an elected government in Nicaragua and replace it with something like the dictatorship of Somoza? On any monster-count, these gentlemen, all creatures of American foreign policy, are as bad if not worse than Saddam. So why go to war against Saddam while propping up dictatorships in so many other places? This argument is met by our enlightened warmongers with the riposte: 'five, six or even 20 wrongs don't make a right. The United States may have supported dictatorships in the past, but in this case they are ranged against a dictator. Surely on this occasion they should be supported?'

The same answer greets the other standard anti-war argument –

that aggression has been one of the constant features of the post-war world, and has never been checked by the American Government (which is often carrying out the aggression). What happened in Grenada and Panama unless it was naked aggression by a vast military power against a small defenceless state? Why was no armed force sent to throw the Israelis out of the territories they occupied by force in 1967; or into Cyprus to eject the Turkish invader in 1974; or into East Timor to evict the murderous Indonesian aggressor in 1975? In all three of these cases unanimous Security Council Resolutions were passed opposing the invasions, all of which were plainly illegal under what is laughably known as international law. No one could argue that Saddam's invasion of Kuwait was any more brutal in its execution or disastrous in its consequences than these other three invasions. If aggression should bring instant and huge retribution on the aggressor, why was not a man, not a gun sent to deal with the aggressors in the occupied territories of the Middle East, Cyprus or East Timor?

Our middle-of-the-road warmonger waves all this aside. International force was not used in the past, he agrees. It should have been. The United Nations lost face because it could not enforce its Resolutions. Now, thanks to the end of the Cold War, it is able to walk tall and enforce what it resolves. Roll on the war – or, as the *Sun* so tastefully put it, 'Bye Bye Baghdad'.

The grand old tradition of British empiricism, which hates to see patterns in politics and shuns as Marxist claptrap any attempt to discover an economic motive for the foreign policy of great powers, has, through these arguments, reached its logical climax. It has led middle-of-the-road politicians and journalists into outright support for what is, after all, the crudest and probably the nastiest of all modern imperialist wars.

For what is the common denominator which explains the twists and turns of US foreign policy and UN U-turns? Commercial interest – which in the Middle East can be reduced to a single word: oil. There is (and was at the time of the invasion) no oil in the Israeli-occupied territories, no oil in East Timor, no oil in Cyprus. No commercial interest in the US or Russia or any other great power was threatened by any of these invasions. Indeed, all three greatly assisted the commercial and strategic interest of the US, tied as it is so closely to Israel, Turkey and Indonesia. The toppling of Somoza in Nicaragua in 1979 threatened the hegemony of United States capital there, as did the democratic government of Chile from 1970 to 1973, the left-wing dictatorship of Grenada in 1982, and the dictatorship in Panama last year. In these cases, US business interests did just as well if not better as a result of old-fashioned aggression, and therefore old-fashioned aggression prospered. None of this had anything to do with the Cold War. All three UN Resolutions calling on the withdrawal of Israel from Gaza and the West Bank, Turkey from Cyprus and Indonesia from East Timor were passed unanimously in the Security Council. The US, Britain, France, Russia and China supported them all to the hilt – provided, of course, that no one was expected to do anything to enforce them.

Commercial interest and oil provide the only coherent explanation of US policy over Iraq. After the Iranian revolution of 1979, Iran appeared as the main threat to 'stability' (cheap oil) in the region. Thus Iraq was encouraged by the United States (and by Kuwait and by Saudi Arabia) to invade Iran and start a war for a strip of territory which was eventually conceded. During this war, in which a million people were killed or maimed, Iraq, the aggressor, was supported by the US and Britain. When complaints were made about Saddam's genocidal attacks on the Kurdish people in north Iraq, critical UN Resolutions were watered down by the US, and formal British government protests were suitably muted. When an Iraqi missile accidentally hit an American warship killing 38 people, the US Government immediately sympathised with Saddam: 'these things happen in time of war', they said. After the war, for a brief moment, Saddam became a hero in the Western world. Arms-traders queued up to sell him the weapons he now uses against his former benefactors. British cabinet ministers flocked to Baghdad to tie the knot of friendship with the dictator. During the visit of Tony Newton, now Secretary of State for Social Services, Saddam pronounced Britain a 'most favoured nation'. All this stopped only when Saddam, weakened by war and threatened from within, threw his huge army into Kuwait to increase the price of oil. Suddenly the champion of stability in the region (cheap oil) became its enemy. Suddenly, 'poor little Kuwait' (a greedy little dictatorship which exploits its migrant labour as horribly as anywhere else on earth) became a symbol of liberty and independence, and the Government of the United States of America moved to obliterate the monster it had created and had armed.

There is no other credible conclusion but that the war in the Gulf is a war for oil, a war to maintain the central strategy of British and American foreign policy in that region for half a century – ensuring that the Arab people do not get control of the oil produced in their countries. It was for this purpose (as has coincidentally just been clarified by the release of government papers) that Britain offered Kuwait military aid in 1961 to protect it from an Iraqi invasion.

If this is the thrust behind the war effort, the real purpose of the UN Resolutions, then where does that leave our Modern Empiricists, our Peter Jenkinses and Hugo Youngs, our Edward Mortimers and Gerald Kaufmans and Paddy Ashdowns? Their 'practical approach', their faith in the 'cock-up theory of history', their insistence that political events must be judged as they come, each by each, without pattern or precedent and most particularly without any economic drive or thrust to them, leads them to a mealy-mouthed support for 'a military initiative' which is likely (at best) to kill tens of thousands of people, most of them, as always, poor, defenceless and civilian.

If this is, as seems plain to me, a war to ensure that Britain and the United States keep tight hold of the world's richest and cheapest oil supply, then what will be the result of an allied victory over Saddam? Will it really lead to more influence for the United Nations, a better world order, a bleaker prospect for dictators? Or will it simply mean that the most powerful state on earth becomes more powerful, and the dictatorships which it supports in its own commercial interests all over the world will become more secure? Will it mean that the UN, instead of exercising more influence over its member states, will become even more grovelling a satellite of the great powers which control the Security Council: that the Cold War will be replaced by a new condominium of the United States Government, invaders of Panama and Grenada (and Iraq), the Russian Government, invader of Afghanistan and Lithuania (who knows where else?) and the Chinese Government, oppressors of Tiananmen Square? Will it not prove, after all, that the biggest Might is the biggest Right, and that the only way to dispose of a small world bully is by calling in a much bigger and more aggressive world bully whose victory will lead to the further throttling of the voices and aspirations of ordinary people everywhere?

I write this, half-watching early-morning television, on January 17, 1991. A BBC nincompoop in battledress, safe in his bunker in Riyadh, is reading out jingoistic nonsense from *Henry V*, and now Margaret Thatcher regales us with the horrors of Saddam's attack on Iran, an attack she supported. The air is thick with chauvinist drivel. When the dead are stretched out, and the hideous cost of this crazy war is counted, the blame must not be allowed to stop at the

Sun, the prime minister and his exultant predecessor. The Modern Empiricists, the 'practical politicians', the 'sensible' journalists are every bit as responsible.

NEWS – AND PROPAGANDA
Phillip Knightley
The Times, January 21, 1991

There was a huge anti-war demonstration in Trafalgar Square. The *Guardian* carried a full-page advertisement announcing the formation of a league to stop the war. Leading citizens, including mayors, politicians, businessmen and church leaders signed manifestos urging Britain to keep out.

It all happened, in this instance, in the summer of 1914, on the eve of war against Germany. The government of the day suddenly had to face the fact that it lacked the most essential element for successfully waging war: the wholehearted support of the nation. What could be done about it?

The propaganda campaign developed by the government over the next four years was probably the most brilliant ever waged – it became the model on which Goebbels based his moulding of German public opinion some 20 years later. Although propaganda had been around since Sun-tzu, the Chinese author, wrote *The Art of War* some 2,400 years ago, it was Britain in the First World War which lifted it to the organised scientific level used today.

In the intervening years propaganda has become so much a part of our society that there is no need now for a Lord Northcliffe ('the minister for lying', as the Germans called him) to direct it. Today propaganda seems to occur almost spontaneously as the government and the media slip into gear for war.

The parallels with 1914–18 are striking. First, demonise the enemy and its leader. The Germans were never able to popularise so striking an epithet as 'Hun' or 'Boche' and never able to attack British leaders with equal skill and vigour. In a single report on September 22, 1914, the *Daily Mail* referred to the Kaiser as a 'lunatic', a 'barbarian', a 'monster' and a 'criminal'. Saddam Hussein has been called all these – and a 'little Hitler' as well.

Next, always seek to portray the war as one of civilised nations defending themselves against a menacing aggressor with all the wrong on his side. 'There are only two divisions in the world today,' Rudyard Kipling wrote, 'human beings and Germans.' In the Gulf, Saddam is the aggressor, the allies are upholding the civilised values of the new world order. There has been little discussion of Iraq's long-standing claim to Kuwait.

Third, attribute to the enemy all forms of atrocity, true or false. The allies accused the Germans of raping nuns, bayoneting babies, slicing off women's breasts and torturing children. So many atrocity allegations surfaced so often that the French press grew tired of putting individual headlines on them, and simply ran them week after week, headed *Les Atrocités Allemandes*. Similar accusations have been made about the behaviour of Iraqi soldiers; as in the First World War, one suspects that the truth will not be known until the fighting is over.

Next, arouse the nation's patriotic spirit by appealing to past glories and drawing historic parallels. In 1914–18 the call went out to the Empire – 'our common history, our common language, one King and Emperor'. This time we are reminded that the 7th Armoured Brigade was part of the Desert Rats division that fought with distinction in the Second World War and took part in the battle of El Alamein, one of Britain's greatest victories.

Finally, promise a short war with minimum casualties. In August 1914, the British generals promised that the troops would be home for Christmas and that the power of massed artillery would save infantrymen's lives. In the Gulf, the Pentagon predicted that the war would be over within 10 days, the Americans would suffer only 100 casualties to the Iraqis' 30,000, and the awesome might of the allies' high-tech weaponry would save infantry lives. (Given the way the war has gone so far, this could be true.)

A good example of the propaganda value of drawing historical parallels was the Israeli statement after the first Iraqi missile attack that 50 years ago a brutal dictator had tried to kill off the Jews by gassing them, and another was now trying to do the same. This comparison was bound to arouse powerful memories and thus sympathy for Israel's predicament.

But it is the media itself to which we must look for the influence of propaganda, international or otherwise. Governments know that most people are not convinced by logic but seduced by stories, and the First World War showed that no one could spin a story better than a journalist. He knew how to get the war over to the man in the street, how to exploit the popular vocabulary, prejudices and enthusiasms. Journalists were not hampered by what Dr Johnson called 'needless scrupulosity', and they had a feeling for the public mood.

So how today can the ordinary newspaper reader and television viewer distinguish the news from the propaganda? The answer is that he cannot. Good propaganda is too subtle to be instantly identifiable. The only protection is to treat all good news of the war with scepticism and to remember that history teaches us that in human affairs it is very rare for all the right to be on the one side.

A MILLION MEN WAIT FOR THE CLASH OF ARMS

Robert Fisk

Independent, January 15, 1991

With Saddam Hussein's refusal to withdraw from Kuwait by tonight's United Nations deadline, the most powerful armies in Christendom are now poised to fight the largest military force in the Muslim world. The last, abortive mission to Baghdad on Sunday by the UN secretary-general, Javier Pérez de Cuéllar, appears to have set the stage for a tragic and bloody war.

Mr Pérez de Cuéllar's almost total pessimism last night suggested conflict was inevitable. In Baghdad, the members of Iraq's National Assembly voted to support Saddam Hussein with their 'blood and souls'; his wrath would have been turned on them if they had not.

Last night, great storms raged over the deserts of Kuwait and Saudi Arabia, inundating the sand and *sabka* depressions across which the armies would have to fight, stranding thousands of tanks on both sides in a sea of mud. Thick cloud prevented almost all reconnaissance flights.

A few extra days of life may thus be granted to the tens of thousands of young men who are likely to die in the coming weeks. For a million or so soldiers now face each other across the Kuwaiti frontier; half of them are Iraqis, doomed – if the American and British military planners have their way – to be destroyed in the massive air attacks before the ground offensive. But wars also destroy the best laid plans and the Pentagon's gloomy if anonymous predictions of a long and gruesome conflict are beginning to gain credence.

Driving through the soggy desert yesterday, past the American Marines, in their soaking combat jackets, the lines of tank transporters, the Scimitar armoured vehicles bearing the pennants of the British 16th/5th Lancers, one could only reflect on the crisis in history that had brought all these men – teenagers, most of them – to so alien a land. In many cases, no doubt, to die.

For what? Many of the British soldiers here are quite frank about it. They say that Saddam Hussein is an evil man but they also say, quite frankly, that the war will be about oil. There is no mention of George Bush's 'new world order'. There was some cynicism over a British editorial which advised Western troops they could take the offensive with 'clear consciences'. It was not their conscience which concerned these young soldiers yesterday but their survival.

Here, for example, are the unexpurgated thoughts of Captain Ronald Thomas, from Stoke-on-Trent and A Squadron of the 16th/5th, as he watched his soldiers load their missiles for what might be the last hours of peace: 'Yes, I'm frightened of dying. Everyone's thinking about it now.' (A pause here.) 'But you know, I'll be really pissed off if I didn't see my family again. I've got four kids. I'd be fucking angry if I was killed.'

There are other Captain Thomases, many of them, no doubt, in the Iraqi Army awaiting the allied onslaught. Yesterday's meeting of the Iraqi Assembly can have given them no comfort. Its Speaker announced that Iraq's soldiers were 'ready to sacrifice everything for the cause of Palestine'.

The man who invaded Kuwait, set his torturers upon all who opposed him in the captive emirate, held thousands hostage and defied the UN to the end, gave no sign yesterday that he might break his promise to attack Israel. If he does, he will almost certainly achieve what other Arab leaders have sought in vain: a wartime alliance of America and Israel.

If Saddam Hussein is ready to fight the Americans, the Saudis are now asking themselves, does he perhaps believe he can win? And how? With gas and biological weapons? British and American troops were last night receiving anthrax injections.

Or with the breakup of the Middle East in a series of uncontrollable, frontierless states that will turn against the West?

The Gulf oil states showed no signs last night of flinching in their support for the Western armies. Saddam Hussein's latest attack on the 'treacherous Saudi regime and Arab stooges' left them in no doubt where they stood. Yet there are Arab Gulf ministers who still ask privately why sanctions could not have been continued for longer. And what of President Bush's promise not to launch an offensive from Saudi soil? It is now almost certain to be dishonoured.

It is also difficult for many Arabs, however much they hate the Iraqi regime, to shake off the suspicion that the West has embarked on a moral crusade in the Middle East, as undefined as it could prove disastrous. How is the 'new world order' to be applied in the aftermath of war? Is there to be a US protectorate in Kuwait? Or in a defeated Iraq? What if Israel uses a war to expel the Palestinians from the West Bank? What if Jordan disappears? Are the lands of the Middle East then to come under UN mandate as they came under that of the League of Nations in 1920?

Last night, these questions remained unanswered. There appear to be no allied plans for a post-ceasefire world, save a vague resolution to restore Kuwait to its immensely wealthy ruling family and ensure an undefined 'security' to the region. The probable war with Iraq has instead focused, at least in its initial stages, on whether the West's technology – its bombs and rockets, its radar, its satellite surveillance – can break the power of Saddam's Hussein's army. For the West, this is an essentially military question.

In the Muslim world, however, it is also a religious one. Even today, Islamic scholars ask themselves why Muslim armies were once beaten back from the gates of Vienna: was it because they lacked faith or because the armies of Christendom possessed better weapons?

Thus the events of the next few days and weeks will contain a far deeper significance than the mere settling of accounts with a brutal dictator by a world supposedly grown tired of tyranny. It is this which lies behind the tragedy unfolding in the Middle East. Last night, airports were preparing to close as airlines suspended their commercial flights. Tardily, the Saudis began to distribute gas masks to tens of thousands of their population with little attempt to demonstrate how such vital protection should be used.

The border town of Khafji was almost deserted, its inhabitants fleeing down the long highway to Dhahran in the opposite direction to the military convoys. Extra trains were laid on from Dhahran to Riyadh, which the Saudis – rather optimistically – believe will not be the targets of Iraqi missiles.

They leave behind them in the desert young men from Stoke-on-Trent, Manchester, New York and Wyoming preparing to kill or be killed by young men from Basra or Kirkuk. It is just possible that the storms will delay their battle and give sufficient time for just one more peace initiative. But there was no sign last night – least of all from the Arabs themselves – whence it might come.

If it does not, then the final irony may prove to be that the overture to a new world order takes the form of one of the most awesome bombardments in the history of modern warfare.

'GOD BLESS OUR NATION'
George Bush
January 15, 1991

'Just two hours ago, allied air forces began an attack on military targets in Iraq and Kuwait. These attacks continue as I speak. Ground forces are not engaged.

This conflict started August 2 when the dictator of Iraq invaded a small and helpless neighbour. Kuwait, a member of the Arab League, and a member of the United Nations, was crushed, its people brutalised.

Five months ago, Saddam Hussein started this cruel war against Kuwait. Tonight the battle has been joined.

This military action, taken in accord with UN resolutions and with the consent of the US Congress, follows months of constant and virtually endless diplomatic activity on the part of the UN, the US, and many, many other countries.

Arab leaders sought what became known as an Arab solution, only to conclude that Saddam Hussein was unwilling to leave Kuwait. Others travelled to Baghdad to restore peace and justice.

Our Secretary of State, James Baker, held a historic meeting in Geneva, only to be totally rebuffed.

This past weekend, in a last-ditch effort, the secretary-general of the UN went to the Middle East with peace in his heart – his second such mission. He came back from Baghdad with no progress in getting Saddam to withdraw from Kuwait.

Now, the 28 countries with forces in the Gulf area have exhausted all reasonable efforts to reach a peaceful resolution, have no choice but to drive Saddam from Kuwait by force. We will not fail.

As I report to you, air attacks are under way against military targets in Iraq. We are determined to knock out Saddam Hussein's nuclear bomb potential. We will also destroy his chemical weapons facilities. Much of Saddam's artillery and tanks will be destroyed.

Our operations are designed to best protect the lives of all the coalition forces by targeting Saddam's vast arsenal.

Initial reports from General [Norman] Schwarzkopf [allied commander] are that our operations are proceeding according to plan. Our objectives are clear: Saddam Hussein's forces will leave Kuwait, the legitimate government of Kuwait will be restored to its rightful place, and Kuwait will again be free.

Iraq will eventually comply with all relevant UN resolutions, and then, when peace is restored, it is our hope that Iraq will live as a peaceful and co-operative member of the family of nations, enhancing the security and stability of the Gulf.

Some may ask, Why act now? Why not wait? The answer is clear. The world could wait no longer. Sanctions, though having some effect, showed no signs of accomplishing their objective. Sanctions were tried for well over five months, and we and our allies concluded that sanctions alone would not force Saddam from Kuwait.

While the world waited, Saddam Hussein systematically raped, pillaged and plundered a tiny nation, no threat to his own. He subjected the people of Kuwait to unspeakable atrocities, and among those maimed and murdered, innocent children.

While the world waited, Saddam sought to add to the chemical weapons arsenal he now possesses an infinitely more dangerous weapon of mass destruction, a nuclear weapon. And while the world waited, while the world talked peace and withdrawal, Saddam Hussein dug in and moved massive forces into Kuwait.

While the world waited, while Saddam stalled, more damage was being done to the fragile economies of the Third World, the emerging democracies of Eastern Europe, to the entire world, including to our own economy. The US, with the UN, exhausted every means to bring this crisis to a peaceful end.

However, Saddam clearly felt that by stalling and threatening and defying the UN, he could weaken the forces arrayed against him. While the world waited, Saddam Hussein met every overture of peace with open contempt. While the world prayed for peace, Saddam prepared for war.

I had hoped that when the US Congress, in historic debate, took its resolute action, Saddam would realise he could not prevail and would move out of Kuwait in accord with the UN resolutions. He did not do that. He remained intransigent, certain that time was on his side.

Saddam was warned over and over again to comply with the will of the UN, leave Kuwait or be driven out. Saddam has arrogantly rejected all warnings. Instead he tried to make this a dispute between Iraq and the United States of America. He failed.

Tonight 28 nations, countries from five continents – Europe and Asia, Africa and the Arab League – have forces in the Gulf area, standing shoulder to shoulder against Saddam Hussein.

These countries had hoped the use of force could be avoided. Regrettably, we now believe that only force will make him leave.

Prior to ordering our forces into battle, I instructed our military commanders to take every necessary step to prevail as quickly as possible, and with the greatest degree of protection for American and allied servicemen and women.

I've told the American people before that this will not be another Vietnam. Our troops will have the best support in the world, and they will not be asked to fight with one hand behind their back.

I'm hopeful that this fighting will not go on for long, and that casualties will be held to an absolute minimum. This is an historic moment. We have in this past year made great progress in ending the long era of conflict and Cold War.

We have before us the opportunity to forge for ourselves and for future generations a new world order, a world where the rule of law, not the law of the jungle governs the conduct of nations.

When we are successful, we have a real chance at this new world order, an order in which a credible UN can use its peacekeeping role to fulfil the promise envisioned of the UN's founders. We have no argument with the people of Iraq; indeed, for the innocents caught in this conflict, I pray for their safety.

Our goal is not the conquest of Iraq; it is the liberation of Kuwait. It is my hope that somehow the Iraqi people can even now convince their dictator that he must lay down his arms, leave Kuwait and let Iraq itself rejoin the family of peace-loving nations.

Thomas Paine wrote many years ago: "These are the times that try men's souls." Those well-known words are so very true today, but even as planes of the multinational forces attack Iraq, I prefer to think of peace, not war. I am convinced not only that we will prevail, but that out of the horror of combat will come the recognition that no nation can stand against the world united.

No president can easily commit our sons and daughters to war. They are the nation's finest. Let me say that when the troops finish their work, I'm determined to bring them home as soon as possible.

Tonight, as our forces fight, they and their families are in our prayers.

May God bless each and every one of them, and the coalition forces at our side in the Gulf, and may he continue to bless our nation, the United States of America.'

A JUST WAR

Robert Runcie, Archbishop of Canterbury

Thought For the Day, BBC Radio 4, January 17, 1991

'There doesn't seem much good about the first day of another war – especially for those living in the Gulf, serving in the forces, or their friends and loved ones at home.

Sometimes I'm asked about the words "Good Friday". It wouldn't be good if the suffering on the cross were the whole story. But the tragedy of the cross was followed by the triumph of Easter. Death gave way to new life. This *good* morning, we pray that war will give way to peace – and quickly.

We all want peace. And there have been many efforts to obtain peace without conflict in recent months. But peace must never be separated from justice.

The Bible does warn us against an easy peace. Jeremiah complained about those who ignored the demands of justice by saying:

> They dress my people's wound, but skin-deep only,
> With their saying "Peace, Peace"
> When there is no peace.

Often we say we're leaving someone in peace when we mean we are simply ignoring them. We cannot ignore the people of Kuwait. The longer we leave them suffering at the mercy of a barbaric aggressor, the more difficult it will be to create a just order and a lasting peace there or elsewhere in the world.

The tragedy of war is its cost in human suffering. As a soldier I've seen too much of that to wish it upon others. And it's true that a Christian has a built-in resistance to the use of force. We are to be peacemakers.

But to do justice sometimes compels us to use force. The harsh reality of history is that the use of force has been caused as much by human virtues – our sense of justice, our belief in and the difference between right and wrong, our readiness for self-sacrifice on behalf of others – as it has been by any of our failures or wickedness.

This war is not with the Iraqi people, but with Saddam Hussein and those who surround him.

Dietrich Bonhoeffer, the German pastor who was killed by the Nazis in the last week of the Second World War, once said that God is among us in our lives, but not on any side. That's another instinctive Christian insight which helps maintain our reserves of compassion and mercy as we seek to do justice.

Not even in a just war should we forget that pity is God-like. Nor should we forget, as we seek to do what is right and good, those words of Jesus: "There is only one who is good, that is God." And he does not change, nor will he fail us. That is why we can say with conviction even on this bleak day: "*Good* morning."

Lord, make thy will our will in all things, and so give us peace.'

WAR DECLARED

'PALLS OF BLACK SMOKE, THE HOTEL IS SHAKING'

John Holliman and Peter Arnett

CNN, Baghdad. Quoted in the *Guardian*, January 17, 1991

'Thick palls of black smoke are rising from the city . . . the skies are illuminated now by large flashes . . . the entire city is blacked out.'

Breaking the news of the air attack on Baghdad, John Holliman of Cable News Network reported that white flashes were everywhere as bullets shot into the night sky.

'There is tremendous lightning in the sky,' he said. The city was still lit up and there was no sound of explosions.

'Now hear loud reports, this hotel is shaking, Baghdad is still not blacked out,' Holliman said, looking out over the Iraqi capital.

'We are not sure if the blasts are bombs or shells landing.'

He said he could see no flames or other visible signs of the city being attacked and the firing petered out after a few moments. He said the city was beginning to be blacked out.

'There were loud explosions, obviously bombs, in three parts of the city,' CNN said in a news report. It quoted a pool report from Saudi Arabia saying that a squadron of fully laden F-15 fighter-bombers had taken off.

'It looks like the Fourth of July display at the Washington Memorial,' said Holliman.

'You can hear the bombs now. They just got the main telecommunications centre . . . the planes are circling . . . apparently coming back for more targets.

'There is a lot of fire going up . . . there is no sign that any of the aircraft have suffered any damage . . . we've seen no sign that any have been hit,' Holliman said.

'They are bombing from quite a height . . . no swooping, dive-bomb attacks,' his colleague Peter Arnett reported.

'A bomb came down near the hotel . . . you can feel it shaking the building [the Rashid hotel from which the CNN team was reporting late last night].

'There's a very bright flash at a refinery building,' Holliman went on.

'Theres something on fire . . . an explosion near a mosque . . . there is another refinery under attack.

'There have been at least three waves of air attacks so far . . . there seem to be multiple explosions taking place on the outskirts of the city,' Arnett said.

He said that four waves of bombers, reported to have taken off from Saudi Arabia at 12.50 am local time (21.50 GMT) had passed high over Baghdad.

An oil refinery was said to have been bombed. Planes also seemed to have been attacking near the airport and the telecommunications centre.

Iraqi anti-aircraft guns opened up 'but they seem to be shooting at what they cannot see,' Arnett reported.

Holliman said they could continue to hear bombs landing in the distance.

CNN reporters in Baghdad said that at 00.55 GMT, anti-aircraft fire lit the skies again. 'It looks like a million fireflies,' said one.

There was another wave of anti-aircraft fire to the south of Baghdad.

They said a huge red explosion lit the sky about 10 miles from the city.

Nearly two hours after the first strike, CNN reported from Baghdad that the bombing has moved out beyond the perimeter of the city.

'The anti-aircraft fire is going up . . . the planes are moving so rapidly,' its reporter said.

'Wow, that was a bright light, everybody get down,' the CNN reporter shouted as a bomb landed in the heart of the Iraqi capital.

John Holliman and Peter Arnett are correspondents for the Cable News Network, the 24-hour satellite news television service based in Atlanta, Georgia.

VIEW FROM THE RASHID HOTEL
Nancy Banks-Smith
Guardian, January 17, 1991

'Something's happening outside,' said Bernard Shaw. 'Let's try and describe to the viewers what we are seeing.' It was the start of the most incredible piece of television since astronauts played golf on the moon.

On the ninth floor of the 14-storey Rashid Hotel in what they called downtown Baghdad, Peter and Bernie and John (we are talking about Americans here, we are automatically on first name terms) reported the Baghdad blitz from the eye of the hurricane. 'We see the sky lightening up to the south with anti-aircraft fire. It looks like a million fireflies, sparklers on the Fourth of July. There's a huge red rose explosion lighting up the sky. Holy cow, that was a huge outburst.' Again and again they saw it as the Fourth of July.

Several times they went off the air. Wolf Blitzer, CNN's aptly named military reporter, said it was probably electronic jamming. He spoke knowledgeably and at some length about electronic jamming. He was wrong. 'For the last 20 minutes,' said Bernard Shaw, 'I've been hiding under a table. The security people have been making a sweep.' Hotel security kept trying to force them down to the shelter and they were equally determined to keep at least one reporter on duty. Bernard Shaw is black and quite a handy man to hide under a table in a blackout. Peter Arnett had covered the Vietnam war. 'Peter said to the security man "I spent years in Vietnam. Those bombs don't bother me. If I go down to the shelter, I'll go crazy." And he conned them.' John Holliman had never been under fire before.

By the end of the night you had known them all your life. John's light, bright, almost excited voice: 'Peter, that looks like a shooting star.' Peter's amused assurance: 'I think that shooting star is an F-15.' Bernie's habit of entering on all fours, having crawled across the hotel to get another view point, then making some grave observation: 'Clearly I've never been there but this feels like the centre of hell.'

The Rashid stands taller than anything else in downtown Baghdad. You can't miss it. 'Peter, let's see if we can make that light go out. If we have to smash it, let's do it.' But what they really feared was the knock on the door.

'Let's go back to the boys in Baghdad,' said David, the CNN anchorman, giving them their label for life. 'We've gotta run, we've gotta run,' said Peter. 'There's someone knocking on the door.' 'We'll assume,' said David as the line went dead again, 'that that was not the Fuller brush salesman.'

They had no electricity. No television. No telephones. No sleep. They were okay for tuna though and A-okay for ratings. At one point the BBC, ITV and Channel 4 were all showing CNN. At his first press conference in the Pentagon Dick Cheney, the US Defence Secretary, said that the best press coverage of Baghdad was CNN and everyone laughed. They had been watching too.

By the end of the night Peter and Bernie and John were passing the commentary to each other like football players. Now and then they held the microphone out of the window and let the night speak for itself. 'And now we hear planes actually overhead. I'm going to be quiet and let you listen.' The air shook till its teeth rattled. 'That was really targeting. No kidding. The sound of those planes overhead was a little bit unnerving.'

Bernie entered on all fours. 'I'm really wearing trousers out. Gentlemen, does it occur to you that it is not accidental we are still on the air?'

The bombing had been going on for three hours now. They were all hunkered down on the floor, carrying on uncensored what Peter Arnett called this phenomenon of continued communication. He thought it was deliberate on Iraq's part. 'We help to tell their story and I believe all sides of this story should be told.'

A rooster crowed, mistaking the illuminated air for dawn.

Then it was dawn. They looked out of the window and saw, astonished, Baghdad still stood. The statue of the Unknown Soldier was not damaged. The power station was pouring out thick smoke as if to hide the city. 'As I look around people are going about their business on the street. Birds are flying against the sun and flags are flying on the parade ground. People are picking up the garbage, folks. Baghdad is a very orderly place.'

Then the sound of a plane was heard. 'A taxi cab is going down the street at about 30 miles an hour. In reverse. It's like a picture played in reverse. Birds, they look like doves, are flying round our building, all shaken up.'

Bernie, who had heard the plane, came rushing in. ('What are you doing awake?') 'One reason I haven't been able to sleep, it's been, oh, 40 hours, is I can't turn my mind off. I can't find the key,' he said. 'I come back to the men and women of Iraq, who have the misfortune to be on duty when modern warfare falls upon them. Behind all this are human beings.'

'What are we going to do through tonight,' said Bernie.

'We'll never know till it's over,' said Peter. 'Something's happening outside,' said John.

THE FEAR OF FLYING

Jon Swain of the *Sunday Times*

Pooled despatch, January 18, 1991

The exhilaration and fear of flying in a night-time bombing raid over Iraq was clearly etched on Flight-Lieutenant Ian Long's face as he climbed down from the cockpit of his Tornado ground attack aircraft, still sweating but with a glint of triumph in his eyes.

'It was the most scary thing I have ever done in my life,' the pilot said with real conviction as he headed for the debriefing room.

'We went in low over the target – as low as we dared. We dropped the bombs and then ran like hell.'

Long had trained for months for such a mission. Now that it had become reality he added: 'It was absolutely terrifying. There is no other word for it. We were frightened of failure, frightened of dying.'

It was shortly after 6.30 am. The giant air base in eastern Saudi Arabia that is the hub of the massive air war the allies launched at 3.00 am. yesterday against Iraq had already experienced a couple of air attack alerts in the course of the night. They turned out to be false alarms but made the atmosphere understandably tense.

But even as they pulled on their chemical warfare suits and gas masks and raced from their offices for the shelters, most RAF personnel's thoughts yesterday were clearly focused elsewhere. They were fixed on the lone British bomber pilots who three hours before had launched the first wave of air assaults on Iraq and were now flying back to their Saudi base.

One of those pilots was Long. Twenty-five years old, he was married only three weeks ago. Day One of the Gulf conflict was his wife's birthday, the early part of which he celebrated at the controls of his Tornado GR1 ground attack jet dodging flak and tracer. The latter part he spent fast asleep at base.

Such a demanding mission as Long carried out tends to leave a bomber pilot in the immediate aftermath of combat anaesthetised with fatigue.

Long belongs to RAF 31 Tornado Squadron, nicknamed the Gold Stars. His mission began when he was scrambled in the middle of the night. His Tornado, guided by navigator Jerry Gegg, 43, was refuelled in mid-air *en route* to the target. It crossed the Iraqi border at 500 mph hugging the ground all the way to the target, an unidentified air base deep inside Iraq.

Long's was the last plane in his formation to bomb the target. Its main weapon was a 1,000lb bomb that craters an airfield runway rendering it unusable for enemy aircraft and its radar was so sophisticated that he could see on it the corner of the airfield's perimeter fence, the only fix he had as he approached the target.

'We could not see the ground but it looked a pretty good hit,' he said.

'We went in just to the right of the aircraft in front and we are confident that we got it.'

Having dropped its bomb, Long's Tornado streaked away. Gegg, the navigator, shouted 'Height' to Long, and the Tornado rose in the air.

A few seconds later it ran into bursts of flak from Iraqi anti-aircraft guns but managed to avoid being hit.

As they headed for home Long and Gegg observed two other airfields under attack about 30 miles away.

'The sky was a mass of yellow explosions, it was flak and went on for about 20 minutes,' he said.

Racing for the Saudi border the young pilot from Croydon guided his Tornado down a wadi, a shallow valley. As he and Gegg crossed the frontier and reached the safety of Saudi airspace they shouted out with sheer relief.

Their ground crew was waiting to congratulate them. It was a moving moment.

Only half an hour before, Wing Commander Sandy Davis, Deputy Force Commander of RAF Fighter and Bomber Squadron in Eastern Saudi Arabia had been standing beside the runway waiting to welcome them home.

At the time he still did not know whether the bombing raid had been successful. When he spotted the Tornado's landing lights approaching the airfield his face broke into a grin. 'It has been a truly remarkable feat,' he said.

According to Davis, allied aircraft flew more than 2,000 missions in the first two hours of the air war against Iraq.

It was an intensity of one-day bombing not seen since the 1,000 bomber raid against Nazi Germany during the Second World War. To keep the Tornados in the air tankers made 299 mid-air refuelling sorties.

Commanding officer Group Captain Cliff Spink was waiting in the operations room for the Tornado jets to return safely. 'When they arrived it got very noisy in the Ops Room,' he said.

Also waiting to welcome them back at the base was welfare officer Squadron Leader Clive Parnell-Hopkinson.

He said: 'The boys are elated. They are pleased with their success and are pleased to be back in one piece.

'We are proud of what they did – because it had to be done.

'We're all looking forward to the day we can say "that's the job done. Let's go home."'

HUMAN SHIELD

THE NEW KNIGHTS OF WAR
Paul Johnson

Daily Mail, January 19, 1991

We are the first civilians in history with a close-up view of a great war as it happens.

Thanks to round-the-clock TV, we see not only the military pyrotechnics but the human dramas too.

From our seats in the electronic stalls, the most striking aspect of it all is the demeanour of the young fighter and bomber pilots as they return from successful but ultra-hazardous missions to face the cameras.

These are the new knights of heroic warfare. They might have fought at Crecy or Agincourt.

They certainly could have belonged to one of the rival 'circuses' of Flanders, flying Sopwith Camels or Fokker tri-planes in the days when the Red Baron held the record for the number of kills and enemies were not merely rivals but gentlemen.

Saddam Hussein is certainly no gentleman and these young knights of the skies are hunting down the monster with terrifyingly accurate laser-guided bombs and a range of technologies so new they were unknown five years ago and have never been tested in action.

All the same, it is the human factor which pulls at our heartstrings and, not least, the traits of national character which the TV cameras catch.

The Saudi pilots, bearded and handsome as desert sheiks – which is exactly what their grandfathers were – are greeted on their triumphant return with great smacking kisses on both cheeks, administered by ground crews, commanding officers and waiting relatives alike.

Most striking and significant, however, is the contrasting behaviour of the British and American pilots.

The RAF flight lieutenants are bang in the tradition of the Battle of Britain pilots – shy, laconic, self-deprecatory, with that inner confidence which allows them to confess to fear.

'You're scared of failure, you're scared of being killed,' one admitted, unabashed. 'And when you've seen your weapons on target, you get out of it as fast as you can.'

They don't boast. They smile rather than laugh. And they certainly don't shout.

The US pilots, by contrast, are boisterous, extrovert and – well – very American.

They slap backs, hug and punch each other, jump and wisecrack, make a great deal of noise.

Like their huge and jovial boss, 'Stormin' Norman Schwarzkopf, they don't mind blowing their own trumpet.

They are giving Saddam hell and they love it. It's as much as they can do to stop themselves telling you they are bombing Iraq back into the Stone Age.

But before we start getting snooty and draw disdainful attention to the difference between becoming British reticence and Yankee gung-ho cockiness, not to say vulgar arrogance, consider this:

We are looking at young men who have just returned from the jaws of hell.

They are lucky to be alive and they know it. The way they celebrate the fact and release the tensions is their own business.

Let the Americans bellow and vaunt if they want. They have earned it.

Moreover, beneath the surface, the similarities are much greater than the differences. It is not just that British and American pilots are alike in that they are carrying out extremely difficult (as well as dangerous) tasks with some of the most complicated pieces of machinery ever invented, tasks in which a split second's inattention can mean failure and death.

What, above all, they have in common is their dedication, high seriousness and old-fashioned sense of duty.

A markedly high proportion of the British pilots are regular church-goers. Many come from old service families.

They are second-, third- or even fourth-generation military servants of the Crown.

They are devotedly raising families themselves, boys, and perhaps girls too, who will one day embrace the same tradition.

They have a lot to live – and to fight – for. They are a million light years away from the football yobbo and the lager lout, and the Hooray Henries for that matter.

As a rule they don't get the headlines at all. But this week has served to remind us how much of Britain's future will rest on their shoulders.

As for the American fliers, their high spirits conceal the same deep professionalism and sense of duty. These are young men who have escaped the drugs culture and all the other horrors of the modern US.

They too come mostly from old service families. They too belong to churches, albeit sometimes exotic ones.

They are raising young families. They work at the frontiers of technology but they share with their British colleagues old-fashioned notions like patrotism.

They stand up when a lady enters the room. They salute the flag. The national anthem brings a catch to their throats.

Both groups of young men have something else in common – team spirit.

It is here where British and Americans differ so sharply from the French, who *have* to be different.

In accordance with some inscrutable Gallic logic, the French insisted they would fly sorties into Kuwait but not into Iraq.

The British and the Americans shrugged their shoulders and got on with it.

They enjoy resolving difficulties, rather than raising them. They seem to get a kick out of working together in one of the most complicated battle plans in military history.

What is also striking, and touching, is the way the Anglo-Americans have taken under their wing the young Saudi and Kuwaiti pilots who are proving they can fly and fight with the best.

So there it is – the modern-style chivalry which has again brought the Special Relationship into vigorous life.

The British and American nights make different noises but beneath their breastplates beats a valuable communion of hearts.

It is a long way from Tennyson's Idylls of the King. But it is going to win us this war.

SCUDS OVER ISRAEL

Ian Black

Guardian, January 19, 1991

It looked, said a man who saw it seconds before the first blast, just like a falling star.

For nearly five million Israelis, unusually experienced in adversity, the Iraqi missiles that landed yesterday were a terrible warning that this war may be very different from any they have known.

Most people were asleep when it happened. Air raid sirens wailed in Tel Aviv and Haifa only after the explosions, and in some parts of Jerusalem the job was left to civil defence loudspeaker vans touring the deserted streets.

It was a bad end to what had looked like being an encouraging day.

Initial euphoria at the allied pounding of Iraq had given way, as dusk fell on Thursday, to caution that not all President Saddam Hussein's missiles had been destroyed.

The missiles came suddenly: only minutes separate the enhanced

Scud-Bs' camouflaged launching sites in the south-western Iraqi desert from Tel Aviv.

Direct casualties were astonishingly low. Only 12 people suffered superficial injuries from the blast and shrapnel produced by conventional high explosives.

In Tel Aviv, a textile factory and two homes were destroyed. In Haifa there was little damage and no injuries. A three-yard-wide crater in an empty lot was all that was left of one missile.

Fifty other people were admitted to hospital, several – including newly arrived immigrants from the Soviet Union – as a result of prematurely injecting themselves with an anti-nerve gas agent.

'There was a big flash and a boom,' said Mani Barkan, one of the injured. 'It was like something from the movies.' Another Tel Aviv man said simply: 'It was a miracle no one was killed.'

But three elderly people died because they forgot – I did too, briefly, before I started choking – to remove the plastic stopper that protects the gas mask's screw-on filter when it is not being used.

An Arab girl, aged three, suffocated as her parents struggled to force her to wear the breathing hood for infants.

Precise locations of the seven or eight Scud hits were not revealed, to prevent the Iraqis from improving their aim if there is a second salvo.

Israelis were ready for an attack. A state of emergency had been declared early on Thursday, but at that stage people were told not to open their sealed gas mask kits.

Not since 1940, when Italian planes bombed Tel Aviv and killed 42, had civilians been in the front line.

As the news flowed in from Baghdad, Dhahran and Washington, it had seemed that the Jewish state, for once in its short and eventful history, was to be a spectator cheering from the sidelines in a war against a country that had threatened it long before Kuwait was conquered.

It was not to be. The moment the alert was sounded, people tumbled out of bed and into their safe rooms, windows sealed with plastic masking tape, bleach-soaked towel stuffed under the door.

Even the keyhole had to be blocked.

For many, the worst part was the uncertainty. In our flat in central Jerusalem, my wife and I entered the sealed spare bedroom donned our masks easily enough, but took several agonising minutes to adjust the black rubber straps.

It was an unnerving experience. As aircraft roared overhead, the radio offered only repeated warnings to stay put and listen to civil defence instructions in a babel of languages – Hebrew and Arabic were followed by English, Russian and Romanian.

The telephone was a lifeline. Friends and relatives rang each other constantly, reassuring, offering advice and expressing a solidarity and warmth that briefly took the rough edge off a country where brusqueness is the social norm.

Children vomited: my nine-year-old son worried about his dog, which had run off as the alert sounded.

And he was unable to use the special rubber drinking straw attached to the mask issued to his age-group. Babies were placed in transparent protective infant carriers.

After the all-clear, people ventured out into the winter sunshine to buy milk and bread, carrying their gas masks naturally now, no longer with the sheepish is-this-all-really-necessary look they had when they collected them from the distribution centres. The longest queues were for newspapers.

No one knew what another night would bring, but the sealed rooms were ready and the masks at hand. And no one knew whether or how Israel's government would respond – under immense international prssure to stay out, but also buffeted by domestic fury at the Iraqi attack.

One effect of the missile salvo was a wave of international sympathy. Get hit by a Scud, someone quipped bitterly, and suddenly you are an underdog again. After years of being cast as the Middle East's Goliath – with others playing plucky little David – it was an unfamiliar role.

HOW I ESCAPED SADDAM

Chaim Bermant

Observer, January 20, 1991

And so they finally came, seven rockets out of a cloudy sky. The noise was tremendous. The damage was minimal, a few houses were destroyed and a dozen people slightly injured. And I nearly lost my beard.

Every Israeli building has a bomb shelter in the basement but, thanks to Saddam, every home must now have a sealed-off, airtight room. When the alarm went off just after two in the morning my father-in-law, an ancient Brit who retired to Jerusalem 10 years ago, refused to stir or don his gas mask.

'If I have to die, I would rather die in bed,' he said. My daughter, who also lives in Jerusalem, wouldn't don her mask because it worried her cat. And the cat, of course, didn't have a mask at all.

I, for my part, wanted to remain in bed because I was very tired, but I was staying in a hotel and was allowed no such option. There was a banging at my door and my phone began ringing and the switchboard girl pleaded: 'Please don't make difficulties, this is an emergency.'

So I put on my best suit and packed a couple of books, a packet of cigarettes, a bottle of duty-free, a pack of cards and went down to the sick-room.

The room turned out to be a suite of rooms with two bathrooms – no small matter in such a situation – and two telephones. A burly young man gave us a gas mask and told me to remove my beard, just like that, as if it were a muffler (which in a sense it is).

I've had my beard for 20 years and have grown attached to it. It was one thing being roused from my bed and another being separated from my beard. I refused point-blank. 'All-right,' he said, 'it's your funeral.'

In fact my beard fitted fairly snugly into the mask, and I was able to breathe with little difficulty, but it was about the only thing I could do. I couldn't smoke, I couldn't drink but, worst of all, I couldn't read because I couldn't get my reading-glasses to fit under or over my mask, and I could see myself dying of boredom long before a gas attack. A gas mask has a built-in baleful look, and we sat there for the better part of an hour glaring at each other in glum inertia.

There were about 20 of us in the room, mostly journalists, and the phone kept going all the time with calls from impatient editors in Holland, Belgium, Germany, Japan and South Korea, who demanded to know what was happening. As far as we knew, at that time nothing was, but that did not prevent several of my colleagues – their gas masks on – from making lengthy reports. I admired their professionalism.

It was nearly four before we could remove our masks, and nearly six before we emerged from our sealed compartment into the streets. I have never known air to smell sweeter.

Jerusalem, in common with most holy cities, is not the most ebullient of places. But it normally comes alive on a Friday, with families rushing around doing last-minute shopping in preparation for the Sabbath.

On Friday it was like a Sabbath in its own right, with little traffic and closed shops. Buses were picking up recently mobilised reservists.

There were also numerous camera crews who, for want of something better, seemed to be busy filming each other. I was stopped for a vox pop interview, until they discovered I was one of the pack.

This is an oddly frustrating war for most Israelis. Many thousands of them assembled at the Western Wall last Monday to pray for peace, but that was before the war broke out and the rockets landed. Now they must be passive onlookers where they would have preferred to be active participants.

There is almost something millenial about the whole Gulf war. This is where history began and this – as many a rabbi has agreed – is where history could finish. Jews, who have always had a central place in that history, are not happy about assuming the role of 'noises off'.

In the past, Israel has always had to act on its own. Here was an occasion where it could have been part of a grand alliance, but it still has to stay apart, like Jews throughout the ages.

The Israelis, with the sort of pride in their air force which Britain took in the 'Few', would have loved to see their F-16s demolish the Iraqis' launching pads, and perhaps a good part of Baghdad. Turning the other cheek doesn't come easily.

CASUALTIES OF WAR

John Naughton

Observer, January 20, 1991

'You furnish the pictures,' cabled William Randolph Hearst to his photographer, Frederic Remington, 'and I'll furnish the war.' Much the same deal seems to have been struck between General Norman Schwarzkopf and Ted Turner, proprietor of Cable News Network.

The only problem is that when Stormin' Norman provided the war Mr Turner was unable to deliver. All CNN could manage on the night was live *audio* coverage from Baghdad, screened over singularly uninformative maps of Iraq.

Not since the early days of the Test Card has a static image received such concentrated attention. As Peter and Bernie and John held excited conversations in their hotel bedroom and pushed the mike out of the bedroom window so that the president could hear the bangs, the rest of the world eavesdropped with bated breath.

This, after all, was History in the Making. At one time, Peter and Bernie and John were being run live by both BBC and ITV, an honour usually extended only to Gazza and HM the Queen.

As the networks cleared their schedules for the greatest Outside Broadcast of all time, we were confronted with a new possibility – that wars will henceforth be conducted live on television.

From which point it will be but a small step to having wars conducted – like general elections – *for* television, with major strikes planned to coincide with news bulletins, interviews with returning pilots, and photo-opportunities laid on with picturesque craters and plucky survivors.

"LET'S GET OUTTA HERE, IT'S A GRAPHICS ATTACK!"

We are already part-way there. On Friday we were presented with a live televised briefing given in Riyadh by Generals Horner and Schwarzkopf on the alleged success of the allied air offensive.

This in itself was remarkable enough, but what took the biscuit was the sight of the USAF boss giving the voice-over commentary on a video or laser-guided bombing. We saw cross-hairs superimposed on targeted buildings, followed by satisfying puffs as another 'surgical strike' went home.

General Horner knew what he was doing, for the video footage proved irresistible to the Western networks, and the sequence has been run on an endless loop ever since, often with a gung-ho commentary from the broadcaster's resident military correspondent.

In the process, what somehow got lost was the kind of scepticism that serious journalism demands. Nobody seemed interested, for example, in knowing whether this dramatic footage was statistically representative of the aerial assault. And, of course, nobody asked whether it was the genuine, undoctored article. If it's good enough for Stormin' Norman, then it's good enough for us.

The amazing thing about the non-stop, live, real-time news avalanche which has engulfed us since Wednesday is how little hard information it has contained. It is the journalistic equivalent of candy floss: delicious to consume, but devoid of substance.

Here we are, several days into the war and we still have no objective assessment of the effectiveness of the allied aerial bombardment, no information about civilian casualties, little idea of what has been destroyed, and total ignorance about what has been done to the Iraqi forces in the desert. We know very little beyond what the military PR boys want us to know. And we have no idea whether they are levelling with us.

Was it not ever thus? Yes, but the 'real-time' nature of contemporary television coverage is having a disastrous effect on our judgement. The medium's pathological need for moving pictures delivers it into the hands of those who control access.

This is why we have endless footage of what the allied commanders are prepared to let us film, and no pictures at all of the situation in Iraq. The inevitable result is that our coverage is biased because the story has to be led by the pictures.

More importantly, the sheer speed of the communications technology has eroded our capacity to reflect, interpret, sift. The imperative is to get the story on the air, no matter how dubious or uncorroborated it is.

The most striking example of this came on the night when Israel was first attacked by Scuds. The story of reported explosions in Tel Aviv was broken shortly after midnight by Channel 4's *Midnight Special*. By 1.38am, BBC1 was reporting that 'Israel is retaliating' and Channel 4 was relaying an American report that the Scud missiles had been fitted with chemical warheads.

As the colour drained from one's face with the thought of what this might mean by way of an Israeli response, it was hard to remember that these reports might be nonsense – as in the end they proved to be. Satellites have turned Martyn Lewis and John Suchet and their colleagues into little more than hi-tech rumour-mongers.

But truth and scepticism were not the only casualties last week. As reporters salivated over arcade videos of laser-guided bombing, archive footage of fragmentation bombs and a Patriot missile seeking and destroying an incoming Scud, they spoke the language of computerised warfare – in which 'assets' are 'taken out', buildings 'plugged' and launchers 'neutralised'.

One was reminded of Heidegger's observation that the purpose of technology is to arrange the world so that we do not have to experience it.

We expect arms manufacturers to use this sanitising jargon to obscure the fact that, ultimately, the point of the exercise is to kill, maim and burn human beings. Journalists ought to be more discriminating.

THE FOG OF WAR
Robert Harris
Sunday Times, January 20, 1991

You can tell us at once from the way we look. Our eyes are red. Our faces are white and puffy from lack of sleep. When we open our mouths, a strange new vocabulary spews forth; we talk of Scuds and Patriots, of 'interdiction' and 'degrading capabilities'. For us, the most ordinary phrases have suddenly taken on fresh and sinister meanings: I was genuinely nonplussed for a moment last week on being asked to open the oven and 'take out' the dinner.

We are the Gulf war news junkies. We start getting our fix with the BBC's breakfast news at 6.00am, switch to ITV at 9.25, back to BBC at 10.00, ITV at 12.30pm, BBC at 2.00, ITV at 5.30, BBC at 6.00, Channel 4 at 7.00, ITV at 8.00, BBC at 9.00, ITV at 10.00, Newsnight at 10.30. At 11.30 there is bound to be a discussion about the media's saturation coverage on *The Late Show*, during which we can snatch 45 minutes' sleep before settling down to ITN's Gulf News Report at midnight. That takes us through until 6.00am, when the whole cycle begins again.

During a lull for *Neighbours* last week, I worked out that there are now only two hours out of 24 when you cannot watch the war on one of the four main television channels. I am not even including in this calculation *Sky News* and – the real hard stuff – *CNN*; the LSD of the Gulf-war addict.

Inevitably, certain Conservative MPs have started complaining that this round-the-clock coverage is providing useful information to Baghdad. To which the best answer is to misquote the Duke of Wellington before Torres Vedras in 1810: never mind what it's doing to the enemy; by God it's frightening me.

For it is fast becoming apparent that the Pentagon *wants* its military briefings to be watched in Iraq. When General Colin Powell and Dick Cheney, the defence secretary, delivered their extraordinary illustrated lecture last Wednesday, one had the clear impression that they were talking over the reporters' heads directly to the enemy. They wanted Saddam Hussein, sitting watching *CNN* in his bunker, to see the inexorable, ruthless pressure they intend to bring to bear on his forces.

More precisely, they were aiming their talk at the Iraqi general staff, inviting them to draw the obvious conclusion and remove their dictator before their military machine is utterly destroyed. It was as if General Eisenhower and Marshal Zhukov had broadcast jointly to the German high command in the autumn of 1944. Television executives may believe they are merely providing an unparalleled news service to their audience. They are. But they are also a megaphone, pointed by Washington at Baghdad, faithfully carrying the message the joint chiefs of staff want the enemy to hear.

This time it is not the military who are complaining most about television's coverage of the war. It is the viewers. By Thursday, 4,000 had run the BBC to complain about its coverage; only 150 were complimentary. ITV has logged similar figures. One sees their point. Between the rare hard nuggets of fact – the numbers of sorties flown, the video pictures of bombs hitting their targets – television has been serving up a suet pudding of chatter which John Birt, the deputy director-general of the BBC, is pleased to call 'depth of analysis and inquiry'.

As an addict, I make no complaint. But even I must admit that it is rare that one gets up from the television without feeling more confused than when one sat down. On the BBC's lunchtime news on Tuesday, for example, one expert warned us that the allies were a high-tech force ill-adapted to fight a low-tech opponent like the Iraqis. A few moments later, a BBC defence correspondent declared the exact opposite: that Iraq's high-tech weaponry was precisely what we were trained to fight. This see-sawing of views is not analysis. It is verbiage.

Indeed, expert comment is ruled by an iron law of diminishing returns which runs roughly as follows; one distinguished ex-serviceman on a programme clarifies; two confuse; three baffle. What is the point of having General X saying the land war will begin in two weeks, when Admiral Y says it will take two months, and Air Commodore Z hovers in between? This is simply the range of opinions one can pick up free of charge in the average saloon bar.

The grammar of television, established over decades, has led us to believe that when David Dimbleby sits behind a desk during daylight hours he is bringing us facts: a budget, say, or the results of an election. Now the poor man is reduced to reading out scraps of unsubbed news agency copy, with no idea whether it is accurate or not. His morning show follows a pattern: read out claim; cut to correspondent in the field who knows nothing about it; cut to studio full of experts who erect a great mountain of speculation; cut to Mr Dimbleby with second piece of news agency copy flatly contradicting the first.

From time to time, out of this televisual fog of war, stories loom, never to be seen again. What became of Iraq's capture of some Saudi territory, announced by that fountain of truth, Tehran Radio, and solemnly repeated to British viewers? Where are the great fires supposedly raging in the Kuwaiti oilfields? What about the stealth bomber allegedly shot down? Gone into the ether, every one.

The irony is that Mr Birt is supposed to be the great advocate of 'contextualising' the news; the opponent of television's dreaded 'bias against understanding'. This bias was supposed to be combated by analysis and extended coverage. Now, the scale of the analysis and the coverage is adding to the lack of understanding. It is like gorging on junk food and promptly suffering a monosodium-glutamate attack on the brain.

There are a number of dangers. One is that our senses will be deadened by the time the grimmest phase of the war, the land battle, gets under way. Another is that we are losing our sense of proportion. For example, the Scud attacks on Israel and Saudi Arabia, brought to us in such dramatic fashion, keep being compared to the V-1 flying bomb assault on London. The comparison is crazy. As I write, three people have been killed by Scuds; 24,000 British civilians were killed or wounded by the V-1. What hyperbole, what reserves of drama, is television keeping back for when the war gets really nasty?

I am second to none in my admiration for British broadcasting and its armies of correspondents in the field. But at the end of the first 10 days of war, the television executives would be well advised to conserve them, and us, for the struggle that lies ahead. British television, like the RAF, needs to change its strategy. And this is an addict speaking.

STORMIN' NORMAN

Observer, January 20, 1991

Here is a quiz about some of those most intimately involved in the Gulf war. Which major figure, currently making perhaps the most key decisions of all, is also a conjurer who once belonged to the International Brotherhood of Magicians? Who insists, despite his involvement, that 'war is a profanity'? What strategist based at HQ in Saudi Arabia speaks fluent French and German? Ballet and opera are the principal pastimes of which crucial personality? And, lastly, who is 6 feet 3 inches tall and weighs 18 stone?

Perhaps the last question may provide a clue. Indeed, the answers to *all* our questions are the same: the one person is none other than the massive, enigmatic figure of General H. Norman 'Stormin' Norman' Schwarzkopf, Supreme Commander of the Allied Forces in the Gulf.

It was Schwarzkopf, speaking into a red phone in his Command Centre in Riyadh, who kept President George Bush informed of the progress of the beginning of Operation Desert Storm on Wednesday night and the early hours of Thursday morning. And it will be Schwarzkopf – at least until he retires next summer after 35 years in the United States Army – who will continue to be in overall charge of military tactics until the war against Iraq reaches its conclusion.

Though there are numerous minor gripes about his personality – his real army nickname is 'The Bear', because of his gruff and often downright bad temper – there is an almost universal consensus in the American military establishment that Schwarzkopf, at 56, is exactly the right man to be running the war. In the words of US General Robert Sennewald: 'He doesn't suffer inefficency and mediocrity too well. But if you want someone to lead you into conflict, this is the guy you'd like to have.'

His list of credentials seems almost too good to be true: a graduate of West Point, an IQ put at 170, two Purple Hearts and three Silver Stars earned during two tours in Vietnam, a Master's degree in guided missile engineering, and unrivalled military expertise on the Middle East. He argued as far back as 1983 that the US should be preparing for a war in the Middle East on the grounds that American interests might be compromised by a hostile takeover of one country by another; as a result he drew up contingency plans as thick as a phone book for just such a conflict. Five days before Saddam Hussein invaded Kuwait, Schwarzkopf ran a command exercise for 350 of his staff, rehearsing what would need to be done in such an event.

It all meant that as Commander-in-Chief ('Sink' in military parlance) of the US Central Command – the country's rapid reaction force – he was the natural choice to be sent to take command in the Gulf last autumn. He cuts an unmistakable figure there, purposefully striding across airfields and desert camps while a surrounding brace of Special Forces bodyguards – in civilian clothes so that they should not be instantly recognisable – hold M-16s with fingers at the ready.

He knows, too, how to speak to troops in their own language; hence the not-altogether apt label of 'Stormin' Norman', given to him by the media rather than his colleagues. 'If Saddam crosses that line [the Kuwait–Saudi border],' he told his soldiers in one typical aside meant for media consumption, 'I'm confident that we're gonna kick his butt!'

Behind the scenes, though, he is a master politician-soldier of the Nineties. In the five-and-a-half months of the Gulf crisis, he has always exuded confidence and pride in the manner of a Patton or a Montgomery; in reality, he has been fighting ferociously to press the Bush Administration to apply continual pressure to keep the multi-national military coalition intact and under his command.

That it has done so, Pentagon officials say privately, is largely due to the efforts of Schwarzkopf. 'He has held the coalition together in almost the way Eisenhower did in the Second World War,' said one. In public he is very careful to defer to his Saudi Arabian counterpart Prince Khalid – technically Joint Commander with him on the allied forces – but in practice no one questions his authority. The result of such careful diplomacy is the maximum possible co-operation with the Saudis in a sensitive situation where there is much potential for mutual antagonisms and aggravations between rival religions, traditions, armies.

His background is as colourful as his persona. His father was also a General Norman Schwarzkopf, who played a key role in putting the Shah of Iran on the throne (with, inevitably, the help of the CIA) – and then helped train his security forces. Before that, the elder Schwarzkopf had been a swaggering detective who led the investigation into the kidnapping of Charles Lindbergh's baby. The young Norman spent a year in Iran when he was 12, followed by spells during his formative years in Switzerland, Germany and Italy. He went to West Point and graduated in 1956.

There remains one cloud over his career. In his second tour as a battalion commander in Vietnam, he was in charge of an operation in which several young soldiers were killed by what is known as 'friendly fire' – in this case, artillery shells fired by their own side. The parents of at least one of the dead soldiers blamed Schwarzkopf, and threatened to sue him. The incident became the subject of a book, *Friendly Fire*, and even a subsequent television film. Both exonerated Schwarzkopf, as did the US Army's own investigation at the time.

It is a cliché that like all American officers of his generation the general is haunted by Vietnam. Yet it is probably not so much the memory of the horrors of war that troubles him, although from time to time he has alluded to these if only to reassure the parents and spouses of the men and women under his command that he is not some latter-day Custer. What really seems to trouble Schwarzkopf is the thought that he may make the kind of gross blunder that the men who commanded him in Vietnam did.

He hinted at it again during Friday's press conference in Riyadh when asked about the number of Iraqi casualties. 'I have nothing to say about it,' he said. 'I am never going to get into the body count business.' Body counts, the practice of making detailed claims about the number of enemy killed after an individual action, were the brainchild of General William Westmoreland in Vietnam. It has been argued that they led to some of the worst American atrocities against civilians there.

Perhaps because of the *Friendly Fire* episode, Schwarzkopf is keenly aware of his own image, collecting press cuttings and profiles of himself and underlining passages he considers specially relevant. He is quite capable of assuring reporters that all is well, when in reality he is fighting tooth and nail to unite the disparate American political and military bureaucracies into one common and agreed path of action – not always as easy a task as it may appear. Good public relations, he believes, help instil pride and self-confidence in his soldiers – which, in turn, gives them a winning edge in combat.

Notwithstanding his famously bombastic words – he has told journalists, among many other things, that Iraqi commanders are 'a bunch of thugs' and their troops 'lousy' – Schwarzkopf is a cautious commander whose military philosophy resembles that of some of Britain's Second World War officers, who could never forget the rashness of the generals that a generation before had despatched so many of Britain's young men to their deaths on the Somme and at Passchendaele. Seven years ago Schwarzkopf was deputy in charge of the US invasion of Grenada, when careful planning meant that deaths were kept to a minimum. 'Nobody is more anti-war than an intelligent person who has been to war,' he says.

He met his wife Brenda, a TWA stewardess, at a West Point football game 21 years ago and married her eight months later. They have three children, aged from 13 to 20, who have led the nomadic life of the offspring of an ambitious US Army officer.

'He's very much a family man,' his wife says. 'He cares about people. He cares about his "warriors of peace," as I call them, all those wonderful men and women over there. Their safety is his main concern. He talks about it all the time.' As hostilities broke out so dramatically last week, Schwarzkopf found time to phone his wife and family. 'Hang in there,' he told them.

That, precisely, is what H. Norman Schwarzkopf himself now has to do in the Arabian desert. An awesome burden now rests on his ample shoulders: the lives of a million or so troops on both sides of the combat, the future stability of the Gulf and the world's oil supplies, the political future of President George Bush and other leaders of the international coalition.

There is, alas, one further question in our quiz which none of us can answer with any certainty: when will the war end? All one can say with confidence is that if General Norman Schwarzkopf has his way, it will be very soon indeed.

'DEVIL DOGS' LONG FOR HOME

Patrick Bishop

Daily Telegraph, January 22, 1991

Evening chow had just finished and the Marines were placing bets on what time the Iraqi shells would arrive.

79

'I'm picking 8.22,' said one as we stood in the fast-descending dusk. 'It'll definitely be between 8.00 and 8.30.'

'No, it'll be later, that's for sure,' predicted another.

Inside the mess hall a corporal examined a jagged piece of shell casing, the evidence of a round that had exploded down the road the night before. 'I'm going to put this in my war room when I get home,' he said.

Out in the desert the reality of a land war is creeping up on the Marines.

So far, it is a matter of a few mysterious bangs in the night as Iraqi gunners lob over haphazardly aimed rounds in the hope of hitting something important.

The Marines are mildly excited. For most of them it is the nearest thing they have experienced to coming under fire. But they are also apprehensive.

In a short time, in all likelihood, a few incoming shells will be barely worth mentioning. In a short time, the Marine Corps' lovingly tended image as the world's most efficient fighting machine will be tested.

Even to those familiar with the extravagant self-regard of British paras and French Foreign Legionnaires, the pride of the Marines is impressive, rather 'awesome' and 'outstanding', to use two favourite words in their own rich vocabulary.

'What does it mean to be a Marine, sir? To be the best there is,' is the usual response from computer clerks to tankers when you ask why they joined.

The ethos they would like to protect is a mixture of *Marvel* comics, ancient Sparta and 1950s Hollywood. They refer to themselves as 'devil dogs', a nickname that dates from the First World War, and joke about having to have killed a parent as a prerequisite for membership.

In preparation for combat, the company barbers have been tidying up the brutal 'zero to three' haircuts, in which the victim's head is shaved up the sides leaving a 3-inch Mohican tuft on top.

Marines from the commandant down chew tobacco, packing it into their lower lip and punctuating their speech with squirts of yellow juice.

'I learned when I moved up north that girls didn't like kissing you with a wad in your mouth,' said a Marine corporal. He compromised by switching to a scented brand.

But at the same time they are thoroughly modern Americans, fluent in the argot of popular psychology.

Talking about his wife's reaction to the news that he was going to Saudi Arabia, 23-year-old Corporal Charles K. Piceno solemnly informed the Marine publication *Brown Side Out* that 'she went through a process of denial, rejection and withdrawal, as many wives do'.

In the next few weeks these children of the shopping mall may be called upon to test the truth of Saddam Hussein's assertion that American society cannot withstand the shock of losing tens of thousands of its citizens in a battle.

So far, some 85,000 Marines, about 90 per cent of their combat strength, have been drafted into Operation Desert Storm. Bases all over the world have been denuded of personnel and 18,000 reservists called up.

Their role in the looming land battle has yet to be stated. Logically, their seaborne capability could be used for an amphibious assault on the Iraqis' Gulf flank in Kuwait.

The infantry, supported by tanks, armoured personnel carriers and artillery, will undoubtedly take part in the thrust through the Iraqi defences.

Until last week, the prospect of fighting still seemed far away. When the air war began, most Marines at the logistics base from where this dispatch is being filed expressed reactions of relief, welcoming the end of the stultifying waiting game.

'I'm just glad it's started,' said Lance-Corporal Greg Terna, a muscular 21-year-old from Kinsman, Ohio, as he queued for breakfast. 'Hopefully it's going to be over soon. I hope they keep bombing. They should go on for another 21 days. Now the time is starting to tick down. Now we can hope on going home soon.'

Life in the desert, even for barrack-dwellers, is stupefyingly boring, a routine of hard work, massive stodgy meals and long dark nights in which one day merges indistinguishably into the next.

Since the start of hostilities it has become more interesting, but also more alarming. Several days ago, the pre-dawn torpor of the camp was shaken by the long-drawn-out wail of a siren giving warning of a chemical attack.

Inside the 'hooches' there was just enough light to find canvas gas mask bags and pull out the clumsy apparatus with its sinister sci-fi monster green plastic hood.

A loudspeaker announced a 'MOPP [Mission Oriented Protective Posture] Level 4', the highest state of chemical alert, requiring troops to put on full chemical suits.

81

Eventually, an hour and a half later, the all-clear sounded and everyone thankfully took them off again.

It had been a false alarm – exhaust fumes apparently set off a detection device – but an uncomfortable experience all the same. One effect of the masks is to amplify breathing, reminding you of how easy it would be for it to stop.

Since then, the alarms have grown to be part of the routine. Moving into the shelters, the Marines resume the conversations they were having in the mess hall or the 'hooch'.

Money is a common topic. There is a story going round that King Fahd offered to give $1,500 (£780) a man but was turned down, to the troops' dismay, by President Bush on the grounds that they were not mercenaries.

According to the (unfounded) rumour, the British accepted the money.

The death benefit is also discussed. Fifty thousand dollars (£25,680) does not seem so much when the prospect of getting killed is lying just over the sandy horizon.

There is little talk of politics and little animosity towards Saddam Hussein and the Iraqis, except as the agents of their being in Saudi Arabia.

The main contact with Iraqis, apart from a few under-nourished PoWs brought in at the weekend, are the anonymous gunners responsible for the – so far ineffective – nightly fire. The Marines joke that they like the gunners. They keep missing.

The women Marines, who are present in sizeable numbers in the forward areas, have done little to soften the atmosphere of the locker room at war, and seem to be regarded by their comrades as honorary men.

The concerns of the young men and women are much the same as those of any other American of their age. 'They're older and more literate than my generation,' said a journalist who served with the Marines in Vietnam.

'Our average reading was a comic book. That was about the level. The average age of a field unit in Vietnam was about 19½. We had a guy with us who was 24 and we called him "Pops". These guys are in their early to mid-20s.'

The considered opinion of the Marines concerning Saudi Arabia is that 'this place sucks', a conviction that is all the more lowering to the spirits when the length of time they are going to have to spend there is so difficult to gauge.

Even if there is a quick end in the fighting, few expect to be out before the end of August as the process of packing up is likely to be even longer than that of deployment.

The prospect of escaping when your period of service expires has vanished for about half those eligible to do so now that certain categories are required to stay on until the end of the operation.

In the darkened 'hooches' at night, country-and-western and soul play softly on the boom boxes, a reminder of home. And even for 'devil dogs', home is where they want most of all to be.

SPEAKING OF DEATH
Richard Kay
Daily Mail, January 24, 1991

There are few moments in war when it seems better to be a soldier than a correspondent, but this is one of them.

The infantrymen of the Royal Scots and the cavalry of the 14/20 Hussars in their tanks deployed across miles of empty sand must take for granted their part in the conflict that will surely soon begin.

For those of us who little more than a week ago found ourselves pitched into service alongside the British build-up at the front, it has at times meant a conscious effort of will.

Not only about transforming ourselves from, let's face it, a free, easy and independent civilian life into a soldier's routine of orders obeyed, but also about coming to terms with our own confusion about what is ahead.

How shall we cope with the fog of war? I hope we shall be permitted our apprehension. For me these past 10 days have been a revelation.

While not in any way trying to diminish the role of the magnificent men who face long, hard and certainly bloody battles ahead, we too have had to undergo intense self-examination, a kind of battle-preparation if you like.

I suppose it was Brigadier Christopher Hammerbeck, commander of the 4th Armoured Brigade, who pulled it into sharp focus.

On my arrival he looked me over in my newly pressed desert pattern fatigues, a helmet hanging with the strap undone for all the world like

Audie Murphy, and asked if I had thought through what was going to happen. Not to the troops but to me.

He didn't say it, but he was talking about death. About a 7.62 calibre bullet that comes out of the dark, or a mist of poisoned chemicals that dusts the ground like a deadly drop of spray.

But surely, you think, as a reporter you are a mere observer? That impressive white identity card in your tunic pocket bearing your picture and Ministry of Defence crest says war correspondent, not soldier.

A week later in the dead hours before the dawn, the realisation that there is no distinction, no room for mere spectators, begins to sink in.

The air is alive with the sound of shrieking klaxons and the fearsome yell of 'Gas! Gas! Gas!'

And the Iraqi special forces, said to be at large in our area, will surely show no quarter with their piano wire and stealth.

It is a comfort to think of the sentries at night in their foxholes, although how they distinguish between friend and foe when every piece of desert brush takes on the form of a man I can only guess.

For someone used to a daily newspaper office, where the lights of industry burn late into the night, life without so much as a candle is an extraordinary experience.

There are, incidentally, enough perils in venturing out after nigthtfall in the shape of trenches, traps for the unwary, without worrying about Saddam's killer squads.

In a way these past days – and in the desert you have little concept of time or date – have been something of an initiation.

One of our number has left already, ground down by routine as much as anything. Perhaps there will be others. In times of war, though, routine can be life preserving. So let me tell you about a day with the Desert Rats.

We rise each day at 6.00am when the flat half-light looks as I imagine the Western Front did in the First World War. The sand is wet and clammy and in the gloom you can see heads moving about the parapets of the guards' slit trenches.

My home has been the alcove of a tent with a rickety old camp bed under sheets of pink CARM – chemical agent repellent material. In the days to come, I think I shall long for such primitive comforts.

Washing over a basin dug out of the sand with a jug of cold water may not be the most dignified way of starting the day, but it does wake you up.

In the cookhouse at 7.00am, the World Service News is listened to intently by men who at home would rarely tune their transistor dials to Radio 4.

The successes of Patriots in knocking out Scuds are greeted with cheers. The losses of aircraft acknowledged in silence.

Scud has become the word of this war, in the same terrifying way as the name Exocet filled every household with a sense of dread during the Falklands.

In this build-up to battle, the day revolves around meals. We eat on our feet off disposable plastic while wearing full combat gear, helmets and flak jackets, ready to move in an instant.

For all of us, the respirator that could be the difference between living or dying in a horrible way does not leave our sides. It hangs in its green pouch like a six-gun ready for the quickest of quick draws. We have a ditty about getting it on in under 10 seconds. *Be in time. Do it in nine. Stay alive and make it five.*

Shoulders once familiar with nothing heavier than the cut of a grey flannel suit have grown used to a backpack of kit that would do credit to a sherpa. And added to that are chemical-proof charcoal-lined smock and trousers, clumsy rubber overshoes and water.

We have been accustomed to the stages of alert for donning the gear. Just the other night I lay in my sleeping bag perspiring gently in the respirator for what seemed like hours as Scuds flew out of hearing above our heads.

At a field casualty station, I lined up for an anthrax jab with our Scottish driver, Jock Johnson. 'Better not turn us into badgers,' he said, suspicious of the needle. If Saddam has his way it could be the most vital unpleasant moment we ever have.

To increase our resistance we are all taking NAPS – anti-nerve gas pills – washed down three times a day with stewed army tea.

Morning can mean 'administration', the quaint army term for washing clothes, or if the water supply has got through a cold shower.

Being clean is just a distant memory. Sand permeates everything. Like the soldiers I have my hair shorn to the scalp.

At night we turn our socks over the tops of our desert boots to keep out scorpions.

Orders to strike camp come abruptly and must be followed swiftly. Camouflage netting is packed away and trenches, over which we seemed to labour for so long, are filled in. That way we move on without showing sign of our presence.

Driving is another unforgettable experience. At night it is like navigating in a blindfold. All the fuses must be removed from lamps. In daylight, every halt has to be accompanied by throwing a 'scrim net' over the vehicle so it melts into the sand.

Night falls quickly like a great black curtain dropping across the skyline. By 8.00pm the camp is silent. Men are sleeping or alone with their thoughts. These hours are a time to reflect on the momentous days that lie ahead.

What will it really be like? We have spent long hours with battle groups to give us the taste, sound and sight of war. But then no one was firing at us.

To escape from those thoughts, I have burrowed under my sleeping bag to write 'blueys', the soldiers' lifeline to family and friends and loved ones, by torchlight. It brings memories of boarding school flooding back.

There have been lighter moments in these past days. At a first-aid class, my task was to heave Private Steve Smith, 16 stone and as solid as a rugby international, into a fireman's lift. He slammed over my shoulder with such force that we both hit the sand.

Or the afternoon of rest and recreation spent playing with a miniature crossbow when the correspondents proudly outgunned the army sharpshooters.

They will be moments to treasure, faces to remember, to sharpen the mind when we are baptised by battle.

Now it is dark. Allied planes are rumbling overhead on their nightly run to Baghdad.

The last week with the Desert Rats has been a privilege. The next few promise to be the most testing of their lives and certainly of mine.

THE BASTARDS OF BAGHDAD

Sun, January 22, 1991

The faces of captured British airmen Adrian Nichol and John Peters will haunt us all for many a long day.

So brave when they went into battle, so helpless when captors paraded them on television.

Adrian's mumbled and hollow words, like those of the two American fliers with him, were obviously **DICTATED** by an Iraqi propaganda writer.

How they must have stuck in his throat as he was forced, under what threats we dare not even imagine, to denounce the allied mission in which he had played such a gallant part.

No one can believe the sentiments uttered by Flight Lieutenant Nichol, in a voice drained of emotion, were his own.

They were the words of an evil monster, Saddam Hussein, and the Bastards of Baghdad.

Our thoughts and our compassion are with the captured allied servicemen and their families.

But what anger, what contempt we feel towards Saddam Hussein and the creatures around him.

ANYONE who doubts that we are at war with an evil monster should study these shameful TV pictures.

ANYONE with a scrap of human compassion and dignity will recoil with horror at Iraqi threats to keep prisoners near military installations which are legitimate targets of allied raids.

The conventions about the treatment of prisoners of war are clear and precise among civilised nations.

They must be held with humanity and dignity, without any kind of duress, physical or mental.

That is the honourable tradition.

They must certainly not be gleefully paraded as tools of propaganda.

Yet what does Saddam know about honour or decency?

His cowardly forces have not had the guts to face our men in open combat.

So he turns his cruel malice on the captives at his mercy.

Our prayer is that the war will speedily be over and Adrian Nichol, John Peters, and our other prisoners, will be safely back with their families.

And when the war is won, the time will come for Saddam and his henchmen to pay the price for their crimes.

Forty-five years ago the Nazi leaders were tried and executed as war criminals.

The Bastards of Baghdad deserve the same fate.

For holding Our Boys as human shields, they should hang, long and slow.

Death by a swift bullet is too good for them.

PARIS LIFE

Suzanne Lowry

Daily Telegraph, January 24, 1991

My friend 'E' has changed her route to work in the mornings. The barriers on the Rue du Faubourg Saint Honore, the police and CRS, the body and bag checks, the random demands for her identity papers were bad enough. It was when she saw marksmen on the roof near the British embassy that she decided to take the long way round, thus also avoiding the Elysee Palace, the American embassy and the Ministry of the Interior and their prophylactic troops.

She has insisted on a guard at her child's school and is cancelling a skiing trip that involved flying Air France. She will not go to the cinema or risk shopping in the Galeries Lafayette. The Metro is out and the bus just tolerable.

She has bought tickets for Bejart's ballet in February and hopes that by then the war will be over so that she can go to it. Meanwhile, she presided over the installation of a hefty armoured door at her office, which caused a collective nervous breakdown among the building's other inhabitants. The night-time electronic code is now on all day. There are nine policemen on the street corner.

Only nine? Certainly not enough to deal with the general level of panic that hangs in the air. Paris, within a week, has become paranoia city. Paranoia *de guerre,* paranoia *de terrorisme.*

E does not want me to give her full name for fear of attracting a terrorist's special attention, but she is not alone in her fears. Everyone is afraid of someone or something. The government has had to ban the sale of arms to private individuals, such has been the run on hunting and hand guns.

In the suburbs, of late the setting for violent troubles in the lycees, racial tension has been replaced by war anxiety. Peace protests abound. In at least one establishment, one child per class is permitted to have a radio plug in its ear and re-broadcast the news to classmates as it breaks.

In the old Jewish quarter of the Rue de Rosiers, residents are nervous of Arab neighbours. In Barbes and Belleville, the Arabs fear

National Front reprisals. Street musicians and shoppers have almost vanished from the Forum des Halles. Buskers, gypsies and *clochards* of the Metro have been flushed out above ground. Throughout the republic, 200,000 gendarmes and police are on full alert, waiting for Saddam Hussein's suicide squads or Abu Nidal's hit men.

Fringe nerves are comprehensible, predictable. But in the jewel-box centre of Paris, the fear is both less reasonable and more palpable. The Americans and Japanese seem to have deserted: hotel palaces are half empty. The world capital of luxury, whose main customers came from the area and the nations now immersed in conflict, is having a bad case of nerves.

The couture fashion collections scheduled for next week have not been cancelled, although much of the flummery surrounding them has. Many American buyers and customers are not going to show.

The cocktail circuit was the first to go dead. A party for the dog portraitist and sporting artist Cecil Aldrin was so thinly attended that doggy-bags of food were handed out to departing guests.

Was all Paris at home rearranging kitchen cupboards? Certainly the people of the Cote d'Azur last week engaged in a wave of panic buying of staples – flour, sugar, oil, bottled water. Rumours that Saddam would somehow poison the water supply by remote control found a ready audience. The Ministry of Finance has constantly, but to little avail, told people there is no petrol shortage and forbidden people to hoard it at home. Rumour has it that some have filled their baths with the stuff.

A French military man apparently announced on television that the Midi would not be spared if chemical or nuclear warfare erupted at the other side of the Mediterranean, which may explain the South's alarm. A reason closer to home might be that people there harbour the bitterest and longest memories of the last war. It has an elderly population, and a large number of North African immigrants who recall the *penurie* of the Algerian war.

Paris has lived all year with such tales, this being the 50th anniversary of the German occupation in 1940.

Culture, luxury and megalomania have an embarrassing inter-relationship. When Hitler came to Paris in 1940 he and his gang systematically removed paintings to take to Berlin. The Nazis luxuriated in the best Paris had to offer; it became a rest and recreation base for the officer corps.

This time, the Gulf crisis and its ensuing war are said to have caused mass cancellation of Middle Eastern orders for jewellery, glass and other trappings of western civilisation – not just on the Kuwait/Saudi side.

Saddam has a taste for such goods, too. It seems he placed an order for Limoges porcelain worth five million francs (£500,000). However, since the invasion of Kuwait, nothing has been heard of him.

French television is covering the war round-the-clock. *Envoyes speciaux* are dotted round the Gulf region, the usual talking heads replaced by generals and colonels dragged out of mothballs to give their views. My favourite correspondent is the TF1 man in Dhahran who livens up his commentary by talking as if permanently under missile attack, ducking and rolling his eyes and looking over his shoulder all the time, gas mask on and off.

France, too, has bowed before the all-embracing coverage of CNN but the incorporation of the American material into the French footage is not wonderful. Listening to Saddam speaking in Arabic being translated into English being translated into French makes the war seem distant indeed.

'I COULD SEE ITS LITTLE FINS'
Marie Colvin
Sunday Times, January 27, 1991

Hussein stood alone in the carpet souk on the eastern bank of the Tigris, fingering his ivory worrybeads and gazing at the huge sun setting behind the Ottoman tenements on the far side of the river. The dying sunlight washed his *dishdasha* robe a wintry red.

The market square of the souk usually bustled at this time of early evening as people stopped to gossip or do last-minute shopping on the way home from work. But it was January 15, the United Nations' deadline for Iraq's withdrawal from Kuwait. Baghdad was silent and edgy. The souk was deserted.

Hussein greeted me with far more warmth than our acquaintance merited. I had visited him on and off in his shop over the past five months, using the excuse of fingering a Kurdish bangle, or looking at a carpet, to pick up the rumours and rhythms of daily life in Baghdad. For him, it had been an excuse for a rare talk with a foreigner, something that for an Iraqi is akin to a visit to the confessional.

Now, in this chance encounter, we seemed the only people left in the capital. We walked to his shop under the vaulted roof of the souk. Inside, there was none of the usual salesmanship or the ritual cup of sugared tea. 'Would you like a whisky?' he asked, and picked up a half-full bottle of Whyte & Mackay. He poured us two tea glasses full.

Amid the clutter of piled-up carpets, silver necklaces, antique frames, heavy Kurdish belts – and, beside the ubiquitous picture of Saddam Hussein, a likeness of President John F. Kennedy beaten into a copper plate – we discussed whether he should stay in Baghdad or take his family to a place safe from American bombs, as other merchants had.

Tareq, who owned the House of Antiquities across the street, had taken his wife and sons to Kurdistan in northern Iraq. 'The Americans like the Kurds, they won't bomb them,' he had said.

Hussein agonised. Baghdad was home; perhaps thieves would come to the empty souk and steal his carpets; but there was no business anyway because everybody was hoarding their money.

We drank another tea glass of whisky, standing up, too edgy to sit down. His wife, five children aged two to 12, younger brother and a mother were at home waiting. His children had their school exams on the 20th: if they missed, it would mean losing a year of school. 'But perhaps it is better that they lose a year than that they lose their lives,' he said.

Darkness was falling and we walked out of the shop. He said: 'If you have any problems you can come to my house. Really.' For an Iraqi, it was an enormous act of faith. A visit by a foreigner in this tightly controlled society meant a follow-up visit by the security police. But these were extraordinary times. It was a way of saying we were not enemies. I drove back to the Rashid hotel through dark and deserted streets.

Baghdad is normally a bustling city. Although its glorious antiquity was long ago buried under drab concrete, its spirit was irrepressible, even at the height of the first Gulf war, when taxis returning from the front with coffins on their roofs raced among the fierce traffic on its highways. To see the city now was chilling.

Many middle-class families had closed their homes and left to stay with relatives in the country after the failure of the talks in

Geneva between Tariq Aziz, the foreign minister, and James Baker, the American secretary of state. Others held out, fiddling for good news between the BBC, Voice of America and the Pan-Arab station, Monte Carlo.

They had heard the ominous tone in Saddam's speech on Friday to an Islamic conference in Baghdad. They had heard Joe Wilson, the American chargé d'affaires, dramatically announce as he left on Saturday: 'This is the last flight out.' They knew most Western diplomats had left with him.

But even illiterate taxi drivers held an irrational faith that Javier Pérez de Cuéllar, the United Nations secretary-general, might be able to avert war when he arrived to see Saddam at the weekend. 'Maybe Saddam will leave Kuwait,' the taxi driver said as he drove me to Pérez de Cuéllar's news conference at the airport. When the secretary-general said 'only God knows' if there would be a war, it was the last straw. Iraqis knew Saddam was ready to take on the world.

Everybody was jumpy. We lost our way leaving the airport and when we drove up to a checkpoint to ask a soldier for directions, there was an audible click as he flipped the safety catch off his AK-47 and walked up to the car with the barrel pointed through the window.

There were many poignant moments in those days overshadowed by the deadline. The most striking thing perhaps, to somebody who had been visiting Iraq on and off since the crisis began, was the sudden openness of the usually careful and closed Iraqis.

This is a society that usually keeps its head down and offers no political opinions. Most dissidents are dead or in exile. The tiny middle class would, in general, be glad to see Saddam's regime fall; but the merchants did well out of the war against Iran and reached an accommodation with those in power. The urban poor, who have enjoyed cheap, and even free, housing and subsidised food under Saddam, are compliant to his will. The long war against Iran united society and now I found that his stand against the world was filling many Iraqis with pride as well as fear.

After seeing Hussein in the souk hours before the deadline expired, I went into the Al-wiyah club with Falah, an Iraqi businessman. It is a former British club now frequented by Iraq's elite, a place of contrasts. A huge Saddam portrait greets arrivals in the club car park, but members still leave their own private bottles of whisky behind the bar, their names printed on them, in the old British club tradition. We were the only customers, but there was still food, some salads and chicken.

Falah spoke over dinner about statistics, trying to put on a brave face that Iraq would somehow continue. He had been helping as a consultant to the government in what he called 'food security' since the crisis began. He had managed to cut sugar consumption by 60 per cent by closing down ice-cream and confectionery shops; Iraq was now making its own liquid sugar from dates. Farmers had had to kill most of Iraq's chickens because of the shortage of grain, but cows had been switched to grass and still gave milk. Wheat was a problem; Iraq produced 4 million tons annually and consumed 6.5 million but increased subsidies for farmers would make up much of the shortage. Meanwhile, rationing filled the gap: his office had made charts of human consumption, added 20 per cent and produced rationing amounts and distributed coupons.

Such statistics are usually impossible to come by; but I had barely the energy to commit them to memory (you don't take notes in public in Iraq). Falah relaxed, dropped his beloved subject and lapsed into tales of his childhood.

The club was significant to him and to the current situation. He had come here first as a young and proud university student, the first Arab of his generation to visit it, brought by a British professor as a reward for being number one in his class. 'You realise for us this is much more than a war between Iraq and America. For us, even for the Arabs who are not with Saddam, it is a struggle for our dignity. The West has humiliated us and we see Saddam as a leader who has finally stood up to the West and said we want our dignity.'

On the way home, I went by the French embassy where André Jenier, the last Western diplomat in Baghdad, was preparing to leave in proper French style. He had laid out the embassy's last French cheeses, pâtés and salamis and served champagne until midnight, when he and his few remaining staff clambered into their cars and drove through the night to the Jordanian border.

At the Hotel Palestine, previously the Meridian but now run-down and shabby after a change from French to Iraqi ownership at the start of the economic embargo five months ago, I stopped at a 'challenge the deadline' celebration, an Iraqi version of an end-of-the-world party.

Kadum Al-Sahir, a popular singer, was on the floor amid a group of men who danced and waved Iraqi flags. But most of the rest of the hall was filled with sombre beer drinkers, sitting at their tables without much enthusiasm. Most were government recruits; the only guests who seemed to have paid the 20 dinar ($35) entry price were 10 Palestinians who had come in a delegation from Jordan to show solidarity with Iraq. A wedding party had been recruited to build up the numbers.

I went to bed in my room at the Rashid hotel and waited for the worst.

The Americans had announced that the deadline would fall at midnight New York time, 8.00am local time next day, Wednesday the 16th. When I woke, a heavy fog had settled across the flat city. For a moment, looking out of the hotel window, unable to see anything but white mist obscuring the skyline, I thought perhaps the attack had come and I had slept through it.

Downstairs, among the government 'minders' who watched the comings and goings of the few of the 40 or so journalists left at the Rashid hotel, there was premature euphoria. 'You see, I told you there would not be war,' said Karim, one of the men from the information ministry.

Baghdad thought otherwise. Driving around town, I saw only a few knots of men in quiet discussions. Rashid Street, the main thoroughfare, lined with colonnaded mock-Ottoman buildings from the 1930s, was usually packed with cars. Instead, it was a wide deserted avenue at 9.00am.

Windows were taped over against bombs for the first time. The Mandarin restaurant on Karada Street, once Baghdad's busiest fast-food joint but closed for months because of a ban on serving meals, had its wide windows taped in large Xs. At the Shorjah souk, Baghdad's most popular market because of its cheap clothing, household items and canned goods, only four of the 200 stores had opened. One man, hanging up flannel robes from the ceiling of his shop, said: 'We still open for an hour. If it stays like this, we will close.' Schools had opened, but with few teachers and fewer students they quickly closed for the day.

There was no sign of backing off by Saddam. The headline of the government newspaper, *Al-Jumhuriya*, said: 'We shall never compromise on Iraqi and Arab rights.' Midday television news showed perhaps the unluckiest people in the world that day: 177 former prisoners of war descending from an Iraqi Airways flight to Baghdad after years of captivity in Iran.

Sources were fast disappearing. I telephoned the foreign ministry to try to see Nizar Hamdoun, the under-secretary. But the ministry's number had changed and its officials had moved to a new location. The last time I had seen Hamdoun, he was sitting in his office, morosely watching CNN television. 'I feel like I'm watching a bad fiction movie,' he had said.

During his tenure as Iraqi ambassador to Washington, Hamdoun had been the architect of the Iraqi-American *rapprochement* of the 1980s. He still felt Iraq could be America's best ally in the Middle East. It was the only local power able to enforce stability in the region under Bush's new world order; it had oil America needed; it was a potentially wealthy market; and it would guarantee American interests. But by January 16, 1991, policy was long out of the hands of thoughtful diplomats such as Hamdoun.

At the ministry of information that evening, the receptionist at the office of Naji Hadithi, the director-general, was watching cartoons. Inside, Hadithi and I watched a film showing Saddam visiting troops in Kuwait. The president looked confident as he had in every appearance that week, although rather awkward as he sat wrapped in a huge greatcoat with troops who looked terrified by his presence. He asked them oddly personal questions. 'Have you had your dinner?' he said to one. A long pause . . . 'Is this place warm?' he said to another.

Hadithi switched to CNN and we watched a demonstration of allied fire control in Dhahran, where Saudi, American and British forces are based. A lieutenant-commander was interviewed, saying his men were prepared. Hadithi commented: 'The only thing missing from this is reality.'

He meant on the allied side. It was a cherished belief of many Iraqis I spoke to, even those who were desperate to avoid war, that if it came to a battle, Iraqi soldiers, hardened in the war against Iran, would defeat their better armed but inexperienced enemy.

As Wednesday evening drew on, Marlin Fitzwater, Bush's spokesman, caused the first real worry among the foreign press corps. He said any journalists in Baghdad were in danger and should leave immediately. All American print reporters had left on the 14th, but the American television networks remained. Now they started getting prearranged signals from Pentagon sources that an attack was imminent.

Larry Doyle of CBS received the message: 'Your family is fine but your children have colds.' Doyle, a veteran journalist who reported on the Vietnam war, put down the phone and said simply: 'Shit.'

A delegation of journalists hurried to Hadithi's office. Some wanted to move out of the Rashid hotel, located in central Baghdad near most of the ministries and the presidential palace, all obvious targets for attack. But Hadithi said: 'We are still here. Our ministry is a dangerous place and yet we did not evacuate.'

John Simpson of BBC Television said in his understated manner: 'The Americans have 2,000lb bombs which could make things extremely unpleasant.'

Latis Jassim, the information minister, arrived and reassured us. 'You are safe. This is a commitment on our part. We are willing and eager to offer you the necessary services so that you can report the facts as you see them. But at no time will communications fail completely.'

It was midnight. We went back to the hotel. The attack could come at any moment. Nobody knew how bad it might be. We waited.

I took a small bag down to the bomb shelter below the hotel, just in case. Already women and children were huddled along the walls wrapped in blankets. Somehow the warning had swept through the hotel.

The lights in the shelter flickered. I had to see what was happening. I turned and started up the steps but was met by a flood of panicked people coming down the stairs, women with crying children, Sudanese waiters still in uniform, an Iranian delegation staying at the hotel.

At entrance-hall level, I could hear booms from outside. Upstairs, from the 5th-floor BBC office, we saw out of the window a spectacular display of tracer fire shooting across the sky. Tracers spewed up as if from a roman candle. Others shot across the sky as if following an unseen and unheard enemy. White flashes illuminated the tops of buildings on which, during the last five months, we had watched the crews of anti-aircraft guns shelter first from the August sun and lately from January's rain and cold.

Strange video game noises filled the air. The staccato thud-thud-thud of heavy artillery sounded. Bob Simpson of BBC Radio had a microphone out of the open window and leaned on his elbows on the windowsill as he calmly described the spectacular display. Down the hall, a CBS cameraman knelt on the floor, his camera out of the window, and filmed through a down-tilted eye scope.

Huge yellow flashes appeared on the horizon. Something to the right thudded and the impact threw me back across the room. Smoke rose from the building. There could no longer be any suspicion that it was a false alarm or jittery anti-aircraft gunners. It was 2.35am Iraqi time and Baghdad was under attack.

Doyle, spotting the flashes on the horizon, narrated for those of us less knowledgeable about armaments. 'Those are the big boys, the cute 2,000lb bombs,' he said. 'Unfortunately I've been through this before. They are just pounding the hell out of that place.'

The bombing appeared to be about 20 miles off, probably at the Rashid military complex. The attack slackened off, then started again at 3.35am. The city, which had remained lit up, went completely black. The anti-aircraft fire stopped and started again in almost 15-minute intervals, sometimes directed above our hotel, filling the skies but seeming to have little effect.

About 4.25am, hotel security guards came into the room and tried to drag us downstairs to the shelter. They settled for taping over the emergency light that had gone on when the hotel lights failed. From below, during a lull, an earnest ABC reporter yelled up: 'What are your departure plans?' Somebody yelled down: 'Up in the air at the moment.'

I wandered back to my room at 6.00am as dawn broke and the attack appeared to have stopped. A man I had never seen before was asleep in my bed still wearing large boots. I went down the hall and took a nap on the floor of the BBC office.

Morning came cold and misty again when I woke at 7.30am. After the drama of the night, it was strange to see the city skyline unchanged. Smoke from a fire behind the hotel drifted through the hallways. But little damage was visible from the hotel room.

We clustered around to hear Baghdad radio for the first communiqué of the war. 'This is communiqué number one. The mother of battles has begun. President Bush will regret this attack. Victory is near.' The voice announced the immediate call-up of reserve soldiers born in 1954, 1955 and 1956. The radio returned to martial music.

My driver had disappeared. He was born in 1955 and had been worrying about the call-up for the last month. 'War is very bad,' he had said to me. 'I fought eight years in the war with Iran. No wife, no children. Now maybe I have to go to Kuwait.' His fears had been realised.

I grabbed a taxi on the street and drove around the city. The first evidence of attack was at the international post and telecommunications building. It had been hit by at least four missiles that had left gaping holes and dangling wires. Chunks of building and glass littered the streets, but no surrounding buildings suffered damage more than broken windows.

A bit further on, the Ba'ath party headquarters had taken a direct hit in the roof. Again, no surrounding buildings were touched. On Abunawas Street, across the river from the presidential palace, a car tilted crazily into a 30-foot crater already filled with water. But, other than that, there seemed to be almost no damage to civilian targets.

Anti-aircraft guns sounded again at 9.00am and 10.00am. Soldiers in uniform lined the roads at bus stations trying to flag down cabs or cars to head south to register with their units. The few families that had left it too late to leave stood, suitcases and children in hand, trying to do the same.

At 10.30am I was standing in front of the ministry of information, now deserted despite the minister's brave words just hours earlier, as a thud sounded and a mushroom of smoke went up from the defence ministry about half a mile away. Two more thuds shook the building. Neither a plane had been visible nor an engine heard. Anti-aircraft fire went up but it was too late.

Driving by the ministry – an old Ottoman building still marked the Abbassid Palace on tourist maps and so secret that a government official once told me it was a musuem – I could see flames in the central section. A wing had been flattened as if by a giant fist.

The reaction from soldiers in the barracks across the street from the defence ministry was as surprising as the suddenness of the attack. They stood standing and watching the fire as if it was a show unconnected to them. Nobody seemed to be in much of a hurry to put it out. Like the foreign ministry, the defence department must have transferred its operations elsewhere in the days before the deadline.

As I drove around town, the calm and lack of panic were impressive. Orderly lines formed for bread and cars queued for petrol. It was a far cry from the day after the bombing of the Libyan city of Tripoli, when Libyans crashed their cars into each other trying to flee, the government disappeared and rumours that Colonel Gadaffi had been overthrown filled the capital.

Baghdad's militiamen had appeared overnight to keep order. In the Amriyah area, a civilian neighbourhood, six teenagers dressed in jeans and jackets walked along the streets with Kalashnikov assault rifles casually slung over their shoulders. A man in a cheap suit and a *keffiyeh* Arab headdress manned an anti-aircraft gun placed in the back of a Nissan pick-up truck at a crossroads. But there were no new checkpoints, nor was there hostility towards foreigners.

Saddam came on Baghdad radio at 12.40 in the afternoon, speaking in calm and confident tones: 'At 12.30am the great duel started. The valiant sons of Iraq, your brothers, sons and fathers confronted the invaders. Damn King Fahd, the traitor of Mecca, damn the invaders, damn these criminals. We shall win. The dawn will break and they will be damned.'

My taxi driver, taking me back to the hotel, said he was not at the front because he had a piece of shrapnel still in his head from the Iran war. It hurt when the weather got cold. Like most Iraqis that day, he appeared worried but unfazed. 'I did not think we should have taken Kuwait,' he said. 'I don't agree with this. But the Americans should not come to Iraq. Iraqi soldiers will fight for Iraq and for Saddam. We have fought for eight years against Iran and they cannot frighten us.'

This was the mood of Baghdad under fire. An Iraqi businessman explained to me why people were so calm. Listening for weeks to the propaganda from Washington, they had expected Armageddon. Now that the bombing had come at last and they had survived, he said, their attitude was: 'Well, if that's it, we can take it.'

People had even begun to listen for the first time to Iraqi radio, and to believe its propaganda, because they felt that the BBC and Voice of America had lied about allied successes against the air force and missile sites in the first attack.

In addition, the government maintained at least a semblance of control. The city was without water or electricity, and the streets began to smell of sewage and cordite. But soldiers directed traffic in place of traffic lights, papers continued to publish daily, and the television news appeared every night at the same time, with its usual announcer, and on the same television studio set.

Only a few shops opened; and prices were astonishing: I saw a bottle of whisky, a packet of cigarettes and three Mars bars bought for 147 dinars, the equivalent of $441 at the official rate and equal to three-quarters of the monthly salary of a middle-ranking government official.

But in the poor neighbourhoods such as Saddam City, where more people had remained because they had no way of escape, and which the regime regards as its centres of support, government lorries distributed bread under normal ration regulations.

Anti-aircraft fire erupted sporadically during the day. Tracer fire, the thud of guns and falling bombs filled the night, but there were few civilian casualties.

There were makeshift shelters to be found almost anywhere in the city. Driving back to the Rashid, I ducked into the Baghdad hotel when anti-aircraft guns went off at the nearby presidential palace. The discotheque had been turned into a bomb shelter and guests were handed candles at the door. People were worried but there was still an air of unreality. 'Palestine seems closer than it has for 40 years,' said a Palestinian businessman also sheltering inside.

Baghdad's survival — and the news that Saddam had launched Scud rockets at Israel — had many Palestinians and their Iraqi supporters still believing that he would achieve his goal of somehow freeing Palestinian land from Israel.

As the sun set on Friday, I watched two orbs of light streak low across the city skyline, just missing the rooftops, and smash into the Dora oil refinery. A huge ball of fire erupted and smoke drifted back over Baghdad.

Bombing continued sporadically that night and at dawn the refinery had only three instead of four chimneys. The 20-storey communications tower — which had lost its top three storeys to an unseen missile on Friday, as if to an invisible hand — had completely disappeared from the skyline by Saturday morning.

On Saturday afternoon, I was gazing idly from a 5th-floor window across the Zawra zoo park opposite the hotel when I suddenly realised that a cruise missile was heading above the trees straight for us. It seemed to be white. I could see its little fins. There was no smoke trail coming from it.

I thought it was going to hit the hotel, and I yelled out. But it turned right and skirted the building, as if following a street map, and hit the old parliament building about half a mile away, sending up a white pall of smoke.

Another cruise landed even closer, disappearing with a deafening crash into breeze-block staff quarters next to the hotel. The huts burst into flames and shrapnel showered the lawn and swimming pool. Glass from broken windows littered the hotel lobby as hotel workers dragged an electronic circuit board into the air-raid shelter, dancing around it, ululating and shouting that they had downed an American plane.

It was a relentless afternoon attack. At least two more missiles hit the Dora refinery again, sparking a fire that lit Baghdad with a beautiful rose glow late into the night.

Conditions at the Rashid hotel were becoming primitive. Electricity remained off and journalists worked at night by candlelight. Sanitation had broken down, toilets could not flush, and we had been washing in the swimming pool.

The officials minding us had had enough. They had stayed in the shelter for days and had not seen their families nor been able to contact them by telephone. They were worried about our safety and about the detail of what we were reporting. We were ordered to leave.

On Saturday night, as I packed and sat up late with other journalists discussing our departure, a Palestinian friend stopped by to say farewell. An articulate, educated man, he was trying to explain why so much of the Arab world had come out in support of Saddam despite his invasion of Kuwait and oppressive policies.

'You must understand that if Saddam goes, no Westerner will be safe walking down an Arab street. I will pick up a machine gun and fight the Americans. A year ago I would have told you I hated Saddam and his regime. But he has become a symbol for us. Saddam is the result of the humiliation of the war of 1967 and of all the humiliations we have suffered from the West. If we let you destroy Saddam now, you will destroy all of us Arabs again.' He added: 'It is a question of dignity. Saddam came along with his rockets and stood up to you and we said, "Why not?"'

I rose at 5.00am to the incongruous sounds of a cock crowing and another barrage of anti-aircraft fire, this time a light and sparkling scattering of shots of tracer into the air. The government newspaper headline read: 'Hussein rockets answer the call of Palestine. The road to Jerusalem is open.' Uniting under attack behind Saddam, people might even believe this hyperbole.

Downstairs the taxi drivers demanded the exorbitant sum of $3,000 a car to the Jordanian border, because a convoy of cars that had left on Saturday had been bombed near the town of Rutba in the western desert.

We drove out of Baghdad on the deserted highway, past military camps on the city's perimeter that appeared surprisingly intact, with anti-aircaft guns still manned on mounds along their boundaries. Government army lorries trundled south towing anti-aircraft guns, but there was little other traffic. The journey through flat, unbroken rocky desert was uneventful. Iraqi guards stamped exit visas into our passports at the desolate border station of Trebil. Among the shabby breeze-block buildings we left behind the stacks of abandoned cheap luggage from earlier refugees and drove across the no man's land into Jordan.

A DIFFERENT KIND OF WAR

John Simpson

Spectator, January 26, 1991

It isn't what any of us expected. I have seen various wars, from the sudden bush skirmishes of Angola and Rhodesia to the mindlessness of Beirut and the occasional ferocity of Afghanistan; but none of these was remotely like what has been happening in Baghdad and the other cities of Iraq. In the 20 hours between the expiry of the United Nations' deadline to Saddam Hussein and the moment the first air raid started, those of us who were in the Rashid hotel in Baghdad talked obsessively about the likely pattern of the war. The repeated warnings of President Bush and his spokesman were deeply disturbing. So was an expression used by an American air force general on American television: the Rashid was to be a 'turning-place' for cruise missiles. These things worried away at us like an infected bite.

By the night of January 16 the main topic of conversation among the journalists was the power of the 2,000lb penetration bomb. A large, unshaven man from one of the American networks who was planning to get out said, 'Man, I wouldn't be down in the shelter when one of those mothers comes out of the sky. I saw them in 'Nam. You'll be dead meat. The vibration's gonna shake the fillings right outa your teeth.' I ran my tongue round my fillings, familiar and smooth: how bad would the vibration have to be to shake them? Finally I summoned up a response. 'Not half as bad as the vibration on the road to Jordan,' I said; 'that'll shake the money out of your pockets, and in your case it's a lot more serious.' He was notoriously tight-fisted, and the going rate for a taxi to the Jordanian border was $3,000.

Other people, also leaving, worked out our margins of safety for us. 'I've seen penetration bombs land in Beirut. One hit by the swimming pool here, you ain't gonna be alive. If it hits away over the street you might make it.' These thoughts penetrated our imaginations with considerable effect and exploded there. I dozed for an hour or two and dreamed of penetration bombs. And yet none of these things came to pass. Our mistake was to associate the destructive capability of the new weapons technology with the hit-and-miss delivery systems of the past. The missiles I had seen landing on Teheran in the Iran-Iraq

103

war were closer to V-1s than the Tomahawks which the Americans were to use against Baghdad. Only the Iraqis fought the old war of indiscriminate attacks against Tel Aviv and Riyadh with their elderly Scud missiles. If the Americans had used the equivalent of Scuds it would have been another war of military men against civilians. There would have been fearful casualties, yet the economic and military infrastructure of Iraq would have remained largely intact. Instead, the American missiles and smart bombs have worked their way through the centres of population and done the maximum damage, not to life but to Iraq's ability to prosecute the war. When the air force general said the Rashid hotel was a turning-place for cruise missiles, he meant it literally: one flew across the front of the hotel, turned at the corner and flew across the back of it before striking its target just opposite. No one in the shelters seemed to lose their fillings.

As I looked out from the 5th floor at the skyline it felt like being in the middle of a very big chessboard: every now and then, at apparently random intervals, a gigantic hand would reach down out of the sky and take away one of the major pieces on the board, without touching any of the others. One day the piece might be Baghdad's electricity supply. The next it would be its communications or its stocks of fuel. With great deliberation, Iraq was being bombed back to the age of the Abbasids. Baghdad became a city lighted only by candles and oil lamps, where information passed by word of mouth rather than television or radio or phone. At night the only sources of light you could see from the Rashid were the headlights of a few speeding cars and the fearful glow from some big chemical plant which had been hit earlier. Otherwise there was no light and no sound.

The Iraqi government was plainly taken by surprise. Such evidence as there was indicated that President Saddam Hussein expected a massive onslaught in which thousands would die. This is presumably why he thought the American will to prosecute the war would be short-lived. It may also be the reason why he refused to authorise the evacuation of women and children from the cities. The plan to evacuate Baghdad was made public by the minister of the interior, a portly, scar-faced man who turned up at a camp for refugees which we had been taken to inspect. It seemed a very small camp, considering it was supposed to take a quarter of the population of Saddam City, a vast surburb of great barrenness on the north-east edge of Baghdad. A million people lived there; but the refugee camp contained only 80 medium-sized tents, each sleeping a dozen or so. No one could explain where the remaining 249,000 inhabitants of the relevant quarter of

Saddam City would stay. Not that it mattered at the time, since all but a few of them had decided to ignore the order to be evacuated, and stayed at home with the curtains closed.

The interior minister bustled across the sandy ground towards our cameras, children and dogs scattering in the path of his bodyguard. The bodyguards fought us back while we tried to get close enough to hear what the minister was saying. Next Friday, he promised (it would be the Friday before the UN deadline), there was to be an evacuation drill for the whole of Baghdad. After that the city would be evacuated in earnest. Friday came and went. So did January 15. On January 16, the day before the war began, the speaker of the Iraqi parliament gave a small news conference. A slight, smiling man, he explained there would be no evacuation after all. When their fathers were preparing to be martyrs in Kuwait, he said, the children were equally prepared to be martyrs.

Back in our cutting room we put together our report. We had pictures from a girls' school in Baghdad: the pupils making their way through the early morning mist, the school bell ringing, the girls settling down in their classroom. The camera-work was good, and I looked at the dark, eager faces of the pupils as they started the examinations which the government had deliberately refused to postpone. The girls were in their mid-teens: a little younger than my own daughters. When we had edited those pictures we added on the Speaker's news conference. I was tempted, when he came to the part about children longing for the opportunity to become martyrs, to overlay close-ups of the faces of those girls, rational and earnest, on his words. But the producer had a better grasp of the BBC's principles than I did, so we let the viewers make up their own minds about it, and decided not to load the issue. But it was hard to ignore the suspicion that if an American missile had landed on the school the Iraqi government would have felt it constituted excellent propaganda.

A train was hit in one of the earliest attacks, and people aboard it were killed. But Iraq's own casualty figures seemed to indicate that the number of deaths was remarkably low, given the destruction that was going on by day and night. In Baghdad itself the losses were lower than anywhere else. That, presumably, is the result of having Western journalists in the city. The Americans must have taken especial care to avoid civilian casualties in Baghdad, where they could have reported back to every television viewer in Europe and America.

In the end, of course, we were obliged to leave. We tried hard to stay. Having cracked a couple of ribs during a bombing raid, I did my best to persuade an Iraqi doctor to say I was unfit to travel; it didn't work. Some of us thought of barricading ourselves in our rooms, but we were told politely that the order to leave had come from the president's office and would be enforced in whatever way was necessary. The ministry of information, which knew the value of having us there, had fought a spirited rearguard action on our behalf; but the security ministry was determined to get rid of us on the grounds that we were acting as artillery-spotters for the allies, informing the outside world which targets had been hit and which were still standing. The decision to allow Cable Network News, Saddam Hussein's favourite viewing, to remain in Baghdad looked like a compromise between the two ministries. When we found that CNN was staying, there was a good deal of anger among my colleagues; but privately I was glad that someone at least would still be there as a continuing protection for civilians.

As our $3,000 car took us through the suburbs of the city in the direction of the Jordanian border, we saw the big communications buildings and the defence installations split like cans of corned beef opened with a hammer and chisel, while the houses and shops around them were mostly untouched. Everywhere was silent and empty, with a few shell-shocked people standing about dully on the street corners. We passed the restaurant which I had visited on New Year's Eve in search of a party to film. It had been a frenetic affair, with people clambering onto the tables and wearing masks and silly hats and squirting one another with foam. Young girls danced with portly old men, and with other girls, and with their boyfriends. Older women made a lot of noise, and pretty women looked at the floor and giggled. When people found out that we were British they gathered round to kiss us or shake hands. There was a lot of very bad champagne and reasonable Scotch, and everyone sweated a great deal. The New Year would bring terrible things, and no one wanted to remember it for a night. When midnight came and the lights went back on and the shouting and laughter was louder than ever, I watched an old man, bald and fat, his face shining with the heat of the room. He was sitting silently by himself, and opposite him at the same table was a woman who looked like his daughter. She was beaming, and bouncing a child on her knees, making it clap its pudgy hands together in time to the loud dance music. The old man sat there in the noise and the jollity and looked at them, the tears running unchecked down his fat grey cheeks.

Now the restaurant was deserted. The windows were taped against blast, the New Year decorations long since taken down. It was just another silent, tatty building in the city which expected its next air raid at any minute. I had been frightened many times during the previous nights and days, but as I looked back from the car and watched the restaurant receding into the distance, remembering the old man and his daughter and grandchild, I knew there was nothing I wanted more than to come back here.

SADDAM AND THE MEDIA
Max Hastings
Daily Telegraph, February 5, 1991

On the Gulf battlefield today there is a struggle for dominance between two agendas: that of Saddam Hussein and that of the allied coalition. However complex in reality, the coalition agenda is straightforward in concept. The allied armies are preparing a major ground offensive, to drive Iraq's forces out of Kuwait.

All the evidence so far suggests that General Schwarzkopf is sticking firmly to the plan for his 'big push' (if that phrase is not rendered pejorative by its First World War origins), and no 'sideshows' are being undertaken to impress the public or please the media.

Meanwhile, in Washington and other allied capitals, there are fervent hopes that Saddam will be shot or deposed by disillusioned underlings in the wake of defeat. There is no clear political plan for the later phase of the war, because there seem too many uncertainties. The war is being addressed simply as a military operation to liberate Kuwait with minimum casualties.

But Saddam's agenda appears entirely different. Soon after the beginning of the war, I suggested that he was seeking to keep his forces in being. The key question was whether he intended to commit them in the ground battle, or was thinking further ahead.

It now seems likely that Saddam is indeed looking beyond the loss of Kuwait to a scenario in which, even amid military defeat, he can claim heroic status in the Arab world for having stayed in the ring against the Western-led alliance through a 'mother of wars'. Thus, he has mounted a succession of militarily futile but headline-grabbing operations, and thus his apparent confidence. Saddam is not running a war in the expectation of military victory, but a political and publicity campaign in which his weapons merely chance to be lives rather than government hand-outs.

At a briefing last week by General Schwarzkopf it was fascinating to see this struggle between rival agendas being fought out before our eyes. On the day after the much-publicised, if trivial, border ground battle, the general talked for 10 minutes about the progress of the allied air offensive, with much detail and resort to maps and videos, before he deigned to mention Khafji.

Even for those watching on television in an office several thousand miles away, the tension was apparent between the host of journalists and onlookers aching for the commander-in-chief to 'get to the point', and General Schwarzkopf himself, determined to show what he considered *was* the point.

We are seeing a confrontation between two sets of logic: that of the West, which argues that military defeat signals nemesis for Iraq's leader; and that of Saddam, who seems to believe that, even in defeat, glory can be achieved and his own influence in the Middle East maintained. Such a cultural chasm is not new. Many allied soldiers in north-west Europe in 1944–45 shared a bitterness that they were forced to go on risking their lives fighting an enemy who had no rational hope of escaping defeat.

Argentina's diplomatic and, later, military behaviour in the months following its seizure of the Falklands in 1982 was, in British or American terms, founded upon fantasy. Yet the Argentinians were viewing events and prospects with the eyes of a wholly different culture.

Vietnamese logic ran wholly contrary to that of the United States for a bloody generation. I do not for a moment believe that Iraq, unlike North Vietnam, can avoid military defeat. But there seem valid parallels in the enemy's belief that even tactical military defeats can be turned to propaganda and ultimate political advantage.

Here, we approach one of the most sensitive issues of this war; the role of the media. We shall not be able to judge for many months how far Saddam's efforts to make the world's media address his agenda, rather than of the allied coalition, have served his cause. But he is not faring badly.

While the allies prepare for their ground offensive, their air forces are waging the war. But the air campaign is taking place far beyond lens range of the media in Saudi Arabia. Every night, commanders are subjected to probing questions from journalists about bomb damage.

The commanders' responses do not sound very convincing, for the simple reason that they do not know. Nobody, not even General Schwarzkopf, will be able to assess the effectiveness of the bombing campaign until the ground war comes.

But, amid one of the most serious conflicts of modern history, the media feel compelled to trawl the Middle East, searching for aspects of the conflict that they *can* write about or film. First and foremost, thanks to Iraq's generosity in granting facilities, cameramen and reporters in Baghdad are allowed to film damage to civilian life and poperty. Acres of film and newsprint are being daily exposed on this theme.

Yet no foreigners in Baghdad can perform the function of a proper journalist – to search for information and report this in context – because they are being granted no access whatever to news or pictures of the effects of bombing on military objectives. Saddam is thus successfully exploiting the media to place injury to innocent civilians on the world's front pages.

Although the *Daily Telegraph* has kept no correspondent in Baghdad, precisely because this situation seemed inevitable, I accept the existence of a dilemma. We carry agency reports from Iraq. There must be a case for maintaining some link between Baghdad and the outside world. A more serious charge against the media concerns their apparent determination, which pervades vast areas of the television coverage and newspaper analysis, to seek evidence of allied failure and incompetence.

In recent days, we have seen the prominence given to news that American Marines had been killed by friendly fire (which happens with depressing but inevitable frequency in every war); enthusiasm for some uncensored journalists' reports claiming that the American build-up is in something between disarray and chaos; and constant claims that the war is 'running over time' because of setbacks to the bombing. It is no exaggeration to suggest that the litmus test for a reporter to win plaudits from his peers so far in this conflict is to outdo the competition in expressions of disbelief about official allied claims.

It must be right for journalists to maintain instinctive scepticism about official claims and government statements, in war as in peace. This responsibility deserves more credit than it receives from some media critics. But I remain unconvinced of the case for displaying 'objectivity' as between the allies and Saddam, when even the most generous moral assessment of his deeds already in this war suggests that he is an exceptionally evil man.

I hope I am not succumbing to either jingoism or deferential journalism when I say that nobody I respect in military circles can yet see the smallest evidence that (a) the allied war effort is being conducted other than competently, or (b) the allied timetable is being unduly disturbed, given that a war cannot be run like an airline schedule to Paris.

Here is the old, old problem that occurred in Vietnam, where American atrocities were visible, communist ones were not; where American blunders and failures could be reported immediately, while those of the enemy could not.

Every journalist covering the Gulf war needs constantly to conjure up a mental image of the enemy's predicament: of the havoc in Iraq's infrastructure and lines of communications; the misery and fear among many of its military units (yes, even or especially after Khafji); the demoralisation at its shattered air force and naval bases; the bleak prospect facing any Iraqi soldier capable of rational reflection. All this is out of sight. But it should not be out of mind.

The public is sometimes insensitive to the difficulties of reporting wars. We are all struggling amid a fog. We journalists are speculating no more than every allied general and politician is speculating.

We are bound to get it wrong sometimes, with so many pieces of the jigsaw missing. The *Daily Telegraph* has made its share of mistakes, including a front-page prediction for which I was personally responsible, that Israel would retaliate for the Scud attacks launched on her cities.

But, amid the big and important struggle between the rival agendas of the allies and of Iraq, I do not believe it is excessively chauvinistic, or a betrayal of professional principles, to express the conviction that we, the media, should do our utmost to ensure that we are not addressing the agenda of Saddam Hussein.

'WE WILL TALK ABOUT GOD'

Philip Jacobson of *The Times*

Pooled despatch, February 4, 1991

In a spick-and-span tent in the forward zone of the British ground forces, the commanding officer of a regiment earmarked to assault the Iraqi front line is talking quietly about the conquest of fear on the battlefield.

For Colonel Arthur Denaro, who will lead the Challenger tanks of the Queen's Royal Irish Hussars into action, the need to confront, examine and ultimately unmask the terrors of combat is a crucial element in preparing his men for the unbelievable intensity of armoured warfare at close quarters.

'We should actually be talking about battlefield stress,' he observes, 'because shock, fatigue and even disgust are also ever-present. I can't begin to define what courage is, except in terms of being prepared to face the unknown out there in the combat zone.

'I can assure you that if a guy told me he was not frightened about what lies ahead of us, I would be genuinely concerned.'

Leaning back in his canvas chair beneath a signed photograph of Field Marshal Montgomery in the desert, Colonel Denaro spoke of the curiously British reluctance to discuss something as intimate and personal as fear.

'I have tried to read as much as possible on the subject and I talked to experts before the regiment was sent out here because I firmly believe that the more this subject is talked through among my troops the less they will worry about not being able to cope when the shooting starts and there is the chance of letting down their comrades.

'In a tank regiment where crews commonly train together for months on end, the level of personal trust and mutual dependence has to be total. One chap who is not up to scratch at the wrong moment could be disastrous for all the others,' Colonel Denaro noted.

'Talk about male bonding is really nothing but the process by which soldiers who expect to fight together develop a brotherly, even tender, regard and respect for each other that transcends background and rank. Call it comradeship if you like, because that probably best expresses the feelings of the men themselves. One definition would be the certainty that, if you were trapped in a burning tank, the other crewman would always try to get you out.'

For Colonel Denaro, the only man in the unit with any experience of active service (and that is what the military calls low-intensity operations rather than armoured warfare), comradeship is the building block on which any regiment that takes pride in its tradition and battle honours must lay the foundations of high morale.

'If soldiers are happy about their equipment, their spares, if they are eating OK and getting mail from home, they develop a deep confidence in the system they are a part of. Without that, the prospect of going into action, facing the unknown, will become an even greater burden,' he said.

Unsurprisingly, Colonel Denaro is happy that the unit's approach will pay off handsomely.

Before the regiment moved into the forward zone, officers and senior NCOs gathered for informal sessions at which they were encouraged to talk frankly about how they viewed the prospect of going into combat.

The idea was to chase away the fear of fear that makes soldiers worry about how they will react to seeing a comrade's tank in flames, to getting hit themselves, to destroying another human being.

'We are getting letters from wives and mothers saying "Thank you" for looking after their men so far and how they pray this will continue when the battle starts.

'Obviously, that places an awful burden on the shoulders of individual troops' leaders and their non-coms, but the discussions that this sparked off were truly remarkable, of great personal intensity.'

We asked Colonel Denaro what his soldiers would be told when the regiment begins the final advance that will bring it up against an entrenched enemy in Kuwait.

He answered in a quiet voice: 'We will talk about God, certainly, probably about home and families and, being good Irish, there will definitely be some joking to break the tension.'

As Colonel Denaro accepts, even the best troops sometimes 'freeze in action', but the speed with which they can bounce back reflects the depths of their physical and mental reserves.

'My aim is to bring the regiment back alive', he concluded, before taking down the photograph of Monty to show what the former QRIH officer who had sent it over to Saudia Arabia wrote in his letter – 'May the force be with you.'

BOGGED DOWN IN THE DESERT

Robert Fisk

Independent, January 23, 1991

Journalists officially accredited to the British and American armies in Saudi Arabia are not brought to this particular forward divisional location. Outside these hundreds of square miles of waterlogged desert, allied check points have been instructed to turn back reporters. And when you drive into this swamp of mud and water, it is not difficult to see why.

For the gathering of allied armies here in preparation for the great land battle against Iraq bears little relation to those comfortable, efficient scenarios outlined by American and British commanders in Riyadh. The mass of troops and armour gathered here for the offensive have had to fight their way through a logistical nightmare, which at times left armoured units unable to find their headquarters.

Officers who talk about their difficulties to the press without authorisation are subject to military discipline and must therefore remain anonymous. Their problems are easy to identify:

1) Many junior officers are leading their units to the front lines without even the most basic road maps. The *Independent* has twice had to donate its tourist maps of the region to convoy commanders hopelessly lost within 30 miles of the Kuwaiti frontier. Once this week, an allied military convoy travelled to within 20 *feet* of the border – and within sight of an Iraqi artillery position – before being turned back. The convoy was 200 miles from its correct location and of 220 military personnel aboard, only 14 carried rifles.

2) The location of the main allied offensive against Kuwait and the units scheduled to take part in the principal attack have become an open secret, not just here but around military bases at Dhahran and al-Jubail. Every officer I spoke to is concerned that the Iraqis must long ago have acquired this information.

3) Convoy 'discipline' near the front lines has largely broken down. Transport drivers are often paying little heed to notices ordering them to maintain a good distance between vehicles. Armour and trucks were moving along a supply route littered with the wreckage of disabled or smashed vehicles.

4) Forward medical units have been instructed to give priority to battle

casualties with hope of recovery, leaving terminal patients 'to take second place'. Although this is standard military procedure in battle, allied medical services are uncertain of their ability to cope with the number of seriously wounded casualties who may die in their care. In the words of one doctor: 'We can handle hundreds of patients and perform operations eight at a time and we have transport aircraft to take them out.

'We have refrigeration trucks to take bodies to the rear but we may be overwhelmed. So we have dug two mass graves. If necessary, they will be used for any of the dead – Americans, British, Iraqis . . . they would be disinterred later for official burial at home. I'm not having bodies lying around during a battle.'

Medical staff are trained to care for gas victims but admit they could do little, on coming under chemical attack, to help patients undergoing operations.

Almost incredibly, allied military doctors claimed that the precise location of every American, British and French field hospital has been forwarded to the Iraqi government. 'We know where their hospitals are, and they know where ours are,' a medical officer said. 'This is the usual practice. We have to trust the Iraqis to respect this.'

JOURNALISM AND PATRIOTISM

Independent, January 18, 1991

Truth is inevitably the first casualty of any war. Journalists are bound by rules designed to ensure that they do not immediately tell the whole truth about the conflict that they are reporting. Many of these restrictions are justifiable. Reporters and their newspapers or television networks should not be allowed to disclose information that would be of value to the enemy. Few would wish to do so. But, given modern technology, this restraint can be unexpectedly comprehensive. For example, live television coverage of the damage caused by Scud missile attacks on Israeli cities could enable the enemy to identify the random sites on which the projectiles had fallen and to readjust their targeting.

Equally, it is right that undigested information or rumour that could undermine morale either at the front or at home, or which might endanger lives in the course of a current military operation, should

114

generally be held back until confirmed. This is a matter of growing importance now that both television and radio have live or 'rolling' news channels. As a matter of common humanity, the publication of detailed information – including names and photographs – identifying those killed, captured or gravely injured in combat should be withheld until the next of kin have been officially informed.

Problems would arise if the media believed they were being censored (or invited to indulge in acts of self-censorship) to avoid embarrassing the military, the politicians or individuals with careers at stake. Patriotism does not and should not mean telling lies on behalf of the government of the day. If newspapers and television stations become mere conduits for offical propaganda, they undermine their own independence and lose their value to a democratic society. When editors or the government subsequently attempt to deliver messages of importance the public will be inclined to discount them.

The principle of accountability would be eroded by a supine press. Wars should be fought under political control with ministers answerable to a well-informed people. There are few activities that do not benefit from public scrutiny. Reports of incompetence or unpreparedness at the front are inevitably distressing to the friends and relations of those risking their lives for their country. Those at home fear for their loved ones, and they worry lest alarmist reporting gives comfort to the enemy or encourages him to attack at a vulnerable spot.

Such attitudes are natural, and a sensitive editor will have them constantly in mind. This is why such reports must be meticulously edited to ensure that sensitive information is not published. What remains may be a valuable snapshot or vignette of the chaos and confusion of war; or it may be an indication that something more fundamental has gone wrong and should be rectified. The reporting by William Howard Russell in *The Times* of the manner in which the Crimean War was being conducted, and the danger and suffering to which troops were exposed as a consequence, was a bold and patriotic act. It was certainly not an act of irresponsibility. Those who systematically censored their own reports during the First World War did their readers and their fellow countrymen at the front no service. War reporting demands sensitivity and restraint. But it also demands honesty and courage.

NOSTALGIA IN BRITAIN

Richard L. Hudson

Wall Street Journal, Europe, January 31, 1991

London – The Battle of Waterloo, it has been said, was won on the playing fields of Eton. If so, the ancient English school is keeping up the side in today's Gulf war. Should any terrorist bomb threaten, school policy dictates, pupils on playing fields are to 'continue games'.

Let the Americans, perturbed by terrorist threats, cancel their travel plans. Let angst-ridden Germans protest in the streets. Here in Britain, no mere dust-up with an Iraqi dictator is being allowed to ruffle the national spirit.

'When you've got 1,000 years of history behind you,' explains Robert Adley, a Conservative Party member of Parliament, 'you tend to take these things stoically.'

Just as the country stood firm under Hitler's bombing Blitz, so today Britain's mood is one of quiet determination. Without fuss, British hospitals are readying wards for the expected Gulf casualties, while charities prepare to help bereaved families. Even prostitutes are

116

answering the civic call, if one tabloid newspaper, the *Sport*, can be believed. Its front page asserts that some are donating their wages to a gulf charity: 'Call Girls Bonk for Britain,' the headline screams.

There is an eerie feeling of *deja vu* in all this: Britain is at war – but which war? The Second World War references are back on everyone's lips. The prime minister's war cabinet meets daily. The 'Desert Rats', Field Marshal Montgomery's old North Africa brigades, are in the battlefield again. Vera Lynn, the now elderly wartime crooner, is once more serenading troops with her famous song 'We'll Meet Again'. Newspapers compare every manoeuvre of the US-led coalition and the Iraqis with Allied and Axis tactics and dust off old photos and quotations of Winston Churchill. 'This Could Be Our Finest Hour', one paper editorialised.

Nor is television immune to the nostalgia. Since the conflict began, viewers have been treated to such wartime treasures as *A Yank in the RAF*, a black-and-white chestnut featuring Tyrone Power and Betty Grable in wartime London. The film was sandwiched in between live telecasts of war briefings in Riyadh and London.

Newspaper letter columns are crowded with missives from old soldiers relating their war stories. One writer to London's *Daily Telegraph* recalls how he shot German mines out of the water when serving on Atlantic convoys. Another recalls his grandfather's battalion, in the 1941 desert battle of Sidi Barani, taking prisoners 'about five acres of officers and 200 acres of other ranks. May we only pray that history repeats itself at the earliest opportunity.'

A third writer, to the *Guardian*, asks, 'When and in what circumstances could the Gulf war justifiably be named the Third World War?' (The *Guardian* invites readers' opinions.)

Of course, even in peacetime, war memories aren't far below the surface here. But the current orgy of remembrance is a useful way to gird for an uncertain future. Though the Gulf war is nowhere near as immediate here as was the Second World War, 'one does always hark back to the past,' says Carol Mayers, an official of a British charity that is helping soldiers' families. 'The war is part of our history.' Moreover, she adds, rallying to support the nation 'is something traditional here. In time of crisis, everybody wants to do something to help.'

Colin Moxson did his part at a blood donor centre in London's financial district. 'I never gave blood before, but I'm here because of the crisis in the Gulf,' says the telephone-company office manager as he and a throng of donors, of all ages, recover from their bloodletting with English tea and biscuits in a cramped waiting-room. 'I like to think we're all doing our little bit, however small it might be.'

In the first days of war, the queue for donors at this office stretched out onto the street. Nationwide, according to a spokesman for the National Blood Transfusion Centre, more than 70,000 people telephoned or visited blood banks in the first week of war. Daily collections jumped 80 per cent before the blood banks called time out and asked people to make appointments for later on. Blood has a shelf life of just 35 days, and few expect the Gulf war to end that quickly.

Mr Moxson and his fellow donors at the London centre represent a fair cross-section of British public opinion. Not all agree that the war should have begun. 'I don't know how hard we really tried the economic sanctions,' complains 28-year-old Ian Matthews, a junior bank employee who frets about getting drafted if the war drags on. But he brushes aside such qualms, noting that, like it or not, the soldiers abroad will need blood – and so will civilians at home if the Iraqis carry out their terrorist threats.

Other parts of British society are rallying to the cause, too. The Archbishop of Canterbury, a past critic of government policies, buried the hatchet and declared the war 'just'. Both Queen Elizabeth II and Diana, the Princess of Wales, with press in tow, have been visiting servicemen's families while Prince Charles tours defence factories.

British Broadcasting Corp. told its disc jockeys to avoid such controversial tunes as the old John Lennon number 'Give Peace a Chance'. And members of Parliament, in a subtle but much noted signal of heightened vigilance against terrorism, have taken to facing the TV cameras with their security identification tags pinned prominently to their pin-striped lapels.

The ever-rowdy British tabloid press is in full cry. The *Sun*, Britain's biggest-selling newspaper, reports a (dubious) survey finding that 81 per cent of respondents want to 'nuke Baghdad' and admonishes its readers to fly the Union Jack everywhere. Its Page Three Girl feature, a daily nude pin-up photo, has a special wartime logo: 'Page Three at the Front'. Most of the models are photographed with – or, rather, posing beside – gun belts, army helmets and camouflage jackets. Reads one caption: 'Dashing Donna needs no reinforcement at the front'.

Another tabloid, the *Daily Star*, has 'adopted' a British battleship and is running a contest to find Saddam Hussein look-alikes. 'Are You Mad Sad's Double?' the newspaper asks readers.

In stark contrast to such flippancy, many here complain, is the widespread American dread of terrorism. Since the war began, thousands of US tourists and businesses have cancelled trips to Europe to avoid terrorism – enraging many British politicians and commentators. By penalising British hoteliers and tour operators, such panic aids Saddam Hussein, *The Times* of London harrumphed.

'The great American wimp' is back, *The Times* opined. 'Grounded chickens', agreed the *Spectator* magazine.

Chimes in Mr Adley, the Conservative MP: 'The behaviour of Americans is entirely ridiculous. I would far rather walk the streets in Britain [in a war] than New York' in peacetime.

Of course, a stiff upper lip may come easier in Britain than elsewhere. This is a country accustomed to terrorism. 'We very much doubt that Saddam Hussein can do anything nastier than the IRA have already done,' says John Keegan, a prominent British war historian now acting as the *Daily Telegraph*'s defence editor. Besides, the national spine is stiffened by its citizenry's broad support for the war; polls indicate that Prime Minister John Major now enjoys the highest public-approval ratings of any British leader since Churchill in wartime.

'This war rings very, very familiar imperial bells with the British,' Mr Keegan says. 'The British are used to over 200 years of expeditionary forces going overseas, fighting the Africans, the Chinese, the Indians, the Arabs. It's just something the British take for granted.'

MOZART ALWAYS WINS THE WAR
Bernard Levin
The Times, January 24, 1991

An ancient Russian proverb says: 'When the cannons are silent, the muses are heard; when the muses are silent, the cannons are heard.' Once in a rare while, though, they make a fearsome counterpoint, and the baying of the hounds of blood mingles with the airs and sweet sounds that give delight and hurt not.

Perhaps there has never been a more profound and terrible experience of the coming together of death and art than what happened, during the Second World War, in Terizen. Terizen, more usually known by its German name, Theresienstadt, was one of the Nazi concentration camps, but a special kind. For some time it was a '*Potemkin*' camp, used for propaganda, including films, and for that reason conditions in it, though harsh, were much better than in most of the other cities of hell. But the credulous neutrals who saw the camp or the films did not know that as more men and women were sent there, the numbers were kept stable by a regular delivery to Auschwitz.

Most of the inmates were Czechoslovak Jews, and these included a substantial number of musicians. The commandant of the camp, himself a music-lover (artistic folk, the Germans), allowed the doomed musicians to rehearse and perform; one of their highlights was *The Bartered Bride*, another the Verdi Requiem. (There is a tradition – I hope it is true – that in the middle of the performance one of the musicians abandoned Verdi's score and began to sound the four notes which begin Beethoven's Fifth Symphony, the phrase which had been adopted as the call-sign of freedom.) The members of the orchestra all knew that they had no hope of rescue or reprieve, and they did not imagine their heroic dance on the cliff of death would be noted and remembered. Yet the instruments of the condemned orchestra spoke for history, and can still be heard over the cries of evil, be they never so loud.

Here I must cross a very frail bridge. Last Sunday evening, I went to the Royal Festival Hall to hear a concert performance of *The Marriage of Figaro*, conducted by Sir Georg Solti. The chasm between the music in Terizen and my joyous evening in a warm, bright hall, followed by my safe and simple return home, is grotesquely wide, and the bridge is *very* frail. But I had to cross it because, you see, another of the performances by the condemned of Terezin was *Figaro* itself.

And death shall have no dominion. I had left for the Festival Hall with the latest news of the Gulf war in my ears, and I could not but reflect that as the number of bombing raids increased, however precise the aim, human beings, including women and children, would be killed. Some of those would die in agony, their innards ripped from their bodies, their eyeballs melted, their legs smashed; the very crews of the planes which delivered such death might be burnt alive in their aircraft, as the tanks, when the ground offensive begins, will for some become ovens in which they are roasted.

Did those reflections destroy my pleasure at what turned out to be one of the finest of the 70-odd performances of *Figaro* I have ever heard? No; indeed my evening was grounded in a way that made the work even more profound and moving than Mozart invariably and eternally is.

There is war in *Figaro*; Cherubino is called up in Act One, and

Figaro tries to make his blood run cold with the prospects, but of course the *farfallone amoroso* is never going to get the smell of gunpowder in his nostrils; directors of the opera who make him truly frightened at the prospect have misunderstood Mozart. The war in *Figaro* takes place not on the battlefield but in the human heart, where the *concerto di tromboni, di bombarde, di cannoni* rages for ever, or at least until the true peace of full understanding is signed by all the High Contracting Parties.

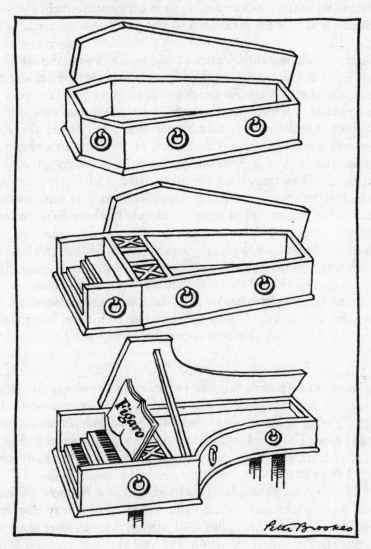

Meanwhile, though we must not be so foolish as to think that if Saddam Hussein could be persuaded to listen to *Figaro* he would come out with his hands up (Hitler was devoted to *The Merry Widow*), we must not fall into the opposite trap and allow ourselves to believe that art can offer no more practical service than consolation. It is not just a romantic fancy of mine to believe that Mozart changed the world, even though I suppose that most of the people in the world have never heard, or heard of, *Figaro*. The scientists tell us that matter is ultimately indestructible, however many times it changes its forms, and it is no great leap to the belief that the same is true of sounds.

Mozart dealt in truth, and nothing in his work, not even *The Magic Flute* or the Jupiter symphony, demonstrates his dealing more clearly and deeply than *Figaro* does. Remember: it is the only one of his operas in which no character is a symbol, but everyone and everything is real and of perfect human scale. Remember also that it is the only one of his operas that starts and finishes in a single day, from sunrise in a homely room to sunset in a stately garden. The souls of the characters have been laid bare, and the reconciliation in which it finishes is not just a happy ending; it is a testimony to a truth more glorious even than the earthly truth of the harmony in which the story and the opera finish.

Shaffer's Salieri instantly recognised that Mozart was a conduit through which God's truth entered the world. And Salieri knew also, and as immediately, that the work which demonstrated most clearly this breathtaking truth ('Whatever else shall pass away, this will not . . .') was this tiny tale of human beings which flowers in that single day into a tree under which all humanity can shelter.

That does not help with Saddam Hussein. But goodness and beauty, particularly goodness and beauty touched by an eternal hand, have a literally miraculous quality: they can spread independently of any human agent. The very fact that an extra item of goodness and beauty has entered the world makes the world better, even if nobody knows that it has entered.

I make so bold as to claim that the men and women of Terezin would have understood what I am saying. They were murdered, hideously. But, after all, they had always known that they were human. Their defiance of death and evil did not mean that they might escape mortality; it was an affirmation which said that music could and does so. The performance of *The Bartered Bride* announced that their blood, even as it was shed, was Czechoslovak and Jewish blood, and they were proud of it; the performance of the Verdi Requiem announced that man must learn to die as well as live; but the performance of *The Marraige of Figaro* announced that although five sparrows are sold for two farthings, not one of them is forgotten before God.

'Men must endure their going hence, even as their coming hither; ripeness is all.' There will be death in the Gulf, and hypocrisy, and a kind of justice; after all, the commandant of Terizen was hanged. But beyond the furthest stars, where love alone rules, all earthly stains, be they of blood or tears, are expunged. *Figaro* abides.

MAD DOGS AND ENGLISHMEN

Guardian, January 23, 1991

We have	They have
Army, Navy and Air Force	A war machine
Reporting guidelines	Censorship
Press briefings	Propaganda

We	They
Take out	Destroy
Suppress	Destroy
Eliminate	Kill
Neutralise or decapitate	Kill
Decapitate	Kill
Dig in	Cower in their foxholes

We launch	They launch
First strikes	Sneak missile attacks
Pre-emptively	Without provocation

Our men are . . .	Their men are . . .
Boys	Troops
Lads	Hordes

Our boys are . . .	Theirs are . . .
Professional	Brainwashed
Lion-hearts	Paper tigers
Cautious	Cowardly
Confident	Desperate
Heroes	Cornered
Dare-devils	Cannon fodder
Young knights of the skies	Bastards of Baghdad
Loyal	Blindly obedient
Desert rats	Mad dogs
Resolute	Ruthless
Brave	Fanatical

Our boys are motivated by	**Their boys are motivated by**
An old fashioned sense of duty	Fear of Saddam

Our boys	**Their boys**
Fly into the jaws of hell	Cower in concrete bunkers

Ours ships are . . .	**Iraq ships are . . .**
An armada	A navy

Israeli non-retaliation is	**Iraqi non-retaliation is**
An act of great statesmanship	Blundering/Cowardly

The Belgians are . . .	**The Belgians are also . . .**
Yellow	Two-faced

Our missiles are . . .	**their missiles are . . .**
Like Luke Skywalker zapping Darth Vader	Ageing duds (*rhymes with Scuds*)

Our missiles cause . . .	**Their missiles cause . . .**
Collateral damage	Civilian casualties

We . . .	**They . . .**
Precision bomb	Fire wildly at anything in the skies

Our PoWs are . . .	**Their PoWs are . . .**
Gallant boys	Overgrown schoolchildren

George Bush is . . .	Saddam Hussein is . . .
At peace with himself	Demented
Resolute	Defiant
Statesmanlike	An evil tyrant
Assured	A crackpot monster

Our planes . . .	Their planes . . .
Suffer a high rate of attrition	Are shot out of the sky
Fail to return from missions	Are Zapped

All the expressions above have been used by the British press in the past week

A BUFFALO SOLDIER GOES TO WAR

Martin Walker

Guardian, February 11, 1991

On the wall of General Colin Powell's Pentagon office hang three pictures. There is one of Lieutenant Henry Flipper, born a slave in 1856, the first black man to attend West Point. He was hounded out of the US Army on trumped-up embezzlement charges in 1881 and was finally posthumously exonerated only 12 years ago.

The other two pictures are of the men Flipper led: Buffalo Soldiers, the black men who made up the 9th and 10th cavalry regiments. Ill-equipped, with cast-off uniforms and antiquated weapons, they were the troops who won the West, just as much as Custer's more famous, all-white 7th Cavalry. History had almost forgotten them.

'I was jogging around Fort Leavenworth and noticed a couple of gravel alleys named 9th and 10th Cavalry streets,' Powell explains. 'I wondered if on this most historic army post in Kansas, in the centre of the region where the 9th and 10th spent so much of their blood, these two gravel alleys were all there was to signify their incredible contribution to the American West. That was a situation that had to be changed.'

Powell began a campaign to get an army monument built to the Buffalo Soldiers, and last July they broke ground for the 16-foot bronze statue of a black trooper on horseback, gazing across the fort to the endless plains they patrolled.

125

Late last year Powell joined the caucus of Black Congressmen on Capitol Hill in welcoming the new Buffalo Soldiers. Dressed in 19th-century cavalry uniforms, they are black teenagers with criminal records who are being inspired and with luck rehabilitated by the example of the black cavalrymen. 'No group of Americans ever served this nation with greater devotion, greater loyalty, greater sacrifice than African Americans,' he told them.

Such stories make it tempting to get a touch sentimental about Colin Powell, who as chairman of the joint chiefs of staff at the Pentagon can probably be described as the most powerful black man in the world. He is a living refutation of the glib slogans about America as an incorrigibly racist society, and by all accounts an exceedingly fine and decent man. Saddam Hussein apart, he seems to have no enemies, and there are no unpleasant anecdotes about him.

His hobby is to rebuild elderly Volvo cars, and to the dismay of his wife of 28 years, their driveway is often scattered with oily parts. Powell likes to tell stories against himself, like when he was speeding through Alabama in 1964 in a VW Beetle with an 'All the way with LBJ' bumper sticker, and was stopped by a patrolman wearing a 'Goldwater for President' button. 'He looked at me, the German car, the New York licence plate, the LBJ sticker. There was a moment of suspense. He finally said, "Boy, get outta here. You ain't smart enough to hang around."'

Powell has an easy conviviality. He enchanted Israel's Yitzhak Shamir by speaking Yiddish to him, a language Powell picked up as a teenager working in a New York shop. The son of immigrants from Jamaica, he seems free of any racial chip on his shoulder. 'In New York City, everybody was a minority. I grew up with other black kids from the US, black kids such as myself, Jewish kids, Italian kids, Polish kids . . .' All rather like the army he now commands.

Talk to senior officers he worked for in Vietnam, or the men he commanded there, or Pentagon officials who know him in power, and they all agree that he was a good and loyal subordinate, and an intelligent and immensely able commander. He is not only the first black man but also the youngest officer to head the Pentagon. President Reagan's two defence secretaries, Caspar Weinberger and Frank Carlucci, who guided Powell's meteoric rise up the bureaucratic ranks still sing his praises.

And yet the more one investigates the planning of America's response to the Gulf crisis, the more clear it becomes that this awesome

126

confrontation is Colin Powell's war. Last April, soon after Saddam's speech about 'bringing fire to half of Israel', Powell quietly ordered an overhaul of contingency plans for a Middle East crisis. The plan to stop a Soviet drive through Iran no longer looked relevant. He asked for a plan to protect the Saudi oilfields from regional threats.

As a result, in July General Norman Schwarzkopf, as head of Central Command which was based on the Rapid Intervention Force, put his staff through a series of war games. The assumption was a need swiftly to deploy US air power and about 100,000 troops into Saudi Arabia. Within 48 hours of the Iraqi invasion, Powell was at Camp David, briefing George Bush. Initially the president envisaged a more modest commitment; the Saudi ambassador, Prince Bandar (who was one of Powell's regular squash partners), had been told that three squadrons of jets could be sent to Saudi Arabia within days. 'That was enough to get us into trouble, but not enough to get us out of it,' the prince recalls.

Powell pressed Bush for a much bigger commitment for three reasons: to show the whole Middle East the US was serious about defending Saudi Arabia, and about its demand that Iraq leave Kuwait; because Saudi airfields would have to be protected by sufficient US ground troops; and because of the lessons Vietnam had taught him. He had served two tours in Vietnam and been wounded each time. The quagmire there had sucked in the US Army inch by bloody inch and, like most career officers, his Vietnam motto is 'Never again'. 'Powell has a simple conviction. You go in with overwhelming force, you go in very quickly, and once it's over you get out,' said Weinberger.

That was the way Powell met his first challenge, the Panama crisis. He scrapped the initial plan, for limited intervention, and demanded a full-scale attack. The results endorsed his doctrine of overwhelming force.

The difference between Vietnam and the Gulf is that this time the escalation took place during the planning phase. Once Powell had convinced the President that US air power would need ground protection, he realised that the Paratroops of the Rapid Intervention Force were too lightly armed to hold off Iraq's 5,000 tanks. 'Light and lethal is good,' is one of his sayings. 'But you also need heavy and lethal.'

The US Marine Corps was supposed to provide the heavyweight punch, and thanks to a remarkable pre-positioning of $1 billion worth of military equipment at regional airfields and bases, it had its heavy armour and artillery on the Indian Ocean island base of Diego Garcia. But they were equipped with obsolescent M-60 tanks, and their field artillery was mainly elderly M-114 howitzers. So Powell called for some of the army's heavy armoured divisions.

All this was worked out in one weekend planning session with Schwarzkopf. Powell had commanded the US Army V Corps on Nato's central front before becoming deputy national security adviser at the Reagan White House at height of the Irangate scandal, so he had convincing Nato credentials.

In October and early November, as Bush was realising that diplomacy, threats, and UN resolutions would not prise Saddam from Kuwait, the question of force between urgent. Powell had been studying the satellite photographs of the defensive lines the Iraqis were building along the Saudi border, and the US Army War College study of Iraq's performance in the eight-year war against Iran, which concluded: 'Iraq is superb on defence . . . Its *modus operandi* is to establish a deep, integrated, fortified zone augmented with large quantities of artillery.' He was convinced that the 200,000 men already in Saudi Arabia would not be sufficient for a land war, and this time he turned to the Nato central front: he would need 500,000 men, and the cream of the armoured divisions in Germany.

But this, he pointed out, was no longer a purely military decision. The Bush Administration, its secretary of state, its National Security Council, and its CIA must jointly help the president judge if the new East-West relationship would allow Nato's central front to be denuded safely. The decision was taken in that happy month leading up to the Paris summit, when the Conventional Forces in Europe Treaty was signed; the Soviet military seemed reconciled to the loss of Eastern Europe; and Gorbachev seemed firmly in power with the agreeable Eduard Shevardnadze as foreign minister.

Had Powell delayed his recommendation for the build-up to 500,000 men until Christmas, when the resignation of Shevardnadze was chilling fact, the decision to strip Nato might not have been taken. The nervous attention Washington is now paying to events in Moscow can hardly be overestimated. Even the slightest possibility of cold-eyed military men taking over the Kremlin makes the US and British redeployment of crack troops from Germany look like a huge gamble.

These are command decisions of a stunning, global scale. Not since Eisenhower in the Second World War has a US officer had to make them and, as with Eisenhower, there is already a movement to draft Powell as Bush's vice-presidential candidate in 1992. It would be a dream ticket for Republican strategists who see Powell bringing back the black vote and the patriotic vote, and outflanking Democratic critics of Bush's feeble record on the poor and inner cities. Nobody seems to have asked if Powell is a Republican; he certainly has never registered with either party, and the Reverend Jesse Jackson sees him regularly.

In Powell's career as soldier-cum-bureaucrat he has served Democrats and Republicans alike. His rise began after his second tour in Vietnam where he won a medal for pulling troops from a burning helicopter. He went to George Washington University on an army scholarship, took a master's in business administration in 1971, won a one-year White House fellowship: at the Office of Management and Budget he hugely impressed Weinberger, the director, and his deputy, Carlucci, with his appetite for work, for getting on with Congress, and for easing smoothly into the bureaucratic snake-pit of the Nixon White House.

After commanding a battalion in Korea, he went to the War College on a staff course, and then took over a brigade of the 101st Airborne. In the Carter years, he went to the Pentagon as senior military assistant to the deputy secretary of defence. He wanted, and got, a proper soldiering job – deputy commander of the 4th Infantry Division – then went to Fort Leavenworth as deputy chief of the Combined Arms Development command. There he helped to thrash out the tactical doctrine of the air-land battle, which combined ground-support aircraft and helicopters with ground troops to make up for Soviet superiority in tanks.

But Weinberger, then secretary of defence, pulled strings to get Powell back as his senior military aide, just as Carlucci was later to promote him from commanding V Corps in Nato to the rebuilding of a demoralised National Security Council after Irangate. When Carlucci succeeded Weinberger at defence, he told Reagan there was no better choice to run the council than Colin Powell.

Like Alexander Haig, Powell had a reputation for being more politician than military man. Bush picked him for the Pentagon to help to preside over the peace dividend, a hugely political job in which he had to deal with Congress and the stubborn Pentagon bureaucracy. Last summer Powell unveiled his strategy: much heavier reliance on reserve troops, and the preparation to fight one major and one minor war (fortunately perhaps, it was still on paper when Iraq invaded Kuwait).

What startles many army colleagues about Powell's career path is not his colour but the way he entered the force. He did not come up the gilded route from West Point but through the humble Reserve Officer Training Corps programme at the City College of New York. His father was not happy, in those segregation days of 1956, to see his son go off to Fort Bragg in North Carolina. 'He wasn't sure I would ever return from this adventure in the South,' Powell recalls, 'and it was only then that I had it brought home to me with stunning clarity the way things were in other parts of the United States.'

He got married, and then went to Vietnam. 'My family was living in Birmingham, Alabama, in 1963. When Bull Connor and his damn dogs were running up and down the street, I was in Vietnam, while my father-in-law was guarding the house with a shotgun,' he says. 'Because of my position and the things I was doing in my career, in my life, I didn't have a chance to participate in that struggle in an active way. I did it my own way, by my own example, and by helping other people who were coming along as best I could. But you better believe that I identified with that struggle, and continue to identify with that struggle.'

This weekend, as General Powell discussed with General Schwarz-kopf the launch of the ground offensive into Kuwait, another struggle takes precedence. The heir of the Buffalo Soldiers is going to war.

POWELL

131

'WE COULD LOSE A MILLION'

Richard Beeston

The Times, January 22, 1991

Mrs Wahabi waved her hand dismissively in a gesture intended to brush aside any concerns for her safety during one of the allied air attacks on Baghdad at the weekend.

She was putting forward a familiar argument, repeated frequently by Iraqi civilians and soldiers alike, that after eight years of a bitter and crippling war with Iran, the Iraqi people have become inured to privation and the prospect of sudden and violent death.

'What the West fails to understand about us and Muslims in general is our belief in destiny,' she said. 'I could die today in an air raid, or escape to Paris and be killed in a car accident. It is all the will of God.'

To some extent these sentiments are borne out by the behaviour of the citizens of Baghdad, such as the taxi driver who dropped me – arguing about the fare – just before the start of an allied missile attack. We ran for cover together. Having reached the safety of a nearby building, and hardly pausing for breath, he resumed the argument where we had left off.

It was not so much an exhibition of courage as of nonchalance, and is typical of a nation that has been obliged to display patience and resilience in the face of a decade of hardship. But like most of the people in the Middle East, the Iraqis remain acutely aware of developments in the region which override even the most determined efforts by the government propaganda machine to obscure the true implications of their present predicament.

For instance, when the UN ultimatum expired last week, the government and its officials spoke confidently about a last-minute peaceful solution of the dispute and made little attempt to prepare Baghdad for allied air attacks. Even so, hundreds of thousands of people left the city, and when the first raids began, most of the others were indoors – where they had been for some hours.

Among the people I spoke to in Baghdad was a man of 34 – I shall just call him Mohammed – who spoke with great trepidation of his call-up, to join a missile battery in Kuwait. Like many men in their late twenties and early thirties, he feels strongly that his years of compulsory military service have denied him not only many pleasures in life – such as his wish to visit the West – but the basics. The poor army pay – only 80 dinars a month (about £130) – means that he has been unable to marry, and the new conflict means that his marriage prospects will remain slim.

A regular listener to the BBC Arabic service and the Voice of America, he accepts that his chances of coming home intact when the allies launch their ground offensive are slight. 'I fought in all the big engagements of the Iran-Iraq war on the southern front,' he says. 'If we lost 100,000 men in those battles, then we shall lose a million in the fight against the Americans.'

The realisation that Iraq is up against a very different enemy has been driven home by the accuracy of the allied bombers and missiles. Armed with detailed intelligence of every significant strategic site in the country, most of which were built by foreign contractors, the allies are able to knock out targets at will with relatively light losses at the hands of the largely obsolete Iraqi anti-aircraft defences.

Because of the allied mastery in the air and the remarkable precision of their attacks, Baghdad is without electricity, following the raid on the power station on Friday night. There is no running water and the telephone system is wrecked. The already acute fuel shortages will get worse with the destruction of the Dora refinery south of Baghdad on Saturday.

Although locally grown fresh produce is still available and food continues to be trucked in from Jordan, most shopkeepers have either fled the city or are staying indoors, and even prestige establishments such as the government-owned Rashid hotel – normally reserved for visiting VIPs – cannot adequately feed their few remaining guests.

Saddam Hussein has made much of the stoical resolve of his people in the defence of their motherland, but the Iraqi people who are being asked to make this sacrifice know that they are now expected to defend Kuwait as well as their own communities.

If Iraqi servicemen are tempted to desert or mutiny, they are likely to be deterred by the knowledge that although they run the risk of death at allied hands, that will be their certain fate if they fall into the hands of Saddam's all-powerful secret police. And it will not only be they who die but, *pour encourager les autres,* their families too.

While the attacks against Israel are presented as a moral crusade

133

against the longest-standing enemy of all, they have nevertheless failed noticeably to draw the same ecstatic response which they did from Jordanians and Palestinians.

While President Saddam is certainly feared by his people – and probably respected – he is certainly not loved. Even the clumsy last-minute attempt to arouse Islamic fervour with his call for a holy war against the infidel armies lacks credibility in a secular state that has ruthlessly suppressed any display of Islamic fundamentalism among the majority Shia Muslim population.

Officially, the government contends that the people can stand up to any challenge, and when asked how much more punishment they can be expected to withstand, the information minister, Latif Jassim – a Saddam confidant – replied that material sacrifices are irrelevant when the cause is justified.

However unpopular Saddam may be, there is little to indicate that he might succumb to the sort of popular revolution that toppled the dictators of Eastern Europe in 1989. However, he no doubt recalls that when his forces were losing ground to the Iranians in the mid-1980s, his leadership was under serious threat from within his own close-knit group of advisers, many of whom are established figures in the various arms of the military and security police. His immediate followers are well aware that if the allies defeat him, the present adventure will bring them down too.

As the time approaches for the decisive ground battle for Kuwait, Saddam may find not only that he loses what little popular support he ever had, but that he is threatened by the very men now pledging their loyalty to him.

THE BOMBING OF THE BUNKER

Alfonso Rojo of *El Mundo*

Guardian, February 14, 1991

Hassan Ali Hussein pursed his lips, struggling to hold back the sob fluttering in his throat.

'The boy went to spend the night in a shelter. They'd linked up a television to the generator and used to show videos. Clint Eastwood, Bruce Lee. That sort of thing.'

Over his cassock-like *abaya* he was still wearing the check dressing-gown he had thrown on when he heard the second of the two explosions.

'The windows were blown out and we started to hear shouts from the street. It was just before 5.00 in the morning.'

Mr Hussein covered his face with his hand. He was ashamed that we should see him cry.

'Then I remembered Ahmed, and I went running to the shelter. We were sure nothing could have happened to him. It's a nuclear shelter with walls of concrete three metres thick. But it was burning like a kiln. We still haven't been able to get in.'

Mr Hussein shook his head slowly. His slippers squelched in the mud.

'Everyone inside must have died. Ahmed too. He was only 14.'

Amiriya is a middle-class district of detached houses in the north of Baghdad, near the road to Ramadi. Next to the mosque is a block of concrete, 10 yards high and 50 wide. It has no windows. Underneath it was the shelter.

'President Saddam Hussein ordered it to be built in 1984 when we were at war with Iran,' said Abdul Razak Hassan al-Janaby, who was in charge of the shelter. 'We always thought it was impregnable.

'Each evening since the start of the war, local people would come along with their food, blankets, pillows and their things to the bunker. Nothing had ever fallen on Amiriya, but people preferred to spend the night down there for safety's sake. Last night, there must have been at least 400 people inside.'

Mr al-Janaby said that the first explosion was at 4.45 in the morning and that earlier some people had heard the distant roar of planes.

'The two missiles arrived one after the other, within less than five minutes. They both hit the same spot. When we got there, we saw two children and five adults getting out. Some of them were badly injured,' he said.

'I pulled out one boy, who was trapped in the rubble near the door, with my own hands. The rest have died.'

In the roof of the shelter there was a smoking hole about 10 feet across into which firemen were continuously pouring water. 'There are shelters like this in lots of parts of Baghdad,' said Mr al-Janaby. 'They have room for 2,000 people. We always thought they were the best civilian shelters in the city. It seems impossible.'

Inside, the firemen had spent four hours in the suffocating fumes trying without success to cut through a thicket of steel with axes and oxyacetylene equipment to the main room of the bunker.

Out in the street, hundreds of people were milling around. A lot of the men were weeping unconsolably, but there was no hysteria. The impression was that people had still not recovered from the terrible surprise of it all.

'Mister! Mister!'

A boy had come up to the other side of a cordon of soldiers and was beckoning us towards him. He was holding a chunk of green metal. It was a bit of the tail of the missile. On it, clearly visible in English, was an engraved warning that the guarantee was only valid to the end of June 1988.

From time to time, firemen, their faces blackened by the smoke, would emerge dragging a blanket full of human remains and throw it into the back of a lorry. The corpses, which looked as if they were made of pumice, were very small and seemed to have shrunk by the heat of the fire.

When the lorry was full, it started off for the Yarmuk hospital where a group of women, with their heads covered, laid out the corpses in the yard – 47 black bundles laid out in a line.

Dr Bogosian, a softly spoken Armenian with a sad demeanour who studied in Britain and the US, said that until yesterday hardly any civilians had been admitted to his hospital.

'Most days since the war began, we've received some casualties and the odd fatality, but there were very few of them,' he said. 'This is different. This is the most terrible thing I have seen in my life, and in my life, I swear to you, I have seen many dreadful things.'

The two women who survived the attack were both in the same room. When the television cameramen, barging and shouting, asked the doctor to pull back the blankets so that they could film her ghastly burns, one of them did not even move. But the other howled like a wounded animal as soon as she saw the lights and the strange faces behind them.

Outside, the Iraqi health minister, Abdul Salam Mohammed Said, said at a press conference that the Americans had blocked the exit to the bunker with a missile 'in order to be able to incinerate with impunity the people in the shelter'.

I asked Dr Bogosian if the injured and their relatives only blamed the US and its allies for the tragedy overtaking Iraq.

'I'm not a politician,' he replied, shrugging his shoulders. 'I'm an Armenian. I belong to a people who know full well what persecutions and massacres are. I'm a Christian. Remember what the Turks did to us at the beginning of this century and all that we Christians have suffered in these countries. All I can tell you is that war is a dreadful thing, and that all of us should have done more to avoid it.'

In the hospital courtyard, some boys, overcome by grief, were beating their heads against a wall until blood ran. They were screaming: 'Gone! Gone!'

A HOWL TO MAKE YOUR HAIR STAND ON END

Alfonso Rojo

Guardian, February 15, 1991

It was an electrifying cry – a howl to make your hair stand on end. The men advancing down the street were shouting it over and over, their voices hoarse and their stares feverish.

'*La ilaha illa Allah!*'

As the five simple coffins draped in the Iraqi flag passed by, icy-eyed civilians marshalling the funeral let off bursts of fire from Kalashnikovs slung across their chests.

'*La ilaha illa Allah!*' – 'There is no God but Allah!'

The people of Amiriya, lined up on either side of the road like so many extras in a Greek tragedy, chorused hysterically: '*Allahu akbar*', '*Allahu akbar*' – 'God is great.'

There was not one woman in the cortège.

It was just after 10.00am, and the crowd at the funeral for these five who died in Amiriya's bunker was sweating hatred.

For the first time since the start of the war, 28 days ago, aggression was directed at the foreign correspondents here. A stone and a couple of punches were thrown, but all it took to stop people dead in their tracks was for the information ministry officials who shadow us everywhere, or the armed activists of the ruling Ba'ath Party, to raise their voices.

Two blocks away, firemen wearing gas masks were still picking at the bowels of the bunker. More than 24 hours after the explosions, dozens of corpses remained inside.

'Everything caught light in a flash,' said Hassan al-Sadin, the chief rescue worker. 'Everything – blankets, clothes, people's hair, the polyurethane in the ventilation ducts, the plastic insulation on the cables. In a fraction of a second, all the oxygen went and they were all burned to death.'

The air inside was unbreatheable. There was a sweet, acrid smell and bits of scorched flesh hung from the twisted girders. Every time they picked up a charred bit of a corpse, the stretcher bearers ran gasping towards the exit, their boots squelching in a black mud composed of water, ashes, and human remains.

As they ran, they shouted like men possessed: '*La ilaha illa Allah!!*'

Outside, a dark knot of women had gathered by the metal barrier. They were loudly insulting us and imploring Heaven for the death of President Bush and the extermination of the Saudis.

'Is this your civilisation?' a woman wearing European dress whom the soldiers had allowed through the crowd howled in English. 'Look! Look!' She pointed at the people on the other side of the wire fence and, looking straight to camera, she added: 'They can't even identify their loved ones. They're not even going to be able to bury them!'

When the television cameramen who had not got there in time asked her to repeat it – 'In French, if possible,' said one – the woman hesitated, but then went on: 'I hope you're proud of yourselves. Is this your civilisation?'

All it took was for a camera team to bring them into focus, and from the other side of the wire fence the screaming and shouting would at once start again.

WHEN THE CAMERAS SWITCH OFF

Jeremy Bowen of the BBC

Guardian, March 9, 1991

Once the camera had been switched off the man pushed his way through the laughing, vile-smelling crowd of bazaar traders and started to tell the truth. 'What I just said,' he smiled, 'was all lies.'

A few minutes before, he had been on camera praising Saddam Hussein. President Bush was a criminal, he had said, an insane killer of children. Saddam was loved by his people, feared by the coalition. Iraqi soldiers would win the mother of battles.

It was a few days before the ground war started, and for some reason the ministry of information had given us a Spanish-speaking minder. His English was weak and he was bored by filming. He had wandered off to buy cigarettes, leaving me standing in a mess of rotten vegetables and rainwater to talk to the man I had just interviewed. I suggested we moved out of the drizzle towards one of the red Honda saloons which journalists in Baghdad had to hire for more than £300 a day, excluding petrol. The man refused. 'It's probably bugged,' he said. 'Most of these cars are, or they wouldn't make you use them. I am a deserter from Kuwait. Do you want to know what it's really like down there?'

The deserter talked of the misery of life in the Iraqi trenches, about the bombing and the bad food. He predicted the defeat which happened soon after.

Three weeks before, he said, he had been given a few days' leave from his unit in Kuwait. He had not gone back. 'They'll hang me if they find me,' he said, 'but I don't care. I've had enough.'

He said he was 31, but he looked at least 10 years older. Tears started in his eyes as he talked about the waste of his youth. He had wanted to earn a little money, have some fun, perhaps get married. Instead he had been in the army, conscripted like all his contemporaries early in the war with Iran. The English he had learned at school so he could work with tourists was useless.

'All we've done since I grew up has been to fight,' he said. 'What have we got out of it? Nothing.'

He broke off and started shouting at me in Arabic. The minder was returning. It was time to restart the charade which people in Iraq use every day to protect themselves against the state. 'I will show what the butcher Bush has done,' he said. 'Let's go to see how he bombs civilians.' He said it loudly in English and louder in Arabic.

As the car was about to move off, a stranger got in next to the minder who was busying himself with his cigarettes in the front seat, pretending not to notice that a six-foot man was almost sitting on his lap.

In Iraq, it is sometimes better to stay silent. The deserter, sitting next to me in the back, drew a cross on my knee with his finger, pointed at the new arrival and shook his head. I stopped shouting and we drove off to the bomb site.

We did not use the sound-bite the man had provided in praise of Saddam. Neither could the other things he said be relayed from Baghdad. The Iraqi censor would have taken them out of any report. I wanted to wait, as well. A few weeks' time and a few details left out will, I hope, be enough to stop our minder and his employers identifying the deserter.

In the last month in Baghdad it has not been hard to find people who would speak out against Saddam Hussein. Some of them insisted on doing so while the cameras were running. We didn't even try to get those interviews past the censor. The words would have been cut and the people who said them would have suffered.

The Iraqis, who always came out when they saw foreign reporters, were usually polite. Arab traditions of hospitality aside, it might also have been a way of distancing themselves from the regime and from a war few ordinary people wanted.

Even some Ba'ath Party activists, in their green uniforms, were courteous once they had stopped denouncing the coalition, its leaders and the Zionist conspirators they believed ran the BBC.

One man delivered a long lecture on the pavement about Iraq's historic right to Kuwait and its duty to lead the Arab world: 'Iraqis are the sons of Nebuchadnezzar, the people who drove the British out. Your grandfather was probably killed here by Iraqis in the 1920s.' But once he had run out of slogans he smiled and asked what I thought of his English.

A man nearby appointed himself cheerleader and made the crowd go through the litany which had been standard before the authorities started to fear that a Ba'athist pep-rally might turn into a demonstration against the dictatorship. 'Down, down Bush,' the cheerleader shouted. 'Down, down Major.' But then he stopped, shook hands with the BBC cameraman and invited us to drink tea and eat kebabs.

In almost every encounter like that, someone would want a whisper about the latest rumours once the minder's attention had been distracted.

Some of the latest are about Takrit, Saddam's home town. Takritis are reported to have demolished property belonging to Saddam Hussein and to have damaged the tombs of his family. Some prominent Takritis are said to have vanished. Arshad Yasin, the head of the presidential bodyguard, is rumoured to have been killed during an attempt on President Saddam's life in the first week of February. People wonder whether he was attacking or defending the president, who is his cousin and brother-in-law.

Others remark that very little has been heard of Taha Ramadan, the first deputy prime minister. He is rumoured to have fled during the bombing.

None of the usual journalistic checks can be applied to such reports because of the restrictions in Iraq, but some people there take them seriously. They are careful, though, about passing them on. 'Saddam has killed the good things that were inside Iraqis,' one man told me before I left Baghdad. 'You can't trust anyone. If three Iraqis are in a room, at least one is an informer. What kind of future do we have?'

DON'T SHOOT THE MESSENGER
Robert Harris
Sunday Times, February 17, 1991

Confronted by the shrivelled images of women and children burnt alive in a Baghdad bomb shelter last week, a large section of the brave and independent British press did not hesitate. It immediately attacked those responsible for the harrowing scenes: not America or Iraq, but the BBC.

'Outrage over BBC war bias,' shouted the *Daily Express*. 'Viewers rage at TV "bias",' pronounced the *Sun*. In the *Daily Mail* it was: 'Outrage as TV's bunker bomb bulletins "show bias to Saddam".' Three Conservative MPs, Jonathan Sayeed, Nicholas Soames and Sir Dudley Smith (let us remember their names), promptly joined in the chorus.

Even mild little John MacGregor, leader of the House of Commons, announced that the government ('very informally') had made 'representations to the broadcasting authorites'. How courageous. One can imagine the scene in the MacGregor household: 'What did you do in the Gulf war, Daddy?' 'I made very informal representations to the broadcasting authorities.'

People are weird, are they not? Watching blackened pieces of mothers and babies being shovelled on to sheets and laid out in the sun prompts many feelings: anger, chiefly at Saddam Hussein for having led his people into this hopeless struggle; horror, that the innocent must always suffer so dreadfully; shame, that the human race, after all it has gone through this century, is still capable of doing this to itself. Most of us, I expect, felt all this and more.

But what kind of person is it, whose first reaction is to get on the telephone and complain about 'bias'? How much bias can a dead baby have? Does a corpse in Baghdad have to be balanced by a corpse in Kuwait before it can be shown, in some sort of ghastly parody of Woodrow Wyatt's version of 'impartiality'? Or were the broadcasters supposed to pretend the massacre in the shelter hadn't happened? Lose the film? Save it for the archives?

Certainly, that is what some people believe. Twenty years ago, in a famous article in *Encounter*, Sir Robin Day (as he then wasn't) advanced the argument that television, unless strictly controlled, could make it impossible for a democracy to fight a war at all:

'However good the cause – self-defence, resisting aggression, or even fighting under the United Nations flag – the brutal details of military action may be there on the television screen to shock and to horrify, sapping perhaps the will of that nation to resist the forces of evil or even to safeguard its own freedom.

'When people are horrified by the sight of bloodshed and mutilation they are not easily convinced that a cause may be at stake. The sight of a dead child, a burning home, a dying citizen-soldier – all these may have a much more powerful impact than abstract concepts like "liberty" or "collective security".'

This has since become a classic text for those in favour of censorship. Indeed, it has been taken up with enthusiasm by several right-wing commentators during the present conflict. But it is, in my view, utterly wrong.

To begin with, it rests on the assumption – a rather perverse assumption, if you claim to be fighting to preserve democracy – that the bulk of the population is inherently untrustworthy and has to be shielded from 'brutal details' by those who think they know better. I am less contemptuous of my fellow citizens. The *Daily Express* notwithstanding, there is a great reservoir of common sense among the general public, most of whom reluctantly accept that dead children, burning homes and dying soldiers are a fact of war. I would not expect a sudden lurch to pacifism as a result of last week's television coverage.

What would start raising suspicions, and fuelling anti-war sentiment, would be censorship. Nothing, I am sure, would suit the likes of Mr John Pilger more than to be able to claim that wicked, militaristic governments were preventing their electors from seeing what was being done in their name. After last week, it has become much harder to argue that this is a completely 'sanitised' war.

Behind the present lust for censorship lies one of the most threadbare and fraudulent accusations ever levelled against television: that

142

it somehow 'lost' the Vietnam war; that nightly images of burning villages and napalmed children sapped the American public's will to fight. Nonsense, or 'bovine scatology', as General Norman Schwarzkopf quaintly calls it.

The United States lost that war because it could not win on the battlefield, and the cause for which it fought was eventually perceived not to be worth more than 50,000 American lives. Television reflected that reality, it did not create it; if, by those reflections, television helped hasten the American withdrawal, so much the better.

Ah, say the armchair censors, but what about the Second World War? What would have been the effect 50 years ago if the television cameras had been in Hamburg, Berlin or Dresden to report the effects of allied raids there on women and children? Again, would the images not have eroded the British and American public's will to go on?

On the contrary, this is a powerful argument in *support* of television. For if public opinion had been stirred between 1942 and 1945 by television coverage to demand a change in allied bombing strategy, the results would have been wholly beneficial. Tens of thousands of lives would have been saved, both among German civilians and allied aircrew. The bombing effort would have been switched to industrial targets, notably the Nazis' oil refineries. And, as we discovered after the German surrender, the war would have been shortened as a result, for the terror raids served little military purpose. Humanity and good military tactics do not necessarily conflict.

Far from crippling democracies in time of war, therefore, I would argue that television has done nothing but good. Precisely because they know that cameras may be present, the military have had to be more careful about their targets. They have had to develop laser-guided bombs and computer-controlled missiles to limit civilian casualties. Today, in the Gulf, if a mission fails, returning pilots are forbidden simply to unload their ordnance on whatever takes their fancy; they have to carry it back to base.

One of the sickest clichés of war is 'they did not die in vain'. Of course those people in Baghdad died in vain. But at least they did not die unseen. Already, allied commanders have been obliged to review their targets to reduce the risk of further civilian deaths. And for this mercy we must thank that much maligned medium, television.

IRAQ'S LOST GENERATION

Martin Woollacott

Guardian, February 15, 1991

It was the tragedy that we had all been waiting for. It was the tragedy, perhaps, that we had all been consciously or unconsciously seeking. The massacre of the innocents in a Baghdad basement, whether the victims turn out to number 100 or 1,000, could become, for Arabs certainly and for some Westerners as well, the Guernica of the Gulf war.

The human loss is undeniably a cause for sadness and for outrage. But before we allow this particular bombing to assume mythic proportions we ought to look at the elements of coincidence and collusion that seem likely to inflate it, masking the far greater tragedies that are taking place in Iraq.

There is a kind of conspiracy – linking such otherwise entirely disparate groups as the Iraqi propaganda agencies, the Western press, Arab governments and peoples, those opposed to the war in Europe and America, and even the US government and the Pentagon – to make the bombing of civilians into the primary moral issue of the war. So broad a consensus must invite the suspicion that what these actors all have in common is an interest in avoiding or suppressing some of the real truths about this conflict.

The Iraqi government has, from the beginning of the war, sought to publicise civilian casualties in every way, inviting back for that purpose alone Western journalists whom it had expelled. By doing so, of course, Iraq appeals to Arab sentiment but, equally important, it can to some extent conceal from Arabs, including its own people, the real damage by allied bombing.

There are, no doubt, some considerations of military security here, but the dominant motive is surely political. What is being knocked to pieces by US and British bombing is not the Iraqi civilian population, but the army in Kuwait and southern Iraq and the country's physical plant, its whole expensively achieved equipment as a modern nation.

The price that Iraq is paying for this war is not to be counted in civilian deaths. The greater immediate tragedy must be the death of soldiers from bombing. Regulars, conscripts, and reservists, they constitute a huge proportion of its able-bodied young male population.

How many have died already in situations that it would be ludicrous to call combat, is not known, but they must be many. The US military, which normally cannot resist figures, has sedulously avoided anything that might look like a body count. Tank kills it will estimate; people kills it will not. In this its interests coincide with those of the Iraqi authorities. Far better to emphasise to their own people, and to other Arabs, the deaths of a relatively few civilians than to expose what may turn out to be the crippling of a whole generation of male Iraqis; and, even more, to invite public examination of the perhaps irreparable damage being done to the physical and the political structures which hold Iraq together.

For Arabs outside Iraq, the temptation to seize on civilian casualties, however few they are in reality, seems irresistible. They need the US to be the kind of moral monster that would deliberately target civilians. The uneducated among them require the immediacy and sensationalism of such alleged atrocities. And, with their old-fashioned views of soldiering, they are constrained to see the Iraqi troops as Islamic fighters, and thus as martyrs rather than as victims.

The physical and political damage that will affect the lives of millions of Iraqis is something many shy away from examining. It

145

raises difficult questions about Arab responsibility for the war, and even harder ones about the nature of Iraqi politics and Saddam's gross miscalculations on the likely price to be paid for annexing Kuwait. Far easier, then, to bury yourself, in anger and tears, in the psychodrama of US villainy versus Arab innocence.

The uneducated actually believe civilians are the targets. The educated would argue if pushed that representation of the Americans as baby-killers, while not factually accurate in this instance, has an underlying truth in that Arab women and children have for generations been sacrificed to Western, US and Israeli interests, in Israel, Palestine, Lebanon, and elsewhere. Such a position, combining intellectual dishonesty and ethical fuzziness with justified grievance is typical of the moral muddle in which the Arabs find themselves.

Whether by accident or design – probably by a bit of both – the allies have also found it useful to concentrate on the question of civilian casualties. In spite of the real embarrassment that a hit like that on Wednesday can cause, the allies have so far been winning the propaganda battle over civilian deaths as far as the Western public is concerned, and probably holding their own, until this week, in terms of Arab opinion.

The Western public knows that civilians are not being targeted, and has been reasonably convinced that great care was being taken to avoid civilian casualties near military targets. But the overall effect of all this virtuous avoidance of Iraqi civilian casualties has been to obscure what is actually being done to Iraq; and that cannot be unwelcome to this war's public relations managers.

First, by emphasising the distinction between combatants and non-combatants in this watertight way, it is easier to present the bombing of soldiers in an abstract, technical, manner. They don't die, they are degraded.

Second, the constant discussion of the necessity to avoid civilian casualties tends to pre-empt inquiry into what is the full purpose of the bombing missions in Iraq (as opposed to Kuwait). Undoubtedly there are important military reasons: above all, if Saddam and his top generals can be prevented from talking to their field commanders, Iraq's centralised and hierarchical army will suffer grave disadvantage in the coming land battle.

Similarly, to cut the supply lines brings obvious advantage. Yet in each case there must be some doubt about the objectives. Iraqi duplication of communications makes it highly unlikely that all telecommunications can be taken out in time, while Iraqi stockpiling in the battle area means that damage to roads and bridges may not be vital.

To which the military argument may well be, reasonably enough, that anything that may help ought to be done. But the damage being inflicted on Iraq's physical assets carries another message, and aimed at those around Saddam. This is surely that the destruction of Iraq will continue – even after the battle for Kuwait – as long as Saddam is in power. The bombing of ministries in Baghdad quite unrelated to the war effort seemed to many to ram home that message, which is in essence that there will be no Iraq left to govern and no means by which to govern it unless Saddam is removed soon.

This is an incitement to a coup, understandable enough given what we all know are the real war aims of the allies. But it must prompt further thoughts, which are that getting rid of Saddam may involve getting rid of the centralised Iraqi state which, whatever its excesses under him, may be the only way of running this varied country. The ramshackle coalitions of opposition groups now hopping about in the wings do not inspire huge confidence.

Here, in other words, we may have another case where the Arab impulse to dramatise, regardless of the immediate facts, could have a sort of basis. The allies have no formal intention of 'destroying Iraq' – the charge laid by some Arabs – but that may nevertheless be the result of Western actions. The future lives of millions of Iraqis will be damaged if their country becomes an arena for the ambitions of contending outside powers.

These are the sort of questions that the continued fuss about civilian casualties enables the US and Britain to avoid. It is not that the policies themselves are avoidable. Perhaps they could, and perhaps they will, be modified. But the bombing of Iraq and Kuwait has to continue for all the reasons, military and political, that have been outlined. It is more that our governments can evade the moral responsibilities such drastic action ought to imply for the post-war period.

In this situation the Western press is undoubtedly acting as a bridge between Iraq, the West, and the Arabs, serving their common need to make civilian casualties into a powerful issue. Individual reporters in Baghdad have been scrupulously careful in their dispatches, which have been full of signals about censorship and have painted an over-all picture of low civilian casualties. That is, they have done so in the

West; but for many Arabs who ignore the caveats and the nuances, television reports in particular have supplied the images of destruction that were needed to clothe their already firm belief in America's evil intentions.

Men always look for parallels and symbols from history, but it is especially true of war that the past provides an often misleading vocabulary for new tragedies. Guernica, Coventry, Dresden: the whole grim panoply of air war on civilians has been conjured up in both Western and Arab minds. Some Arabs seize on the flimsiest of evidence to accuse the Americans of aerial atrocities, while the Americans and British find too much moral comfort in the knowledge that we are striving to keep civilian casualties to a minimum.

In behaving like this, we are all, Arabs and Westerners alike, avoiding much bigger and more difficult issues.

BLOODLESS THEATRE OF WAR AT THE RIYADH HYATT HOTEL

Robert Fisk

Independent, February 13, 1991

There is no blood on the floor of the Regency Room at the Hyatt hotel. And although the talk is all of war, there is no hint of pain or fear between the television arc lights and the wood panelled walls.

The ashtrays are regularly emptied. The wall-to-wall carpet is spotless. The flags clustered at one end of the room – American and Saudi and a curious banner labelled 'Joint Forces' with a map of the Arabian peninsula in yellow protected by palm leaves – might be stage props in a televised drama. Which is, in one sense, what they are.

The style is informal, sanitised, occasionally infused with laughter. For it is here, under the eyes of the world, that the allied briefers in Riyadh tell reporters how the war is going.

Watch television at your fireside and you will know the faces well; but attending this extraordinary ritual is probably essential to an understanding of its meaning. Old hands say that Saigon's 'Five O'clock Follies' had nothing on this, and one can see why.

Brigadier-General Richard Neal, US Deputy Director of Operations, gave the first performance yesterday and he made us feel the war was a world away.

He is a short man with a chunky face who talks warspeak. 'Battlefield preparation' was still going on, as well as 'restrikes of strategy targets'. There had been 65,000 sorties 'to date' and the allies continued 'to interdict . . . roads, rail and bridge systems'.

He divulged that 'three TELs were attacked in Scud-related areas' – a TEL, it transpired, was a Transporter Erector Launcher for a missile – and there was much snickering when he suggested that there was an Iraqi technician 'trying to check his fuel' moments before an allied bomb exploded beside him.

Six Iraqis had surrendered to US forces. Iraq 'continues to disregard the Geneva Convention and also the International Committee of the Red Cross'. He placed a 'high confidence value' on reports that execution squads were roaming behind Iraqi lines to shoot deserters. But what the general really wanted to talk about was pride and the young men bombing Iraq.

'We've got such kids doing the job . . . These young kids . . . Super equipment . . . Unbeatable combination.' He spoke of a 'combined arms attack' that was 'well-orchestrated' in a 'target-rich environment' although he regretted not being able to give us 'a good BDA'. A BDA is a Bomb Damage Assessment. Was Baghdad airport being used? 'I wouldn't buy a ticket on a local airline to go to Baghdad.' Much laughter. The general spoke of 'a lucrative target' that was 'hunkered down'.

There was, of course, no mention of the suffering of war, least of all was there reference to civilian casualties in Iraq (in warspeak, 'collateral damage'). There was, in fact, no war at all, rather a husk of words from which all reality had been sucked. The speech was packaged, a word which itself appeals to the generals. The Americans now speak, for example, of a 'package' when they mean a collection of aircraft participating in a raid.

General Neal is not the only American briefer. There is the slightly more elegant US chief of staff, Major-General Robert Johnston, whose experience of the Middle East extends beyond the Gulf. I last saw him chatting to a senior PLO officer in West Beirut in 1982 when, as a colonel in the 32nd Marine Amphibious Unit, he arrived in Lebanon to help to evacuate the guerrilla army now one of Saddam Hussein's closest allies. I even have a picture of a smiling Johnston shaking hands with a certain Lieutenant Colonel

Basagh Zarab of the Palestine Liberation Army. War is rich in ironies.

But no ironies are allowed to intrude in Riyadh. At the end of Neal's peroration, the floodlights and cameras and tape recorders are switched off for an 'off the record' briefing at which, in semi-darkness, exactly the same performers go on talking on condition they are referred to as a 'US military source'.

We learn then – from a US military source – that road bridges carry communication lines beneath them (thus one reason for their destruction). We even hear that there now exists a group of officially accredited reporters known – heaven spare us all – as the 'Scud debris pool'.

The Saudi colonel recorded the death of a Saudi soldier in a booby trap at Khafji, and a few more Iraqi deserters. He remarked that 'the weather in this part of the world is very difficult to predict. Clouds come one day, rain the next day, the sun will rise next day. It's very difficult to predict.'

The event ends with the appearance of Air Commodore Ian MacFadyan, Chief of Staff of Headquarters, British Forces Middle East. What he has to say is very peculiar indeed. He tells us that the Royal Navy is 'ever watchful on patrol in the Gulf,' but that 'life at sea is much the same in peace and war'.

For some unfathomable reason, he then starts talking about 'Tommy in the desert' and 'Ginger on the airfield'. It takes a while before we realise that 'Ginger' must be a reference to Biggles's friend.

'I have to recount a story from my time in the Falklands . . .' the air commodore goes on. The British services are 'three large families in which everyone has a part to play'. There are, he goes on to assure us, a 'very small minority' in Britain against the war. Still no mention of human life and pain. So what would be the air commodore's advice to Iraqi civilians who wanted to avoid being accidentally wounded in air raids? 'Stay at home,' said the air commodore. And if they had to travel? 'Stay away from bridges.' And from roads, too? 'As you wish,' the air commodore replied testily.

It was an uninformative and embarrassing performance. It was also the finale to something which closely approximated – because of the cameras – a stage show.

The allies will have to do better to counter the wickedness of

Saddam Hussein's propaganda. It was not that the participants told lies, although what they said was undoubtedly sifted and highly selected as well as rambling.

But it was a form of theatre. And one was reminded, in the end, of Samuel Taylor Coleridge's contention that drama requires a 'willing suspension of disbelief'.

WHEN TRUTH TAKES A DIRECT HIT

Simon Jenkins

The Times, February 18, 1991

There is a point in most wars when public opinion, frustrated at the lack of swift victory, turns on its messengers. The worse the news, the more vehement the condemnation, as if attacking the media could substitute for a sudden loss of will. Thus it was last week when bombs fell on a building in Amiriya, with the death of many civilians. What happened? Was the event misreported? If not, should it have been reported at all?

After the Amiriya bombing, *The Times*, in common with most other media organisations, went to lengths to find out which was true, the Iraqi claim that the building was an air raid shelter, or the American claim that it was a command bunker. This meant risking reporters' safety, risking deception by Iraqi censors, risking the credibility of allied spokesmen and risking readers' confidence.

The alternative preferred by many MPs in Britain and congressmen in America was not to try. The media should have decided that our side of the war should always be believed and the Iraqis regarded as liars, for which thesis there was plenty of circumstantial evidence. British newspapers did not have reporters in Berlin in the Second World War. Why have them in Baghdad?

Set aside the fact that no newspaper would send a reporter to certain incarceration or death (as in Berlin during that war), modern limited wars are now conducted on two levels: fighting and politics, with its concomitant of publicity. In the Amiriya case, to have suppressed the Iraqi claim would have been fruitless. It would have been all over foreign broadcasts and newspapers, in the reports of visitors. If television companies felt bound at least to give Iraqi footage, with the appropriate caveats, the public would have demanded to know if the footage was true. Hundreds dead in a shelter went beyond the normal pabulum of propaganda.

Some news organisations, including some British newspapers, have taken the view that all journalists should be withdrawn, to avoid becoming tainted by the difficult task of validating counter-claims. They have decided that no journalist can possibly work normally in Baghdad. A journalist requires two freedoms to do his or her job: freedom to move and see, and freedom to write what is seen. If both are curtailed, reporters are worse than propagandists; by their professional status they validate propaganda.

In carrying reports by two reliable correspondents in Baghdad, Richard Beeston and Marie Colvin (of the *Sunday Times*), *The Times* took a different view. We should try to give our readers the nearest we could get to the truth. Every war is a casualty to censorship. Few journalists see military action. If they do, they see only a microcosm of it, They are dependent on raw material that must come from one or other side and are plainly vulnerable to bias. Reporters who plead for an 'uncensored' war are naive. War reporting does not start pure and become tainted by censorship. It starts censored and is an act of de-censoring. That de-censoring must take place at every stage in the journalistic process, listening, writing and editing.

'Reporting restrictions' have long surrounded news from the communist bloc and from much of Africa and Asia. Restrictions operate on journalists in Israel. Yet the media rarely mention these. After an initial burst of protest, they settle down either to working within the controls or to working round them. American journalists who sought to boycott South Africa in the mid-1980s were conceding professional defeat. They proposed no similar boycott on military news from Israel, or on 'facility trips' from their own defence department.

In war as in peace, the task of a newspaper is simple: to make the best possible stab at the truth in the time available. No responsible newspaper gratuitously aids and abets an enemy of the state. No responsible newspaper offers its readers what it knows to be partial information from either side without the appropriate caveats. In the Gulf, censorship has been tighter from the Iraqis than from the allies, but only relatively so. Disinformation has come (in the early days) from many military sources in Saudi Arabi, including news of defecting tanks and defeated Scuds.

The Times has sought, in carrying reports from journalists whose writing was overseen by a censor, to tell readers clearly of this fact. We carry such reports only where they convey information that we and the reporter regard as likely to be true. Readers can then judge whether they feel the context is blatantly partial and make the appropriate adjustment in reading.

The extreme view was well put during the Falklands war by an admiral: 'Tell them nothing; when it's over, tell them who won.' Were such draconian censorship feasible, the silence might just help the war effort, but I doubt it. I believe the public in a democracy are better able to support a war by feeling they have been properly informed of its course, victories, defeats, mistakes, warts and all. For rulers to shield their publics from the horror of war is certainly unwise. It is also immoral.

AN ARMY FIGHTS ON ITS STOMACH

Patricia Wilson

Daily Telegraph, February 12, 1991

It is as if a city of half a million Americans had picked up and moved to Saudi Arabia.

Meeting the awesome task of sending so many people half-way around the world, feeding, clothing and sheltering them, has won Major-General William Pagonis a nickname of which he is quite proud: The Grand Mover.

Now, as the ground war looms, he is facing the challenge of moving hundreds of thousands of troops and their supplies to the front.

As the US Army's chief logistician in the Gulf, General Pagonis is compared by other officers to Milo Minderbinder, the supply genius of Joseph Heller's *Catch-22*, who bartered, traded and wheedled what he needed to keep his forces happy and up to scratch.

On a less whimsical note, President Bush has recognised General Pagonis's skills by recommending him for promotion from major-general to lieutenant-general.

Keeping America's forces poised for combat is expensive and difficult. In the past six months, the general's staff has served 90 million meals, delivered 160 million gallons of water and pumped 100 million gallons of petrol.

General Pagonis had a staff of five working from the boot of a car when he arrived in Saudi Arabia in early August. Now his team has grown to 16,000 working round the clock.

He is supported by 4,000 men and women at the Defence Personnel Support Centre (DPSC) in Philadelphia, Pennsylvania, who spend their days at computers or on telephones seeking contractors, filling orders and ensuring the right items are sent to the right place at the right time.

Once goods have arrived in Saudi Arabia by ship or plane, more than 2,000 lorries distribute them. Each vehicle makes an average, one-way haul of about 230 miles every day across the eastern province of the vast desert kingdom.

By the end of last month, the DPSC had dispatched food worth £347.5 million medical supplies costing £209 million, and clothing and other textiles worth £414 million in support of the Gulf operation.

Subsistence items – as the military refers to food – included 7.6 million Meals Ready to Eat (MREs), not the dinner of choice for American Servicemen, who have nicknamed them Meals Rejected by Ethiopians. More popular among the troops are the Meal Ordered Ready to Eat (MORE) selections prepared under a private contract. They include chicken breast, spaghetti, beef pot roast, sukiyaki with rice and lasagne.

Another firm has been awarded a contract to deliver 14 million 'lunch bucket' meals such as beef stew, chili and beans, pasta and chicken.

A treat for the American soldier could be one of the 12 million heat-resistant Hershey chocolate bars already shipped to the desert. Staples such as sugar, flour and coffee, so far totalling almost 15lb million, have also been sent.

The supply of medical goods sent to the Gulf costs an average of £1.2 million a day. Along with 2.2 million tubes of lip salve, 715,000 cans of foot powder and 558,000 bottles of sunscreen are more sobering items as 790,000 atropine injectors containing an antidote to chemical agents and 60,000 pyridostigmine bromide tablets, an anti-nerve gas drug.

America's troops have received 3.2 million pairs of desert camouflage trousers, 376,000 pairs of goggles to protect against sand, wind and dust, 1.4 million pairs of tan desert boots and 1.34 million chemical suits.

The comforts of home include mail delivery, a huge operation involving almost 300 tons of mail a day to men and women scattered from warships in the Red Sea to outposts on the Saudi-Kuwait border.

Much of the post is from children and well-wishers and is addressed simply to: 'Any soldier, Saudi Arabia'. One recipient of such a letter in the Marines has successfully proposed marriage to the young woman who sent it.

A staff of 350 sorts and delivers the mail from distribution centres in Dhahran, Riyadh and Bahrain. 'We use everything available short of Bedouins and camels,' said Major Michael Whitaker, commander of postal services in the Gulf.

General Pagonis described the importance of logistics. He pointed out that in the Second World War, the Germans lost battles to the British because of a lack of logistics.

'They would attack and take ground and then have to go back and resupply. When they moved back, the Brits moved forward,' he said.

Think of a number, add a few noughts . . .

Packing up an army of half a million men and women and sending it a third of the way around the globe can produce some impressive numbers.

● The total air and sea movement of equipment and personnel to the Gulf comes to 58 million miles so far, according to military authorities at allied headquarters.

● Nearly 13,000 missions have been carried out in the strategic airlift, ferrying 450,000 tons of cargo and 450,000 passengers.

● Last week, more than 100 aircraft arrivals were being recorded in the strategic airlift every day.

● Within the theatre of war, 9,500 missions have been flown, carrying more than 100,000 tons of cargo and 75,000 passengers.

● There are 150 four-engine, propeller-driven C-130 cargo planes in the Saudi Arabian theatre of war. Other aircraft hauling personnel and supplies include the C-5A, the world's largest aircraft, and the C-141 Starlifter.

● Keeping all the transportation going, including combat missions over Iraq and Kuwait as well as the myriad military vehicles, has consumed 550 million gallons of fuel so far.

● Saudi Arabia – the world's largest filling station – provides 16 million gallons of fuel per day to the American effort.

● More than five million tons of equipment has been delivered to the theatre of war by sea. A total of 187 cargo vessels, not including US Navy and Marine ships, has been used in the sealift. The number of ships unloaded as of last week was approaching 400. Sixty more ships are on their way to the Gulf.

• Of all the dry cargo vessels used, 38 per cent have been US government ships, 1 per cent US-flag chartered vessels and 50 per cent chartered ships of other nations.

ORDEAL OF A PALESTINIAN IN PENTONVILLE

Abbas Shiblak

Guardian, February 15, 1991

Abbas Shiblak, a writer and researcher at the Arab League, was arrested on January 17 with six other Palestinians and several dozen Iraqi nationals and served with a deportation order on the grounds of 'national security'. On February 6 he was released. This is his account of his ordeal.

Thursday, January 17. It was the second day of the Gulf war. My adult education class on sailing finished at 9.30pm. It took me less than 15 minutes to drive to my house in Kilburn. My wife, Farehan, was standing in the entrance, shaken and in tears. 'Four security men came and asked for you. They're carrying an order to detain and deport you.'

A knock soon came at the door and Farehan let the four men in. They showed me the order. I noticed there was a mistake both in the spelling of my name and of the street in which I live.

They took me first to Willesden police station and I spent the most terrifying night of my life in a detention cell not half a mile from my home. The conditions were appalling.

Next day they took me to Pentonville prison. The majority of the other detainees were Iraqis, mostly postgraduate students. I had never met any of them before. I made my views on the war and my opposition to Saddam Hussein clear to them from the first day.

Many were either of a religious persuasion opposed to Saddam or non-activist Ba'athists, who had to be members of the Ba'ath Party in order to have further education. They were mainly worried about their families.

On the second day, I met a Palestinian, Mahmoud Ayyad, who had worked as a public relations officer in the Qatar embassy for many years, and whom I knew slightly.

He is an apolitical person whose main interest is to have a good life. Ayyad could not believe what had happened to him.

The second Palestinian I met was Ali al-Salih, whose English friends called him 'Nemo'. When I first came to London in 1975, Ali was leader of the Palestinian Student Union in Britain and close to the rejectionists who opposed the mainstream's proposal of a two-state solution for the conflict between ourselves and Israel. But he was opposed to extremism and foiled attempts by the Iraqis to finance and control the union.

After this period Ali abandoned politics and for the past 12 years he has lived in Bedford, married and raised a family, and pursued a career first in journalism, then in management.

I had never met the third Palestinian detainee, 'Mr B', before. He seemed to be an innocent, lonely person with a quiet voice, who had committed only one unforgivable sin, that of being born the nephew of a man who is hated and feared throughout the world.

For the first two days we had not even an inkling of what lay behind our detention. But on the third day we read a leak to the newspapers that the security services had broken a cell of seven Palestinian terrorists planning bomb attacks in Europe and the US.

I realised suddenly that we were these seven: me, Ayyad, Nemo and his wife, Mr B and his wife, and a businessman of Palestinian origin who was released early on.

But this was very strange, as the authorities never interrogated us, they never searched any of our homes, and no one was ever asked about his links to the others.

Our lawyers were trying to bring our case to court, to require the charges and evidence to be produced, but these challenges failed. We appeared to have no legal rights whatsoever.

Our only hope seemed to lie with the British and other friends who visited us, with our fellow writers and journalists. They initiated a debate on the rights of people in Britain, and on civil rights in time of war.

I am relieved that the home secretary revoked his order of deportation and released me and a few others, including Ayyad, Nemo and Mr B. But I am sad to have discovered the other face of a system I had always assumed was just and fair. This was a terrifying experience for my family and myself. After we lost two countries, Palestine and Lebanon, we made Britain our home for the last 17 years. It is a country which gave me an education, shelter, and a sense of freedom.

Out of this episode two facts emerged for me, which I will not find easy to forget. The first is this. Here we are in a democratic and free society. Yet suddenly I found myself completely helpless and defenceless, held in prison and threatened with the destruction of my future without any reason given, without any legal defence.

The second fact is brighter. There are democratic institutions here, a long-standing tradition of free speech, a free press, civil liberty groups and many individuals who are ready to stand up and speak out for these rights.

A CLUMSY ABUSE OF POWER

Independent, March 9, 1991

Britain's disgraceful treatment of Iraqi and other detainees during the Gulf crisis must not be forgotten amid rejoicing over the outcome of the war. Nor should the belated release of the detainees provide an excuse for burying the whole episode, which in its way has done almost as much to discredit British justice as the case of the Birmingham Six.

What is at issue is not simply the extraordinary ineptitude of MI5, which acted on flimsy and often out-of-date information, nor the credulity of the government in not questioning that information, but the existence of laws that so manifestly invite abuse. The powers under which the government acted were not special emergency powers of the type that Parliament can grant in time of war. Had they been such powers, and had the nation been facing a threat of such gravity that they were justified, the grounds for objection would have been much weaker. But these were the normal powers available at all times to the home secretary under the Immigration Act of 1971, and often used by him in cases that normally attract little publicity.

In effect, the home secretary can override all the protection that the law normally accords to suspects when some unspecified, unproven and largely unchallengeable issue of national security is at stake. He can detain suspects indefinitely without brining them to court and without granting them bail or the right of appeal. As the Act puts it, 'a person shall not be entitled to appeal against a decision to make a deportation order against him if the ground of the decision was that his deportation is conducive to the public good as being in the interests of national security or of the relations between the United Kingdom and any other country or for other reasons of a political nature'.

A modicum of protection is supposed to be provided by the right to appear before 'three wise men', often known as 'three blind mice', since they have no power and little information. They are selected by the home secretary – in effect, by the prosecution – so their impartiality will hardly be evident to the detainee, who is anyway granted very limited rights when appearing before them. He is not allowed legal representation, though he may be assisted by 'a friend' if he wishes. Nor will he be given any particulars of the allegations against him, or evidence to support them, that might entail disclosure of sources. And even if he does succeed in impressing the 'wise men', their opinions are merely advisory. The home secretary can ignore them in the same way that he can ignore the reasonable rights of the accused. The result is that people who have committed no crime at all, and may not even be thinking of committing one, can in certain circumstances have less protection than those who have actually committed a crime.

The most basic assumption on which plural democracy rests is, as Lord Acton observed, that power tends to corrupt and absolute power corrupts absolutely. That is why power has to be subjected to checks and balances. It is not easy to understand why this principle should be suspended when it comes to dealing with foreigners. That the British government should be able to accuse and imprison foreigners more or less at will, denying them the protection of due process accorded to British citizens and probably breaching the European Convention on Human Rights, is a scandal that should be quickly remedied.

The recent detentions have provided evidence enough of the corrupting effects that these unchecked powers have had on the authorities. Spared the need to present evidence or submit to proper scrutiny, their procedures were sloppy, their behaviour lazy, and their initial response to criticism smug, reflecting the comfortable inertia of the too-well-protected.

No doubt the threat of terrorism was real, and the government was obliged to take serious precautions. The fact that during the crisis there was not a single terrorist incident in Britain attributable to Arabs or Palestinians neither disproves the need for precautions nor vindicates those that were taken, although, given the casual inefficiency of the countermeasures, it seems unlikely that they would have been effective against a seriously planned operation. More significant is that no other member of the coalition against Saddam Hussein felt it necessary to act in such an arbitrary way against foreign residents. That Britain was alone among the democracies in being willing and able to disregard elementary human rights so blatantly is a matter for shame, and an invitation to less scrupulous nations to misuse power in the same way.

A MIDDLE EAST TRIP
FOR MACHIAVELLI
Edward Pearce
Guardian, January 16, 1991

The first casualty of war is Lithuania. That at least is obvious. The war of George Bush's dapper vanity will start on a minus as the Soviet Union synchronises its watches and surrounds another parliament building in another capital city with the same familiar tanks. Eighteen months ago I stood in a Hungarian town watching, with a lovely double-take, Soviet tanks being shipped out on railway freighters: the undoing in symbolic form of the rolling of tanks across the Chain Bridge in Budapest in 1956.

I remember the cool indifference then of a Foreign Office officialdom not programmed for human sympathy or other defects of character. Today we hear the loud, crushing, arrogant representatives of British awfulness declaring the total impossiblity of doing anything, and making very clear their contemptuous indifference to the wretched little oddities under the tanks.

There is – in trade, aid, and diplomatic terms – a great deal we can do. There is also, on the other side of the hemisphere, a great deal that we should not have been doing. But listening to Sir Julian's old-style realpolitik about small countries after four months of non-stop pulpit-grief about wronged, profitable Kuwait, is something of a conversation-stopper.

Kuwait is worth 45,000 body bags, provided in thoughtful anticipation; Lithuania is worth a quick cluck of the tongue. I really don't want to hear again about 'sacred duty to legality', or 'rights of independent peoples'. Soldiers will shortly be burned black as hamburgers, but not for the sacred rights of independent peoples. This will happen, of course, a little for oil and investment, but eyes will pop out of bodies in burning tanks more than anything else because someone called the President of the United States a wimp.

The abrupt shift of policy in late November, when the US moved from siege and embargo to war threatened on non-negotiable terms, will be explained by historians. Perhaps the boy-Clauswitzes, heroic to the last dead other man, got the upper hand. But my own guess is that the inadequate man in the White House began a gamble. If it was meant as a bluff, it represented an unconscionable risk; if meant as the choreographing of a war, it was a crime. But nobody would ever again be able to say that George Bush couldn't cut the mustard, or devastate a population.

Consequently in the Soviet Union every force for undoing liberalisation has been armed. The supplicating Soviets find themselves courted again, and their little lapses into heel-on-windpipe dialogue are seen in a long, wise perspective. We stand where we stood in 1956, doing wrong, and making possible another wrong about which we will wring our hands before washing them.

Of course, we were at that time engaged in what is now widely acknowledged as a piece of criminality which Anthony Eden – 'half-mad baronet, half-beautiful woman', in R. A. Butler's elegant phrase – set rolling because he was affronted at the impertinence of President Nasser, described as 'another Hitler', in nationalising the Suez canal, a British asset in a sovereign country.

Eden, with his bile duct severed by an incompetent surgeon, could at least plead diminished responsibility; Bush, a feebleton rolling his pectorals, can plead only his vanity. Nothing has happened which makes the declaration of aggressive war – to take the term from the Nuremberg indictment – justifiable to the United States or its uncritical, unreflective, war-happy lieutenant.

But what will flow from this war? There is a school which thinks that once the private soldiers have done their disagreeable but necessary dying and regrettable civilian casualties have been brushed away, a great enlightenment will take place: an American-led, UN-respecting grand plan of law and light will descend. To some notions 'Garn' is an inadequate answer.

161

Saddam, however nasty, is an Arab leading Arabs, a Muslim leading Muslims. His opponents are Westerners, Christians, foreigners, infidels. His destruction will take on the qualities of martyrdom to other Arabs. Saddam was encouraged and promoted by the West as a counterpoise to Iran and militant Islam. Those forces must, by the rules the Americans set themselves, be contained by the presence of more forces. (One should at this point congratulate the professional military: no peace dividend; no scaling down of the military budget; no drop in the useful manufacture of armaments; no premature departure of superfluous captains to Cheltenham or Florida. Somebody is going to have a very good war!)

But we shall with luck have an Arab world in permanent crisis. Not only will Iran – and Syria – loom larger but so will Israel, for ever unwilling under its government of old terrorists to concede a bone button. If anyone supposes that Bush is going to give the Palestinians the state which is the pre-condition of any calm in the Middle East, they misunderstand priorities. It is one thing to fight a colonial war and kill a few score thousands, but quite another to take on a rich, well-wired lobby able to deliver a bagful of votes in key states.

There will be a lot of healing talk after the killing – there always is – along the lines of 'a land fit for heroes', and it should be dismissed for the public relations tosh it will be. In the actual Middle East the US will have working for it, for a little while, Machiavelli's doctrine of the preferability of fear to love. It is really something to be known as a killer who will lightly reach for his guns. On this principle the US police maintain the high standard of urban peace and low levels of violent crime for which US cities are admired.

But if America is not equipped in temperament or talent to be a peace-keeper, the truth is that nobody is, and that nobody should try. Consider past involvements: Suez; the US intervention in Lebanon in 1958, which prolonged the vicious, stupid rule of the Christian families; support for Israel in all circumstances; the Israel and US involvement in Lebanon in the early Eighties; the shoring up of the Shah; the commitment of Britain and the US to the Arab family power of unelected medieval rulers, guided into their loot at the end of the First World War and heading regimes loyal to us out of innate fragility. Suez, remember, was followed in 1958 by the overthrow and murder of King Faisal, 'our staunchest ally in the Middle East': his dismembered body and that of Britain's greatest friend, Nuri es Said, were carried through the streets of Baghdad.

You cry for war, you can have war, and you can win war. But

when war is over, who will keep your friends and allies safe from the rage you have called up? Machiavelli's doctrine is good only for the shortest of time spans. It is never good to be hated.

In the part of England where I live, Amersham hospital has prepared a burns unit of 20 beds, High Wycombe 30, and Mount Vernon 60; Harefield has set aside two wards.

I usually write to music: Rossini or Mendelssohn for the happy pieces, Bach or Bruckner for the grave ones. This I have written to Verdi's Requiem.

THE BATTLE OF VINDALOO
Jim White
Independent, February 9, 1991

There were four of them, sitting at the table opposite us, clearly under the influence of lager. They were all in their early twenties, wearing well-tailored suits and expensive haircuts. It was a pricey theatreland curry house, after all.

They were discussing money: how much they earned on the foreign exchange dealing floor and how much their cars cost to run. As the rounds of beers went down, the lads became louder and more extreme in their language. When their main courses arrived, one of the boys, who had ordered beyond his spice tolerance, wheezily complained about the heat of his vindaloo.

'Christ,' he shouted. 'That's not a vindaloo. That's the stuff what they put in bleeding Scud missiles.' This line inspired a round of Scud jokes; nan bread, napkins and then cutlery flew in mock missile attacks.

After each object was chucked, the lads tittered into their curries like schoolboys at the back of class. When a spoon landed at the feet of a well-dressed couple who were being ushered to a table, a waiter went over to remonstrate. Times are hard enough in the restaurant business without a visit from the militant pilsner wing of British yobbery frightening the regulars. The waiter asked them to moderate their behaviour. His intervention may have been a mistake.

'What you trying to say?" asked the man with the vindaloo. 'Listen you black bastard, this food is shit. This isn't vindaloo. You're trying to poison us, you bleeding Muslim.' With this he tipped the food on to the carpet.

By now mere unease among the other patrons had developed into a nauseous tightening of the stomach muscles. No one said anything because these were big lads, whose rapid mood swing from boisterous to vicious suggested it would be unwise to intervene. In any case, the manager, a small man with a combative edge, seemed capable of handling himself. He asked them to leave, after they had paid their bill.

'We're at war with you bastards,' said one of them. The manager looked confused and said he would never allow them in his restaurant again.

'Well, that's your fault for letting us in in the first place,' said one, with a nasty curl of his lip.

The manager replied with a naivety that was almost touching. 'That was my mistake,' he said. 'You are dressed like English gentlemen, but you do not behave like English gentlemen.'

During the argument over the bill, the staff moved into a well-rehearsed battle plan, three waiters surrounding the table, another standing by the emergency exit, a fifth covering the door.

'We know the laws of our country, we don't have to pay if we're not satisfied,' said one of Britain's finest, rolling up a £10 note and throwing it on the table to show this was a matter of principle, not lack of funds. Another said they weren't going to contribute to Saddam's war effort.

'Why do you say that?' asked a waiter. 'This is not our war.'

'You Muslim bastards support him, don't you? I hope your relatives get blown to pieces.'

In the end they were bundled out of the door, the small one of the party left behind, muttering apologies as he struggled to put on his coat. The manager told him he was scum, and a disgrace to his country.

After they had gone, rolling and cursing down the street, the remaining diners returned to their curries. As we ordered another couple of pints to calm our nerves, my mate told me that his girlfriend, a teacher in Tower Hamlets, has had Bengali children in her class staying at home since the war began. They had been bullied by whites who made them take the part of Iraqis in role-playing games in the playground. At knife point.

In Bradford, Asian taxi drivers are finding customers on Saturday nights who refuse to pay their fares, using the same logic as curry-eating money dealers in London. 'I'm not paying you,' a friend heard an old woman tell a Pakistani London bus conductor last week. 'Haven't you people caused us enough trouble already?'

As our brave boys, jolly Jack Tars and surgically skilled airmen battle for freedom in the Gulf, the lads left behind are opening up a home front. Pop your *Sun* Union Jack in the back window of the Montego and target the enemy within. They're all Muslims, uppity bastards who come over here, take our jobs and try to murder our best literary brains. Or they're Arabs, rich sods who soil the Dorchester's bed linen and shoplift from Marks and Spencer.

The war has come at a time when the Muslim community is at its least popular level ever, after Rushdie and the *fatwa*. On a Friday, after a night in the pub, the war is a good excuse to behave like pigs; never mind that Bangladeshi curry house waiters come from a place that is further from Baghdad than is the Mile End Road.

'This is something that has been going on for 1,400 years. Don't forget, the Crusades never really ended,' said Shabir Akhtar, of the Bradford Council of Mosques.

'These are terrible times,' said Rana Kabani, a writer who has been monitoring attacks on British Muslims. 'You only have to look at the deportation of moderate Palestinians. It is a witch hunt that permeates all levels of society.'

Both Shabir Akhtar and Rana Kabani are not alarmed so much by the tabloid jingoism as the moral and ethical support given the war from respectable quarters. 'If the Church of England says it's a just war, what are these Muslims complaining about?' asked a contributor to Radio 4's *Call Nick Ross* earlier this week.

'It shows that somehow we in Britain believe the Arabs, the Muslims, deserve it,' said Rana Kabani. 'How often have you heard someone say "Well, they put a different value on life in the Middle East"? That's as racist as you can imagine.'

'My fear is that incidents like these might occur on a larger scale when allied casualties mount,' added Shabir Akhtar. 'In the meantime our message to the host community is that we are powerless to stop this war. It is not our war.'

Try telling that to Our Boys with the nan, the lager and the chicken vindaloo.

INTO BAGHDAD

Brent Sadler of ITN

Mail on Sunday, February 3, 1991

The one-ton white Mercedes truck was loaded with 300 litres of petrol in green and blue plastic containers, 200 litres of boiled water, a satellite communications dish and 100 circles of pitta bread.

It was driven by a young Jordanian called Ayman, whose family is from Israel's occupied West Bank. His friend – another of our drivers – was a little younger and called Moussa.

He was also a West Banker with a fiery temper and Jihad or Holy War in his soul. The third in the trio of enlisted drivers, guides and translators was Latif Alawni, a 40-year-old Jordanian whose wife and five children begged him to stay away from Baghdad.

But Latif desperately needed the money and war bonuses. After all, his translation services with the Kuwaiti Ministry of Foreign Affairs were no longer needed after the invasion on August 2 last year.

Latif has a slight limp, chain-smokes a choking brand of Arabic cigarettes and was terrified of the journey ahead.

We were all scared. The road from the Jordanian border at Al Ruweished had been heavily bombed by allied planes. Reports were coming in at our time of departure that the Jordanian government was protesting that four of its citizens and one Egyptian civilian had been killed on the road to Baghdad.

The Hashemite Kingdom of Jordan is being economically crushed by the Gulf war. The King of Jordan is a politically cautious man and charming to meet over dinner. We have something in common. The King is hard of hearing in his right ear – the legacy of test-firing an anti-tank missile that damaged his eardrum. Similarly, my left ear is virtually useless from standing too close too many times to artillery fire in Beirut. We have both experienced war and its painful consequences.

'This Gulf war will change the standards by which Arabs judge their governments and leaders', said the King. His support for Iraq sits uncomfortably with the US-led coalition forces. 'I tried to find a way to peace but no one was prepared to listen,' he continued. 'If you ever go back to Iraq take great care – many people are going to die there.'

166

As we left his kingdom and entered the no man's land between the Jordanian and Iraqi frontiers I felt really afraid for the first time in my life.

Two Turkish journalists had earlier pleaded to join our Baghdad-bound convoy. They squashed on to the front seat of the Mercedes alongside the Palestinian driver Ayman.

Packed behind the threesome was enough fuel to blow them all sky-high if the vehicle was hit by a bomb.

One of the journalists, Ali Haydar reassured Angela Frier, our ITN producer, that she need not worry for their welfare. They wanted the ride to Baghdad.

They had sent a signal to the Turkish foreign ministry suggesting the authorities in Ankara inform the US Pentagon that a convoy of journalists was passing through western Iraq. They gave the estimated time of departure and the approximate route in.

'Hopefully the allied pilots, if they have orders to attack the area, will try to avoid hitting us,' said Ali, smiling nervously.

By now we were running several hours late. Fat chance of that warning doing the slightest bit of good, I thought.

'If we're hit, we're hit and there is nothing we can seriously do to avoid it. But let's pray it doesn't happen,' I said to my three ITN colleagues.

I have seen Beirutis play Russian Roulette in Lebanon. They put a single bullet in the chamber of a revolver and bet on the outcome. Punters come out either alive and rich or very dead.

This drive into Iraq was a little like that – a journey across several hundred miles of war zone under the constant threat of an allied raid. We four had firmly decided the ground rules.

One, the entry to Baghdad should not be attempted in the dark because that was far too risky.

Two, that the cars should space out and avoid any appearance of a convoy-like formation.

And thirdly, drive steadily and carefully because the road was bomb-cratered and extremely dangerous.

At Triebel, which is the Iraqi frontier post, we met Saffudin Talid, a representative from Iraq's Ministry of Information in Baghdad. We were dishevelled, tired, cold and hungry. Saffudin was immaculately dressed in a smart suit and carrying a Kalashnikov AK-47 sub-machine gun.

He was the man who told me on the eve of the war that America would never attack Iraq. Saffudin always likes to be right.

The moon was full. The sky a little cloudy and no one in their right mind would think about moving any further into Iraq from Triebel that night.

'Let's open some pilchards, a tin of tuna fish and a bag of that Arabic bread the drivers brought with them to bribe people,' said Phil Bye, the ITN cameraman. 'Who's got a Swiss Army penknife with a can opener?' He sounded a little frustrated.

A bottle of Cognac miraculously appeared in someone's hand to help meet the icy cold wind cutting into our al fresco banquet. Later I settled into a sleeping bag in the back of Moussa's blue Mercedes with its plastic-encased miniature of the Holy Koran stuck over the dashboard. Obviously we would be spending the night safely here. It was, I thought, the correct and sensible way to approach matters.

Then came an enthusiastic cry from someone who didn't know any better.

'Great, Saffudin said we could all go to Baghdad now. It means we will get there after lunchtime tomorrow,' said the voice of inexperience.

At 10.00pm London time the BBC World Service reported that the first major ground battle was going well for the allies. A quarter of Iraq's electricity generating capability had already been destroyed, according to America's senior general in the Gulf. And Jordan, said the radio, was still condemning the allied raids on the road we were driving along.

My exhaustion eventually overcame the fear and I gave in to sleep. A jab in the ribs by Patrick O'Ryan-Roeder ended that snooze.

My contact lenses had dried out and my eyes were bleary but I could see the blaze ahead of us. It was the wreck of a tanker with Jordanian plates carrying Iraqi oil for King Hussein. Latif, in a Toyota Corolla, was wobbling his way behind the Mercedes truck. He was paralysed with fear and ran off the road twice, narrowly missing a gigantic bomb-crater.

At the edge of one crater we looked critically at a minibus lodged at the bottom. It was a civilian vehicle with a civilian inside. A man had survived and was sleeping the night away. He had no means of doing anything else but stay where the bomb had blown him.

Shortly before dawn we could hear the allied bombers somewhere overhead with a distant drone. 'Get in the cars and run quickly – go fast for they will bomb us here,' yelled Arabic voices.

There wasn't much use in running and the cars needed petrol so we carried on filling the tanks hoping the allied planes would fly away.

Thankfully they did. The game of Russian Roulette in the desert had just ended and there were no losers.

Now that we could see in daylight, the journey was a little less nerve-wracking. Moussa the driver had picked up an officer in the Iraqi Army along the way. They were kindred spirits, talking loudly about the war, allied aggression, the liberation of Palestine and the destruction of Israel.

The new passenger was called Mohammed. He was Kurdish. He hated America, hated Britain and did not appear to like journalists. His English was broken but his meaning quite clear. He reminded me how Iraq executed by hanging the journalist Farzad Bazoft as an Israeli spy.

Not all Iraqis are like that. Saadoun Al-Janabi is a bear of a man with a mission in life to keep a rein on foreign journalists in his country. When Saadoun and I shook hands again on my return to Iraq two Tomahawk Cruise missiles streaked past us at the height of a three-storey house.

Our Palestinian drivers Ayman and Moussa had no stomach for this. They had braved the drive. But no amount of war bonus would persuade the two of them to stay a second longer than necessary and they fled back to Jordan.

As chief minder of the Western media Mr Al-Janabi has a difficult task. We journalists need to know more than we are told and so Saadoun reads every word I write and listens to every word I say that is pre-recorded or even when I talk live in ITN's radio or television broadcasts.

There have been no major deletions from my stories, although there is, of course, much more I would like to report but cannot.

The day after I reached the city I was to get some of the most dramatic pictures of the war – the Cruise missiles, probably launched from a ship at sea, roaring overhead. It was quite phenomenal and proved the most remarkable TV news pictures for years.

We had been taken to see the wreckage of the factory which the Iraqis claimed was a baby milk factory but the Pentagon insisted had been producing chemical and biological weapons.

We were allowed to see what we wanted and I must say it did look and smell like a milk-producing factory. But a watch-tower on the edge of the complex and the camouflaging of part of the building did leave me with a nagging doubt.

Rooms 404 and 406 at the Rashid hotel in Baghdad are our office, editing room and kitchen. A chamber maid comes round some days but the hotel services have all but collapsed – like the rest of the city.

Our work and eating place is beginning to smell. The generator, a small motor that sounds like a lawn mower, is providing us with just enough voltage to report the war electronically. We purchased the generator and hundreds of feet of cable before the war. It was money well spent.

I am writing by the light of a low-voltage bulb and I can see Iraqi anti-aircraft fire swirling into the sky. The explosions, when they are close and loud, make me jump.

Phil Bye, the cameraman, has switched on his lens with an image-intensifier to pick out the nightly pyrotechnics. We cannot edit the video reports and eat at the same time because there is not enough power to run the tape machine and the microwave cooker at the same time.

Whoever invented long-life non-refrigerated microwave food packs has saved us from hunger and illness. But the packs are running out and the last driver who attempted to bring in fresh supplies from Jordan turned back with fear. In between filing reports, cooking food, maintaining the generator and sleeping, there is the hardship of finding and maintaining water in which to wash. But one learns the tricks of survival very fast.

If the water is running we use the bath as a personal reservoir. You can then use a litre-size plastic bottle to wash and shave in. I can now soap my hair, rinse it, brush my teeth, scrape off my whiskers and catwash in a single bottle of water.

Life is both an endurance and an obstacle course. The flashlights we each carry at all times are an essential tool in Baghdad where there is no form of mains electricity. There are many ways of getting hurt in the darkness, like tripping over cables and tumbling down the stairs.

This is one of those rare occasions in a story of global magnitude when only a few can report first-hand what is actually happening now to Iraqis in Baghdad.

When ITN was told to leave Iraq three days after the start of the war we left a newly appointed freelance Jordanian cameraman to help us return.

His name is Mohammed Ali Assad and his family comes from Bethlehem on the occupied West Bank of the River Jordan. For the 10 days I was out of Iraq, Mohammed Ali ran our operation single-handed.

ITN owes him an immense debt of gratitude. Without him it would have been impossible to come back so soon and before any other British broadcaster.

The demands on our time are limitless because of the world's insatiable appetite for any news from Baghdad.

Providing the Iraqis agree, I will stay on here for as long as the generator and my team keep running.

WHERE SCUDS ARE GOOD FOR BUSINESS

Geraldine Brooks and Tony Horwitz

Wall Street Journal, Europe, February 6, 1991

Amman – When the first Scud missile crashed into Tel Aviv three weeks ago, a secondary boom sounded at Fouad al-Afghani's souvenir shop here.

At one end of a makeshift assembly line, Mr Afghani's cousin cuts pieces of zinc in the shape of tiny missiles. Another cousin polishes and cleans the metal. A third paints the tricolor flag of Iraq on the projectile's tiny warhead. The finished product, fitted with a pin or key chain, is a miniature Scud engraved with the words *Allahu akbar* – 'God is greatest'.

'Scuds are the best thing for business since the *intifada*,' says Mr Afghani, who moulded hands clutching stones to commemorate the three-year-old uprising by Palestinians in Israel. When demand for these slumped, he fell back on worry beads and olive-wood figurines of Bedouin. Now, sales of Scud souvenirs are so brisk that Mr Afghani and his family are working 16 hours a day to keep up with orders for everything from buttons to wall hangings adorned with the weapon.

'Brooches are the most popular,' Mr Afghani notes, 'because people can wear them close to their heart.'

Scudmania is breaking out all over Jordan, as well as in other states where Iraqi leader Saddam Hussein and his missiles have become symbols of Arab strength and pride. On the mean streets of Lebanon, young militiamen have adopted 'Scud' as a *nom de guerre*, and also use the word as a term of respect.

The Iraqi president himself is revered as Abu Scud – 'Father of the

Scud'. In Algeria (where youths have changed the traditional Arabic greeting *salaam aleikum,* or 'peace be with you', to *Saddam aleikum,* or 'Saddam be with you'), thousands of Islamic fundamentalists carried cardboard models of Scuds in a march last week supporting Iraq's 'holy war'. One Algerian family is even reported to have tried (unsucessfully so far) to register their infant son's name as Scud.

The current craze may be just the tip of the missile. Scud songs haven't yet rocketed to the top of Arab charts, but at the Raouf Centre music store here, youths besiege the counter in search of a new album of such tunes recorded by a local Palestinian band. They groan when Maklouf Mohammed, the sales assistant, tells them they will have to wait two more weeks. In consolation, he offers a collection of songs about the Iraqi leader, including 'Saddam the Arab' and 'Our Friend Saddam'.

'We have sold 200 copies of this' since the war, Mr Mohammed says. 'Nobody wants Michael Jackson anymore.'

Across town, at the Quick Meal Restaurant, Mahmoud Ibrahim plans to honour Iraq with a Saddam Burger or torpedo-shaped Scud Sandwich. The problem, he explains, is that the war has cut beef imports to Jordan. 'I have chicken,' he says, 'but I think this is not right for such a sandwich. I will wait until we have real meat.'

Others are making do with available ingredients. Mouther Khouri and Mahi Abu Kaf, two Amman pastry chefs, are accustomed to strange orders: cakes in the shape of computers or topped with characters from 'Tom and Jerry' cartoons. But a request last week for a cake modelled after a Scud was something they hadn't anticipated. Working from a newspaper photo, they crafted a sponge-cake missile two feet (about 60 centimetres) long, with marzipan icing and two phrases squiggled on top: 'Happy Birthday' and 'Al Hussein', the name Iraq has given to its improved version of the Soviet-made Scud.

'It looked so real,' Mr Khouri exclaims, 'I wanted to climb aboard and launch it!'

When Nasser Lattouf turned 30 last week, his cake came with a smaller, edible Scud in place of candles. Midway through the party came news that Iraq had lobbed another salvo of real Scuds onto Tel Aviv. 'I thought: What a nice birthday present from Saddam,' says the Palestinian pharmacist, who is raising money to buy medicines for Iraq. Asked if he worries that Israeli civilians died in the attack, Mr Lattouf responds: 'For the first time, Israel is experiencing what we've been through. Maybe next time an Israeli pilot flies over a refugee camp in Lebanon, he'll think: Let's stop the bombing.'

Even in the hushed corridors of Al Amal Maternity Hospital, Scudmania is having an impact, notes Mahmud Taher. 'Last night, we had two Scuds,' the obstetrician says, referring to Iraq's salvos the previous evening. 'So this morning, we should have at least two Saddams.' One of them is already sleeping soundly in a blue crib in the hospital nursery. His mother, 30-year-old Shireen Mosuli, says she decided on the day of the US attack on Iraq to name her baby Saddam if she had a boy. 'I am just waiting for my husband to come to discuss whether we should give him the full name – Saddam Hussein,' she says.

By the time he reaches kindergarten, this new Saddam will have lots of company. Jordan's Civil Affairs Department says 412 babies – six per cent of male births – were given the name between August 2 and January 22, with numbers soaring since the US attack.

'When I ask the parents why they give this name, they say it's because they have felt humiliated a long time, and he has restored their pride,' says Dr Taher, who has delivered three Saddams so far. He thinks the name will remain popular even if the Iraqi president is ultimately defeated. 'It was the same with Nasser,' he says of Gamal Abdel Nasser, the former Egyptian president. 'He lost two or three wars, but at least he fought.'

Older Jordanians want a piece of Saddam Hussein, too. At a Palestinian refugee camp, a barber named Abu Mohammed wields a pearl-handled cut-throat razor on the beard of an elderly client. Like most of Mr Mohammed's customers, this man aspires to a Saddam-style moustache. 'Every Palestinian wants to look like him – to *be* like him!' says the barber, as likenesses of the Iraqi leader peer down from the shop wall.

Saddam Hussein's Scud attacks have also inspired Arab writers. Mohamed al-Khysi published an experimental medley of poetry and prose in a Jordanian paper last Friday, describing how the first missile strike restored Arab pride. 'From far away, I hugged him,' he writes of the friend who telephoned with 'this great piece of news'. The verse concludes by extolling the Iraqis as they march to war: 'I can hear their footsteps as if they are dancing.'

At Mr Afghani's souvenir shop, new and unusual orders continue to come in, even as the Scud attacks wane. One customer wants a Scud in flight, which Mr Afghani is constructing with a wooden base and a thin wire to hold the missile aloft. He recently asked the Iraqi embassy to provide copies of Saddam Hussein's speeches so that he can choose quotes to print on T-shirts. And he is already producing buttons with such messages as 'Saddam, one like you makes dreams come true' and 'Israel is Cancer. Scud is the Answer'.

For the Palestinian shopkeeper, who fled his native Yaffo in 1948, crafting such products isn't just business. It is 'political advertisement,' he says, adding that of the first $3,300 he has made since the war, he has donated almost half to a popular army in Jordan pledged to support Iraq. While he has buttons and watches featuring Palestine Liberation Organisation head Yasser Arafat and Jordan's King Hussein, he dropped Libya's Colonel Moammar Gadhafi soon after Iraq's invasion of Kuwait. 'Now that we need him, he is invisible,' Mr Afghani says. 'This is not a true Arab leader.'

As for future projects, Mr Afghani says 'it depends on Saddam – what weapons he uses.' He draws the line, though, at chemical weapons and won't produce anything honouring them. 'This will be a long war,' he predicts. 'I am sure Saddam will come up with many more surprises.'

UPPER CLASS DECADENCE

Sunday Times, February 10, 1991

The Queen needs urgently to summon the royals to Windsor for a chapel meeting. This country is at war, though you would never believe it from the shenanigans of some members of Her Majesty's clan. As usual, it is not the most important members of the royal family whose behaviour has been less than we have a right to expect, though the performance of even the inner circle since hostilities broke out has hardly been faultless. It is the exploits and public demeanour of the minor royals and nearly royals which causes most offence. Britain's armed forces are waging war against the fourth-largest military machine in the world. They stand on the brink of the biggest land battle since the Second World War, a battle in which some of the nation's finest young men and women are expected to risk their lives. Yet, on the home front, too many of the young royals and their entourages carry on regardless with their peacetime lifestyles, parading a mixture of upper-class decadence and insensitivity which disgusts the public and demeans the monarchy. The Queen should put a stop to it.

It is unfortunate that no member of the royal family is on active service in this war. The Duke of York served bravely in the Falklands but there are no royals, or nearly royals, in the Gulf. That is a great pity, for it is important in a democracy at war that the first family in the land is seen to be making the same sacrifices as ordinary families throughout the country. But the Gulf War has brought different images from Prince Andrew's helicopter missions in the South Atlantic. He is still a serving officer in the Royal Navy, but this time his ship is far enough away from the war to allow him recently to enjoy a couple of days' golf on a sunny Spanish links. The Duke of Edinburgh and the Prince of Wales have taken up arms, but only to go hunting birds. Not even war, it seems, can stop the last shoot of the season at Sandringham. Sadly, there has been worse.

Lord Linley, the Queen's nephew, has gone to the Caribbean island of Mustique, though royal publicity has concentrated on the decision of his mother, Princess Margaret, to cancel her trip there. He graced the front page of Thursday's *Sun* in fancy dress, wearing red lipstick and holding on to various males in drag. The Duchess of York, who went skiing last month as the country stood on the brink of war and returned only when the hostilities actually broke out, must still have her fun too: this week she was playing with her gang, very publicly, at a high-spirited dinner in a London restaurant. Both royal frolics followed hard on the heels of the confessions of Lord Althorp, the Queen's godson and brother of the Princess of Wales, about his recent adulterous fling in Paris. This could be regarded as a royal contribution of sorts to the war effort since his revelations, especially when they failed to kill the kiss-and-tell tale of the 'other woman', did give the nation some light relief from page after page of war coverage. It is an example Prince Edward has chosen not to follow. He could be regarded as the only other young royal with something to contribute to the war since he runs his own theatrical company. But so far he has not offered its services to entertain the troops. Indeed, anything related to the Gulf has been noticeably absent from the prince's royal schedule, despite the £100,000 he receives from the civil list.

Nobody expects the royal family to cease to have any sort of social life until the war is over. But wartime does demand a sense of proportion and a degree of decorum out of respect for those unable to enjoy any social life because they are risking their lives on our behalf. That applies above all to the royal family, whose behaviour in time of conflict should symbolise the purpose and concern of the country. Some royals, notably the Princess of Wales, have been seen to do their bit with visits to the families of those serving in the Gulf and other war-related appointments, and by following a social schedule which does not attract attention. The Queen, of course, has behaved impeccably. But too many have made only token gestures and have continued to lead social lives which make no concessions to a country at war. Their behaviour at a time of national crisis is helping to undermine the very role of the royal family.

Questioning the position of the monarchy in our constitution now goes well beyond the usual small minority of inveterate republicans. A growing number of young people, by no means all on the political left, are also beginning to question the purpose of the monarchy, perhaps encouraged to do so by the behaviour and lifestyles of too many of their royal contemporaries. Their inadequate, sometimes insulting, response to the demands of the Gulf war has encouraged such questions, as have reports about the monarch's wealth. The recent study which claimed the Queen earned £1.8 million a day on her investments is probably wrong, because it includes many royal assets which properly belong to the state and which the Queen could not dispose of even if she wished. The more important matter is that, whatever her wealth (and nobody denies it is very great) she pays no tax on income generated by it. Her unique status as the only person in the kingdom not to pay tax is rooted in our feudal past, when the monarch was personally responsible for raising all national revenues and deciding how they were spent. The constitutional position of the monarchy has clearly altered radically since those days but its ancient financial privileges remain, even though they are beyond justification today.

The Prince of Wales seems to realise that such privileges will not wash with future generations. He already volunteers some tax on income from his personal assets. He has also spoken of funding the cost of the monarchy from its own revenues rather than from the civil list. And he has recently concurred with a theme, first raised in this column several years ago, that too many of the royals are behaving as if they were in a soap opera, with the result that the media now treat the royal family like a soap opera. The Queen needs quickly to write such roles out of the royal script while we are a nation at war. In the longer run, the best hope of the monarchy lies with the Prince of Wales.

SCHWERPUNKT

John Keegan

Daily Telegraph, February 22, 1991

As the ground war gets under way, how can General Schwarzkopf best maximise the advantages the allied army enjoys and exploit the weaknesses of the Iraqis? To do that is, of course, to practise the art of generalship.

All the classics of strategy ever written, from that of Sun Tsu in ancient China to Clausewitz's *On War*, insist that the duty of the commander is to make the enemy fight on unfavourable terms. How is Schwarzkopf to impose such terms in the Kuwaiti theatre of operations?

The advantages that the Iraqis enjoy are those of strong fixed defences and short lines of communication. The principal advantages the allies enjoy are those of superior firepower and mobility.

Air supremacy heightens the advantages of firepower and mobility, to an almost inestimable degree against an enemy which has lost all air cover, without constituting a separate advantage in itself.

Allied firepower and mobility are further enhanced by a magnificent logistic system of transport and supply, while behind that system an enormous defence industry produces the munitions and replacement equipment that the war consumes in vast quantities with every day of operations that passes.

Iraq has a logistic system which is probably adequate for its needs while its army remains static, but which is under heavy attack and will be severely strained when the army is forced to manoeuvre.

It never had the defence industry necessary to equip or munition its forces. Every day that passes not only depletes its stock of munitions but also the tanks, artillery pieces and armoured vehicles that make it formidable. None of these can be replaced.

A final advantage that the allies enjoy is a virtual intelligence monopoly. The Iraqis may derive some intelligence of allied deployments from signal eavesdropping and from within Saudi Arabia by spies, but their intelligence plot must be patchy at best and cannot work in 'real time'.

The allies, by contrast, have a magnificent 'real time' system, supplied by its JSTARS surveillance aircraft, which transmit virtually instantaneous images of enemy movement, and a huge array of other information-gathering devices. The allies, in short, can see deep into the enemy's operational area.

All this is very reminiscent of the situation prevailing in Normandy before the great allied break-out of July 25, 1944 – with the difference that the desert better favours an offensive and that the Iraqis, unlike the Germans, are fighting without a defence industry behind them.

What the allied high command contrived in 1944 was to stretch the German mobile forces to the utmost, causing Hitler to commit his tank divisions on a sector far distant from the chosen point of attack. That point was then deluged with airborne fire-power, falling on static troops which lacked air cover, before the allied tank forces crashed in and broke through.

The Germans call the point where decisive strength is concentrated the *schwerpunkt* – roughly 'heavy point' – a term so useful that it is now often used by British and American staff officers.

The allies know where the Iraqi *schwerpunkt* lies. It is in Kuwait itself, a country only eighty miles square, and behind that on the Kuwaiti-Iraq border. General Schwarzkopf's problem is to choose the best *schwerpunkt* for his own forces.

That choice must not overstretch his own logistic resources. It must not commit the assault troops to an advance that cannot be supported with reinforcements from the rear. Above all, it must not commit allied troops where the Iraqis are strong in men, in equipment and in fortifications.

That being so, the chosen *schwerpunkt* ought to be west, though not too far west, of the large Iraqi concentration in Kuwait. Such a choice would open up a line of advance that would threaten the Iraqis with being outflanked from the desert side.

To counter such a threat, the Iraqi commanders would then have to bring forward their own tanks from their protected positions and to concentrate them for a counter-attack.

To move and concentrate armour on the face of the open desert when the enemy possesses overwhelmingly strong tactical air power is to invite crippling loss. The danger would be further enhanced if the Iraqis could be confused into reacting to several apparent threats at the same time, only one of which would be at the real *schwerpunkt*.

General Schwarzkopf possesses such a capability. The two Marine Expeditionary Brigades afloat force the Iraqis to keep troops and tanks concentrated in the coastal sector, whether the Marines stage a landing or not.

The helicopter-borne units of XVIII Airborne Corps could be used to stage strong diversions on the desert side of the theatre or even to mount powerful hit-and-withdraw raids inside Iraqi positions.

Given the situation, such raids might develop into ground-holding operations to be continued until tank forces made a link-up. Air power and artillery will no doubt continue bombarding the front to simulate the preparation preliminary to an armoured attack.

The two Marine divisions ashore, which are close to the coast, constitute a grave menace to the Iraqis. A local offensive by them against the Iraqi front would sow serious confusion in the enemy's mind.

Ultimately, however, it is the commitment of the allied heavy armoured force – the American 1st Cavalry, 1st Armoured and 3rd Armoured Divisions and the British 1st Armoured Division – and its supporting tactical air force which will decide the issue.

The selection of the heavy armoured force's *schwerpunkt* is therefore the key to victory. It will be chosen to impose maximum overstretch on the Iraqi counter-attack force, so that its dense columns of vehicles will be thinned out on the move by air attack. The terms of the ultimate tank-to-tank encounter should largely be settled by attrition from the air before the ground battle is joined.

One thing is certain. Once the tanks roll, under their umbrella of air power, there can be no turning back. The *schwerpunkt* is not a place where the appeals of diplomacy are heard.

WAITING FOR BATTLE

Max Hastings

Daily Telegraph, February 21, 1991

There is sometimes an impression that, while the diplomatic manoeuvring goes on, the battlefield remains in a state of suspended animation.

On the contrary. In the past few days, the preparations for the ground offensive have continued without interruption.

Patrols, probing operations, engineer activity, harassing fire by aircraft and artillery are in constant motion, above all in the hours of darkness.

Few Iraqi soldiers on the border with Saudi-Arabia are likely even to be aware of the diplomatic activity that has been taking place.

Most will know only of the bombing, strafing and allied ground deployments that have been taking place across their front.

It is hard for an outsider to gauge the loneliness and misery that must prevail among men short of food; watching such terrifying weapons as fuel-air bombs and multiple rocket salvoes detonating around their positions; waiting to receive an attack from overwhelming forces. Some commentators convey the view that the Soviet peace initiative has caused undue delay to the launch of the ground offensive. Military sources in London and Washington say this is untrue, that the allied forces are still operating to their pre-ordained timetable, from which they will not be deflected unless Iraqi forces are seen to begin to withdraw from Kuwait.

Each day of air attack, of which the principal weight is now being carried out by aircraft carrying precision-guided weapons, further depletes the Iraqi defending forces. Every 24 hours, somewhere between 100 and 200 Iraqi tanks and armoured vehicles are removed from Saddam Hussein's order of battle by bombing. Every 24 hours, therefore, the task facing the allied ground forces becomes less difficult.

The only balance to be struck is that between the military advantage thus gained, and the political and diplomatic difficulties that inevitably increase, as the world nurses its unease about the apparently one-sided pounding of Iraq from the air.

For the men of the allied ground forces, this phase before the main battle begins is in some respects the most critical. The difficulties and losses they will sustain when their advance begins will be heavily influenced by the success of the patrols and engineer reconnaissance that takes place before H-Hour.

The principal allied purpose at this stage is to maintain tension and uncertainty across the greatest possible breadth of front. Helicopter attacks on isolated Iraqi positions, and softening-up fire are designed to keep the enemy in doubt until the last moment about where the decisive allied thrusts will come.

Every night now, the engineers are at work on the dangerous and lonely task of exploring the Iraqi minefields and obstacles, marking the paths along which the tanks will advance. They would laugh at our distant notion of a war that has not yet begun. For them, the war is in full swing, and they are bearing the stress and danger of one of the most important jobs of the campaign.

The artillery are ranging their guns, testing the freaks of ballistics that variations of climate impose upon the performance of high explosives, practising the rapid shifts of position that the gunners expect to carry out, when they are faced by dangerous counter-battery fire, such as Iraqis are, at least theoretically, capable of.

It is a strange business for artillerymen, who have spent all their service careers subject to the tight restrictions upon expending training ammunition that prevail in the Rhine Army, now to find themselves shooting salvo after salvo in the course of an afternoon.

The gunners, of course, seldom or never see their targets, 15 or more miles ahead of them. It is a journalistic misnomer to say that they are in the front line. They are shooting to the wireless orders of their battery commanders, who are located alongside the infantry battalion and armoured regiment COs, thousands of yards further forward. It is a curiously cold-blooded business for a gunner officer, watching through binoculars as the fire that he directs by remote control falls upon his target.

Gunnery is a science in which the British have always excelled; in the Second World War it was the one branch in which the Germans conceded that the British Army was their superior. In the Gulf now, the role of the artillery will be critical, against the formidable equipment the Iraqis possess. We have been told little so far in this war about the activities of allied special forces.

But we know that the SAS and its American counterparts are strongly represented in the theatre, and are playing an important role in directing air and artillery strikes.

It is impossible to guess how far behind the Iraqi lines they are operating, in three and four-man teams. But their perspective is critical, in building General Schwarzkopf's picture of the state of the Iraqi forces, in a fashion that aerial photographs cannot achieve.

Are the enemy vigilant? Do they wash? How well fed are they? How well led and disciplined? These are all questions to which only direct and constant ground surveillance can provide answers, and this is the reason that special forces are never likely to find themselves out of a job on the battlefield.

Focus your sympathy today, though, upon the thousands of men of the allied armoured divisions, cleaning their weapons and polishing their vehicle optics for the hundredth time, men who have not yet glimpsed an Iraqi, who know that they are at war only because they hear the crump of the guns and the bombs, and see the distant columns of smoke on the horizon they have yet to cross.

They yearn for the suspense to be ended. They do not want to risk their lives, or to kill Iraqis. But they desperately want to get on with the job.

There is one thing worse than braving the fire of the enemy, and that is waiting to brave the fire of the enemy. They are unsure whether they fear more the battle to come, or the sense of self-ridicule they will feel, if having come so far, a diplomatic settlement takes them home without firing a shot.

Each man asks himself, in the silence of his sleeping bag in the darkness, how he will behave when the test comes.

It is the same before every battle, in every war.

It is unlikely that the allied ground forces will have long to wait before they know the answers.

THE LONG WAIT IN
NO MAN'S LAND

Con Coughlin

Sunday Telegraph, February 17, 1991

To the allied soldiers dug in along the no man's land of the Kuwaiti frontier it is known as the *'bomb et lumière'*: for the Iraqi soldiers on the receiving end of the relentless allied bombardment, it is a personal hell from which they hope Saddam Hussein's last-ditch gamble to avert a land war may yet deliver them.

As darkness fell each night last week, the sky along the border was illuminated as barrage after barrage of shells, bombs and rockets rained down on the Iraqi positions. The explosions sent great shafts of light soaring into the darkness.

To the uninitiated, the varieties of weapons were almost indistinguishable as they hit their targets with an earth-shaking rumble. But the young British and American soldiers took great pride in identifying the cause of each *'lumière'* by its *'son'*: the whistle of the bomb, the whine of the artillery shell and the roar of the missile. So spectacular are the sights that many soldiers sit up most of the night to watch the bombing display, running the risk of sleep deprivation.

At the very time that the Revolution Command Council in Baghdad was formulating its heavily hedged offer to withdraw from Kuwait, fuel air bombs – the poor man's nuclear bomb – were dropped for the first time to clear the vast minefields which are all that now separate the armies – an action widely held to be the final preparation for an allied ground offensive.

In the circumstances, the peculiar brand of diplomatic brinkmanship being practised by Saddam to save what is left of his army suggests the action of a would-be suicide who jumps over a cliff and then calls for a rope to save himself.

Face-saving formulas are a perennial feature of Arab diplomacy, so it was to be expected that Saddam would attach a handful of fanciful conditions to his offer to withdraw from Kuwait. The only objective open to him is to save the remnants of his once-mighty military machine from annihilation.

Indeed, Saddam may consider himself fortunate that he still has the opportunity to forestall a ground attack by ending the occupation of Kuwait. According to front-line troops in Saudi Arabia, orders had been passed down the line for the offensive to liberate Kuwait to begin last Wednesday night.

After months of preparation, the best equipped, best trained and most sophisticated military force ever assembled was on the point of going into battle. The divisions were in their allocated places, the men psychologically prepared for action and the strategy decided. Even the weather cleared – the vicious sandstorms of the preceding weeks being replaced by cool, sunlit skies.

Then, at the last minute, the soldiers were told to stand down. That decision was a direct result of the visit by President Bush's most senior military advisers, Mr Richard Cheney, the American Defence Secretary, and General Colin Powell, chairman of the Joint Chiefs of Staff, to General Norman Schwarzkopf, the allied commander, in Riyadh last weekend.

Against the advice of the more practical allied commanders, the demand of the coalition's political leaders that casualties should be kept to a minimum resulted in the decision that the land offensive should be postponed until more of Iraq's heavy armour had been accounted for by air strikes.

When the history of this conflict comes to be written, that decision will no doubt be seen as an uncharacteristic loss of nerve on the part of an allied command which had hitherto shown a clinical determination to pursue its objective of securing the liberation of Kuwait.

Postponing the land offensive left the the front-line troops in something approaching a state of suspended animation. 'We were all geared up for the Big One,' said a staff sergeant with the Queen's Own Highlanders. 'Now we don't know what to do with ourselves.'

British commanders hurriedly devised new training exercises to keep their men in prime fighting condition. Ordinarily, the garrison town of Hafr al-Batin, about 60 miles from Kuwait's western border, is strictly out of bounds, but commanders turned a blind eye as groups of soldiers filed into the ramshackle hotels in search of a shower and to sample the debatable charms of the local cuisine.

After the intensity of the night bombing, the atmosphere at an Egyptian front-line observation post I visited last week was almost pastoral. While some soldiers dozed in the shade of their trucks, others took advantage of free time to wash clothes, write letters and sunbathe.

A circle of sandbags originally intended as a defensive wall had been adopted as a communal meeting place. Packets of Egyptian Cleopatra cigarettes were passed around while young officers closely scrutinised the film review pages of week-old copies of the Egyptian *Al-Akhbar* newspaper.

About the only indication of the war's proximity were the arcs formed in the sky by the vapour trails from B52 bombers as they wheeled away after their missions and headed back to the safety of bases in the Indian Ocean, Spain and southern England.

Not even the presence of a group of Iraqi prisoners – who had escaped to the allied lines the previous night by crawling through their own minefields – disturbed the general atmosphere of conviviality. Captive and captor alike sat crouched on the ground easily reaching a consensus on Saddam Hussein's abiding lack of merit.

Even the massive supply columns of recent weeks have subsided to the extent that spare trucks are being used to ferry non-military supplies to the front. One truck carried a portable field mosque towards Saudi Arabian units.

Whatever arguments may have weighed in favour of postponing the land war last weekend, the controversy provoked by the death of Iraqi civilians when allied aircraft bombed a bunker in Baghdad, believed to be an Iraqi command and control centre, brutally exposed the dangers of relying upon air power alone. After four weeks of intensive allied bombing, there was a certain inevitability about the bunker incident.

The decision to persist with the air war was taken primarily because the more conservative allied commanders wanted to destroy as much of Iraq's military infrastructure as possible before initiating the land war.

When Cheney and Powell visited Riyadh, only 750 of Saddam's 4,000 tanks had been destroyed. Some allied ground commanders wanted to see at least half of the Iraqi heavy armour taken out. After a week when allied aircraft have concentrated primarily on destroying armour and artillery, the number of Iraqi tanks out of action has risen to 1,300.

The argument against relying solely on air power was that, with fewer easily identifiable targets, there would be a diminishing return in damage done to the Iraqi Army for each of the sorties flown.

There is also an inherent fallacy in the numbers game. To start with, some of the figures are wildly inaccurate. According to the allies' official count, considerably more of Saddam's Scud missile sites have been destroyed than the allies believe existed – a discrepancy made all the more embarrassing by Saddam's continuing ability to launch Scud attacks on Israel and Saudi Arabia.

Counting guns, tanks and armoured personnel carriers, moreover, provides only one part of the military equation; it does not take into account such factors as the readiness or willingness of the enemy to fight and the quality of his defences.

The nightly briefing sessions of the allied command in Riyadh have also engendered an aura of invincibility about everything the allies do. From the outset the American and British briefers have presented the war as a clinical, humane operation undertaken to uphold an issue of high moral principle.

While there is no denying the overwhelming international consensus in support of the main war objectives, the language used by the briefers, senior officers specially selected for their public relations expertise, portrays the campaign at its most sanitary.

The Kuwait frontier is not a battlefield, but the 'Kuwait theatre of operations'; the allies' successes are reported in terms of the equipment or facilities destroyed, not the human toll. Nor do the briefers ever admit that anything that occurs is other than part of the great master plan for the liberation of Kuwait.

The public has been encouraged to look on this as a bloodless war by the Iraqis' decision to show only a tiny proportion of the damage done by millions of tons of allied munitions. The way in which the West has reacted to the relatively light damage caused by a few score Iraqi missiles is out of all proportion to that inflicted on Iraq.

Now the bunker bombing has caused a fundamental rethink of allied strategy. Whatever the Riyadh briefers may say, this one incident has done more to boost Saddam's standing in the Arab world

185

than any number of Scud attacks. In a conflict in which the allies have claimed the moral high ground, there is a growing acceptance that, if there are going to be casualties, it is the military, rather than civilians, who should suffer.

Before Saddam made his 'offer' to withdraw from Kuwait on Friday, the start of the land war appeared imminent. It will still be launched if Baghdad does not show a clear resolve to withdraw its troops from Kuwait without precondition within the coming days.

However, if Saddam seriously intends to leave Kuwait, he had better be quick about it. The delays in launching the land war have added to the frustration of the battle-ready and eager allied troops who want to get the job done quickly and get home. This frustration could soon be powerfully vented upon the battered remnants of Iraq's infantry divisions.

'BELIEVE IN SOMETHING'

Robert Fox with the 4th Armoured Brigade

Daily Telegraph, February 4, 1991

From the low-flying Lynx helicopter the positions of the British 4th Brigade spread across the bare desert like small Bedouin encampments draped in suitably muted shades of camouflage nets. Beneath the nets the armoured fleet of Challenger tanks and Warrior troop-carriers is ready for battle at a moment's notice.

In the helicopter the brigade commander, Brigadier Christopher Hammerbeck, makes a last tour of inspection of all his units. It is part of a cycle of visits to his men before they are committed to full-scale war.

Infantry companies, armoured squadrons, batteries of artillery and troops of sappers are to hear their commander's last words of exhortation.

The brigadier's speech is a mixture of encouragement and reassurance – to summon the blood – and for sober reflection about the preparation of mind and body for what lies ahead.

Brigadier Hammerbeck thinks that the allies could be on the brink of the biggest tank battle in history, greater in weight of firepower than anything seen in Russia in the Second World War or the Arab-Israeli wars of 1967 and 1973.

'We are getting to the stage where we are going to have to fight,' he explains to C Company of the 3rd Battalion of the Royal Regiment of Fusiliers. 'We are going to have to do some crazy things in crazy places. It is time to kick the front door down.'

Maintenance of the man, maintenance of equipment, and professionalism are the watchwords. The men are told to eat as much as possible and to log up extra sleep. 'Try to get a bit of a lie-in, never mind the sergeant major.'

For the inner spiritual man the brigadier stresses the need for conviction and companionship. 'Believe in something, your family, God, your homes and that will help you to survive, to believe you will come back.' Fear, he says, is to be shared, as this reduces the fear of the unknown.

His carefully balanced words are the work of long thought and discussion with the brigade chief staff, Major Julian James, who commanded a mortar platoon at the Battle of Mount Longdon in the Falklands. The stress of belief and companionship are the echo of the words with which the Paras' padre, David Cooper, sent them into battle nine years ago.

'Remember your professionalism, know your job. Look after your neighbour,' concludes the brigadier. 'Be confident, share your fear. God bless you all. When it happens I'll be there, right up with you.'

In the exhortation there are tips of practical tactical common sense. The brigadier tells the fusiliers to go for the vehicle and not the man. 'If the vehicle is gone, the enemy is finished. Without support and the means to move, their formations will wither on the vine.'

The companies and squadrons at each location give a different reaction to their commander's words. Moving from the company positions of the fusiliers to the Grenadier Guards and the Royal Scots invites military culture shock.

At each position different queries emerge from the brief interlude of questions. 'What do we do about taking a surrender, particularly if the man may be faking as the Iraqis did at Khafji?' asks a fusilier NCO. The answer: 'Act with extreme caution, only move if he has thrown away his weapon. Try to stick to the Geneva rules.'

At the Grenadier Guards' position, where the neat rows of crates and tents indicate severe discipline from the drill sergeant, the questions dwell on more material things. 'Why don't we get the allowances the Americans have?' inquires Sergeant Nick Westwood. He has heard the American GIs get an allowance of $40 (£20) a day.

But here the brigadier has a firm defence. News of the forces' pay rise (12 per cent for other ranks and 18 per cent for officers) has come in overnight. It is also the water money day. Each man receives 700 Saudi riyals in cash (about £125) to buy bottled water for the month.

Most warlike in appearance are the two companies of the Royal Scots – the First of Foot, the oldest regiment in the army, 'Pontius Pilate's Bodyguard'. Men and machines are stripped and accoutred for action. The men sit round as if ready to deal personally with Saddam Hussein at a moment's notice. One or two have bayonets fixed; nearly all have pouches laden with grenades and ammunition.

'What's so special about the Republican Guard?' asks a corporal of B Company. Brigadier Hammerbeck explains that most armies have an elite, and the Republican Guard, formed during the Iran-Iraq Gulf war, is now equipped with the best armour and artillery Saddam possesses. 'Well I don't think they'll feel so bloody elite when they hear the Royal Jocks are on the way,' replies the corporal.

THE MOTHER OF BATTLES

After the long lecture tour, the business of the evening begins for the brigadier at his headquarters. He is briefed, and in turn briefs his staff for a hard night's planning and writing. After supper there is time for reflection, and the huge post bag has to be tackled. It will take at least four hours.

In between the brigadier finds time for reading a few favourites. Top of the list is *Crisis on the Suez Canal* by General Avraham 'Bren' Adan who made the lightning Israeli counterstroke to surround the Egyptian 3rd Army, and effectively end the 1973 Yom Kippur War. The brigadier confesses he has based much of his tactical thinking about rapid movement of headquarters units on Adan's achievements.

Brigadier Hammerbeck, 47, is an addict of the theory of warfare, tank warfare especially. References to Guderian, Liddell Hart, and above all to Field Marshall Lord Carver, who commanded his regiment and brigade, litter his conversation. He also admires the first master of armoured warfare, Hannibal. 'Take the Battle of Trasimene – a classic counter stroke movement; just look at what he did with the elephants there.'

The brigadier in private reveals himself as a staunch family man and a devout Catholic. But in his final message to the troops Brigadier Hammerbeck chose to quote from the gospel according to Star Wars rather than the Bible. 'The force is with us,' he told the headquarter troops of the Royal Scots. 'God Bless you all. We are going to do the business.'

A NIGHTMARE RAIN OF FIRE
Philip Jacobson of *The Times* with the 32 Heavy Regiment
Pooled despatch, February 28, 1991

A long column of Iraqi soldiers trudges out of the driving rain shortly before dawn, their heads bowed, hands high. They are walking like men who have emerged from a nightmare, and there is every reason for that.

A few hours earlier, I watched a terrifying artillery barrage on the position they were occupying.

For nearly 40 minutes the sky rained fire upon them: salvo after salvo of heavy shells and devastating volleys of rockets lit up the dark almost continuously, with sudden blossoms of bright red flame marking hit after hit.

From where I was lying at the side of a 7th Armoured Brigade command vehicle, the flashes were blinding and the earth heaved beneath me.

As the shells passed overhead with a noise like heavy canvas being torn, the air pressure changed perceptibly; then came the double boom of impact and percussion wave, like the slamming of a heavy door.

189

The thought of being under that hail of shrapnel and high-explosive was sickening.

Several of the young soldiers who had joined me to watch this extraordinary and, it must be admitted, riveting spectacle caught their breaths and swore quietly, uneasily aware of the torment their enemies were enduring.

When the barrage lifted, leaving us with ringing ears, a ground attack by Challenger tanks and infantry went in immediately to exploit the numbing effect of the bombardment.

The sky lit up again, this time with long streamers of red tracer drifting lazily across into the Iraqi position.

Machine guns were hammering incessantly and we heard the deep thump of Milan anti-tank rockets seeking out Iraqi armour.

At times, the fire-fight appeared to be advancing towards my position, then a new burst of shooting would begin on a more distant flank.

We could follow the course of the battle on radio in the signals vehicle: the distinctive voice of Brigadier Patrick Cordingley, commander of 7th Armoured, was on the air almost continuously, pressing this unit to get a move on towards a new objective, cautioning another not to get carried away before securing any enemy gun-pit.

A flurry of traffic would indicate that a new attack was under way, yet virtually every voice was calm and composed, even when the first of the British casualties was reported.

Severely wounded, he was rushed to a nearby aid post before being taken to a more sophisticated field hospital. It seemed unbelievable that men were not dying by the score in such intense fighting, but even estimates of Iraqi deaths were well under three figures.

Shortly before dawn, another prolonged artillery attack was called in and the earth began shaking again.

It was the last straw for the Iraqis, who laid down their weapons where they stood and set off in search of someone to accept their surrender.

That was when we came across them, being rounded up by a handful of bewildered gunners from 32 Heavy Regiment.

'They just loomed up out of the rain and stood looking at us,' Staff Sergeant David Serjeant said, gesturing to the PoWs sitting quietly on the sand and whispering among themselves.

'A lot of them looked dazed, punch drunk maybe, and they stood there while we searched them for weapons without saying a word.'

Most of the prisoners were shivering with cold, at least one had no boots. Within minutes, a new pair of British Army issues were produced, plus cakes, chocolate bars and cigarettes.

The Staff Sergeant handed out what was left of his wife's last parcel. 'The war's over for them now and I have nothing against these lads.

'In fact I'm delighted they turned it in instead of getting killed.'

Three-two's RSM, David Hill, took me over to a handful of officers. In passable English, a young captain told me his unit had surrendered because there was no longer any hope of escape.

In a voice betraying the tension he had been under, he told me his wife and two children lived in a small town near Baghdad and he hoped the war would end soon so he might see them.

'British Army good men?' he asked me, and when I assured him that all the prisoners were safe and would be decently treated, he translated the news for his comrades.

An older man said something in Arabic.

'He told me to say you that this is the second time he is prisoner of war, and he know the British are kinder than the Iranians.'

Our column got under way again, the Challenger tanks of The Queens Royal Irish Hussars and The Scots Dragoon Guards grinding towards their next objectives.

Our vehicle, named The Whore of Babylon by someone who knew his Book of Revelations, could not keep pace as Brigadier Cordingley's exhortations crackled out over the radio.

He seemed to be in a good mood, joking with one officer who had reported the capture of a dozen soldiers.

On the way up to the new front line, we passed elderly T-55 tanks dug in by the Iraqis for use as artillery, some abandoned without damage, others blackened by direct hits.

Mercifully, there were no bodies to be seen.

One shattered Iraqi troop carrier bore charred testament to the punishment the allies have been inflicting day in, day out since the war began.

Up at the new attack line, where a more sizeable Iraqi concentration was believed to be dug in, preparations for imminent battle seemed to be almost leisurely.

The tea mugs were out, some late compo ration breakfasts were being heated up and Brigadier Cordingley, back in his favourite floppy beret, was consuming a slice of the excellent fruit-cake provided by his ADC, Captain Mark Shelford.

Both looked grey with exhaustion but were clearly bucked by the brigade's long, hard and successful night's work.

'I think you could report that the plan turned out pretty well,' the brigadier observed, sounding mildly surprised.

'Everyone did what was expected of them and I am absolutely cock-a-hoop.'

In the background, the artillery was forming up once more, a long line of ammunition supply trucks creeping towards the guns.

Soon it would be another Iraqi position, another unit of cold, hungry and dispirited men, absorbing the fearsome bombardment.

We hoped that they would have the good sense to surrender first.

THE ENEMY IS FROZEN IN TERROR
Richard Kay of the *Daily Mail* with the 1st armoured division

Pooled despatch, *Daily Mail*, February 28, 1991

It was a terrible day to go to war. Rain swept the encampment and wind drowned the sound of the F-16s and A-10s patrolling the skies.

By 8.00am on Monday as Colonel Iain Johnston handed out his last orders, we had changed into chemical protection suits. We attached patches of chemical-active paper which would show up the slightest trace of poison.

Passing through the border, where large breaches had been blown in the sand obstacles, we would be at our most vulnerable.

As we waited to clamber into the narrow Warrior troop-carrier the gunner, Lance Corporal Jim Lee, bent his head and prayed. It is one of the most emotional moments I have seen. He was not praying for us but for the troops of the armoured heavy brigade who would lead the assault.

We set off at 1.30pm and, by 4.00pm, were just short of the border. There was an allied grave. It was marked with a white cross, the soldier's boots and a sheet of chemical agent repellent material.

The Americans, our guardian angels, were flanking us every inch of the way. The line of armour and troops was colossal.

At 4.42pm we crossed into Iraq. It was a euphoric moment and a sobering one. In a smoking pile of twisted steel was the shattered remains of an Iraqi artillery emplacement. Beside it, the dismembered remains of a soldier.

Tracers and rockets were stitching a pattern across the sky. This, I thought, was definitely it. Over the radio, a coded message gave Major Potter, of Quebec Bravo Oscar, orders for an enemy position to be taken out.

Excitement and fear coursed through every man, but it was eight hours before we made contact, encountering an Iraqi position that had not been completely abandoned.

For hours we crawled behind A Squadron's 14 tanks. Suddenly the radio again crackled into life.

We had strayed into a suspected minefield. Rockets streaked over our heads, bearing down on the armoured brigade we were after. There was nothing to do but to go on. In the Warrior, under layers of protective clothing and body-armour, it was hard to remain frightened. It was hard to be anything but tired. Perspiration ran down everyone's face.

The tanks identified a target. Their commander, Major James Hewitt, ordered them to open fire and the crump of their 120mm shells hitting the trenches reverberated through our reinforced vehicle.

Bright rounds lit the sky and suddenly the ground was alive. Each blast sent up a fountain of sand.

Red and white tracer ripped through the sky. Then, just as it started, the snarling tanks and chattering Warriors were stilled and, like a mirage, the Iraqi soldiers began to appear – to surrender.

One, two, a third, six marching with hands on their heads.

It was a rout. We had 28 prisoners lying spread-eagled at our feet. Their clothing, for it did not resemble a uniform, was tattered and worn. Their faces were frozen in terror.

Then came the difficult part. Several American soldiers had already died, victims of PoW suicide bombers. Each man had to be checked to see if he was holding a grenade.

Inches from us, Major Potter recoiled. 'Mine! mine!' he screamed. At fingertip reach of one of the prisoners was an anti-personnel device.

The PoW was just as scared. He had not known it was there. From then on, we stuck carefully to vehicle tracks.

Behind us, the tanks roared again, destroying a bunker. We had not stopped. Our destination was a battalion-strength artillery emplacement.

There was another fire-fight at first light.

When it was over, we could see smoking vehicles and the dead sprawled in the extravagant postures of men killed suddenly in battle.

The survivors wanted to give up. Emerging from a foxhole, two surrendered to my colleague, Mike Moore, as he photographed the carnage. I'm not sure who was the more surprised.

Cordite smoke stung the back of our throats and it was hard to breathe, but one of the men had enough poise to throw himself at our feet.

'Please, please, me Christian, love Jesus, don't kill.'

He said his name was Sayeed and he pressed a white scarf into Major Potter's hand. Then he tried to embrace him. It was nearly the last thing he did.

'Christ, I almost killed him and he only wanted to kiss me!' said the Major, slamming back the breech of his SA80.

It was only a temporary diversion. The grid we were heading for took us towards an artillery position behind tanks in formation, their claret and blue ensigns just visible in the poor light.

There was a rattle on the side of the Warrior. It sounded like raindrops on a tin hat. It was Iraqi small-arms fire. It summed up the hopelessness of their position. We shrugged the bullets off.

Our forward platoons were bringing back more prisoners, among them a man with a gaping wound in his chest.

He looked as if he could not survive, but that did not stop Corporal Brian Meechan, the company medic, who quickly began to apply dressings.

The look on the young conscript's face was one of incomprehension. 'Why?' he was trying to say.

'That's the way we do it,' Major Potter mumbled. 'We treat their injured like our injured. And we bury them properly too.'

BLUFF AND DEATH ON THE RUINED STREETS OF BASRA

Karl Waldron

Independent, March 6, 1991

They came down the northern highway, pushing a contraption more reminiscent of the American Civil War than even the First World War; machine-gun barrel protruding through a sheet steel plate, a hastily constructed protection against the bullets of their former comrades.

Fanning uneasily behind it were 30 or so soldiers, single flecks of red exposed on their sleeves identifying them as members of the

Republican Guard. In a city where governance is by armed men acting on information supplied by runner, in the absence of telephone or radio, we had known of their approach for half an hour.

A small boy had run unhindered along the narrow streets to warn of their coming. He was rewarded with a swig of liquor and a dirty pile of banknotes. The currency here is food and bullets, and the dinars he received, once enough to buy a second-hand car, would now require lengthy argument to be exchanged for a loaf of bread.

A sniper opened up from his hiding place within the Hadari apartment block, his bullet corkscrewing a soldier to the street from out of the maze of blasted walls and tunnels which, according to the resistance, now comprise the building.

Suddenly there were perhaps 100 Iraqi soldiers, some carrying rocket-launchers, jogging, taking cover in doorways. This was an organised force from the north, untried in the Gulf war, according to Colonel Ibrahim Bin Hadr, leader of the group that controls the Ashar district, who had brought us to the centre of Basra to witness the chaos.

A soldier peeled back from the advance force to where reinforcements were crouching, his arm clearly visible through the binoculars signalling the window whence he thought the shot came. We saw the explosion a millisecond before we heard the blast, and watched as masonry that was half the building's side fell to the street.

There would have been few civilian casualties, according to Colonel Bin Hadr: much of the city centre has been abandoned since the start of the war. But it is hard to see how the sniper could survive. Knowing they would be outgunned, Colonel Bin Hadr ordered his soldiers back to their base, the old Dinar tourist complex.

For three days there has been no law in Basra: the forces of warlords such as Colonel Bin Hadr control areas rather than make up a seamless opposition. Their philosophy is survival mingled with discontent against Baghdad, and largely dictated by where the troops were at the time of the ceasefire rather than political and religious beliefs.

'Why didn't they come?' asked the colonel, reiterating the most common phrase heard in Basra. This group and others had expected the support of the Americans, the Iranians and the French. Now Saddam Hussein's army was redeploying against them, its superior weaponry seemingly allowed to pass through the allied lines from the north, reasserting the dictator's grip on Iraq's second city.

Colonel Bin Hadr's power now rests on the tank which lies outside his gate, and on the brutalism whence he gained his rank. It does not matter that he has no shells or anyone who can fire them. His soldiers know how to gun the engine, and the few remaining gallons of diesel are expended in the threat of destruction. For a few hours the Republican Guard may be fooled.

'We will need to move tonight,' says Colonel Bin Hadr. 'We have no real weaponry to fight them should they move against us.'

On the quayside our boat is tied, its Iranian crew waiting. Against a pole is the group's shoreside sentry, a Ba'ath political officer, his neck fastened to the pole, bootless, his thorax pierced with a spike: the man from whom the former Private Bin Hadr had stolen his rank.

A RABBLE IN RETREAT

Stewart Payne

Evening Standard, February 26, 1991

I joined the liberating force today as Saddam Hussein's rabble army went into retreat.

With Arab front-line troops we swept across the desert, artillery pounding our path, as Iraq's defeated soldiers surrendered around us.

Across breached minefields, past still-smouldering oil ditches, around tangled barbed wire – the march was relentless. The desert shook with the onslaught.

Everywhere was the proof that what Saddam Hussein had declared would be the 'mother of all battles' was a rout.

Tanks, blitzed by precision allied bombing, had been reduced to blackened skeletons. Artillery lay in twisted heaps. Craters littered the desert.

My jubilant Arab escorts took me to trenches and foxholes abandoned only minutes before. Hand grenades, ammunition, guns and radio equipment had been left in haste.

So too had the personal effects of the pathetic, terrified soldiers. Letters to families, photographs of loved ones and pages from diaries blew across the sand in the bitter, rain-filled wind.

On every horizon thin lines of Iraqi soldiers were emerging, hands in air, from stinking trenches which had been their homes for six months.

The sounds of war filled the air; small arms fire, machine guns, mortar and heavy artillery.

Every now and then our advance was halted by enemy fire. As A10 tankbuster aircraft circled overhead, tanks moved forward to engage the resistance. It never lasted long.

The Iraqi troops couldn't know that, a world away, at the United Nations, their leaders who had brought about this humiliation were trying to bring it to an end. For them the end had come too late. They had seen their comrades die; they were ill-equipped, ill-fed and ill-clothed. Now they waved white flags, surrendering to the inevitable.

The scale of the allied opposition was awesome. In a four-wheel-drive jeep I had crossed the breached defences that separate Saudi Arabia from Kuwait, rain pouring from a grey sky at first light, and poor visibility obscuring the convoys moving north.

I drove past hundreds of ammunition and supply trucks full of cheering, waving Egyptian and Saudi Arabian soldiers.

Some 20 miles inside Kuwait I reached the front line, rows of tanks, APCs and artillery firing in an arc in the general direction of Kuwait City.

An Arab lieutenant called Faisal took me to the limit of the advance. Under cover of machine guns, surrendering Iraqis were being herded into small groups. Wherever resistance was met, the tanks rolled forward, exhaust clouds marking their progress.

Lieutenant Faisal pulled the booty of war from the trenches. Green wooden cases of ammunition, mortars and grenades, most of it of Russian origin.

Several foxholes had scripts from the Koran together with details of allied positions. It was hard to imagine the daily hell of living in these putrid holes under daily allied bombardments.

In the space of just one hour I saw hundreds of soldiers surrender.

The Iraqi defences seem to have caused few problems for the allied advances.

I crossed two minefields which had been cleared using line charges. In front of them huge, blackened ditches still flickered and smouldered from where oil had been ignited.

As the mist cleared the battlefield opened up. In his enthusiasm to show me the scale of the allied victory Lieutenant Faisal had taken me ahead of the front line. The advancing tanks were behind me now, the turrets swinging menacingly.

But my jeep was decked out with military markers to warn against friendly fire. The tank crews simply waved in greeting and roared past.

Ahead lay another battle, another surrender. And then, still in the distance but getting closer by the hour, lay our objective – Kuwait City.

SOMETHING EVIL HAS VISITED KUWAIT CITY

Robert Fisk

Independent, February 28, 1991

What kind of people would do this? That's what we kept asking ourselves in Kuwait City yesterday. Day had been turned into night, so thick was the canopy of smoke, the nation's oil wells burning gold and orange along the black-fringed horizon. Hieronymus Bosch courtesy of the Iraqi Army.

They had even used the modern equivalent of a torture wheel. All day, Kuwaiti men, young and old, approached our car with their terrible stories. 'They twisted my son on a pole and broke his legs with pieces of wood,' a stooped old man said. 'They thought he was in the resistance. Now they have taken him away, with all the others, as a human shield.'

Then there was Heather Rennison, an English woman married to a Kuwaiti. 'A cousin of my mother-in-law was arrested. She was only 19 and they had found two-way radios in her bedroom. Three days later they came to her home to ask her parents for clothes and blankets. So her parents thought she would be all right. Then the Iraqis hanged her and dumped her body outside her home. There were burns from electricity on her arms and legs. Of course, the Iraqis kept the clothes and blankets.'

Perhaps one needed to walk the pavements of Kuwait City yesterday to understand the extent of what the Iraqis did, that it really does amount to a war crime. 'I will show you the mosque where they shot 11 men on Friday,' a bearded man shouted to us from his car.

The Abdullah Othman mosque stands in the Palestinian Hawali quarter. The bearded man pointed to a yellow wall. 'The Iraqis said that all those at prayer would be taken away – kidnapped – and 11 men stayed in the mosque and refused to go. So they brought them here, blindfolded them, made them stand with their backs to the wall and shot them in the face.' The bullets that had hit the worshippers' heads were embedded in the yellow wall. 'Don't be surprised,' the man said. 'I had two neighbours who the Iraqis thought were in the resistance. So they pushed them into the drains, closed the grille, poured petrol on them and set them on fire. Their families buried them later – you can't leave bodies in drains.'

The figure of 5,000 Kuwaiti men abducted in the last hours before Iraq's retreat seems fantastic until you find – as I did yesterday – that the first three families who offered lifts to various locations in Kuwait City had all lost sons as hostages. The young men had simply been ordered into Iraqi Army buses as they walked to work. Three thousand men and women murdered here, the Kuwaitis also tell you. Who could do this?

It is comforting, in trying to come to terms with a reign of terror, to search for some logical reason, historical hatred perhaps, or some aberrant unit of the Iraqi secret police. But this would be fanciful. What is one to think when one walks, as I did yesterday, through the smoking embers of the National Museum, fired by the Iraqis on Tuesday? Or the gutted interior of the parliament? Or the still burning library in the Seif Reception Palace – its magnificent golden clock tower smashed by a tank shell – where I found, lying on a chair, the remains of a book published by the government of India, entitled *The Collected Works of Mahatma Gandhi?* What kind of people burn museums and libraries?

Outside the museum, Kuwait's collection of historic wooden boats had been burned to cinders. The 'Islamic house' lay in ruins. The walls of the Emir of Kuwait's Dasman Palace had been torn down with explosions and bulldozers. The Iraqis had used tanks to shoot at the parliament. The great hotels had been systematically fired. The Iraqis had even planted explosives in the bedrooms of the Meridian Hotel. It was like a medieval army which conquered, looted and then burned even on an individual level.

Boat owners found their yachts stolen or deliberately sunk in the marinas. Shopkeepers found their stores burned if they could not be looted. At an abandoned anti-aircraft gun on the coast – where the Iraqis mined the lovely beaches against a non-existent American amphibious landing – I came across piles of brand new women's shoes, made in France, none of them matching, all wrapped inside Iraqi army blankets along with body-building magazines. Why did they do this, these soldiers? Why had they stolen, too, an exhibition display of women's eye shadow? There were cartridge cases across the forecourt of the great museum, bullet-holes in the cracked walls of the building that once contained Kuwait's finest – and long ago looted – national treasures. What was he thinking, this soldier, when he opened fire at a museum?

The seafront restaurants have been torn down, the high, glass-covered landmark water towers machine-gunned. At al-Ahmadi, the Iraqis set off explosives every hour at the two oil farms, each containing 20 tanks. The fine old British 'White House' there was burned down along with the control room that operates the oil pipelines.

I suppose one sensed in Kuwait yesterday that something very wicked, at times evil, had visited this city. Not just an occupation army, not even the Iraqi Ba'ath Party apparatus, but something which intrinsically links dictatorship and corruption. 'Down with the dirty Fahd, Sabah and Hosni [Mubarak]', said a blood-red graffito on the wall of one of the burned palaces. 'Long live Saddam Hussein.' In the little, looted musuem of Kuwaiti peasant art, I found a poster of Saddam stapled to the wall. 'Most victorious of all Arabs, the great leader Saddam Hussein – God bless him,' the caption said.

Whoever uttered such prayers? Colonel Mustapha Awadi, of the Kuwaiti resistance movement, offered to show me. In a bleak housing estate in the suburb of Quwain, he took me to a school – the Iraqis used schools as interrogation centres – and in a classroom I found 16 young Iraqi soldiers. They sat on the floor, legs crossed, moustachioed, miserable, ordinary men with tired, dirty faces and grimy uniforms. 'They were happy to surrender,' the colonel said. 'See? We even given them food and tea. I promise they will be handed over unharmed to the Kuwaiti Army.'

Two of the men had been wounded in the face – their bandages were fresh – and they all smiled when I greeted them and when they heard me tell the colonel in Arabic that I would mention their presence to the Red Cross. One could not help but feel sorry for these defeated teen-agers with their sad smiles. So what kind of men had raped Kuwait?

RIDERS ON THE STORM

Phil Davison with the US Marines

Independent on Sunday, March 3, 1991

The moon, almost full, cast gloomy shadows in the desert where the shadowy figures of Marines flitted back and forth between blacked-out vehicles and I listened to the football on the BBC. Artillery and bombing shook the sand beneath my feet as Crystal Palace went four behind at Arsenal and Trevor Brooking lamented, 'They've just been all at sea, Palace.'

We were heading for combat. Earlier, at sunset last Saturday, Lieutenant-Colonel David Wittle of the US Marines had called his men together. 'A few minutes ago,' he said, 'I sent a message requesting permission to deploy to the berm at H-hour and to initiate combat operations against the enemy. I want to remind you of a few things: first of all, you're Americans. Second, you are Marines or navy personnel. Third, this is a right cause. All I ask of each of you is to do your best and collectively we will succeed. We are going to raise our flag on territory that is clearly occupied by the enemy. Each of you, shoot straight.'

Then he unfurled the Stars and Stripes and led his unit in the Marine anthem. Not for the first time, the US Marines had been chosen to do the dirty work, and they wouldn't have it any other way. They were to strike into Kuwait in a feint to distract the enemy before US Army, British, French and Arab forces launched the main attack far to the west. That thrust would not come until Monday.

The football was a final, surreal prelude to 90 hours in which I saw Iraq's heavily mined defences breached and an infantry division routed, and which ended with us entering Kuwait City in a shower of kisses, flowers and sweets from jubilant Kuwaitis.

At 2.00am on Sunday, we moved up to the border with dimmed lights in pitch darkness, coming together in a convoy of a thousand vehicles. We were not to see them until daybreak, but up front were tanks pushing ploughs and minesweepers, amphibious assault vehicles (used for their heavy armour), artillery pieces, TOW anti-tank missiles, a ragtag array of bulldozers, a Mercedes water-tanker on its last legs and a sputtering armoured ambulance known as Old Smokey.

201

Jokes and songs soon gave way to silence. Radio traffic ended and drivers communicated by hand signals. The Marines could only guess what they were going into. There would be mines; they believed their breach plan would handle that. But would the Iraqis shower them with chemical artillery shells? Would Saddam's planes and helicopters emerge to attack them during the hours needed to make the breach? No one then knew the answers.

Night had given way to rain-swept dawn when we passed the berm that marked the end of Saudi territory. There was no border marker; only a hand-made sign: 'Welcome to Kuwait – Dallas, Texas, USA' – a Texan Marine up the line had left his mark. Lieutenant-Colonel Wittle logged his entry into Kuwait at 06.42. His next words were: 'Incoming. Indirect.' As we feared, we had come under artillery fire just as we entered the minefield. But it was hardly a threat: most of it landed a mile away. The nearest mortar round threw up a sand cloud 75 yards to our left.

There was no doubting the mine danger, however, and no risks were taken. To cross the minefield, the convoy split up across six narrow lanes, some 500 yards apart. Each was cleared of mines by the armoured plough tanks or AAVs firing light-line charges, then the lanes, barely wide enough for a tank, were flagged and the convoy passed through. Each driver carefully followed in the tracks of the vehicle in front.

It took a nerve-wracking four hours for the convoy to get through. We were held up when a gas alert forced the closure of our track. The engineers had to clear a lateral path to get us on to another track, advancing like tightrope walkers across the minefields, tracing, marking and detonating the mines.

As we moved on again, a lone, unarmed Iraqi soldier limped past us, the first of many. The Marines had decided not to slow their progress by taking prisoners. Those who surrendered were fed, given a letter, and told to walk towards Saudi Arabia.

With the minefields behind us, we roared on towards the first objective, some water-wells that could be used for chemical decontamination if needed. As we approached, we came under small-arms and mortar fire. We had stumbled on the field headquarters of Iraq's 14th Infantry Division. Infantrymen piled out of vehicles and edged towards a network of trenches and foxholes, but the shooting stopped as abruptly as it had started, and suddenly Iraqis began appearing from foxholes, hands on their heads.

The 14th Infantry Division simply disintegrated. The Marines took thousands of prisoners, while many more Iraqis fled northwards, aiming rearguard mortar fire towards our position but missing by several hundred yards.

A major-general was led from one bunker by a delighted motor maintenance man. Another logistics man, Corporal Mark Trafny, still trembling with excitement, described how he had gone into a trench. 'It was so narrow. I borrowed a 9mm pistol, stuck the bayonet between my teeth and crawled in. I kept thinking what would I do if an Iraqi appeared, but no one did. I discovered a medical bunker full of drugs, syringes and weapons.'

What we found there was an underground complex that offered some explanation of how Iraqis were able to survive the allied bombing. The HQ was virtually invisible from above-ground. Soldiers had lived in tiny foxholes reinforced by plumbing pipes, cinder blocks, corrugated iron and sandbags. There was not a building to be seen in the expanse of undulating dunes, but beneath the surface was a sophisticated command and control bunker whose operators had still been transmitting as the Marines moved in.

Outside, the hulks of ancient tanks, sunk in the sand, bore witness to Iraqi attempts to deceive allied bombers. Later, we were to see more simple decoys – large, empty mortar tanks or simply corrugated iron shells with pipes protruding like tongues – scattered across the desert.

At sunset on that first night, Lieutenant-Colonel Wittle told his men it had been 'a good day for the Marine Corps and a major success for this unit'. Monday was less successful. In the morning we captured the positions that had fired on us the previous day. More Iraqis gave up, most fleeing north. Then, in the afternoon, a combination of storm clouds, thick fog and smoke from the burning oil wells forced us first to crawl along with guides at front and rear, and then to give up and dig in for the night some way short of our objective.

It was so dark it was difficult at times to tell whether your eyes were closed or open, and the unit's Global Positioning System, a miraculous satellite navigation device in the commander's vehicle, was rendered useless. As Lieutenant-Colonel Wittle and some escorts walked about, trying to check our location, they came across a truck with an Iraqi soldier on board. The commander raised his pistol and edged forward, calling on the man to give up. There was no reply. When the Marines moved closer and shone their red torches, they saw that the figure was nothing more than the charred remains of a man, killed perhaps on the previous night, but still sitting upright. It is typical of the desert that the following morning, when the fog lifted, we could not find the truck.

By Tuesday it was clear the Iraqis were fleeing *en masse* before us. As we wheeled east towards Kuwait City, we could see Iraqi tank tracks heading northwards towards Iraq. We forged on at high speed, passing the evidence of tank battles of the two previous days and of allied bombing. Almost every landmark – abandoned car, oil well, Iraqi armour or Bedouin corrugated iron dwelling – was demolished. Huge craters were dotted on or around anything that resembled a fortification.

To the rest of the convoy, the tank battles of Sunday and Monday had been invisible. We had heard the Marine tanks firing, sometimes ahead, sometimes off to our flanks, but always out of sight. Such is war.

THE GULF STREAM

We hit tarmac – the Jahra-Kuwait City road – and dug in for the night in yet another thunderstorm. Although we were scarcely a mile from the outskirts of the capital, we could not see it. On Wednesday, as artillery and mortar fire gave way to small-arms exchanges, our escorts drove us past the Marine front line and on towards the city centre. Apart from a 12-man team sent in to secure the US embassy, these escorts were the first Marines to go in.

It was, at first, a tense drive. A fire-fight north of the Sixth Ring Road slowed us down, and when we entered the city proper it seemed deserted. Then as we drove on people began to appear on roofs and balconies to wave and greet us, and by the time we turned on to the seafront, on Arabian Gulf Street, hundreds of cars had appeared in jubilant convoys, honking their horns, flashing their lights, carrying flags and posters of the Emir.

We were showered with flowers and sweets amid screams of 'Thank you, USA!' or 'Bush! Bush! Bush!' Our escorts were pulled from the vehicle to hold babies and pose for snapshots. One woman finding I was British, yelled: 'Thank you to Mrs Thatcher. No, I mean Mr Major. No, say thank you to Mrs Thatcher, too. We'll never forget her. And thank you to all the British soldiers. We appreciate their help. We are very proud of them.'

'IT WAS LIKE DOOMSDAY'

Richard Dowden

Independent, February 28, 1991

It was like doomsday. At 3.00 in the afternoon it was dusk – a filthy, lowering smog of oil smoke covering the desert. The sun was a small, pale disc, the air thick and sickly. Occasionally droplets of oily black liquid pelted down. At one stage we counted six oil fires pouring out smoke. Two spouted flames 50 feet into the air.

This was the battlefield. Yet swallows zipped and flipped across the desert into the dark gale and, amazingly, Painted Lady butterflies fluttered by.

On Tuesday afternoon we picked our way from minefield to artillery battery to armoured column, always seeking a route north-east towards the city. By mid-afternoon the Marines had broken through the main line of Iraqi defensive positions and, following them, we came across a network of trenches with tanks and artillery dug in between them. The tanks had had their turrets blown off and the trenches smelt of death. But in most places the Iraqi soldiers seemed to have fled without a fight.

All afternoon the Marines' artillery kept up a steady barrage. Only rarely was there incoming fire, when the clouds echoed with a peculiar, hollow moan followed by a blast which you felt in the stomach rather than heard.

Always following fresh tracks for fear of mines, we reached a road. A T-62 tank was burning furiously, its exploded ammunition scattered across the desert. Several other vehicles lay wrecked and abandoned. By some of them lay the incinerated bodies of Iraqi soldiers. In two places the road was pocked with scores of holes punched by cluster bombs.

In the distance a line of men was walking towards us. We waited for them, guessing they were surrendering Iraqis. But as they approached they did not raise their hands, but kept them behind their backs. A trick – the fear suddenly froze us. But they shambled on towards us. Their hands had been tied by American troops who had told them to walk south. There were so many prisoners the advancing army could no longer cope with them. Further down the road we passed one more – limping and dejected – a terrible example of the humiliated army which had been devastated in just four days. He must have spent the night like that, unable to eat, drink or urinate, frightened and frozen. I will always feel ashamed that I did not cut him free.

A squadron of Marine tanks was lined up on the road, watching north and east. They warned us there had been two chemical attack alerts in the past hour and, soon after, the gas alert went off and we scrambled into our suits. The attacks were not confirmed. The Marines allowed us to travel with them and throughout the long, dark evening they advanced and stopped, advanced and stopped. Their artillery behind us never let up.

A Bronco spotter aircraft droned overhead towards the Iraqi positions and minutes later two F-15 aircraft roared northwards to drop their bombs on invisible targets. At last, in pitch darkness, the Marines formed a circle for the night. 'There are too few targets now and too many units chasing them,' said a sergeant. At dawn we left them and made our way cautiously into the dead, dark city. At first light near the Sheraton we met two Kuwaiti resistance fighters raising the Kuwaiti flag, and we came across the first taste of the horror that Iraq has wrought on this city. Muwaffar al-Ibrahim, a young Kuwaiti fighter, said one of his friends had been executed by Iraqi soldiers. 'I hate them, I hate them. I feel no mercy for them now. In the past few days they have done anything.' A distraught Palestinian said: 'I wish I was in Gaza or the West Bank now – the Israelis have never behaved like this to us.'

Further on, a man held up his child to kiss me and one old man clasped me, wailing 'Welcome, welcome' through his tears. An old woman called out: 'A hug for Bush, a hug for America – and for Egypt.'

Throughout the morning more and more people poured on to the streets waving Kuwaiti flags, the possession of which under Iraqi occupation would have meant instant death. They waved and cheered and young men fired captured machine guns in the air.

Every Kuwaiti seems to have a personal horror story – a brother, a sister or a friend killed or disappeared. Palestinians and Jordanians were treated better, but for an army which claimed to be liberating its 19th province, the Iraqis' treatment of its citizens was unbelievably cruel. At the hospital we saw the corpses of seven Kuwaitis whose heads had been smashed in and one whose body was barely recognisable as human.

According to every Kuwaiti I have spoken to, anyone suspected of being in the resistance was killed. In the past week hundreds, possibly thousands, of Kuwaiti men have been abducted from the streets. Those shops which survived the original invasion have been comprehensively looted, private cars have been taken wherever they could be found and some 80 public buildings have been blasted by tank fire and burned.

The Kuwaitis have much to celebrate, but their celebration is soured by grief and bitterness.

DEATH AT THE PALACE

Tim Kelsey

Independent on Sunday, March 10, 1991

Safah chose four cans of peas. It was a calculated risk. She needed to fetch water from a friend in another street, but to get there she had to pass the Iraqi checkpoint outside her house in the central district of Kuwait City. The three soldiers manning the road block were always hungry. She knew that. She had been able to pass before by giving them tinned food.

It was just after dusk on October 14 – two-and-a-half months after the Iraqi invasion. The silence of the city was broken only by the beating of the rain on the road. It had been heavy for two days. She walked with her 18-year-old brother, Mansour – two years younger than her – towards the soldiers.

There was a fire struggling to burn in the rain by the sandbagged gun emplacement. At first, Safah thought she could pass unnoticed.

207

But the soldiers shouted at her in the darkness and she stopped. She was clever. 'God bless you and Saddam Hussein,' she said. She gave the soldiers the tinned peas, and they waved her through. She told her brother to say nothing, and they walked around the corner to the house of her friend.

A few minutes later they were back at the checkpoint, carrying a plastic bucket of water. The soldiers seemed to ignore them and they passed unhindered. But one of the soldiers followed them up the street. Mansour noticed first. 'Sister,' he whispered. 'Behind us.' Safah continued towards the flat, walking slowly. The soldier saw the pair cross the threshold and he disappeared. They both smiled.

A quarter of an hour passed, and then there was a knock on the door. Safah and her brother were silent. There was another knock, and then a warning: 'We will shoot if you do not open.' Safah told her brother to hide under her bed. She opened the door to two soldiers and a smartly dressed Iraqi wearing civilian clothes – a polo shirt and slacks – who had a pistol in his belt. She must have known who this was: a military intelligence officer. Down the corridor, from his hiding place, her brother could hear the conversation.

'You love Saddam Hussein?' asked one of the men.

'Yes,' Safah replied.

'So why do you work for the resistance?'

'I don't,' she said.

'You're a courier, carrying messages. We've just seen you. But you shouldn't worry. You're a nice girl. We'll help you to leave Kuwait.' He was very friendly. There was no shouting and no harsh words. One of the Iraqis told her to pack a case. Another kept congratulating her: 'Free from here! We hate it too, you know.' Her brother was confused. But he stayed under the bed. Safah came into the room. He could see her fill her case. A soldier suggested what she should take. 'There,' he said. 'A nice dress, you should bring that.' Safah's diary lay open on her chest of drawers. She tried to hide it under a blanket. 'No, you should bring that too,' said the civilian.

By Kuwaiti standards, Safah was not rich. Her young husband was a Kuwaiti policeman, and his pay only stretched to the rent of this small three-bedroomed apartment. The soldiers did not plunder it as they had so many others in the city – there was not much of value to take. Safah could probably have earned more – she had had some medical training – but she was not working. The two had been married only months before, and were planning to have a child.

Two months before her abduction, her husband had been taken by the Iraqis. He was still missing.

The last thing Safah packed in her case was his photograph. And then she left the bedroom and was gone. Two hours later her brother crawled out, and cried. It was the last time he saw his pretty sister, who was so fond of her velvet black hair.

It was this face, a pretty, smiling Safah, that greeted me four days after the liberation of Kuwait. A photograph of her (the one that appears on the cover) was lying face up beside a pile of women's shoes in the Nayef Palace, headquarters for the Kuwaiti police, which the Iraqis converted into a death camp.

By chance, I met Safah's parents shortly after seeing the photograph, and they confirmed her identity. They had not known what had happened to her after her disappearance, until I told them of the photograph. Even then their knowledge of her fate remained vague: nobody, it seemed, had escaped alive from the Nayef Palace; nobody knew what happened inside.

The exception was Lufti, an 18-year-old student who, like Safah, came from the Bneid al-Gar suburb of Kuwait City and had spent more time in the Nayef Palace than anyone. Pale, thin and nervous, he seemed desperate to help, in order to rid himself of the guilt of having survived. I believed him because of that desperation, because he was the most precise of the witnesses to what had happened in the palace, and because what he told me invariably coincided with details independently provided by others. He helped me to reconstruct the story of Safah's short life in the jail, and of her dreadful death.

When the first allied forces entered Kuwait City on the night of February 26, they removed at least 50 bodies from the palace. Some of these were Iraqis, killed as they tried to withdraw from the city. Most were Kuwaiti civilians. But hundreds died here, and the location of the dead remains a mystery.

Last week, the Kuwaiti resistance started to dig up the ground beneath the basement. They found some bodies there, but the majority remain undiscovered. It is more than likely that the Iraqis simply dumped them in the sea before retreating – making some effort to obscure the evidence of the atrocities. The mutilated corpses of Kuwaitis tortured in other locations throughout the city have been easier to find. I was taken by members of the resistance to a mosque near the city centre, within sight of the turquoise-tiled water tower on the Gulf road, to see two dead men.

209

Their bodies were being laid out to be washed before burial. During the occupation, water was scarce. Kuwaiti pharmacists, forced to work for the Iraqis, secretly stored the dead in the deepfreezes of local hospitals until a time when they could be buried with dignity.

The two in the shadows of the mosque's stone colonnade were not members of the resistance; they had been arrested in areas suspected by the Iraqis of harbouring anti-Iraqi activists. Once murdered, their bodies had been returned to the districts, intended as examples. An electric power-drill had been taken to the shoulders and chest of the first man, Nassr Abdullah Al-Aden. They were precise holes which I had at first mistaken for bullet wounds. His fingernails had been ripped off and an electric cable attached to his fingers. Fragments of wire had melted into the flesh. Next to him lay Ali, his eyeballs gouged out, and an electric cable still attached to his genitals. 'We did not touch anything,' said one of the mourners. 'We wanted to be sure you would believe these horrors.'

The tiny courtyard was full of mourners now, relatives bringing their dead from the hospital morgues to be cleaned. Everything stank of wet fish – one of the bodies had been out of the freezer for days. An ambulance drove in, with another corpse. This time it was a woman, 35 years old, who had been shot two days before the liberation. Her husband, who stood sobbing near the body, said she had not been raped. Her 15-year-old son was pale-faced, still in shock. He stood with his back to a wall, beneath a smiling poster of the Emir. The women ululated when the body of Leyla al-Safar was laid out under the colonnade; the men were also weeping. 'Praise the Prophet! Praise the Prophet!' the mourners chanted.

These corpses had been kept in the freezer of the Al-Adin Hospital, to the south of the city. When I visited, there were 18 bodies in the morgue. Several had incisions in the chest, their internal organs removed for the benefit of Iraqi transplant patients. In all, since the invasion, more than 600 dead have spent time in the freezer. This was just one hospital of many in Kuwait, a small part of the accounting. One of the doctors suggested that perhaps 5,000 had been killed in total. There is no way of knowing whether he is right.

It was in one of these hospitals that I met Safah's parents, and told them of the photograph. None of the dead from the Nayef Palace has surfaced in these morgues. The relatives of the prisoners spend their time shuttling between the hospitals trying to find them, but they have had no luck. This can be explained simply. Those taken to the Nayef, unlike those murdered in other places, or simply shot dead against a wall on the street, were not intended to be returned to their home districts. They were not intended to be communal examples.

The Nayef was the centre for torture. It was here that the Iraqis tried to collect information on resistance cells operating in the city. Many of those imprisoned were women, because the resistance used many women after the first few months of the invasion; so many of the men had died. The prisoners were not intended to serve any useful political purpose by the Iraqis. Some bizarre code of moral conduct also seemed to restrain the Iraqis from dumping the bodies of tortured women on the streets, when they showed no qualms about returning men.

The Nayef police station is in central Kuwait City, close to the telecommunications towers, notorious during the occupation as the site of a crane from which the Iraqis had hung a Kuwaiti soldier. For months, the body was left dangling. Everybody knew to keep away from the Nayef.

Safah did not arrive at the Nayef immediately after her abduction. She was taken first to a local police station and repeatedly interrogated about her suspected association with the resistance. She was entirely innocent of any connection, although like every resident – Kuwaiti, Filipino, Indian or Bangladeshi – she relied on the cooperatives organised by the resistance through the mosques and the Diwaniya coffee house for supplies of food and news of the outside world.

She had, however, apparently written in her diary on the day after the invasion 'I hate Saddam Hussein', and the Iraqis had discovered this. She spent four days in the police station, in a cell with other women. Later, in the Nayef, she told 18-year-old Lufti that at first she was most frightened by the prospect of being raped. A Filipino girl who had cleaned Safah's flat had been raped a fortnight after the occupation by two soldiers. Safah told Lutfi that the Filipino had joked: 'If they demand it, you must give it. Otherwise you will have to say you are raped.'

But she was not raped during her stay in the first police station. Her interrogators gave her the impression that they were going to set her free. They said they were satisfied she was not with the resistance. For a day, she was happy. And on the next, she cried. They took her to the Nayef.

The Iraqis had occupied this awful place on the first day of their invasion, after identifying it as an ideal location for interrogation which could also double as a barracks for the torturers. It has none of the architectural panache of some other government buildings in Kuwait. A simple quadrangle of offices surrounds a car park, all enclosed by a whitewashed brick wall. But it is very large. There are dozens of rooms leading off the paved walkways, and space in the car park for hundreds of vehicles. What Safah saw first differs little from what I saw last week, except that the soldiers lounging on the sandbags at the entrance and their armoured vehicles are now Kuwaiti.

Inside, however, there is chaos. The car park is strewn with rubbish: boxes of tea, women's underwear and shoes, electric cable and rotting food. The rooms are in worse disorder. Beds are overturned, tables smashed and everywhere there are photographs.

Like Safah, many of the prisoners had brought with them pictures of their relatives. There is evidence of looting – sometimes bizarre. Besides the radios and televisions stolen from nearby shops, there are boxes of quails' eggs in tins plundered from a delicatessen. Like all the occupying soldiers in this city, the Iraqis left this prison in a hurry: there is still cooked rice on the gas stoves; uniforms hang from hooks on the wall.

And the torturers left behind their equipment: car batteries with cables attached to terminals; bloodstained hunting knives; bowls of water with wires connected to metal mats on the floor and a spider's web of cable leading to the main junction-box; and ropes trailing from the fan, where they had hung people. There is dried blood everywhere – on the clothes, on the mattresses, on the floors.

What makes the Nayef so disturbing is that there is no evidence that any of the Kuwaitis held here were shot dead. There is a small cell-block to the north of the car park, but there are no bullet holes in the walls of the prison yard. There are no bullet holes in any of the walls. None of the people here, it seems, died quickly.

Safah was first taken to a room in the prison block, originally the guard house. It was used by the Iraqis as a barber's shop for shaving prisoners' heads. Around a chair in the centre of the room, there are mounds of hair. It is unlikely that any of Safah's is among the piles there now, but her hair was cut here. Everybody's was – an act of petty humiliation.

212

She was then taken, according to Lutfi, to a former office on the western side of the car park. This was once the police station's computer room; there are some smashed terminals on the floor. It now has beds in it. She was with two other women. The rooms on either side were inhabited by Iraqi soldiers. This was how they planned it. One room of women sandwiched between two of Iraqi men. She was raped three times on the first night in Nayef, and repeatedly over the following two months. Lufti said that one of her room-mates had warned her to submit without protest. 'Others had been killed if they didn't do what the soldiers wanted,' he said. The best plan was to become a soldier's favourite, because you stood a better chance of having enough to eat and drink. Most days, Lufti said, there was no food. Prisoners were occasionally forced to drink soldiers' urine.

At night, the camp rang out with the screams of the dying. The torture was carried out mostly by electric light after dark. Safah was not tortured for the first couple of weeks. The waiting only made her more frightened. She found it difficult not to cry all the time.

I cannot be certain that I have identified the room in which she was finally killed, but along the quadrangle are rooms, bare of most furniture, which were clearly designed for torture. The Iraqis had to choose rooms which were easily convertible: toilets were convenient, and so too were kitchens.

There is one such room two doors along from the one where I found Safah's photograph. Inside, there is a bed on which prisoners were bound by electric cable; a fan; and a bucket of water. Wires trail out of the mains terminal into the room. It is not clear how long people were held inside, but it may have been several days. There are graffiti on the wall – graffiti drawn by Kuwaitis, not Iraqis. On one wall, there is a picture of a man being attacked by a sea monster, a sword in his hand bound by iron shackles to the sea bed. On another, there is a woman's eye, with long eyelashes, shedding a large tear.

There is a terrible smell of fish, a smell that betrays the presence of the dead. It seems likely that there are bodies under the floor, but the police station has been booby-trapped – the Iraqis have left numerous trip-wired grenades – and the Kuwaitis are moving only slowly through the building.

According to Lutfi, most of the time in the torture chamber was dedicated to the men. The Iraqis separated them from the women.

They were kept in the cells of the prison block before their interrogation. Although Lufti was a member of the resistance, he was not tortured and managed to survive. But he is now remarkably thin.

I do not know how he lived, but he must have made some compromise with his Iraqi jailers. His friends would not say what he had done to save himself, but the resistance has decided that he will stand trial next week for whatever crimes he was forced to commit.

The women tended to survive longer than the men in the prison. 'They gave the Iraqis entertainment,' Lutfi said. But none of them lived, whether or not they had worked for the resistance. They had simply witnessed too much.

What happened to Safah was not unique. She became pregnant by one of the Iraqi soldiers and was taken for her final interrogation almost exactly two months after her arrival. It was during the early evening. Two soldiers first raped her and then walked her – naked – out of the room. She did not cry out. (Lufti said that by then she seemed to have become resigned to dying. She had seen others dead, and had on occasion been forced to clean out the bloodstained torture chambers.) From the Iraqis themselves, Lufti learned that she had been electrocuted, her breasts cut off and her belly sliced open. It all took several hours. He does not know why she suffered so much. 'She wasn't a resistance fighter,' he said. 'I can't understand it.' As soon as she had been murdered, another woman replaced her in the bed.

There were other torture centres in Kuwait City. The Qasma athletic stadium was notorious during the occupation. This was only for women, who were held and killed in the changing rooms before being thrown into the swimming pool. There is a thick green slime on the water now, and there are bodies beneath it. Nobody has had the courage to retrieve them.

But the focus of the Iraqi atrocities was the Nayef. Here the torturers lived – in rooms occupied before by the bodyguards of the Kuwaiti prime minister – north of the prison block. It was possible to identify them as the bodyguards' rooms by the colours of the uniforms hanging on the walls inside them. In other quarters in the police station, there were the standard khaki fatigues of ordinary soldiers and occasionally the desert combats of the Republican Guard. But in these rooms were blue overalls – the working clothes of the military intelligence.

The Kuwaitis remember the men in blue uniforms well – they had priority over ordinary soldiers in almost every aspect of life, at checkpoints, at petrol stations, for food when it was available. The identity of these men remains a mystery. There are some documents in the rooms – members of the resistance are sorting through them. These were men – well known to the Kurds of northern Iraq and to those Arabs who dissented from Saddam Hussein's regime – who knew no normal emotion. The methods they employed went far beyond those necessary to elicit information from unwilling members of the resistance: nor did they serve any useful military purpose. It may be for this reason that Iraqi officers rarely visited the place. Perhaps even they were too appalled by what was happening. Iraqi soldiers held now by the Kuwait resistance insist that it was the reluctance of the officers to command and restrain that enabled the worst of the atrocities to occur. But it had another consequence. Without discipline, the occupying army slowly disintegrated into disorder. Nothing makes this clearer than the squalor of the Nayef and the mindless vandalism visited upon buildings in the city.

It is not clear how central the torturers were in this process of disintegration, but many of these Iraqi prisoners say that the rumours of atrocities had a significant impact in undermining their morale, already weakened by the feeling that this was a war that they did not want to fight.

'We were ashamed to be Iraqis when we heard these stories,' one captured NCO said. 'They worried us, we feared they might be true and we hated Saddam Hussein then. The Kuwaitis are our brothers in blood . . .'

They have as much hatred for the intelligence as the Kuwaitis have. And in one hospital in the city, the animosity is evident. Two days after the liberation, an Iraqi intelligence officer was shot in the leg by the resistance. He had been unable to leave the city with the other soldiers before the liberation and disguised himself as a Kuwaiti civilian to avoid detection. He managed to escape from the resistance after being shot, but after nursing his wound for a day in a stolen car, he was forced to give himself up to a local hospital.

His name is Sabal Alal Zair, 26, from Nasiriyah. He has a handsome face, with green eyes that stare uncompromisingly at you when he speaks. He knows he will be hanged; perhaps for that reason he prefers to be direct. Why, I asked him, had the Iraqi intelligence been so evil? 'Because the government of Iraq feel they lose everything, and

215

when they lose everything then they will do everything to the citizens of Kuwait,' he said without any obvious regret. 'Saddam Hussein, he believes he want to leave Kuwait a burning land. He wants all the Kuwaitis to disappear from their land.'

The Kuwaiti nurse who was bandaging his leg, an elderly woman, looked on blankly as he spoke. She had been imprisoned briefly – not at the Nayef – and her arms were scarred with cigarette burns. The Iraqi denied he had been guilty of any horrors: 'I know in my heart I would not kill a man.' But he acknowledged that he was an intelligence officer.

The speed with which ordinary Kuwaitis became accustomed to living this nightmare is extraordinary. The carnage had become, by the time of the liberation, part of their routine. 'We heard stories in the beginning that we could not believe,' said an official of Kuwaiti Airways who guided me around the city. 'But little by little we realised every story was true.' We talked about Safah. He had other examples of friends and relatives who had also lost their lives in terrible circumstances, but he did not flinch from talking about them. I had not believed the stories at the start. There seemed to be little evidence to support them. It was only on the day after the liberation that the Kuwaitis offered to prove their allegations. I'm ashamed of my scepticism now. Most of the Kuwaitis suffered to some degree. A pharmacist I met had spent a month living in a room one metre square, forced to drink out of the same bin into which he defecated. He was, in fact, an army officer – but the Iraqis never realised, and eventually released him.

With all this, it seems intolerable that the Kuwaitis can want to shed any more blood. But the scale and duration of the tragedy in Kuwait City have had a profound impact on the young. Safah's brother is among those who want retribution: the people who learnt to live under the sword and now want to wield it against those they suspect of collaborating. The impotence of the resistance has made them only more furious.

After the first month, the resistance offered no serious military threat to the Iraqis – they were a nuisance. There is nothing to substantiate Kuwaiti claims of daring sabotage operations against Iraqi targets in the city. Abu Abdullah, a senior member of the resistance who in normal life is the deputy director of the city's public education programme, admitted that Iraqi reprisals against the resistance forced it more or less to end its military operations. 'It was a simple thing,' he said. 'When the Iraqis found one soldier

216

dead, they would go to a house and kill five Kuwaitis. We could do nothing.'

There probably were as many as 10,000 Kuwaitis actively involved in the resistance – some of them armed. No one knows how many of the young boys who now roam the streets in search of Iraqi sympathisers, rounding up Palestinians and staging summary executions, were among them. I myself saw one Sudanese man killed and I hear that there have been other murders. Even Kuwaitis are frightened of the anarchy: the young guns, in balaclavas and *kaffiyehs,* see the Iraqis everywhere around them. One man, who had acted as my host since I arrived in the city, was arrested briefly last week for trying to defend the life of a Palestinian whom he knew to be anti-Iraqi. The elders of the original resistance counsel reconciliation. But the young hotheads do not listen. Nobody controls them. There is no government and no police force in this city.

The matter for the young is, in part, one of dignity. The Iraqis stripped their friends and relatives of any dignity in dying, and now they want to strip it from the Palestinians and the Sudanese. It is a vicious circle of horror which shows no sign of abating.

I asked Mansour, Safah's brother, why he was ready to draw blood when so much had already been spilled. 'It is for Safah that I do it,' he said. The young man carries an AK-47 assault rifle and a rocket-propelled grenade launcher with a paper Kuwaiti flag fixed on its tip. But nothing he does will ever bring Safah back from the Nayef police station.

Safah's body has not yet been found. At her parents' request, her name and those of others in this story have been changed.

DESERT SABRE –
THE 100-HOUR BATTLE

Robert Fox with the 14/20th King's Royal Hussars

Daily Telegraph, April 20, 1991

Two o'clock in the morning. Sunday, February 24. A dank drizzle falling. This was the moment Operation Desert Sabre began. From our bivouac bags under the open sky we watched as a series of dull flashes punctured the darkness on the horizon. At last it was G-Day. G meant Go.

Later that morning, the Americans cleared the way across the border into Iraq through Saddam Hussein's defensive sand ramparts – the 'berms'. I was with the 14/20th King's Royal Hussars Battle Group, one of the three units of tanks and infantry leading the 4th British Armoured Brigade. We were marshalled to our start position some 15 miles south of the border, and by mid-afternoon were ready to move.

My own billet was the Warrior fighting vehicle, code-named Optimist, the domain of the Battery Commander, 38-year-old Major Andrew Gillespie of O Battery, 2 Field Regiment, the legendary Rocket Troop. His role was to travel close to the Battle Group Commander to direct artillery fire.

Besides the major there were Sergeant Steve Allen, the Artillery Assistant, Bombadier Alan Colvill, the driver, and the two signallers – Bombadier Brian 'Pip' Wilkins and Gunner Sean 'Killer' Lyon.

Together we had already passed many days of light-hearted acrimony, drying rain-soaked sleeping bags, fighting off sandstorm and gale, rousing blearily at dawn for sausage, beans and the intermittent egg: in the words of Gillespie, 'the complete heart-attack on a plate'.

Our Warrior was part of the Command Troop of the 14/20th King's Hussars, who proved amiable if idiosyncratic hosts. Recruited from Lancashire, they were men of considerable good humour, their dialogue Coronation Street in uniform. But now they were becoming frustrated. Our progress through G-Day was slow. Stop. Start. Halt.

It was close to midday on Monday, February 26, G plus 1, before we began to move more purposefully – towards the berms, our gateway to Iraq. Inside our Warrior, the carbon linings of our chemical protective jackets and trousers covered our faces and hands with soot. The question uppermost in our minds was not *whether* Saddam's forces would start a chemical or gas artillery bombardment, but *when*. Most of us thought it would be when the armoured columns were bunched together at the breaches in the dunes.

We had spent tedious hours rehearsing the crossing of the berms, but when the moment came it turned out to be an anticlimax. 'The track is now winding away to the right, through what seems to be the main berm,' Major Andrew Gillespie shouted down from Optimist's turret.

'It looks much less formidable than I expected. The Americans have a command post. Everything, enemy vehicles, bunkers and trenches, has been bulldozed flat by the Americans. To the horizon I can see columns and columns of American and British supply convoys. The artillery is starting to fire from either side of us.'

218

The 7th Armoured Brigade, our opposite numbers in the 1st British Division, were ahead of us through the berms. They advanced towards our start line, code-named New Jersey on the allies' maps, and at 15.15 hours they crossed it and began their march on the enemy.

To their chagrin, however, the men of 4 Brigade were told to wait. After the breakthrough at the berms, the swirling concourse of the allied supply columns on the other side was such that Saddam Hussein's heralded 'Mother of all Battles' was about to become the Mother of All Traffic Jams. There was no room for us. Not yet. As the allies' multi-launch rockets whooshed into oblivion and the day's thunder clouds merged into night, we waited.

Suddenly, in a gathering murk, the guns flashed and barked anew, continuing in elaborate orchestration for the best part of half an hour. Between them, jeeps and trucks of the American and British supply convoys wandered like grazing cattle. For the waiting columns of tanks and armoured carriers of 4 Brigade this was the *true* overture of Operation Desert Sabre – the campaign to recapture Kuwait and destroy the heart of Saddam Hussein's invading army, the Republican Guard. Flanked by the artillery, the tanks and infantry of the Brigade formed up by squadrons and companies in their battle groups, waiting for the signal to launch into enemy territory.

The British role in Desert Sabre was to help protect the eastern flank of the American 1st and 3rd Armoured Divisions and the 2nd Armoured Cavalry Regiment (i.e. the heavy armour of VII Corps) as it advanced into Iraq. The British would neutralise and destroy the Iraqi tactical reserve divisions behind their front line, which defended the berms along the southern Iraqi border. The mission for the allied armour was to seek and destroy the Republican Guard, and in particular its elite armoured divisions, the Hamarabi and the Medina. Such was the Schwarzkopf plan.

In pursuance of it, the first tanks of the 14/20th King's Hussars Battle Group, the principal armoured formation of 4 Brigade, crossed New Jersey at 19.30 hours precisely on Monday, February 25. At its head was Lieutenant-Colonel Mike Vickery. As we moved forward, I recalled my first meeting with him, in eastern Saudi Arabia, when his tanks were taking on their full war load of ammunition, their turrets festooned with necklaces of machine-gun bullets. 'It's funny how times change,' he had said. 'Our forefathers went to war with the picture of the enemy, Rommel, in their tank. Now it's Kylie Minogue.'

I thought, too, of Corporal Steve Redgrave, the colonel's 23-year-old gunner and the presiding genius of Command Troop. On December 31, his six years' engagement in the army had ended. But he had decided to stay on for the war. He told me: 'It was part loyalty to the regiment and the country. But it was really my mates – I couldn't let them down.' Then he added: 'I didn't tell the wife, though. She thinks I *had* to stay . . .'

In the words of one officer, the TOGS thermal-imaging night sight of the British tanks was capable of picking up 'anything generating heat – from strings of camels to fornicating rabbits'. But not that night. As the leading tanks of the 14/20th King's Hussars set off into the dark, the rain descended like treacle, the drops thick with soot from the oil fires in Kuwait.

The range of TOGS was down to 1,000 yards and there were problems with new satellite receivers that could fix a tank's position with pinpoint accuracy: they were unable to pick up satellite signals for several hours. At 17.30 hours 7 Brigade came to a complete standstill.

Another difficulty soon made itself manifest. The enemy positions turned out to be more extensive and varied than allied intelligence had indicated. The British and American armoured divisions were to attack a series of objectives – Iraqi emplacements of various sizes – each coded with the name of a metal.

Both 7 Brigade and 4 Brigade were to begin by attacking Iraqi mechanised infantry on a large fortified position called Copper. From there, the 14/20th and Royal Scots Battle Groups were to turn south to attack smaller Iraqi units in the rear on objectives called Bronze and Brass, and at dawn on Tuesday the Fusiliers Battle Group was to strike at an artillery position code-named Steel.

Shortly before ten in the evening, Major Richard Shirreff, the Squadron Leader of B Squadron of the 14/20th King's Hussars, reported 'contact with several heat sources'. 'Find out if there are any friendly forces in front of us,' came the order to Andrew Gillespie. 'Do we have any artillery support troops in the location?' (Artillery ammunition trucks were believed to be moving up behind 7 Brigade.) Frantically, Gillespie called for the identification of all artillery units in the area. Within minutes it was clear that B Squadron had made the first contact with the Iraqis – well before the main position on Objective Copper.

Soon artillery fire from regiments of M109 155mm howitzers, the eight-inch M110s and the Multi Launch Rocket Systems was being called down on the berms and bunkers a few thousand yards ahead. It was this as much as the weeks of pounding from the air by the American B-52 bombers and fighter-bombers that shattered the nerve of the Iraqis. An Iraqi company commander captured after the first day's action said the rockets had killed all but seven of his command of 250 in less than 10 minutes. A captured artillery brigadier said fewer than 20 of his heavy guns had been knocked out in the weeks of air raids, but the artillery bombardment had put paid to the rest, all but six, in an hour.

One of the first of the Hussars' tanks to engage was Colonel Vickery's Challenger, 11 Bravo, nicknamed 'the Emperor'. Firing at more than 1,000 yards, Corporal Redgrave placed a fin round neatly below the mantlet of a T-55 tank where the gun barrel joins the turret. Discovering the position more than a week later, the only external sign was a neat hole drilled through the casing of the T-55's turret. Inside the hull nothing remained but a heap of charred metal and ash: such is the effect of the shockwave set up by the modern high-velocity round.

When we walked later across that battlefield, this image of instant cremation was repeated a hundred times. The Iraqi dead were for the most part without name or number, swallowed by the fire of the sudden attack or by drifting sand. The wounded had simply fled.

The T-55 was later discovered to have been on the outer defences of an immense Iraqi reserve position of 49 square kilometres. 'It was quite a shock when I saw it from the air later,' admitted Brigadier Christopher Hammerbeck, the 4 Brigade Commander. 'It was bigger than anything we had been led to expect at any time by Intelligence.' The complex of command bunkers, defences and storage shelters for ammunition was big enough to have contained the command and support element of a whole Iraqi division.

Later inspection showed the Iraqis to have organised their underground defences in a state of almost domestic cosiness. They had removed the batteries from their tanks and armoured carriers to provide light and heat for their trenches and dugouts. Round the bunkers lay clusters of generators, water containers, tangles of bicycles (the commonest mode of transport in the desert, apparently) and abandoned boots and sandals by the hundred. Though some positions were well placed to give all-round defence, closer examination showed most to have an air of unmilitary timidity and hopelessness. Tanks were dug in so deep that they could not manoeuvre and their guns

221

were incapable of traversing more than a few degrees. 'Whatever else they were,' reflected Major Shirreff, 'the masters of mobile warfare they were not.'

Throughout the Monday night the Hussars drove through the Iraqi lines in a long-running engagement. A few brave spirits tried to fire back from the ancient T-55s. More frequent was the reply of heavy machine guns. Many of the Iraqi crews had abandoned their vehicles – which showed cold on the thermal sights of the Hussars' Challengers. When some of the T-55s were struck, the turrets would lift off in a ball of flame and exploding fuel and ammunition: 'Just like ripping open a can of pears,' according to Captain Jonty Palmer, the 14/20th Adjutant, doubling as loader in Colonel Vickery's Challenger.

At 22.50 hours on G plus 1, the leading Challengers began firing on a new group of enemy positions, catching four Iraqi tanks and carriers on the move, trying to retreat under the cover of the pouring rain. Major Alastair Wicks, Leading D Squadron, which was guarding the flank and rear of our Battle Group, reported prisoners pouring out of the bunkers bypassed by the two leading Hussar squadrons.

Through the darkness, it was difficult to see whether the Iraqis were surrendering, withdrawing, or rallying for a counter-attack or ambush. Or whose side anyone was on. Colonel Vickery had an answer: 'If they ignore you, they are ours: if they shoot or surrender, they're enemy.'

Meanwhile, Major Gillespie was concentrating on ranging the illuminating rounds of the artillery on the positions ahead. Under the glare of the burning magnesium shells, the Iraqis began raising ragged white flags from the top of the berm. 'I am deploying behind you,' came the languid but civilised tones of Major Grant Baker, the Captain of the Queen's Company of the Grenadiers, the Infantry element of the 14/20th Battle Group.

The Guards were ordered forward and to dismount from their Warriors to take charge of the first batch of prisoners. 'I think I'm running a glorified taxi service,' commented Baker over the air. The Guards were to do little more than round up the prisoners and send them back to cages in the rear – much to their regret, since they had come prepared to clear trenches in hand-to-hand combat. Walking the battlefield later, Baker reflected, 'I wish now we had entered into the spirit of the prisoner-handling with more gusto. I was always worried we would run into an ambush or a huge counter-attack, and so we had to be prepared to fight at a moment's notice.' This echoed my thoughts precisely, and those of most of the crew I was with. As much as anything we were battling against the unknown, so ambiguous was allied intelligence of the enemy positions. Right up to the end, a strong counter-attack or ambush with chemical weapons seemed possible and even probable.

Leaving our steel box for a few minutes that Monday night, I was greeted by a scene of astonishing theatricality. The patch of desert was like an enormous stage set from one of Verdi's more epic pieces, *Aida* perhaps, or *Nabucco*, lit brilliantly by the star shells of the guns and the magnesium rounds of the mortars, making a mauve backcloth of the sky. Before us, some hundred yards distant, was the first group of 50 prisoners, hands on heads, swathed in white cloth in token of surrender. A chorus of captives.

From the distance came signals that an action of the Royal Scots to the south was reaching its climax. Their Battle Group, three Infantry companies and a squadron of tanks from the Life Guards, had been assigned to attack a mechanised infantry battalion on Bronze, south of the Hussars' line of attack.

Like the Hussars, they hit pockets of enemy well ahead of the expected targets, because of confused intelligence. The Scots, by all accounts, lived up to their reputation for toughness and aggression as became the oldest regiment in the British Infantry, the First of Foot, Pontius Pilate's Bodyguard.

B Company Commander, Major John Potter, and the commander of the Royal Scots Battle Group, Lieutenant-Colonel Iain Johnstone, were exponents of a new tactic for the British, the Armoured Infantry assault. Potter explained, 'We use the Warrior to get us on to the objective where we can get maximum concentrated firepower from its 30mm Rarden cannon and machine gun.' The Scots had more than generous cover from the Life Guard, whose 14 Challengers gave close support from their 120mm main guns and machine guns until the Iraqi infantry began surrendering in quantity. By the early hours, the Scots had cleared the position on Bronze and at first light were on the way to guard the right flank of the Hussars' Battle Group in their last engagement of the morning.

From the operatic scene of the collecting of the prisoners, the 14/20th had set off east to mount an attack on their main objective, the Iraqi tanks and carriers believed to be holding Brass. The pursuit had assumed a familiar pattern, with many more tanks, trucks and bunkers in the way than had been suggested by intelligence. The commanders, Brigadier Hammerbeck and Colonel Vickery, had decided to lead from the front.

Hammerbeck later summed up his impressions of the night as a 'jumble, thick darkness, flashes and explosions in the distance, gradually feeling more and more fatigued as we received order after order from higher formations'.

Inside our Warrior it was all sound but no sight. Oddly, at times of tension and fatigue like this it can be quite easy to sleep. The heat from the engine and our protective clothes made the atmosphere stifling, and for minutes at a time Killer Lyon, Bombadier Wilkins and I nodded off. After a few minutes halt, Bombadier Covill, the driver, would doze, and as the enemy started fire again both the Battery Commander and Sergeant Allen aimed a few kicks at his back to rouse him.

Brian Wilkins and Killer had to listen to the ceaseless chatter of the Artillery Brigade and Battle Group networks, noting codes, frequencies and grids when they affected us. Most of the time was spent in a soporific and tedious watch. I learnt to sleep upright – a signal achievement in a juddering armoured tin can – and managed to read a few pages of Buchan's *Greenmantle*. From time to time we would brew coffee and tea in the boiling-vessel, and feed the driver and the turret team with chocolate. And so the night passed.

As dawn rose, the firing intensified as the tanks of the Command Troop shot above and around the Warrior. Towards dawn, both Killer and Bombadier Wilkins were dozing. 'Wake up, Killer,' I yelled. 'They want you to find out if we've got friends or enemies ahead – we could save a few lives.' Minutes later the tanks had moved forward and the Warrior was alone, facing an enemy position. Through the turret sight Sergeant Allen could see Iraqis waving and then disappearing into their trenches, while beside them stood an armoured carrier. It was too close to hesitate. Steve fired the Hughs chain gun, a machine gun which made a clicking sound like an electric typewriter.

After an hour or so, the Warrior managed to find Vickery's Challenger. For a few minutes we could wander in the dank daylight to stretch our legs. Before us lay an incinerated T-55 lurched over like a beast slain at a waterhole. The horizon was perforated by tongues of brilliant flame from other blazing tanks. Almost without noticing, the leading squadrons launched into the main attack of the opening phase by crossing a small tarmac road. After this nonchalant beginning came one of the most accomplished manoeuvres of the ground war.

Minutes before the launch of the operation at 09.30 hours, Vickery had decided to switch D Squadron from the flank with B Squadron, to lead the attack on the right of the main axis. 'B Squadron had done a lot of work during the night, much more than expected, and I thought they needed to be rested,' Vickery explained later. The two Squadron leaders, Richard Shirreff and Alastair Wicks, took only two minutes to confer, and their tanks had taken up the new stations less than 10 minutes later, an extraordinary testament to the skill and training of the Hussars.

The attack on Brass was a headlong gallop lasting just over two hours, the Battle Group passing through companies of tanks and MTLB infantry carriers, shooting at everything that moved inside them. Leading the advance on the left was Major Peter 'Garbo' Garbutt, followed by the Guards, taxi-cabbing prisoners by the dozen.

Halfway through their charge, the Hussars' Challengers and the Warriors turned a perfect right angle, a manoeuvre that a Guards drill sergeant might envy, and difficult enough in an exercise let alone during a running pursuit. Then, without warning, the Battery Commander ordered the Warriors to stop. The first phase of the Hussars' mission was over. There were no casualties, but by midday that day, February 26, G plus 2, the 4th Armoured Brigade had neutralised and destroyed more than two brigades of the Iraqi tactical reserve.

We dismounted. Across the sand came groups of prisoners from as far as the eye could see. They appeared to be dancing, from shock and cold, waving white sheets and robes in surrender. A gentle-faced man with a thick beard and the features of a Kurd gestured towards a collapsed dugout. After a few minutes, he pulled out a rusty Kalashnikov assault rifle and a bag of dates and rice which he offered to us. 'I feel really sorry for them,' ruminated Killer. 'After eight years of war with Iran, they have this. Look at the state of them.' 'It was more like an exercise with enemy in it than anything I had expected,' observed Corporal Redgrave. 'A bit like a stroll in the park.'

Several miles to the north of 4 Brigade the battle groups of 7 Brigade had also seen a night and day of heavy action. Leaving Phase Line New Jersey four hours ahead of the 14/20th King's Hussars, at 15.30 hours on G plus 1, their experience paralleled that of 4 Brigade: the rapid advance, the difficulty with navigation, the discovery of confused intelligence.

'We had been given to understand that the Iraqis had five divisions in reserve here, and we would attack two of them, the 12th and the 52nd,' Brigadier Patrick Cordingley, the Brigade Commander, recalled later. 'I am still not sure what *was* in our path.' Soon after nightfall, the commander of the Queen's Royal Irish Hussars, Lieutenant-Colonel Arthur Denaro, ordered a halt.

The Brigade's mission was to clear the northern part of Objective Copper, which was believed to have a major Iraqi communications centre in it; to move through an artillery position called Zinc, and 'go firm' – that is, take up defended positions – on a boundary called Phase Line Lavender. All this by dawn on Tuesday, February 26, G plus 2.

In the early hours of Tuesday, the Royal Scots Dragoon Guards' Battle Group, which included the infantry of A Company the Staffordshire Regiment, attacked the communications complex in the middle of Objective Copper. 'We saw a long berm from which the Iraqis started firing machine guns,' said Lieutenant-Colonel John Sharples, the Battle Group Commander. After his leading squadrons opened fire to clear through the berm, he saw Iraqis running between the trucks and vehicles. 'Every time they fired we fired. As we moved east we took out a lot of tanks and armoured personnel carriers. Infantry positions were lit up with fire from the tanks. From the left flank, C Squadron knocked out everything that moved.'

Once the position had been overrun, Sharples decided not to go forward because he feared tanks might start hitting each other in the dark in 'blue on blue' strikes (so called because friendly forces are depicted in blue on military maps). His next target lay in the distance – a complex of tents around a watering hole. 'We thought we saw a white flag which could indicate a hospital, so we decided to wait for first light.' Meanwhile the Irish Hussars' and the Staffords' Battle Groups had cleared through an artillery position, Zinc, to make their first day's objective. They were at Phase Line Lavender by dawn.

As the sky grew light, prisoners started surrendering to the Scots Dragoons. 'It was clear they didn't have much stomach for a fight,' said John Sharples. An American 'Psy Ops' (Psychological Operation) team called for surrender through loudspeakers, and within minutes more than 500 Iraqis had given themselves up.

By now, Brigadier Cordingley understood the shape of the action to come, and had issued orders to fire warning shots over the heads of enemy soldiers to encourage them to surrender rather than fight. In a brief action at a defensive berm on Lavender, Colonel Denaro found his men showing commendable restraint. 'The boys showed very tight and humane discipline. They knew they had enemy tanks and prisoners coming towards them at the same time in the same area, and took a very nice decision whether to fire or not. They showed the greatest care.'

Shortly after 09.00 hours, the Irish Hussars and the Staffords started south on a big concentration of mixed armour and artillery called Platinum. 'It was our set-piece battle,' says Denaro, 'but the position was much less heavily defended than we expected.'

At first, all sightings of the enemy were obscured by a sudden sandstorm. With the help of helicopter reconnaissance, the tanks of the Irish Hussars moved quickly through the three enemy positions in their path, attacking from the front and enveloping from the side in the classic strokes of armoured mobile warfare. Prisoners soon appeared, two emerging through the swirling sandstorm on camels.

For the Staffords' Battle Group, the fortunes of war were even more bizarre. One of the less glamorous of the county regiments, largely recruited in Birmingham and the Black Country, they were one of the most successful formations in the British offensive, and the one that was to see the most action. They were a large Battle Group of two tank squadrons from the Scots Dragoons and the Irish Hussars and two infantry companies. As one Irish Hussar sergeant put it in an unsolicited testimonial, 'I've worked with good Grunts [infantry] before, like the Irish Guards. But I reckon out here the Staffs beat them all.' Like the 14/20th King's Hussars, another widely underrated regiment, they showed a flexibility in action born of good training and command. Much must be credited to the large and genial figure of the Battle Group Commander, Lieutenant-Colonel Charlie Rogers, whose courteous manner belies the sharpest of tactical brains.

For Rogers, the afternoon and evening of G plus 2 on objectives Platinum and Lead became a tale of the unexpected. 'For a start, we lost the satellite navigation, and then we saw what looked like the beginnings of a serious counter-attack by T-55 tanks. This never got going, and we were soon in a game of hide-and-seek – shooting with Milan missiles. It was like a cracking *Carry On* film. All the time, I was trying desperately not to get into real carnage.' By the time his infantry and tanks had reached the southern end of the Iraqi bunkers and berms on Platinum, Colonel Rogers had more than 300 prisoners on his hands. 'It had been,' he said, 'like driving partridges in a country shoot.'

In the late afternoon, the Staffords turned north-east once more to make the last attack of the day on what was believed to be a unit of mechanised infantry on Objective Lead. This would take 7 Brigade to a northern boundary called Phase Line Smash, the limit of the initial operation given to the British Division by the Americans. They had estimated it could take the British up to 10 days to achieve this line; in the event it took barely two. But then, without any forewarning from Intellience, the Staffords found themselves facing a large and well-defended enemy position. It was held by a battalion group of Iraqi infantry, as large as the attacking force itself.

The leading Warriors of C Company fired over the top of the first trenches, scattering fugitives across the desert. 'I engaged six vehicles myself with the Rarden cannon,' admitted Colonel Rogers. 'It's a most effective weapon. Later, I found out that I had hit six bulldozers.'

Slowly, the Warriors approached the two leading lines of dugouts, two company positions which showed every intention of surrendering. As the leading platoons got out of their carriers to pick up prisoners, the Staffords were caught in the nightmare of trying to take surrenders in the confusion of battle.

'Behind the forward trenches was a cluster of buildings where Iraqis began to form a counter attack,' says Rogers. The men of C company came under heavy machine-gun fire and Private Stephen Moult was killed instantly when a rocket propelled grenade cut through his body. He was their only man to be killed by the enemy. Meanwhile on Lead itself, the reconnaissance force of the 16/5th Lancers and A Squadron of the Queen's Dragoon Guards had become embroiled in a battle lasting some six hours, which they claim to be the longest single engagement of the British campaign.

By nightfall of G plus 2, all three Battle Groups of 7 Brigade had formed defensive positions round Objective Lead (found to be virtually empty) guarding Phase Line Smash. It was on the following day that the Brigade crossed the Wadi Al Batin, which proved to be a dry ravine rather than the Grand Canyon of the eastern desert that had been proclaimed earlier by allied disinformation. Thus the British crossed into Kuwait itself. By nightfall, they had taken a lightly defended artillery concentration on Objective Varsity. By then, however, the whiff of ceasefire was in the air.

In the afternoon of G plus 2, shortly before the Staffords began their action on Lead, the commanders of the 4 Brigade Battle Groups were called to receive orders from the Commander, Brigadier Hammerbeck. The wind was blowing a savage gale from a black sky – the oil clouds from Kuwait. The Brigadier, whose clean craggy features betray his Norwegian blood, was a picture of fatigue, the lines of his face etched in the black grime from the lining of the chemical protective gear.

The mood at 4 Brigade HQ was tense, for news had just arrived that the Fusiliers had been clearing the artillery on Objective Steel when two Warriors exploded one after the other. Such was the ferocity of the explosions that Lieutenant-Colonel Andrew Larpent, commanding the Fusiliers, at first thought the vehicles had struck mines. Soon it became clear that they had been hit by American A-10 Thunderbolt anti-tank aircraft which had wandered from their target areas to the north. It was the kind of 'blue on blue' which the ground commanders had always feared. Diving from 1,500 feet, the A-10s have little time to sight their target. The luminous panels and large inverted chevrons carried by the Warriors and Challengers to indicate their friendly status were to little avail.

Nine Fusiliers died and a further 11 were wounded. Three of the dead and wounded had been some distance away and had run forward to drag their burning comrades from the wrecked vehicles which had been punctured by the Maverick missiles of the A-10s. Some were members of the Queen's Own Highlanders who had joined the Fusiliers to swell their numbers to operational levels for the campaign. It was the biggest single loss to any British unit in the entire war, but it halted the attack on Steel only for a few moments. In less than an hour the enemy had been cleared.

Brigadier Hammerbeck's afternoon Order Group was informal but businesslike. He announced that a signal had been intercepted, ordering the Medina Division of the Iraqi Republican Guard Force to move at 18.00 hours that evening. The Medina and the Hamarabi were the two strongest armoured divisions of the Guard, forming the strategic reserve to the Iraqi forces holding Kuwait: the best-paid and equipped of Saddam's forces. Both divisions were now to manoeuvre, enabling the Iraqi forces pulling back from Kuwait to retreat to Basra. It was what the allies had been waiting for. Once out of their bunkers, the Guard's T-72 tanks would be exposed to American air power and the Abrams tanks of the US Armoured Divisions. General Schwarzkopf's trap had been sprung.

The main target of 4 Brigade were the artillery positions on Objective Tungsten guarding the edge of the Wadi Al Batin, where – a touch obviously – the Iraqis had expected the allies to make their main armoured thrust. It was agreed that the Fusiliers and the Royal Scots should lead, each with two squadrons of tanks – some

27 Challengers each (one or two had stopped for running repairs). This left Mike Vickery, the most experienced armoured battle group commander, commanding two companies of Guards in reserve.

When we returned to the 14/20th HQ the Command Troop were tending to more than 250 prisoners, who were shivering in the chill wind. Corporal Redgrave was throwing bottles of mineral water from 11 Bravo and Sergeant-Major Steve Redhead, the leading signaller of the HQ, was asking questions in the excellent colloquial Arabic he had acquired from a tour in Oman. It seemed that Hammerbeck had taken prisoner a major-general, several brigadiers and 'a slack handful' of colonels who had commanded battalions. He believed his most important captive was a Ba'ath Party commissar who had been in charge of the 'morale police', responsible for shooting any Iraqi troops who threatened to desert.

At dusk, the Challengers of B Squadron came grinding through the desert, churning sand like spray from Mississippi river boats, and 14/20th Command Troop took up its station behind the advancing Scots and Fusiliers. The trickiest manoeuvre was to cross a pipeline marking the start line to the attack on Tungsten. On top of a sandbank nearly 15 feet high, it formed a particular hazard for the 70 tons of a fully armed Challenger. The crew in our Warrior's turret watched apprehensively the movements of 11 Bravo ahead, and, on our flank, of 11 Charlie, commanded by Staff Sergeant Mick Geraghty. Though 11 Charlie came to grief, the pipeline was not to blame. In a second it vanished into a deep tank scrape, dug by the Iraqis for their own protection. It was rescued later: we pressed on.

As the Brigade formed up on the start line, the regiments of artillery and two batteries of MLRS rockets – the equivalent of nearly 100 guns – opened up. The 10-minute barrage subdued almost all resistance, and the Scots and Fusiliers were to clear their objectives in a few hours. Visiting the area later we found heavy guns in almost mint condition. Among them were the G-5s of South African design by Gerard Bull, architect of the Super Gun.

The command posts were well furnished and equipped. One brigade headquarters, with chintz armchairs and sofas, resembled the boudoir of an Ottoman bey. Artillery grids and defensive fire zones had been elaborately plotted – most to the south and east, the directions from which the allies never planned to come. Electronic surveillance equipment was some of the latest from Britain and France. Brigadier Hammerbeck later found an Iraqi intelligence map which depicted the advance of 4 Brigade precisely, location by location and hour by hour. Decoy guns and aluminium reflectors had been carefully laid out to deceive the radar of allied aircraft. Had they chosen to fight, the Iraqis had the means to prosecute a long delaying action.

As the dawn rose we washed and shaved for the first time since action began and Mike Vickery set out on a customarily cheerful and morale-boosing tour of his squadrons. One of the tanks of B Squadron had been shot from behind by a 30mm cannon of a Royal Scots Warrior. 'It lost a gearbox, but it'll be ready for action by this afternoon,' the Troop Sergeant promised.

There was time to mingle. At D Squadron, a young subaltern called Charlie Mowat addressed me with the astonishing intelligence: 'You knew my mother when you lived in Somerset. She sends her greetings.' I had not seen her since her wedding day 22 years before. Either Charlie was too young for this game, or I was too old.

By late morning the Hussars were ordered to be ready to move at five minutes' notice. The Hamarabi and Medina Divisions of the Republican Guard were on the run. Now 4 Brigade was to follow 7 Brigade across the Wadi and into Kuwait, to cut off the units falling back from Kuwait City. The Iraqi retreat was fast becoming a rout.

We set off with the 14/20th in the early afternoon, charging in line abreast towards the Wadi. As the Command Troop approached the low dunes making the valley, Sergeant Geraghty in 11 Charlie reported, 'I have a heat-seeking source, 5,000 metres.' Urgent questions came over the radio net about the wherabouts of friendly forces. The reply was prompt: this part of the Wadi was clear. Around us the tanks cracked and roared. Seconds later, however, we were told to check firing. Passing before us in the Wadi were vehicles bearing the chevrons of allied forces and, to one side, two of our Spartan command vehicles were ablaze.

'It's ours and I think someone's been hurt,' shouted Andrew Gillespie, urging Bombardier Alan Covill to drive towards the burning vehicles. The Spartans belonged to 10 Air Defence Battery supporting 7 Brigade. As our Warrior circled the burning Spartans, Sergeant Steve Allen jumped out to see whether anybody was still inside, only to be beaten back by the burning petrol. 'I'm sure I saw an arm in the wreckage, we must go back,' he shouted and Covill drove back to the fire. Killer and Bombardier Wilkins opened the rear doors of the Warrior and told me to grab the First Aid box. The aluminium hulls of the Spartans now blazed like tinder and we knew the ammunition and the rest of the fuel would go any moment. 'Don't think about it. You just have to go when we say,' yelled the two signallers. At that moment Andrew Gillespie heard over the radio that nobody was inside after all. The three-man crew had been answering a call of nature when their carriers were hit.

It was the fog of intelligence again: the Brigade should have been told about the presence of 7 Brigade's supply echelons in the Wadi by staff officers at Divisional HQ. But by now order and counter-order were flowing thick and fast. That evening, 4 Brigade was given directly contrasting orders from the US VII Corps – either go north to chase the Iraqis running out of Kuwait City, or go south to clear the Wadi of remaining enemy forces.

As things stood, the British Armoured Division and the 1st and 3rd US Armoured Divisions were now heading on a collision course – 'one of the biggest blue on blues in history,' Major-General Rupert Smith was to remark later – so the two British Brigades were ordered to stop for several hours on the eastern lip of the Wadi while the Americans clarified their priorities.

The battle groups were to be prepared to move in the early hours of Thursday, February 27, G plus 4, to support 7 Brigade which had 'gone firm' on Objective Varsity a few miles to the east. In the intervening hours, I took a round trip back across the Wadi to the Divisional Administration Area in an attempt to sort out confusion in the censorship and transmission of copy, the bane of all journalists in the field.

As I travelled in an open Land Rover belonging to a Brigade liaison officer, that moonlit landscape made a strange footnote to the chronicle of the 100-hour war. Criss-crossing the tracks of the Wadi were convoys of American Abrams tanks grinding to the front, supply wagons and engineering tractors for clearing minefields. A crossroads was guarded by a battery of MLRS rocket tubes unmasked for action. Further south, the tarmac road which had been the Iraqi's main supply route was blocked by chunks of twisted metal. An Iraqi convoy was now a row of abstract expressionist sculptures. Beside them the fins of air-delivered mines dotted the sand like desert orchids. In the distance, Iraqi deserters flitted and darted into the night.

We were back in time for the dawn orders of Major Julian James, 4 Brigade's Chief of Staff: 'You'll get your dearest wish: we're going to Kuwait City.' The Brigade was to cut the famous road north to Basra and then take up positions by the coast north of the capital. We did not get far. Shortly before eight o'clock, a ghettoblaster was planted in the sand away from the vehicles, and as we stood round it the World Service relayed the voice of President Bush announcing the ceasefire. Corporal 'H' Harris of the HQ Engineer Troop shoved a shampoo bottle of whisky in my face. 'It's good it's over,' he shouted. 'They've had enough.' Though tasting more of soap than whisky, it was a welcome toast.

Over in 7 Brigade, the ceasefire marked the end of an exciting finale. Shortly before six o'clock they had been ordered to move to cut the Basra road 'at the rush'. In line abreast, the tanks of the Scots Dragoons and the Irish Hussars covered more than 45 kilometres in an hour and three quarters. Colonel Arthur Denaro said later, 'We were terrified of hitting friendly forces by mistake. We were flying every kind of flag we could, the kind of thing I usually hate.' He called urgently for a liaison officer from the Egyptian forces thought to be in the area, and put a helicopter out to locate them. 'I told my HQ to find an LO [Liaison Officer], any LO. I said, "Tell him to come to a tank flying a large Union Jack, a large, green, Irish Hussars flag, and with a commander in the turret with a large chin."' (This was his most notable feature.) The second-in-command replied drily, 'Say again second part of order: not received clearly.'

As they approached the Basra road the sky thickened into a darkness heavier than night. Each commander graphically described the sensation. 'It felt like the beginning of a nuclear winter,' said Charlie Rogers of the Staffords. 'It seemed we were entering Armageddon,' Denaro said. 'It was like the battle against evil in Tolkien,' said General Rupert Smith. 'We were going into the smokes of Mawdor.'

Though the 'Mother of All Battles' had not lived up to Saddam's billing, the British 1st Division had done the job for which it had trained for 40 years in the Rhine Army in Germany. It had been the master of manoeuvre warfare – using the ground in the desert as a medium and not an objective – to disorientate, disrupt and eventually deny the enemy all movement. Only 17 men had been killed, fewer than die in accidents in most major Nato exercises in Europe, and, against all predictions, 96 per cent of the Challenger tanks and Warrior armoured fighting vehicles were fully working at the finish.

Some weaknesses did appear. Logistics suffered from years of government parsimony. The older command vehicles, petrol-driven aluminium boxes such as the Sultans, were scandalously vulnerable, and the light reconnaissance vehicles were at times less than adequate. But the 150-mile gallop from Saudi Arabia into Kuwait via southern Iraq showed General Rupert Smith's Division to be the best prepared and supplied in the allied forces. That it was the only one of the 17 divisions of the coalition forces ready, in cavalry parlance, to 'go again' is a testament to superior discipline, training and command skills. It is probably the best British expeditionary force to have been despatched abroad this century. General Smith was prepared to march his forces to the gates of Basra. As the grim events in southern Iraq and the Kurdish province of the north later unfolded, many under allied command must surely have regretted that their original mission, to destroy the Republican Guard, was not fulfilled.

Only a few hours after our shampoo toast, Brigadier Hammerbeck suggested a trip into Kuwait City itself – 'After all, it's a historic day' – and a small party took off in two creaking Land Rovers. With two somewhat louche Guards officers as drivers, it took us hours to find the road south through the glutinous and apocalyptic storms of oil rain. Finally, outside the capital, we were cheered and embraced by Kuwaiti truck drivers and bands of US Marines and given delicious, sweet, mint tea. The city itself had the aspect of a spilled rubbish basket. Wrecked cars, burned trucks, and bodies bestrewed the highways. The welcome our little band received was extraordinary and it took me some time to work out why. Our Land Rovers flew an enormous Union Jack, and, journalist and soldier alike, we were all wearing the characteristic British desert camouflage fatigues, the clothes we had lived in for the past weeks. Our escorts were probably the first British soldiers from the desert to enter Kuwait City.

There is a curious footnote. A week after the ceasefire, I joined the Squadron leaders of the 14/20th, Second-in-Command Godfrey Tilney and Battery Commander Andrew Gillespie, to walk the battle-field. We were astonished at the sheer size of the enemy positions and the quantity of armaments. In some of the bunkers were the intimate clues to the identity of the occupants – snapshots of girlfriends and passport photos of the soldiers themselves, a few pin-ups of the houris of the Baghdad nightclubs and a pouting siren in a toga by the banks of the Bosporus.

Absent-mindedly I picked up two Iraqi berets with regimental cap badges for my son. Looking at them back in England, my wife said, 'Did you realise these are very old? The cloth shows that. And there are moth eggs in one. They both look as if they were stored for some time, and the badges seem to have been fixed on a long time ago.' It seems they might well have belonged to older conscripts. I fancy, that with the maturity of years, they may have come to the desert to hide from their masters in Baghdad as much as to fight.

'THE GATES ARE CLOSED'

General Norman Schwarzkopf

Daily Telegraph, February 27, 1991

'I promised that as soon as the opportunity presented itself I would give you a complete rundown on what we're doing and, more importantly, why we were doing it – the strategy behind what we are doing.

I've been asked by [US Defence] Secretary Cheney to do that this evening.

This goes back to August 7 to January 17. As you recall, we started our deployment on August 7. Basically, what we started out against was a couple of hundred thousand Iraqis that were in the Kuwait theatre of operation.

I don't have to remind you all that we brought over initially defensive forces in the form of the 101st, the 82nd, the 24th Mechanised Infantry Division, the 3rd Armoured Cavalry.

And in essence we had them arrayed in the south behind the Saudi task force.

In the middle of November, the decision was made to increase the force, because by that time huge numbers of Iraqi forces had flown into the area. And therefore we increased the forces.

We made a very deliberate decision to align all of those forces within the boundary looking north towards Kuwait.

So we aligned those forces so it very much looked like they were all aligned directly on the Iraqi positions.

We also at that time had a very active naval presence out in the Gulf. And we made sure that everybody understood about that naval presence.

One of the reasons why we did that is because it became very apparent to us early on that the Iraqis were quite concerned about an amphibious operation across the shores to liberate Kuwait.

They put in a very, very heavy barrier of infantry, and they proceeded to build an extensive barrier that went all the way across the border down and around and up the side of Kuwait.

Basically, the problem we were faced with was that, when you looked at the troop numbers, they outnumbered us about three to

235

two. And when you consider the number of combat service support people we had – that's logisticians and that sort of thing in our armed forces – as far as fighting troops, we were really outnumbered two to one. In addition to that, they had about 4,700 tanks versus our 3,500, and they had a great deal more artillery than we do.

Any student of military strategy would tell you that in order to attack a position, you should have a ratio of approximately three to one in favour of the attacker.

And to attack a position that is heavily dug in and barricaded, you should have a ratio of five to one in favour of the attacker.

We were outnumbered as a minimum three to two as far as troops were concerned, we were outnumbered as far as tanks were concerned, and we had to come up with some way to make up the difference.

What we did, of course, was start an extensive air campaign.

One of the purposes I told you at that time of that extensive air campaign was to isolate the Kuwaiti theatre of operations by taking out all the bridges and supply lines that ran between the north and the southern part of Iraq.

That was to prevent reinforcement and supply coming into the southern part of Iraq and the Kuwaiti theatre of operations. We also conducted a very heavy bombing campaign and many people questioned why.

It was necessary to reduce these forces, particularly on the front-line barrier that we had to go through.

We continued our heavy operations out at sea, because we wanted the Iraqis to continue to believe that we were going to conduct a massive amphibious operation in this area. Many of you will recall the number of amphibious rehearsals. We continued to have those operations because we wanted him to concentrate his forces, which he did.

I think this is probably one of the most important parts of the entire briefing.

As you know, very early on we took out the Iraqi air force. We knew that he had very, very limited reconnaissance means.

And therefore we took out his air force, for all intents and purposes we took out his ability to see what we were doing down here in Saudi Arabia.

Once we had taken out his eyes, we did what could best be described as the 'Hail Mary' play in football.

236

I think you recall when the quarterback is desperate for a touch-down at the very end, what he does is, he steps up behind the centre and all of a sudden every single one of his receivers goes way out to one flank, and they all run down the field as fast as they possibly can and into the end-zone, and he lobs the ball. In essence, that's what we did.

When we knew that he couldn't see us any more, we did a massive movement of troops all the way out to the extreme west, because at that time we knew that he was still fixed in his area [Kuwait] with the vast majority of his forces, and once the air campaign started, he would be incapable of moving out to counter this move, even if he knew we made it.

There were some additions to Iraqi troops out in this [northern] area. But they did not have the capability nor the time to put in the barrier that had been described by Saddam Hussein as an absolutely impenetrable tank barrier that no one would ever get through. I believe those were his words.

I must tell you, I can't recall any time in the annals of military history when this number of [allied] forces have moved over this distance to put themselves in a position to be able to attack.

But what's important – and I think it's very, very important that I make this point – is these logistics bases.

Not only did we move troops out there, but we literally moved thousands and thousands of tons of fuel, of ammunition, of spare parts, of water, and of food out here into this area, because we wanted to have enough supplies on hand so that if we launched this and got into a 'slugfest' battle, which we very easily could have gotten into, we'd have enough supplies to last for 60 days.

It was an absolutely gigantic accomplishment.

And I can't give credit enough to the logisticians and the trans-porters who were able to pull this off, to the superb support we had from the Saudi Government, the literally thousands and thousands of drivers of every national origin who helped us in this move out here.

And of course, great credit goes to the commanders of these units who were also able to manoeuvre their forces out here and put them in this position.

But by February 23, what you have found is this situation: the front lines had been attritted down to a point where all of these [Iraqi] units were at 50 per cent or below.

The second level – and these were really tough fighters that we were worried about – were attritted to some place between 50 and 75 per cent, although we still had the Republican Guard, and parts of the Republican Guard were very strong.

We continued to hit the bridges all across this area, to make absolutely sure that no more reinforcements came into the battle.

This was the situation on February 23. We put special forces deep into enemy territory. They went out on strategic reconnaissance for us and they let us know what was going on out there.

They were the eyes that were out there, and it's very important that I do not forget those folks.

This then was the morning of February 24. Our plan initially had been to do exactly what the Iraqis thought we were going to do, and that's take them on head-on into their most heavily defended area.

Also, at the same time, we launched amphibious feints and naval gunfire, so that they continued to think that we were going to be attacking along the coast, and therefore fixed their forces in this position.

They wouldn't know what was going on. I believe we succeeded in that very well.

At four in the morning, the Marines – the 1st Marine Division and the 2nd Marine Division – launched attacks through the barrier system. They were accompanied by the 2nd – the Tiger Brigade, US Army Tiger Brigade of the 2nd Armoured Division.

At the same time, two Saudi task forces also launched a penetrator through the barrier. But while they were doing that, the 6th French Armoured Division, accompanied by a brigade of the 82nd Airborne, also launched an overland attack to their objective – Salman airfield.

We were held up a little bit by the weather, but by eight in the morning, the 101st Airborne launched an air assault deep in the enemy territory to establish a forward operating base.

Let me talk about each one of those moves. First of all, the Saudis on the east coast did a terrific job. They went up against a very, very tough barrier system. They breached the barrier very very effectively.

They moved out aggressively, and continued their attack up the coast.

I can't say enough about the two Marine divisions.

If I use words like brilliant, it would really be an underscription of the absolutely superb job that they did in breaching the so-called impenetrable barrier.

It was a classic – absolutely classic – military breaching of a very, very tough minefield-with-barbed-wire-fire-trenches-type barrier. They went through the first barrier like it was water. They went across into the second barrier line.

Even though they were under artillery fire at the time, they continued to open up that breach, and then they brought both divisions streaming through that breach.

Absolutely superb operation – a textbook [operation], and I think it will be studied for many, many years to come as the way to do it.

I would also like to say that the French did an absolutely superb job of moving out rapidly to take their objective. They were very, very successful, as were the 101st [Airborne Division].

What we found was as soon as we breached these obstacles and started bringing pressure, we started getting a large number of surrenders.

We were worried about the weather. The weather, it turned out, was going to get pretty bad the next day and we were worried about launching this air assault, and we also started to have a huge number of atrocities – of really the most unspeakable type – committed in downtown Kuwait City, to include reports that the desalination plant had been destroyed.

And when we heard that, we were quite concerned about what might be going on.

Based upon that, and the situation as it was developing, we made the decision that, rather than wait till the following morning to launch the remainder of these forces, we would go ahead and launch those forces [VII Corps] that afternoon.

This was the situation you saw the afternoon of the 24th. The Marines continued to make great progress going through the breach in this area and we were moving rapidly north.

The task force on the east coast was also moving rapidly to the north and making, very, very good progress.

We launched another Egyptian-Arab force, and another Saudi force, again to make the enemy continue to think that we were doing exactly what he wanted us to do, and that was to make a headlong assault into a very tough barrier system.

At the same time, we continued to attack with the French. We also launched an attack on the part of the entire VII Corps.

The first infantry division went through, breached an obstacle and minefield barrier, established quite a large breach through which we passed the 1st British Armoured Division.

At the same time – and because of our deception plan and the

239

way it worked, we didn't even have to worry about a barrier – the 3rd Armoured Division just went right around the enemy and were behind him in no time at all. And the 1st Armoured Cavalry.

The 24th Mechanised Division also launched out in the far west. Once the 101st had their forward operating base established here, they went ahead and launched into the Tigris and Euphrates valleys.

There are a lot of people who are still saying that the object of the US was to capture Iraq and cause a downfall of the entire country of Iraq.

Ladies and gentlemen, we were 150 miles away from Baghdad and there was nobody between us and Baghdad. If it had been our intention to destroy the country, if it had been our intention to overrun the country, we could have done it unopposed, for all intents and purposes. But that was not our intention.

Our intention was purely to eject the Iraqis out of Kuwait and destroy the military power that had come in.

The next two days went exactly like we thought they would go. The Saudis continued to make great progress up on the eastern flank, keeping the pressure off the Marines on this flank.

The special forces went out and started operating small boat operations out in this area to help clear mines, but also to threaten the flanks and to continue to make them think that we were in fact going to conduct amphibious operations.

The Saudi and Arab forces turned to come in on the flank heading towards Kuwait City. The British passed through and continued to attack. And, of course, the VII Corps came in and attacked.

The 24th Infantry Division made an unbelievable move all the way across into the Tigris and Euphrates valleys, and proceeded in blocking this avenue of egress out, which was the only one left because we continued to make sure that the bridges stayed down. So there was no way out once the 24th was there.

The French, having succeeded in achieving all of their objectives, then set up a flank guard position to make sure that no forces could come in and get us from the flank.

By this time, we had destroyed or rendered completely ineffective over 21 Iraqi divisions.

That brings us to today. We now have a solid wall across the north of the XVII Airborne Corps, consisting of units attacking straight to the east. We have a solid wall of the VII Corps also attacking straight to the east.

The forces that they are fighting right now are the Republican Guard.

Again today, the Arab forces coming from both the west and east closed in and moved in to Kuwait City, which they are now in the process of clearing and assuring that it's absolutely secure.

The First Marine Division continues to hold Kuwait International Airport. The Second Marine Division continues to be in a position where it blocks any egress out of the city of Kuwait. To date, we have destroyed or rendered inoperable over 29 divisions.

I don't like to say destroyed, because that gives you the vision of absolutely killing everyone, and that's not what we're doing.

But we have rendered completely ineffective over 29 Iraqi divisions. The gates are closed. There is no way out of there. We continue of course to have overwhelming air power. The air has done a terrific job from start to finish, in supporting the ground forces, and we also have had a great support from the navy, both in the form of naval gunfire and in the support of carrier air.

The prisoners out there are so heavy and extensive, obviously we're not in the business of going around counting noses at this time to determine precisely what the exact number is. But we are very, very confident that we have well over 50,000 prisoners of war at this time, and that number is mounting on a continuing basis.

Anyhow this is what's happened to date with the Iraqis. They started out with over 4,000 tanks. As of today we have over 3,000 confirmed destroyed.

I would remind you that the war is continuing to go on. Even as we speak right now, there's fighting going on out there. Even as we speak right now, there are incredible acts of bravery going on. This afternoon, we had an F-16 pilot shot down. We had contact with him. He had a broken leg on the ground. Two helicopters from the 101st – they didn't have to do it – went in to try to pull that pilot out.

One of them was shot down and we're still in the process of working through that. But that's the kind of thing that's going on on the battlefield right now.

It is not a Nintendo game. It is a tough battlefield, where people are risking their lives all the time.

And there are great heroes out there and we all ought to be very, very proud of them. That is the campaign to date – that is the strategy.'

In answer to a question, General Schwarzkopf said: 'If I'm to accomplish this mission I was given, and that's to make sure that the Republican Guard is rendered incapable of conducting the type of heinous act that they've conducted so often in the past, what has

241

to be done is these forces continue to attack, and put the Republican Guard out of business.

'We're not in the business of killing them. We have PSYOPS aircraft up. We're telling them over and over again, all you've got to do is to get out of your tanks and move off, and you will not be killed.

'But they are continuing to fight, and as long as they continue to fight, we're going to continue to fight them.'

SADDAM'S MILITARY HUMILIATION

Max Hastings

Daily Telegraph, February 28, 1991

General Norman Schwarzkopf's exposition in Riyadh last night of his army's wholesale destruction of Iraq's forces in the Gulf must rank as one of the most gripping military briefings of all time. The general, scarcely concealing his own exhilaration, was describing an operation that has fulfilled every commander's highest vision.

By painstaking planning, brilliant deception, and overwhelming air preparation, his armies have caught the enemy entirely off balance, divided them into fragments, and now defeated them in detail.

Every general dreams of conducting a battle in which his skill in manoeuvre makes heavy fighting unnecessary. This is what the allied coalition has done in the four-day campaign that began last Sunday and is now almost over. Some Western military analysts, including our own John Keegan, guessed at an early stage, before the battle began, that the allies were deploying forces much further north along the Saudi-Iraq border than they were letting on.

The fundamental problem for the Iraqis from the outset was that they lacked the troops to defend the entire straggling length of the Saudi-Kuwait and Saudi-Iraq border. General Schwarzkopf had 300 miles of front to choose from, along which to make his breakthroughs. He opted for a strong frontal assault with two Marine divisions and Arab coalition forces, just where the Iraqis expected it, on the Kuwaiti border. He intended Saddam to regard this as his principal thrust.

The allies never needed to land their 18,000-strong Marine amphibious force, out on the ships in the Gulf. Its mere presence, a mobile threat capable of landing anywhere on the Kuwait coast, obliged the Iraqis to keep six divisions deployed to face a possible beach assault.

The French light Daguet division drove north on the left wing, facing negligible opposition on its advance to the Euphrates, but providing a flank guard, in case of any unexpected movement from the Iraqi interior. The 101st and 82nd Airborne divisions advanced on the right of the French, again against minimal resistance, exploiting massed helicopter mobility, to close the trap in the Euphrates valley south of Nasiryah.

As John Keegan also correctly told us earlier this week, it was the US VII Corps which provided the *schwerpunkt* – the decisive heavy striking force – that drove deep into Iraq before wheeling right to close in on the Republican Guard. The British 1st Armoured Division made up the right wing of this advance.

From start to finish, it is plain that the Iraqis had not the faintest idea what was being done to them. While allied special forces units were providing on the ground intelligence from deep inside Iraq, and General Schwarzkopf had access to comprehensive air and satellite photographs showing every detail of the Iraqi positions, Saddam's forces were blind. They lacked air reconnaissance, and also the vital signals co-ordination to tell their commanders what was happening, once the ground battle began.

Even Saddam's much-vaunted defensive belt along the Saudi-Kuwait border proved a negligible obstacle – negligible, that is, because its defenders were unable or unwilling after weeks of bombing to lay down effective fire on the allied engineers advancing through it, which alone could have checked the attackers.

In maintaining a sense of proportion about this astonishing campaign, it is essential to stress that the Iraqi defenders have not shown themselves to be a serious enemy. No army of several hundred thousand men, which has killed fewer than 50 allied soldiers in action (excluding the allies' self-inflicted losses), while suffering total defeat itself, can be called an effective fighting force.

When the victors can spare as much pity for the vanquished as the allied soldiers are displaying to the Iraqis, they have not had to suffer much of a battle. It is easy to imagine the overwhelming gratitude and relief among the allied forces, knowing that after weeks of uncertainty and anticipation, they now cherish the prospect of going home alive, with their job magnificently done.

In the weeks and years to come, it will be hotly debated – above all, by airmen – whether the Iraqi Army was ever very good to start with, or whether this may be considered the first war in history in which air power has played a conclusive, decisive role. In the Second World

War, such air enthusiasts as 'Bomber' Harris sometimes claimed that they had 'provided a walkover' for the allied armies in north-west Europe. No 1944–45 soldier agreed with them, and the ground casualties were very large.

But in this campaign, the Iraqis have indeed been so desperately depleted by bombing, the battlefield so effectively isolated, that I believe the airmen may indeed claim to have created conditions in which the ground forces have carried out something more closely resembling a triumphal procession than a ground battle. To find a historical precedent for the scenes of the last four days, one must revert to the Italian collapse in the Western Desert in the Second World War.

Gazing at General Schwarzkopf's map of the battlefield last night, showing the remaining Iraqi forces surrounded by allied divisions, Washington's reluctance to grant Iraq a ceasefire becomes wholly understandable. Not a single Iraqi tank or vehicle can now retire from the theatre of operations, unless the allies choose to let them do so. Why should they allow Saddam Hussein one T-72 or artillery piece? It must surely only be hours now, rather than days, before the remaining Iraqi formations are compelled to surrender, and this bloody business is over.

The military achievement of General Schwarzkopf and his forces is awesome. But so were the risks that he and the allied political leaders ran. It could all have gone terribly wrong.

Now that it has succeeded, at such small if always tragic cost in allied lives, there seems no reason not to ensure that Saddam's military humiliation is exploited to the full, to provide an unanswerable political basis for a peace settlement.

A WAR THAT WASN'T FOUGHT

Martin Woollacott

Guardian, March 1, 1991

Baghdad Radio, whose record of mendacity would have made Goebbels blush, had the gall yesterday to describe the last pathetic engagements of the war as a hard-fought battle which had 'taught the allies some lessons'. The 'battle' didn't teach us any lessons, but the propaganda should, for it seems that myths about the conflict are already taking shape on our side that could be as misleading as the nonsense the Iraqis put out.

Foremost among these are the notions that the war required generalship of a high order, and that it demonstrated the superior fighting qualities of Western over Iraqi troops. It is no reflection on Norman Schwarzkopf's qualities as a soldier to say that he did not truly function as a general in this conflict, partly because of the other side's stupidity and partly because of our side's overwhelming technical advantages.

Generalship involves action and reaction: the enemy commander does a, you do b; he does x, you do y. Out of the cumulation of these decisions, a general takes his armies to victory or defeat. But, in the Gulf, the Iraqi forces were so damaged and demoralised that they neither acted nor reacted. They were, to all intents and purposes, not under command at all. General Schwarzkopf never had to react to a sudden movement of enemy troops, to unexpected resistance, to any impediment other than that offered by the weather or by mechanical breakdown.

General Schwarzkopf may be a good general, but that is not what he has proved himself to be in this conflict. Instead, he has shown himself an able military manager. The essence of the war was that a military machine that had been built to confront the Soviet Union in Central Europe was relocated in Saudi Arabia to deal with an enemy that had not a twentieth of Soviety capacity or offensive power.

That machine had to be set up in a very different environment, and oiled and serviced on a grand scale, and this was done with great efficiency. But once set in motion, it simply chewed its way through the Iraqi forces like a ripsaw through logs, requiring only occasional adjustments of tempo and speed.

This is not to say that at certain moments the soldiers, sailors, and airmen of the coalition did not have to act with courage. At the beginning of the air war there was real danger, but later the bombing became a production process, in which the very occasional Western casualty was more akin to an industrial accident than anything else. Again, at the beginning of the ground war, who could have known, as our men moved off from their start lines, that it would be as easy as it turned out to be? The fact that courage turned out to be not much required does not mean that it did not have to be summoned. But how can these few moments when our own men were at real risk compare with the horrors Iraqi forces faced? Day after day, night after night, the most sustained and effective aerial bombardment in history killed, maimed, and destroyed, with hardly a chance of retaliation.

The Iraqi forces were stripped of everything that makes an army work. At the end, they could no longer see, they could no longer hear, they could no longer communicate with one another. The Iraqi Army resembled nothing so much in its last days as a worm when it is chopped by a spade – the segments wriggle, but the creature is already dead.

Of course it is the business of a general to seek advantage. To imagine that war is about fair fights is to misunderstand its nature. It is, in fact, about unfair fights: a general who is in a fair fight – an equally matched encounter – is usually a general who has mismanaged his job. But there comes a point where the advantage achieved is so overwhelming as to change the quality of the event from something like combat to something like execution.

There is surely a horrifying aspect to the utter disparity in the figures of those killed – 150 on our side; 20,000, 30,000, 40,000 estimated on theirs. We can hardly crow about Iraqi surrenders and retreats. These men did not surrender at the first sight of British or American tanks, but after weeks of bitter experience of the utter superiority of allied weapons.

We should remember, too, that the entry of the allied ground troops into Kuwait and Iraq did not give the Iraqis a chance to fight on more equal terms, as President Saddam Hussein had foolishly imagined. If anything, the terms were even more unequal, with our troops' superior firepower, control of the air and unimpended communications.

Let us admit that there were times when even the experts did not think the war would go as easily as this. Notably, the effectiveness of air power alone in dealing with an inferior opponent was a matter of argument. But the accuracy brought to bombing by electronic guidance systems has changed the calculations that used to suggest that air power alone could never defeat the enemy.

And let us give General Schwarzkopf and the allied armies their due. The general adapted a technology which was untried in war – the air defence machine built for Nato – to the business at hand, and he and his staffs did it well. He measured the extraordinary damage it did, and came to appropriate conclusions. He judged well the moment when the demoralisation of the Iraqi forces had been completed by President Saddam's offers to withdraw, and put in his troops at that moment. And the troops did the job they were sent to do.

246

The thing had to be done, even though we may argue about whether this final act was really necessary. But to start trailing clouds of glory is really too much. About this conflict one might well say, adapting the words applied to the charge of the Light Brigade, '*C'est la guerre, mais ce n'est pas magnifique.*'

A BROKEN COUNTRY
Patrick Cockburn
Independent, March 9, 1991

Old Kuwaiti markings were just visible under the blue and white paint of the single-deck bus as it turned right into Haifa Street in central Baghdad. 'A lot of soldiers died for that bus,' said an Iraqi as he watched it disgorge passengers. Along with other loot from Kuwait – gold, planes and works of art – the bus must be returned under the terms of the ceasefire agreement.

Baghdad is full of symbols of defeat. Some are obvious like the smashed telecommunications towers, the wreckage of the Ba'ath Party headquarters and the hole in the green dome of the presidential palace. Others are more peculiar. The railings of the remaining bridges across the Tigris – two were destroyed and one damaged by bombing – are covered in torn sacking and the pavements of the bridges are strewn with withered saplings. Both sacking and saplings are the remains of an attempt by the Iraqis to alter the profile of the bridges and thus avert their destruction by television-guided bombs.

Officially the government claimed a victory. Last weekend ministry of information officials censoring journalists' copy in the Rashid hotel were carefully excising the word 'defeat'. Generally, they worked by torchlight since, like the rest of Iraq, the hotel is without electricity. When a story was passed it was telephoned from a satellite telephone, usually owned by a television company or news agency, on the lawn of the hotel.

Again a ministry official stood nearby to ensure that no direct reference to the 'defeat' of Iraq should be reinserted.

All concerned were aware of the situation. To Iraqis as much as foreigners the fact of defeat hardly needs to be restated. A phrase like 'the defeat of the Iraqi armies in the south' could be rapidly altered to 'the fate of the Iraqi armies in the south' without feeling that the reader had been robbed of essential information.

Iraqis themselves are acutely conscious of the fate of these armies since almost everybody has a relative called up for military service since the invasion of Kuwait. They listen to foreign radio stations and speak to soldiers back from the front. For weeks it has been common to see taxis with a coffin on the roof wrapped in the green, white and black Iraqi colours indicating that it contains the body of a soldier.

The level of casualties suffered at the beginning of the campaign has been dwarfed by the carnage inflicted after President Saddam had ordered his soldiers to stage 'an orderly retreat'.

Many families in Baghdad are numbed by waiting to see if their sons survived. 'I do nothing but pray for my son to return,' said one old man in Shula, a working-class Shia neighbourhood. The condition in which the soldiers return leaves no doubt about what happened to the armies around Kuwait. One group arriving in Baghdad last week had commandeered a tank transporter and had travelled all the way from Basra.

Others returned more prosaically by bus to al-Nahda bus station. Looking grimy and exhausted, they searched desperately for one of the few taxis still operating.

The government's reaction to defeat has been two-fold. On one hand there is an attempt to alleviate economic suffering. The ration of sugar, soap and milk for children has been increased. Conscripts are all being given 15 dinars (Republican Guards get 100 dinars). Ten divisions have been officially demobilised. Electricity at night has been promised for every district of Baghdad by the end of the week.

Yet there are signs that the government itself has little confidence in these palliatives. The changes in the streets of Baghdad are to do with increased repression, not a return to normality. Destruction of the refineries means there are few cars on the streets but sentry boxes at the main junctions are still manned by traffic police in dark-blue uniforms.

In the last few weeks they have been issued with sub-machine guns. At the bus station the dishevelled soldiers from Kuwait contrast with the numerous and neatly dressed military police with white webbings and red cords in their epaulettes.

Despite the alleged priority given to restoring essential services, the only important change in the government came last Wednesday when Ali Hassan al-majid was appointed interior minister. A cousin of President Saddam, he was head of security until the end of 1986 and then in 1987–88 was responsible for the savage extinction of the rebellion in Kurdistan. In 1990 his appointment as Governor of Kuwait marked an immediate increase in repression. His appointment now underlines the government plans to deal with dissent.

By mobilising loyal troops, security services and the party, the government can keep its grip on Baghdad, the political key to the country where four million people live. The government, always predominantly Sunni, has most to fear from Shia Muslim districts of the capital where live adherents to the same branch of the Islamic faith as the cities which have risen in rebellion. In Shula, for instance, 15 people are said by Iraqi sources to have been killed when they tried to stage a demonstration, though this figure could not be confirmed.

Given the size of the repressive forces, popular demonstrations, even if supported by defecting soldiers with weapons, cannot really hope to succeed. For this to happen it would probably require the mutiny of several regular units with arms and heavy equipment, able to move resolutely against government troops and security forces. But while the president may be able to cling to power, the dimensions of his military defeat and the consequent economic ruin are such that he cannot stabilise his power.

Nor do the government's problems end there. Ordinary Iraqis are politically sophisticated. In the days since the ground war ended there has grown up an extraordinary unanimity of views – shop-keepers, labourers, intellectuals and even some officials – about what went wrong. They see the invasion of Kuwait as very much President Saddam's own idea. Most Iraqis were war-weary from the 1980–88 conflict with Iran. Once Kuwait was occupied the Iraqi leader then refused to withdraw or compromise.

Emissaries from friendly states who said that Iraq must agree to leave Kuwait partially or wholly, if it was to avoid a war it must lose, were all rebuffed. 'Everybody knew we could not fight 33 foreign states and win,' said one Iraqi.

Yet for seven months President Saddam refused to use the word withdrawal. Kuwait was Iraq's 19th province, a child returning to its mother. Right up to the expiry of the UN ultimatum on January 15 Iraq could have come out of the crisis stronger than it went in – though it could never have kept all of Kuwait.

Then when it was too late, Iraq agreed to leave the emirate, a concession unlikely to satisfy the alliance on the eve of the ground war. When the 'mother of battles' did break out the Iraqi leader was asking his troops to die in a battle which they must lose in defence of a province which he had promised to leave. Not surprisingly most refused to do so. Few armies can have voted so decisively with their feet against the plans of their commander.

A real strength of the present opposition is that this indictment of government policy is shared by almost all groups outside the official apparatus. Claims in the press to a mythical victory gain almost no credence. There is also a deep sense of bitterness at the way in which Iraqis became victims of the caprices of their own political leadership.

One Iraqi friend lost a roll of banknotes worth 50 dinars out of his trouser back pocket. 'Well,' he said resignedly after a fruitless search, 'if the government can lose Kuwait and the armies of Iraq and not care, why should I worry about losing my 50 dinars.'

SECRET WAR

James Adams

Sunday Times, March 10, 1991

Huddled under a camouflage net in the darkened desert, the two SAS troopers watched through their night-vision sights as the Iraqi Scud crew prepared a missile for launch against Israel. The drone of an American A-10 warthog reached them from the south.

One trooper raised a bulky instrument, a laser target illuminator, to his shoulder. Its invisible beam found the Scud and bounced up in a welcoming cone into the desert sky to guide an incoming bomb from the A-10. Within seconds, the Scud and its launcher exploded in flame and smoke.

The troopers withdrew into the night.

Hundreds of miles away in Basra, the Iraqi commander of a military headquarters welcomed a dishevelled Arab offering fresh fruit and vegetables after weeks of shortages.

Haggling over a glass of sweet tea, they struck a bargain and the Arab left. But he had hidden a locater beacon by the door. Four hours later an allied air strike buried the commander beneath the wreckage of his bunker.

The fruit seller had been neither Arab nor trader, but a member of the special forces' teams whose operations were the secret side of the

Gulf war, and the key to the allied bombing successes in Basra and Baghdad.

Disguised as traders, salesmen and ordinary citizens, dozens of members of Britain's SAS were among the secret teams operating behind enemy lines. Speaking Arabic and carrying Iraqi identification papers, these men conducted a range of vital missions against key Iraqi targets and helped decide the course of the war.

Some of the units operated from two secret bases inside Iraq, travelling around the country on motorbikes and in converted dune buggies.

There were up to 200 SAS men in the theatre – just under half the regiment's total strength – and about 2,000 American special forces, including Delta Force and three US Navy Seal teams.

As soon as Iraq invaded Kuwait last August, members of the SAS flew from RAF Lyneham in Wiltshire to the Gulf.

Some were infiltrated deep inside Iraq by special helicopters with virtually silent rotors that fly at night 10 feet above the ground. Other SAS men were dropped from aircraft using special parachutes that can 'fly' about 50 miles and be steered with pinpoint accuracy.

Most of the missions are still shrouded in secrecy, so that techniques can be used again, but some details are beginning to emerge.

'What those guys did was truly amazing,' said one Pentagon source. 'Kidnappings, killings, rescues, calling in aircraft, driving around Iraq like it was their backyard. You name it, they did it.'

For the first time in a modern war, special forces were included in all the war plans. Recruits to the special forces tend to be individuals working in small groups outside the regular military structure. As a result the more traditional military commanders distrust them and the black arts they practise and preffer not to have to deal with them.

But in the Gulf war, the special forces had a friend at court in the British commander, Lieutenant-General Sir Peter de la Billière. He served with the SAS in Oman, Malaya and Aden and led the SAS during the Falklands war. He was anxious that General Norman Schwarzkopf, the allied commander, took full advantage of them.

Not all the special forces missions were approved, however. Late last year allied intelligence suggested it was likely that Saddam Hussein would flood the Gulf with oil from the terminals in Kuwait. The special forces put up a plan to destroy the terminals on land and at sea, but it was rejected by the commanders as being too risky.

From the start of the Gulf war, allied commanders were determined to keep the number of civilian casualties to a minimum by accurate bombing using 'smart' weapons. In targeting troop concentrations outside urban areas, or in attacking hardened aircraft shelters inside Iraq, the high-technology weapons worked well.

But inside the three main population centres of Baghdad, Basra and Kuwait City, there was concern that fast jets flying at night might have problems selecting their targets.

The SAS men infiltrated the cities equipped with portable, battery-powered laser designators, which look like small unfurled umbrellas. After finding the target an infiltration squad would direct a designator at the target from a nearby building or other hidden location. After turning on the laser the men would leave. The laser reflected an invisible cone of light into the sky which could be picked up by aircraft. Missiles or bombs would then enter the cone and home on to the target.

According to Pentagon and Ministry of Defence officials, the SAS hunted down the mobile Scud launchers in the vastness of western Iraq that were hitting Israel.

SAS teams found large numbers of missiles and launchers, blowing some up and directing laser beams on others to direct aircraft to their targets.

In the same area, SAS units helped in the search for allied pilots shot down in Iraq, using their fast vehicles to reach the downed airmen before calling in rescue helicopters. The special forces managed to follow two convoys of Iraqi troops with captured allied pilots on board. They were tracked back to a building in Basra, which was kept under observation by the special forces. Consideration was given to mounting a rescue operation, but it was decided that the risk of the prisoners being killed was too great.

The Iraqi military had laid an extensive network of underground communications lines leading from Kuwait to a command centre in Basra. The SAS discovered them and blew them up, forcing the Iraqis to use conventional radio signals, which the SAS intercepted.

From the start of the crisis, the special forces behind enemy lines acted as the eyes and ears of the commanders back in Riyadh. 'On the day the air war began there were a lot of special forces out there,' said Schwarzkopf. 'It was a special operations theme park.'

Two bases were established in the desert inside Iraq, where the special forces had a range of equipment that allowed them to move about the desert at night with total freedom.

The favourite method of transport was a form of dune buggy camouflaged in pink. The buggies consist of a tubular frame, four enormous tyres and a heavy machine gun mounted on a swivel in the back.

Riding in these vehicles, which look as if they come straight from the set of Mad Max, is a terrifying experience, particularly at night. The buggy has almost no suspension, so the ride is rough and the highly tuned engine powers the vehicle over the ground at high speed.

The SAS also used a specially converted Land Rover that recently replaced the long-range desert patrol vehicle, known as the Pink Panther. The modified open-topped Land Rover has a three-man crew and carries two grenade launchers, a 7.62mm machine gun on the dashboard and a 12.7mm Browning on a rear swivel mount. A small satellite navigation system is included in the package. The driver and crew wear Litton night-vision goggles, which can be converted to ordinary binoculars in the daytime.

Each unit had a PRC 319 radio, which weighs only 4.8lb and measures 8x8 inches. The radio hops across frequencies to avoid jamming and sends coded signals in very short bursts. It is powerful enough to send a signal back to SAS headquarters in Hereford via a satellite.

Some units kept Iraqi forces under observation for days at a time. They would arrive at night, dig shallow holes known as scrapes, and then cover themselves with camouflage netting and sand. The only sign of their presence would be a tiny periscope peeping through the sand.

The first clues to more audacious actions came in early January when a report on Iraq's missile capabilities was prepared for the joint chiefs of staff in the Pentagon. Classified 'Umbra', the code for top secret special intelligence, the report set out just what missiles Iraq had and how much of a threat they posed to the allied forces.

One section of the report referred to a joint US-UK special forces' mission to steal a surface-to-air missile guidance system. The system was ferried back to the allied lines by helicopters and analysis of the radars allowed the allies to develop an effective counter measure.

According to Pentagon sources, the SAS and other special forces stole further radar and communications equipment which were taken back to Saudi Arabia for examination.

'There is even a report that we lifted a MiG-23 fighter from inside Iraq and flew it to Saudi,' said a Pentagon source. 'We were concerned about some modifications they had made to the aircraft and so wanted to take a closer look.'

Other special forces' units kidnapped senior Iraqi officers and brought them back to Saudi Arabia for interrogation. There have also been unconfirmed reports that a number of Iraqi officers, known to be political supporters of Hussein, were assassinated so that frontline troops would be more likely to defect or refuse to fight.

Schwarzkopf appeared to confirm the killings when he said there were 'some direct action missions – period'. Direct action is often a military and intelligence euphemism for assassination.

In the middle of February, Britain took its first casualty in ground fighting when Corporal David Denbury, 26, who was on detachment to the SAS from the Royal Engineers, was killed in a battle with Iraqi troops as his patrol was returning to base.

Another member of the regiment was wounded and captured after a six-man patrol was spotted by a convoy of Iraqi troops. In the chase, large numbers of the Iraqis were killed and five of the unit made their escape. The captured trooper was one of seven SAS men taken prisoner during the war who were released by the Iraqis last week. As some were dressed in civilian clothes before being taken prisoner, it is not clear why they were not shot as spies.

'Perhaps they ate their Arab disguise,' said a MoD official.

THE REAL FACE OF WAR

Photograph by Kenneth Jarecke

Observer, March 10, 1991

A NECESSARY SHOCK

Harold Evans

Observer, March 17, 1991

Why did a simple grainy black-and-white photograph of a dead Iraqi soldier in the *Observer* provoke such outrage last week? After all, we had watched with relative equanimity day after day sharply focused moving colour pictures on television of far greater violence.

Death may have seemed remote from the celestial glow of a cruise missile departing the USS Wisconsin or the fastidious cross-hairs of the smart bomb, but it was there directly enough in the bloodied victims of the Scud attacks on Tel Aviv and the remains of those who sought refuge in a Baghdad bomb shelter.

Television is supposed to have rendered the still picture obsolete. It is supposed to have ended the Vietnam war by bringing horror into the living-rooms of America. But in the Gulf war only the pictures of Israelis struggling to put on their gas masks had anything like the power of that single still image of the charred soldier – and he, after all, was not one of ours.

The photograph shocked in the first place for this very reason. It was a solitary individual in the transfixation of a hideous death. Before this, it had been possible to enjoy the lethal felicity of designer bombs as some kind of video game. It had been possible to be caught up in the excitement of people rushing to escape the Scuds. There was no escape from the still silence of the corpse in the *Observer* photograph. Anyone who can replay moving images in his mind has a very rare faculty. Anyone who saw that still photograph last Sunday will never forget it.

It was a necessary shock. The photograph met both the tests I suggested some years ago for the instrusion of images of violence on our peace of mind: is the event portrayed of such social and historic significance that the shock is justified? Is the objectionable detail necessary for a proper understanding of the event? I recoiled from the picture the moment I saw it, as most people surely did. In part that was an elemental human sympathy. Then I was forced to recognise that I had willed this man's death. I believe the Gulf war was a just war, and perhaps the dead Iraqi believed he was

256

fighting a holy war, but here, inescapably, was the consequence of our convictions.

It is right that we should contemplate the results of our beliefs. No action can be moral if we close our eyes to its consequences. Here, in charred flesh and grinning skull, was the price of patriotism. That was the service that publication of this photograph performed.

Critics of the photograph may say that they need no reminding that war is horrible, but they protest too much. The concept that war is horrible is altogether different from the stunning, practical realisation of horror we have willed. The first is easy to live with; the second is hard to forget. I am making an argument for realism, not for pacifism. Equally shocking photographs of mutilation and torture in occupied Kuwait, had they been published, would have confronted those opposed to intervention with the consequences of standing aside. Would those who object to the Iraqi photograph have decried a lack of 'taste' if a newspaper had published pictures smuggled out of Belsen in 1944?

Some critics say the *Observer* would not have dared to print the battlefront picture if it had been of a British or American soldier. It is true it would have been easier then to attack the picture as an obscene mockery of a valiant human sacrifice; but I still believe publication, with one caveat, would have been justified. It would have compelled a more painful recognition of what we ask of our servicemen. The caveat is one of privacy. Such a picture makes its point by anonymity. It would be a gratuitous intrusion into private grief to identify a disfigured victim.

There is something more significant in the protests to the *Observer* than a proper reticence. They suggest that even now, at the end of the bloodiest century the world has known, even now after the trenches, and Hiroshima, and My Lai, popular culture is still largely imbued with a romantic conception of war and resents a grimmer reality.

Perhaps, in a world where evil flourishes and must sometimes be fought, it is necessary to sustain the heroic imagination, but it is also necessary to weight the price. The disputed photograph did something to redress the elusive euphoria of a high-tech war. In its own small way it says what Siegfried Sassoon said of the Menin Gate memorial at Ypres inscribed with its 54,896 soldiers missing in action:

Here was the world's worst wound. And here with pride
'Their name liveth forever'
the Gateway claims.
Was ever an immolation so belied
As these intolerably nameless names?
Well might the Dead who struggled in the slime
Rise and deride this sepulchre of crime.

Staring at the photograph of the immolated soldier, dead in some corner of a foreign field, it was not possible to think of this charred cadaver as a pulse in the eternal mind, a rich dust that will give back laughter learned of friends, and flowers, and gentleness.

THE HUMAN RACE IS GROWING UP

Neal Ascherson

Independent on Sunday, March 10, 1991

Longer than the victory, people will remember the slaughter of the Second Gulf War. They will remember the scenes on the highway to Basra, that solid mass of charred and human corpses stretching for mile after mile near the overpass at Mutla Ridge, where the allied aircraft caught the main Iraqi retreat from Kuwait City. They will remember them mostly from written words (television's nerve failed), and from one photograph: the mask of ash which had been a soldier's face.

It is not yet clear exactly when it happened. Probably on Wednesday, February 27 – less than 24 hours before President Bush called a halt to the shooting. It was a cruel and pointless carnage. The war itself could not, I believe, have been avoided; but the fighting should have stopped the previous weekend, when Saddam Hussein began to accept the Soviet plan for withdrawal. The 'Hundred Hours' offensive, which may have killed 15,000 Iraqi soldiers, was not necessary.

In war, the big killing starts when soldiers leave their positions and begin to flee. It was a French military doctor in the last century, quoted in John Keegan's classic book *The Face of Battle*, who made himself unpopular by establishing that most wounds were in the victims' backs. So it was in the Second Gulf War. Most Iraqi units sensibly stayed dug in until the enemy arrived and then surrendered. Others, though, came out of cover. Some formations prepared to fight. Many simply drove wildly for home. It was on these visible and unprotected targets that the full impact of allied aerial killing-power fell.

By coincidence, a French officer wrote a letter about retreats to the *Independent* last week, abusing its correspondent, Robert Fisk. He blamed Fisk for remarking that Napoleon's *Grande Armée* was 'defeated' by Russia during the retreat from Moscow. France, wrote Colonel Perrodon, was beaten by the weather, not the Russians. Unfortunately for the colonel, I have in front of me a 19th-century graph, drawn up by a retired Inspecteur des Ponts et Chaussées, which proves the opposite.

This horrible diagram is essentially a strip, 422,000 men thick when the army sets out, which has dwindled to a mere pen-scratch representing 4,000 men when the French stagger back to the Lithuanian frontier. The graphic shows unmistakably that it was the battles along the retreat – Vyazma, Orsha, the Berezina crossing – and not the frost which killed soldiers. The colonel claims the retreat was 'organised'. I have spoken to men whose grandfathers saw it. They were told about something more akin to the flight from Kuwait.

The horror on the Basra highway is also a kind of metaphor. In this world, those who cling to their ground and refuse to be put to flight have a chance. But once you lose your soil and take to the roads, you become the target for every cruising executioner, every slave-trader, every despot in search of people to crucify or drive into gas chambers. The Jews know what it means to carry your own killing-field wherever you go, to see your children born into a free-fire zone.

They retreated, on and off, for 2,000 years before their intellectuals invented Zionism and the idea of a physical homeland. The Palestinians have been on the roads of the world for only 43 years, but they have already found themselves more than once at Mutla Ridge. It is easy for the English, especially, to be supercilious about the longing of disinherited nations to have a state of their own. The English have always had a home, a bunker, a patch of earth. Their wounds are seldom in the back.

The Basra highway may seem an odd context in which to claim that the West is growing more squeamish about war. On the face of it, this was absolutely conventional ferocity. Where once the cavalry were hurled after infantry on the run, now fighter-bombers with napalm plunge down to turn rout into massacre. Countless commanders have been disgraced for letting a beaten enemy get away; General Schwarzkopf was determined not to be one of them. And yet attitudes are changing – have been changing, in fact, for some time.

Once, this event would have been described like this: 'The enemy army fled in guilty panic from the scene of its crimes, but was so burdened by loot that it was easily overtaken by our pursuing forces, who gave it the merciless punishment it so richly deserved . . .' But few people today, and fewer soldiers, would buy that as a fair account of what took place.

Death in war is growing steadily harder for governments to justify. In the first place, this means the death of their own soldiers. Commanders now husband their men far more carefully than their fathers or grandfathers did. This was true in the Falklands, and spectacularly true in the Gulf where the purpose of the weeks of bombardment was to spare the lives of allied troops when they finally had to attack. Some of the reasons for this were political: President Bush wanted to show the American people that big expeditionary wars did not have to cost as many lives as Vietnam. Some are more profound: soldiers have grown better educated and more independent. Their readiness to accept an invitation from some twittish young officer to walk into the barrage is even slighter than it used to be. As professionals, they will take risks if they must but consider themselves good judges of that 'must'. When I was a young Marine, my sergeant told me: 'If you get hit, it will be your fault – because you forgot what I'm telling you. And I will put what is left of you on a charge!' I found this anti-heroic approach to death, and wounds, a great comfort.

The real question, though, is whether this laudable squeamishness about taking casualties will extend to inflicting them. On the face of it, the Second Gulf War suggests otherwise – that if the price of losing far fewer of 'our' lives is to take astronomically more of 'theirs', then it will happily be paid. This has always been the promise of new military technologies. Sometimes it has been kept, as with the use of the Maxim gun against tribesmen with spears. Sometimes it has not worked. The Anglo-American bombing offensive against Germany between 1943 and 1945 broke neither civilian morale nor war production, and cost the incredible total of 160,000 aircrew lives. The atomic bomb at first offered genocide for 'them' at zero cost to 'us'. Soon, though, we discovered fall-out.

Now there is fresh arrogance about new weapons. And yet the ritual bombast about killing-power lacks its old conviction. One of the reasons for the unilateral ceasefire on February 28 (which made no military sense) was the genuine panic of Western political leaders at the scale of the killing. They had caused it, even willed it. But they had not imagined what it would be like.

Year by year, people grow more afraid of death in battle, more frightened to ask it of their fellows and – very slowly – less confident about imposing it on others. Few will remember without a flinch that rhetoric which began with 'surgical precision' and 'pinpoint accuracy' and ended with 'turkey-shoot' and 'shooting fish in barrels'. Most of us, though, will remember the face of the man who burned to death on the Basra highway. In such tortuous ways, the human race is growing up.

THE CHARRED BODIES AT MUTLA RIDGE

Stephen Sackur

London Review of Books, April 4, 1991

Major-General Rupert Smith, commander of the British First Armoured Division, was sitting with a mug of tea by his side at the table from which he had directed his troops during the ground offensive. The map on the table told its own story: symbols and arrows indicated the swathes of territory occupied by allied troops in the previous 100 hours, not only in Kuwait, but deep inside Iraq as well. The general had summoned me to his side in this hour of victory. That very morning President Bush had announced a cessation of offensive operations and the other coalition members had rapidly followed his lead. Having made a headlong dash through southern Iraq, the British Division had come to rest in northern Kuwait. Little more than four days after it had begun the ground war was over.

General Smith was tired. This was obvious not just in his face, which looked uncharacteristically drawn and pale, but also in his manner, which was restless and somewhat irritable. He had, he said, been able to grab no more than a few hours' sleep in the previous five days, stretched out on a bench in one of the armoured cars surrounding the command post. Nevertheless the interview had been his idea, not mine. His desire to elaborate on the allied victory outweighed his desire for sleep. I had last seen the general more than a month before, when he had given me, and a handful of other 'pool' journalists, an informative (and of course secret) briefing on the allied war plan and the British part in it. When the ground attack came, he had told us at this first encounter, it would be launched on several fronts simultaneously. It would exploit allied air supremacy to hit the Iraqis in their deep as well as front-line positions, thus providing allied infantry and armour with vital support. It would, he said, be something akin to the German 'blitzkrieg' strategy, applying massive force at very high speed to dislocate and confuse the enemy. 'You saw the plan, and the plan worked.' That was what General Smith wanted to tell me in his moment of triumph. And it was true: looking at the huge map laid out before me, I could hardly deny that the offensive had proceeded according to the plan in a most extraordinary way.

'But the Iraqis didn't put up a fight,' I said. 'There was virtually no return of fire at all.' This observation met with an impatient response. Where they were able to fire back they did so, the general said, but in most cases the Iraqi forces were simply overwhelmed. Military men are, on the whole, convinced that civilians (and journalists in particular) understand nothing about the nature of warfare. As I talked to General Smith, I noticed more than once that a tone not far removed from contempt entered his voice. He positively snorted with derision when I asked him if any steps had been taken to minimise casualties once it was clear that the allies were advancing almost at will through Iraqi territory. On the contrary, he said, while the war continued it was prosecuted with maximum, not minimum force. The general's tone struck me at the time, and still does, as odd, given that it was quite clear during the four days of the ground war that British officers did spare Iraqi lives, and that it became general practice among some of the British tank regiments to give Iraqi tank crews time to abandon their vehicles before they were destroyed.

Notwithstanding General Smith's uncompromising words, I saw for myself the degree to which ordinary British soldiers were disturbed and upset by the wretched state in which many of the Iraqi prisoners of war were found. Having been deprived of food and water for days, with inadequate clothing and third-rate equipment, it would have been hard to imagine an army less suited to the battle-hardened, ruthless image which was peddled on its behalf in the weeks leading up to the ground attack. This mismatch between expectation and reality clearly had a profound effect on many ordinary soldiers. Several came up to me before the interim cease-fire was announced and told me that they felt 'the slaughter' had gone on long enough. The truth about the ground offensive, it seems to me, was that the Iraqi troops simply refused to fight. They were not prepared to commit suicide for a president who had already made clear his willingness to cede Kuwait – the very territory they were supposed to be fighting to keep. So they either surrendered *en masse* or attempted to retreat as fast as they possibly could. Only a tiny minority of British troops experienced incoming fire, and although the statistic has never been confirmed, it seems that only one of the 17 British troops officially described as 'killed on active service' was killed in direct combat by Iraqi fire. The vast majority of the mercifully light British casualties were caused by 'friendly fire' or the malfunctioning of equipment.

Taking their lead from the Americans, British commanders refused to give any indication of the casualties inflicted during their brief but effective ground campaign. There was to be no body count – it was officially regarded as 'unhelpful'. As a result of this allied reticence, we have no idea how many Iraqi troops lost their lives in the ground war. Estimates seem to vary from 40,000 to an extremely unlikely 150,000; all that can be said with certainty is that the imbalance between allied and Iraqi casualties can rarely if ever have been matched in modern warfare.

'Maximum force' was the phrase that stuck in my mind long after I took my leave of General Smith. Was it an approach, I wondered, that remained legitimate against an enemy patently beaten and retreating in disarray? Does warfare of its nature require the application of 'maximum force' from the opening of hostilities to their cessation?

By a quirk of fate my doubts were intensified the very next day. I had been expecting to hitch a ride on a helicopter from General Smith's headquarters in northern Kuwait back to my own adopted army unit, which was still in southern Iraq. But during my encounter with the general the weather had deteriorated, a clinging grey mist had reduced visibility and my return had to be postponed. So it was that the next morning, instead of heading back into Iraq, I took a seat in an army Land Rover heading for Kuwait City. After bumping along a desert track for no more than five minutes we turned onto the main highway – Route 80 – which runs north from Kuwait City to the Iraqi border, and the southern Iraqi city of Basra. As we continued to head south we passed dozens of wrecked civilian and military vehicles, many gutted by fire. Now and again bodies, sometimes covered in rough blankets, sometimes not, could be seen on the side of the road. It was clear that allied aircraft had attacked the highway with cluster bombs – the spent casings were lying all over the area. Cluster bombs are designed to break up into hundreds of little 'bomblets' to saturate the target area, spewing out specially formulated metal shrapnel to maximise damage to both man and machine. They leave tell-tale pockmarks in the area of impact. The Basra road, needless to say, was covered in pockmarks.

Our Land Rover continued on its way towards Kuwait City, skirting round the torn metal and the abandoned corpses. But only two miles ahead the highway was blocked in an altogether more thorough fashion. We had reached the Mutla Ridge, an escarpment perhaps a couple of hundred feet high, from which, on a clear day, you can see Kuwait City itself, some 20 miles away. On the crest of the ridge were a group of buildings, including a petrol station and a police station. The Iraqis had, we were told, established heavily fortified defences on the ridge, on both sides of the highway, during the allied offensive. The Land Rover could go no further, so I got out and walked. To my left was the police station, badly damaged, but still standing. Close by, on the other side of the road, was a grotesque collection of charred bodies, forty in all, some frozen in mid-scream, others so badly burnt that it was impossible to distinguish their sex. In many instances the human form had been reduced to nothing more than a shapeless black lump, the colour of coal, the texture of ash.

Over the ridge, down the highway, this was where they had been incinerated. Across all six lanes of the road, and as far as the low grey cloud would allow me to see, there was nothing but devastation – saloon cars, tanks, military vehicles sitting nose-to-tail in a stalled procession. This was an escape convoy stopped in its tracks. Iraqi soldiers in Kuwait City, and some civilians too, though God knows how many, had realised on the Tuesday of the ground offensive that the game was up – allied soldiers were already approaching the outskirts of the city. They had panicked, seizing any vehicle that looked capable of taking them to Iraq before the allies could close in. The evidence of their desperation was still to be seen on the highway some 60 hours later. Some had commandeered Kuwaiti police cars and fire engines; others had climbed aboard a milk delivery van; somebody had even chosen a civilian bulldozer. Mostly, though, the fleeing thousands had stolen luxury saloons of which Kuwait City could offer a plentiful supply. In their last panic-stricken minutes many found time to stuff these cars with useless trinkets and consumers goods looted from Kuwaiti homes. But Mercedes, BMW or Range Rover, it mattered little: nothing offered much protection from the American bombs and shells which rained down on the convoy that night.

How did it happen? Why did it happen? The only answers I got were from an American major, Bob Williams, who had been part of the tank battalion charged with cutting off the Iraqi line of retreat from Kuwait City. Major Williams, his men and their M-1 tanks – collectively known as 'The Hounds of Hell' – were still on the scene some three days later. According to the major, his tanks had been involved in what he called a 'five-hour fire-fight' with Iraqi troops dug in around the police station at the top of the ridge. As the fight continued the highway became blocked, causing a huge tailback of traffic to build up. There were tanks, military vehicles and thousands of armed troops in the trapped convoy – it was, in short, a legitimate military target, he said. American aircraft bombed the convoy while Major Williams and his men maintained a heavy barrage on the ground. The result, he agreed, was 'apocalyptic'.

Given that I arrived on the scene long after the shooting had stopped, and indeed hours after the inferno on the road had cooled, I have no means of providing an independent account of events. However, to describe what happened on the highway as a five-hour fight seems less than entirely honest. Yes, there were some Iraqi tanks in the convoy, but they, like the rest of the vehicles around them, were trapped. There was a handful of Iraqi tanks to be seen some distance away from the road, but they were almost obsolete T-55s – no match at all for the American M-1 tanks that had taken the Mutla Ridge itself. True also, the vast majority of men trapped in their vehicles were armed Iraqi soldiers: but that they were in full retreat is disputed by no one, and their automatic rifles could present no significant miitary threat in the face of the massive firepower the Americans had brought to the area. Major Williams admitted that during the five hours of the supposed battle he had lost just one man, killed by a bullet from an Iraqi sniper.

As to the number of Iraqis who lost their lives, the Americans would say only that they had recovered more than 150 bodies. But numerous blackened corpses remained inside the twisted metal of their vehicles, and it seemed obvious to me that many hundreds of people must have been obliterated under the sustained American fire. It's hard to imagine how the doctrine of 'maximum force' could have been given a more forcible illustration. Within the international regulations which are supposed to govern the conduct of warfare the American actions on the Mutla Ridge were legitimate. Iraqi soldiers were retreating, but they were armed and (as far as we know) they offered no formal surrender. It was the scale of the American attack that took my breath away. Was it necessary to bomb the entire convoy? What threat could these pathetic remnants of Saddam Hussein's beaten army have posed? Wasn't it obvious that the people of the convoy would have given themselves up willingly without the application of such ferocious weaponry? The hundreds who, by some miracle, did survive were duly taken prisoner. They included two women and a child. Further evidence suggests that Palestinian and Indian civilians were killed, along with other Iraqis and some Kuwaitis who were being taken back to Iraq as prisoners.

When I asked Major Williams to justify what had happened he said: 'As you look at the vehicles down in this area you'll find they are all filled with booty . . . these were thieves, not professional soldiers . . . our cause was just.' A few yards away, American and British troops were rooting around the wrecked vehicles looking for Iraqi military souvenirs to take home and hang on their walls.

I came across one Kuwaiti army officer who was surveying the wreckage from further down the hill. 'I feel very happy when I see this situation,' he told me. 'I feel happy when I see the Iraqi people are killed . . . they tried to escape like we had to when they first came to Kuwait, but they did more than this to the people of Kuwait.'

Who were these Iraqis killed in their hundreds, burnt beyond recognition on the Mutla Ridge? It's a fair bet that most of them were nothing more than conscripts – regarded by Saddam Hussein as expendable. The important men, the commanders and the organisers of the vile campaign of torture and murder directed against the Kuwaiti people, are likely to have quit the city long before that Tuesday night. One can't help wondering what would have happened to this rag-bag convoy, these dregs of a beaten army, if they had reached the 'safety' of Basra. Would they now be required to join in the army's killing of the Shia rebels, or would some of them have joined the revolt?

In the midst of all the looted video cassettes, ornaments and appliances that had spilled onto the road during the American attack, there were pathetic reminders of these soldiers' former lives. Photographs of wives and children, diaries. Those lumps of blackened flesh dumped on the side of the highway were not mere 'turkeys' to be shot, nor 'fish in a tank' – to use the American jargon which gained common currency during the war.

As some of the British tank crew seem to have understood (with or without their senior commanders' specific instructions), there are ways of achieving military objectives, particularly against a demoralised and retreating army, which avoid unnecessary casualties. The soldier who allows enemy troops to abandon a tank before blowing it up surely deserves praise for allowing maximum humanity to overcome maximum force.

THE KILLING FIELDS
Colin Smith
Observer, March 3, 1991

It was the Duke of Wellington who observed that after a battle lost the next saddest thing is a battle won.

Some 30 miles north of this flag-waving, gun-happy capital, along the main desert highway to the Iraqi border, there are low and persistent multi-tonal humming noises in a place where little else moves except the more adventurous human scavengers. It is the sound of engines still idling in the vehicles abandoned intact by the panic-stricken children of Saddam's Mother of Battles.

The allied aircraft arrived as they tried to flee back home with their loot and their weapons. When I visited the spot flames still flickered from some shredded tyres despite a steady drizzle from a sky made even darker by the black smoke from the burning oilfields. Ghastly islands of charred bodies and metal are surrounded by more or less intact transport. Most carry some of the riches of Kuwait so that the convoy often appears more gypsy than military.

Nothing was too big or too small for these soldiers brought up in an oil-rich state that preferred tanks to Toshiba as far as the peasants and the artisans who made up its conscript army are concerned. On the back of one lorry was a complete imitation leather three-piece suite, large grey metal filing cabinets, and a restaurant's soft-drinks fridge still with its Canada Dry transfer on the back. Television sets and videos were commonplace, as was washing powder and bottles of aftershave. A complete chandelier spilled out of its cardboard box. A live chicken picked around packets of Dunhill cigarettes, a woman's handbag, pieces of costume jewellery and strings of imitation pearls.

There were a great deal of new women's and children's shoes, some of them the Italian imitations made in Thailand. An American officer told me he had even seen a steam radiator. 'Suppose it was going back to some little village in Kurdistan where they were gonna hook it up to the log fire.'

He was the commander of an Abrams tank group, part of the US Army's Tiger Brigade which had been attached to the Marines because it was thought the leathernecks' elderly M-60s were not up to the job. This proved to be mistaken.

Several troopers from the Tiger Brigade were picking around the wreckage looking for Kalashnikov rifle bayonets for souvenirs. 'I'd make a fortune if I could get some of this stuff home,' said one private, surveying a great tangle of small-arms on the floor of a bus. 'But we ain't allowed to take no firearms.'

Several hundred weapons, perhaps more judging from the amount of shooting in the air in Kuwait City since liberation, had been taken by Kuwaitis before the Americans got there. Others concerned themselves in more practical matters. Further down the road, before the last American checkpoint, the citizens of the Middle East's richest oil state were busy siphoning petrol from Iraqi vehicles or examining roof-racks and the backs of pick-ups for the greatest prize of all – full gerrycans.

Scattered about were the kind of personal mementoes carried by homesick soldiers everywhere. One snapshot, near the body of a man lying face down with a terrible wound in his right leg, was of what appeared to be a children's birthday party. The children, three girls and a boy in party hats, sat around a table laden with food and dominated by a heart-shaped cake.

Some broken bags contained blank children's exercise books and German colouring crayons. In one truck the radio had been knocked out of the dashboard but was still wired up and faintly picking up some plaintive Arabic air which sounded so utterly forlorn I thought at first it must be a cry for help. The next day, American medics did in fact find one grievously wounded Iraqi in the back of a van and they believed there might be more. Helmets, gas masks and ammunition, including grenades and a few plastic mines that the rearguard may have intended to throw in its wake, lay everywhere. Almost every cab contained a fully loaded Kalashnikov rifle. Some of them had already begun to rust.

A burnt-out quadruple-barrelled anti-aircraft gun, detached from the pick-up that had been towing it, pointed skywards and looked as if it might have been returning fire. There was no sign of its crew.

What occurred here and elsewhere was undoubtedly one of the most terrible harassments of a retreating army from the air in the history of warfare. It must surely rank with Israel's destruction of Nasser's forces in the Sinai Desert in 1967 and what the same allies did in 1944 to Hitler's Panzer divisions at Normandy's Falaise Gap.

They are stopped both sides of a dual-carriageway heading north.

More are just off the road out into the desert on the right where they obviously obeyed some mob instinct to get off the tarmac.

There they are bogged down in a colossal traffic jam for the sand has been turned into a quagmire by recent thunderstorms. At this point the survivors appear to have run off into a night that was being torn apart by explosions and flame.

Most of them are probably now among the estimated 180,000 prisoners of war thought to be in allied hands although there are fears that a few may still be wandering the desert too terrified to give themselves up.

Some of this fleeing mass of traffic was not hit by bombs or cannon fire as the allied planes lined up to strafe them. Travelling in the dark, without lights, they collided with each other in their eagerness to get away.

Several vehicles, including an ambulance, had trapped themselves on a wire net fence on the side of the road. One tank crew had tried to cross the steep central reservation only to discover there are limits to where even a T-62 can go. The Soviet behemoth lay tilted there at an awesome list, its hatches up, the crew's blankets and clothing strewn about it.

In those places where the bombs and the 30mm cannon fire at 4,200 rounds a minute came down the carnage is terrible. Huddled under one motorway bridge, like an animal sheltering from a storm, was a burnt-out petrol tanker whose driver appeared to have been cremated in his cab. Most of the nearby vehicles had also caught fire although a new-looking armoured personnel carrier not far away was quite undamaged, its crew apparently deciding that they would soldier no more.

'Look at that, man. Look what war does,' said a black military policeman, surveying the body of a moustached young man spreadeagled on his back near some cinder black vehicles. 'That man – he didn't even look after his people.'

Many allied troops still seem to be in almost as big a shock over Norman Schwarzkopf's blitzkrieg as the Iraqis. The entire Marine contingent lost a total of three killed in the ground offensive – six less than they had killed by their own aircraft during the Iraqi attack on Khafji three weeks ago.

'I wouldn't even call this a mopping-up operation,' said one bewildered captain of the first battalion, 5th Marine Division, encountered on Kuwait City's seventh ring road on Wednesday morning. At that point the Marines had stopped advancing in order to allow the

Saudi and Kuwaiti elements in the coalition forces to take the city. A considerable barrage of small-arms fire was coming from over the brow of a hill but this turned out to be the Arab soldiers firing in the air in celebration.

The Marines' last encounter with the enemy had been the previous evening when they knocked out two tanks and an APC with their own M-60 tanks and some wire-guided TOW missiles. 'Some of the Iraqis left their vehicles and hid in a nursery – you know, a place where they grow young trees. Two battalions went through and finished them. They didn't fight much but at least they died with their weapons in their hands.'

Now the men of the 1st Battalion's Alpha Company were getting out their gas suits having just had the last alert of the war. It turned out that one of their detectors had picked up some fumes from a burning Iraqi ammunition dump. (American pool reporters have said that in fact two gas shells, thought to be mustard gas, were fired at the Marines on the first day of the ground offensive but there were no casualties.)

The Marines looked grimy but cheerful. Most of them had seen a lot of the men of 7th Armoured Brigade when it was attached to them before the British contingent was expanded to a division. They were well-disposed to the Brits. 'How are the Rats doin'?' one of them asked, and was intrigued to learn that they were reported to be in Iraq.

Alpha Company had taken part in the storming of the second breach made in the Iraqi earthwork defences in southern Kuwait. They said they had had some resistance from a dug-in T-55 tank (a very old armoured vehicle) but their own M-60s had finished it off. Then they started taking prisoners.

'We used to say that we wouldn't take no prisoners unless they came out bare-butt and wavin' a white flag,' said Lance-Corporal George Cadiente, 'but, oh man, some of them were crying. One guy, you know, he defecated himself when they heard we were Marines they were certain we were goin' to kill 'em. They'd been told all sorts of bullshit like to join the Marine Corps you had to kill one of your own family first.

'Some of them wouldn't come out of their bunkers. They were curled up in there and wouldn't come out. We'd throw stones in, pretending they were grenades, and they still wouldn't come out. They'd just curl up some more. And the place was full of guns, grenades, RPGs. They could have fought us. When we tied their hands with the plastic strip some of them were saying, "We love you, we love you." I had one kid who couldn't have been more than 16. He just sat there on the ground and started crying. He was convinced I was going to kill him. He hadn't eaten for days, you could see it. Just a kid.'

Lance-Corporal Cadiente, of San Jose, California, is 22.

Last Monday morning a near-riot took place at a US Marine temporary POW cage about 40 miles south-west of Kuwait City when some 3,500 half-starved Iraqi soldiers fought each other for American combat ration. The Americans did not take steps to convince the prisoners there was enough food for everyone and mass hysteria broke out. It was a degrading and sad spectacle, caused partly by mismanagement by a Marine military police unit and the fact that all semblance of discipline had broken down in the Iraqi ranks. They were a rabble, not an army.

Yet only 200 yards away squatted another group of prisoners, about 500 strong, who were quite differently behaved. They waited patiently for the signal to come up to go six at a time to be searched, a process which involved removing their boots and jackets. They then joined another group when individual combat ration was given to each man. These prisoners were guarded by a reserve unit, the 4th Civil Affairs Group from Washington DC.

'We've got a lot of serving policemen with us,' explained Captain Philip Bennett, who, in civilian life, works for the Department of the Navy. 'They're used to dealing with people. We use the bullhorns and the Kuwaiti interpreters to explain to them what is happening and that they will all get fed if they do what they are told. I don't know why those MPs can't do the same over there.'

As he spoke, nervous young military policemen fired shots in the air from their M-16 rifles and screamed at the prisoners to 'break it up' and 'get f . . . g back'. A group of Iraqi officers with Saddam moustaches, one of them a colonel, looked on but made absolutely no effort to control their men or prevent them from further humiliating themselves. Instead, they indicated that they wanted to be served first.

At one point the Marines were throwing cardboard boxes, full of MREs, much-despised by American troops, over the barbed wire and watching the Iraqis tear them apart. It was like feeding a flock of birds.

Each box of MREs contains at least two pork dishes – pork patties and ham slices – but in their hunger none of the Americans'

271

Muslim captives seemed to notice. 'Meester, Meester,' they implored as the Americans approached with the food, each man definitely an island.

I saw a grey-haired prisoner who in attempting to hug one of the brown plastic MRE packs to his chest was forced down on the razor wire by the scrum. After the Marines had briefly dispersed the mêlée with their warning shots, he tearfully emerged without his meal and with a cut on his face.

The mood of the Iraqis' guards varied from intense irritation to great compassion. 'Poor bastards. You can't even dislike them. All you can do is feel sad for them,' said Captain Kurt Snyder, a bespectacled law graduate from Seattle, who said he was there because he did not know anyone else who had read all of the Geneva Convention.

Even as the MPs were screaming obscenities at them in the manner of very young men trying to be very tough, US Navy Corpsmen were helping an Iraqi Army doctor treat the sick and wounded. The Americans fussed around them, attached intravenous drips fixed to poles in the ground, asked people to search vehicles for extra blankets, and pleaded with their officers to arrange for a helicopter evacuation to the nearest MASH unit which was duly done. One young Iraqi, grey-complexioned and obviously in great pain, had a wound right through one ankle and injuries around his groin.

But the medics only treated two men for battle injuries. They said the rest were suffering mainly from dehydration and thought that this was partly brought on by fear. One stretcher case was shivering so badly he looked as if he had an acute attack of malaria. Others had shown scars they said they had collected in the Iraq-Iran war.

'Basically, they just want some attention, want to know that somebody cares,' said Navy Corpsman David Walden, 21, from Columbus, Ohio.

From behind the prisoners came the occasional sharp explosion as American engineers continued to cut new lanes through the Iraqi minefields. These lanes begin at the gaps cut through the Saudi border earthworks known as berms and are then marked with anything bright that shows up.

The lane I followed was blazed for much of its route by dozens of red plastic trash cans. It wound through the first bunkers of the Saddam Line, which were not the impressive products of five months' engineering some reports have suggested but fairly basic infantry dugouts. The ground around these was littered with the split canisters in which the allied air forces delivered their anti-personnel cluster bomb units.

There was evidence that it had not been entirely plain sailing for the American vanguard. On one side of the lane was an American mine-clearing vehicle with a track blown off and a scorched and buckled sprocket. Otherwise, the vehicle was intact and it seemed doubtful if the crew had been hurt.

The Iraqi fortifications were littered with abandoned equipment, including multiple-barrel anti-aircraft guns and the flat-trajectory cannon sometimes used against tanks known as recoil-less rifles.

A burnt-out Soviet T-62 tank lay in the scrape where it had been dug in as a permanent artillery fixture. The crews of passing American Abrams M1 tanks were constantly hopping off their vehicles to take each other's photograph in front of the destroyed T-62.

There was quite enough time for these sort of antics. The one-way routes to the front were a constant traffic jam. 'What this war needs is an enema!' said a frustrated military police sergeant when a commandeered civilian bus intended for the transportation of prisoners broke down before him.

It was noticeable that when this sort of thing happened people left their vehicles very carefully and made sure that their feet did not stray from fresh tyre marks.

On the Saudi side of the berm, groups of Iraqi deserters who had apparently been hiding in no man's land when General Schwarzkopf launched his ground offensive at 4.00am on Sunday, were still drifting in.

As dawn broke on Monday, photographer Derek Hudson and myself were flagged down on a Saudi border road by 40 very scared and unarmed Iraqi soldiers waving white rags and singlets, in one case tied to a broken-off radio antenna.

They carried pathetic little bundles of food – tomato paste and dried biscuits. They were concerned that they might still be attacked from the air and wanted motor transport to be arranged. We contacted a nearby Syrian outpost but they seemed to think it an unwarranted interruption of their breakfast.

It was only after we crossed into Kuwaiti territory that the full disintegration of Saddam's army could be seen. As we approached what was to become the Marine's POW cage a great black phalanx of broken men was shambling towards it. They looked as if they might have stepped out of a painting of Napoleon's retreat from Moscow. These were the lucky ones.

THE FINAL TURKEY SHOOT

Michael Evans

The Times, March 27, 1991

One of the most controversial incidents of the war with Iraq was the carnage at Mutla Ridge. About 20 miles northwest of Kuwait City, the remnants of Saddam Hussein's fleeing army today lie on each side of the highway, a horrific reminder of the consequences of war. Almost four weeks after the end of the Gulf conflict, the twisted, blackened wreckage of thousands of vehicles – armoured, 'soft-skinned' and civilian – still scars the Kuwaiti landscape. No one has attempted to remove the pile-up of vehicles, though a path has been bulldozed through the middle to allow traffic to use the road.

Mutla Ridge was one of the reasons for President Bush's decision to stop the war when he did. Many in the military and intelligence community wanted to pursue the campaign for another 24 to 48 hours, if only to increase the chance of toppling Saddam. Today, with Iraq stricken by civil war and Saddam surviving only by means of brutal suppression, there are those who believe that President Bush should have continued a little longer, especially now that American troops seem doomed to remain in occupied southern Iraq for months while the turmoil continues on the other side of the ceasefire demarcation line. Some American officials are saying that too many of Saddam's tanks and armoured personnel carriers survived the war.

But a visit to Mutla Ridge explains everything. Despite previous promises of safe conduct to retreating troops, it was a mass killing of Iraqi forces, as they headed out of Kuwait City on the highway to Basra. The attack by American helicopters and aircraft lasted just a few hours. The assault on Saddam's retreating army began when American M-1 tanks lined up on the other side of the ridge, cutting off the escape route. Aircraft were then called in to finish off the job. Nobody counted the bodies found and buried.

The impact this incident had on the politicians back home has not yet been fully appreciated. Marshal of the Royal Air Force, Sir David Craig, who retires as chief of the defence staff next week, admits that having achieved the liberation of Kuwait, the allies would rightly have been called to account if they had continued what was 'more and more like butchery'. He remains convinced that President Bush was right to stop the fighting. If there was to be some degree of magnanimity, the allies could not afford 'more Mutla Ridges'.

War leads to acts of great personal courage, of professionalism and heroism; but it also entails suffering, death, fear and destruction. There were many horrific sights during the brief war with Iraq. British soldiers came across Iraqis who had lost limbs, and bodies charred from burning fuel inside crippled tanks.

But Mutla Ridge was different. Was it justified? The Iraqis were clearly trying to escape. Theirs was not a withdrawal, but a rush for home. So why the carnage?

As the convoy of tanks, tank-transporters, four-tonne trucks, buses, cars, vans and lorries drove out of Kuwait City towards the mountain pass at Mutla Ridge, the only military question was: were the Iraqis planning to regroup for a counter-attack at the border?

General Norman Schwarzkopf, the American commander, had publicly stated that the allies would not attack Iraqis in retreat. But here was a convoy, part of which was armed and capable of mounting an attack. Even though the first two days of the land war had demonstrated Iraq's unwillingness to fight, even though thousands had already surrendered, the convoy moving out of Kuwait City appeared to represent a potential threat. There had also been a shift in allied policy. General Schwarzkopf told Iraqi soldiers they must leave their guns and tanks behind if they wanted to leave Kuwait.

General Schwarzkopf and his field commanders based their campaign on the need to reduce the risk of allied casualties. The fleeing Iraqis, armed with guns, as well as stolen merchandise, could have inflicted casualties as they came up against allied units which had swept across Kuwait and southern Iraq. That was the justification for attacking them, even though they appeared to be following thousands of their colleagues in trying to escape the battlefield.

Brigadier Patrick Cordingley, commander of the British 7th Armoured Brigade and the first to admit that he was distressed by what he saw at Mutla Ridge, reminded me that the Iraqis in the convoy had devastated the Kuwaiti capital. Kuwaiti citizens had been tortured and killed. Homes had been plundered.

Judgements are easy to make with hindsight. But it is difficult to understand why the American bombers were ordered to destroy everything moving up that highway. Once the pass had been cut off, there was nowhere for the Iraqis to go. They were trapped and capable of nothing but surrender. The allied plan was to destroy Iraqi tanks and other armoured vehicles. But the lasting impression at Mutla Ridge is of the mangled remains of private cars. It was the final 'turkey shoot' of the war, and, in retrospect, unwarranted. Further carnage would have been politically insupportable and terrible publicity. President Bush knew it.

THE KUWAITIS' REVENGE

Robert Fisk

Independent, March 4, 1991

Only a week after its liberation, parts of Kuwait City are beginning to resemble the anarchy of Beirut, with gunmen controlling streets, dozens of Palestinians being kidnapped from their homes by armed civilians and the Emir and his Crown Prince still absent. Western ambassadors and relief agencies have been pleading with the few Kuwaiti ministers who have arrived here from Saudi Arabia to restore law and order before they lose control of the capital.

Even the Kuwaiti Army, however, seems set on taking its revenge against the 240,000-strong Palestinian community, some of whom collaborated with the Iraqi occupation forces. Yesterday morning, Kuwaiti forces drove 12 armoured vehicles into the Palestinian Hwali district, shooting in the air, ordering Palestinians to close their shops and beating civilians who fell into their hands. American Special Forces troops accompanying the Kuwaitis did nothing to stop this indiscipline, and shouted obscenities at journalists who asked why they did not intervene.

British embassy staff have expressed their concern to the Kuwaitis and to the Americans about the increasing anarchy in the city and the threat to thousands of Palestinian lives. Palestinians said yesterday that as many as 400 young men had been kidnapped from their homes by armed Kuwaitis over the past three days. As more evidence emerges of the atrocities committed by the Iraqis here, there is a growing fear that allied forces may have to be used to police Kuwait City –

something the American commander, General Norman Schwarzkopf, desperately wishes to avoid.

At night, gangs of armed men are stopping cars in Kuwait City with Kalashnikov rifles left behind by the Iraqis, apparently searching for Palestinians. Little attempt has been made by the Kuwaiti or the Saudi Army to prevent the activities of these gunmen, many of whom claim, doubtfully, to be members of the Kuwaiti resistance movement.

The seafront corniche is filled daily with Kuwaitis still celebrating their liberation, but many are now brandishing automatic rifles, firing in delight over the roofs of nearby buildings, including the British and American embassies.

In Hwali, there is evidence enough that the Palestinian community is in grave danger. Sara Moussa, for example, watched both her sons, Tahseen and Amin, taken from their home on Friday morning by six Kuwaitis armed with rifles. 'They searched our home, they tied their hands and blindfolded them,' she said. 'When they told the Kuwaitis not to touch their sisters, the gunmen beat them with their rifles. Then they put them both in the trunk of a car and drove them away. I have not seen them since.'

Tamam Salman's 23-year-old son, Ibrahim, was taken by gunmen at the same time, thrown into the boot of a car and driven away. She says that when she asked for help from a Kuwaiti policeman, he spat at her 'because I am a Palestinian'. Few Kuwaitis, of course, would shed any tears for the two women, one of whom, weeping bitterly, seized a Koran and swore upon the book that her sons never collaborated with the Iraqis. Kuwaitis also living in Hwali call the Palestinians hypocrites. 'I had a Palestinian friend who worked for the Iraqis,' a Kuwait student told me. 'One day, during the occupation, I saw him on a road checkpoint with Iraqi soldiers, looking for some Kuwaitis. I turned my car away so he would not find me. He was my friend, but he collaborated. How can we trust the Palestinians now?'

But not all Palestinians did collaborate. The Kuwaiti resistance say that five per cent of their members were Palestinians but Yasser Arafat's alliance with Saddam Hussein and the sheer numbers of murders and kidnappings committed by the Iraqis have largely destroyed the relationship between Palestinians and Kuwaitis. The American military authorities, despite warnings from the British and the Red Cross, still seem to act in ignorance of this.

When three Kuwaiti soldiers began to beat up a Palestinian boy on a bicycle in Hwali yesterday, Colin Smith of the *Observer* and I intervened, physically restraining the Kuwaiti troops and ordering them to lower their weapons. Several of the Kuwaiti armoured vehicles were flying American flags. But the Special Forces troops accompanying the Kuwaitis did nothing to help. When I asked the American officer why he allowed the Kuwaitis to beat civilians, he replied: 'You having a nice day? We don't want your sort around here with your dirty rumours. You have a big mouth. This is martial law, boy. Fuck off.'

US officers at the American embassy in Kuwait City confirmed that the troops involved were from the Special Forces when the *Indepedent* provided them with the serial number of their Humvee military vehicle. 'We're having problems all over the city,' one officer said. 'We've had a colonel of ours threatened by armed men. Things are getting completely out of control.'

US Special Forces attached to the Kuwaitis have no names on their tunics, but have small Kuwaiti flags stitched to their uniforms. US policy is to refuse to take any part in internal policing in Kuwait City lest American troops become sucked into a civil war, as they did in Lebanon in 1983. But unless they can impose discipline on the Kuwaiti forces here – and on some of their own Special Forces troops – they may have no option.

The Emir, Sheikh Jaber al-Ahmed al-Sabah, and the Crown Prince, Sheikh Saad al-Abdullah al-Salem al-Sabah, remain in Saudi Arabia, allegedly unable to return home because Kuwait is still thought not safe enough for their presence. In the meantime, opposition leaders are increasing their demands for democracy. Many in the resistance movement support the opposition – and the resistance still has its guns.

THE IRAQIS' REVENGE
Richard Ellis
Sunday Times, March 10, 1991

The body of the teenager dangled from the lamp post. He had been shot through the head. A message, scrawled in Arabic on a piece of dirty cardboard, was tucked into his trousers: 'Death to all traitors.'

The youth, aged perhaps no more than 16, had taken part in demonstrations against Saddam Hussein in the southern Iraqi town of Zubair. According to witnesses, he had been captured by soldiers loyal to Saddam, beaten, then dragged by his hair to the main square, where he was shot and his body strung up.

The summary execution was, according to refugees who have fled southern Iraq over the past 10 days, one of scores carried out by Republican Guards after they crushed anti-Saddam revolts in Basra, Iraq's second city, and other towns in the region.

It was a reminder that while Iraq's downtrodden masses appear to have had enough of Saddam's regime, he retains formidable power. Despite continuing unrest that had apparently spread to Baghdad, he has a merciless, though shaky, grip.

His revenge against those who took to the streets in more than a dozen towns showed, if anyone doubted it, that he has no qualms about using violence against his own people. The repression practised against Kuwaitis during the occupation is now being carried out against Iraqis in a desperate attempt to hold on to power.

The victims reportedly include women and children and anyone suspected of harbouring anti-Saddam sentiments. Hundreds are said to have been shot on the streets while demonstrating: others have been arrested and put in prison. On Friday, the opposition claimed 30,000 had died inside Iraq.

The policy of repression appeared to be succeeding. Despite claims from opposition groups outside the country that they controlled several towns, including Basra, refugees said Republican Guards were back in control. The refugees, mostly Egyptians and Kuwaitis held in jails in southern Iraq since they were seized by Iraqi soldiers in Kuwait City, said they had witnessed the mass demonstrations that followed the end of the war.

Farouk Wadan, an Egyptian who had been in Zubair, said the Islamic-inspired uprising had ended when tanks and armoured personnel carriers from a guard division rolled into the town on Tuesday. 'The demonstrators were armed with rifles and machine guns but it was a very unequal fight,' he said. 'Tanks were firing into houses and other buildings, just blowing them apart. It was complete chaos. Some ordinary soldiers had joined the revolutionaries and it was hard to tell who was on whose side. There were guns going off everywhere.'

Wadan and other refugees said the fighting had subsided by Thursday and they decided to leave. As they set out for Kuwait, they saw troops combing the streets and entering houses. It was then he witnessed the retribution being carried out by the soldiers.

'We saw a teenager, no more than a schoolchild, being dragged by his hair across the main square by three or four soldiers. One of them shot him in the head and then tied a rope around his body to string him up from a lamppost,' Wadan said.

'I saw one of them write out something on a piece of card and stick it in the boy's trousers before they pulled him up. Then they left him dangling there and I went over to see what it said. It was obviously a warning to others. It read "Death to all traitors".'

Yousef, another Egyptian, said he had seen groups of demonstrators shouting, 'Down with Saddam'. Then, he said, the guard began moving into Basra. 'I saw one captain firing his pistol repeatedly into a crowd of demonstrators,' he said. 'Other soldiers fired, too. They were just slaughtering the people.'

Several refugees claimed Iranian soldiers had appeared on the streets of Basra to support the rebellion. 'I saw a group of armed Iranians, in uniform, with the crowds,' one Egyptian said. 'They had come across, they said, to help the Islamic revolution.'

Kuwaitis released from an army prison on the outskirts of Basra on Friday said the people's revolt had come close to gaining control of the city but had finally been defeated. Yousef Basri, a 33-year-old flight engineer with Kuwaiti Airways, said soldiers guarding him and 1,200 other Kuwaitis had come to them one night last week saying they were about to leave and that they would unlock the doors to their cells.

'In the end, though, they didn't go,' said Basri. 'I think the rebels had come close to us – we could hear fighting all around us – but were then beaten back. Basri and his fellow Kuwaitis came home in triumph on Friday after the Iraqi Army asked the Red Cross to organise their return. There were tearful, chaotic scenes at a Kuwait

City hospital as the men were reunited with their families.

They had been held, 350 men to a barracks measuring just 15 feet by 120 feet, in appalling conditions. They survived by collecting rainwater through holes in the roof. Even when they were about to be freed, the Iraqis exploited the prisoners, demanding money for the lorries that were to take them to meet the Red Cross near the Kuwaiti border.

The ordeal for the snatched Kuwaitis had ended. For others, though, the nightmare continued. At the Kuwaiti-Iraqi border a burgeoning roadside refugee camp has grown up, composed mostly of Egyptians, Indians, Sri Lankans and even some Kuwaitis without proper papers who have been refused entry.

Wadan, the Egyptian who fled Zubair, was sheltering there with his wife and five young children, their home made of cardboard boxes. For warmth, many of the camp inhabitants have been forced to take blankets which had been covering the corpses of Iraqi soldiers.

Without any proper relief organisation yet set up, they rely on handouts of combat rations, Meals Ready To Eat, from nearby American troops. Many of the children beg from any passing soldier. Wadan, holding two of his listless children in his arms, said they had walked for two days to reach the sanctuary of Kuwait. 'Doesn't Kuwait have a heart?' he asked. 'I worked there for years, and is this now how they repay me?'

HE WHO FIGHTS AND RUNS AWAY ... LIVES TO FIGHT ANOTHER DAY.

THE ZIGGURAT –
NEARLY A CASUALTY

Richard Dowden

Independent, March 7, 1991

It is, they say, where Western civilisation began – one of mankind's first towns and identified in the Bible as the home of Abraham. Standing on top of the Ziggurat, the scene looked more like the place where civilisation ended.

To reach it, we had come through apolcalyptic scenes of destruction reminiscent of the Somme in 1916 or Hiroshima. And although the war is officially over and the allies are going home, the dying may not be done.

A biting gale drove the rain horizontally across the deserted mudflats around Ur. The whole site, including the tombs, which go down 100 feet, has been neglected and some are collapsing. The great mounds of excavated earth and pottery are forming into mud slides which threaten to refill the huge hole dug by archaeologists, as if the earth had chosen to re-bury such a civilisation which had come to this. Every few moments the wind carried the sound of another explosion as US demolition teams detonated ammunition dumps, military vehicles, bunkers and weaponry.

The Ziggurat itself, one of the oldest man-made monuments in the world, was within seconds of being destroyed by allied fire last week. Colonel David Wood, of the 101st Airborne Division, said he had targeted the Ziggurat among bunkers and other military installations when his strike force attacked the nearby airfield. He had been about to order his men to fire when one of his officers noticed the monument on the map.

The building, about 300 feet high, has suffered no damage, though we found 50mm cartridge cases on top and there was evidence that guns had been installed. The modern building near by, which had housed the curator, was occupied by Iraqi solders and is severely damaged. A few hundred yards from the Ziggurat are two burnt-out Iraqi Army lorries – a tribute to the accuracy of allied targeting. Less than a mile away is the entrance to an air base. Along the runway allied bombing has blasted holes you could drop a bus into, along lines of fighter aircraft. I counted 28, ranging from the latest Soviet-built MiG-29 to ageing MiG-23s. Some lie broken-backed or flipped over in the mud as if some vengeful giant had kicked and stamped his way across the airfield. Others are no more than shattered heaps of melted metal. On the few that survived the onslaught, camouflage netting – which failed so spectacularly to hide them – flapped in the gale.

On the way north to here, the little oasis settlement of Busayyah had been continually bombed by allies, then hit by a French armoured column. It had once had about 200 buildings. None of them was untouched and many were simply heaps of rubble. You could smell death from some way off but, incredibly, 200 Iraqi soldiers walked out of these ruins to give themselves up.

The road past Ur is a six-lane motorway, now virtually deserted except for American patrols. All along it are the sickening remains of convoys and civilian cars hit by allied air fire a week ago. The bodies and bits of bodies still lie across the road or have been fixed in cremated motion as they tried to scramble to safety. Near some lorries which have not burned are boxes and suitcases, burst open and exposing the sentimentality of soldiers bringing home a brightly coloured scarf or dress or a pair of children's shoes.

The US forces set up a Civil Affairs Department post on the motorway five nights ago. On the first night they gave food and water to 1,200 people and provided fuel for the trucks and cars loaded down with household goods. Most stayed the night in their cars to keep out of the cold, but American soldiers said the keening and wailing of those who had lost relatives that day had kept everyone awake all night. They are Iraqi Army deserters, Kuwaitis returning from captivity in Iraq, Kuwaiti families looking for abducted relatives, or local people made homeless by the war.

One group of 34 people from one village had lost 16 killed and suffered 13 wounded during a tank battle. Others are Bedouin or Palestinians who have lived and worked in Kuwait all their lives but who were never given Kuwaiti citizenship. Many were forced to go to Iraq during the occupation but now, when they try to return home, the Kuwaitis are turning them away.

Captain Sholla Swift, the commander of the camp, said he had seen horrific shrapnel wounds, severe burns and many other injuries in the past five days as well as measles, dysentery, malnutrition and dehydration. Two nights ago, when I stayed overnight in the camp, there was one family of 13, eight of whom had been turned back from Kuwait. Five had been let in. They were in a saloon car piled high with mattresses and suitcases. The children were dehydrated and hungry and the four-month-old baby died in the night. Captain Swift exploded with rage next morning, demanding to know why his men had not woken him so that he could have got the baby to a field hospital. This unit, like all US forces on the Euphrates, is expected to leave today or by the weekend. When they go, the last drop of outside help will be lost as the region, already smashed by a month of bombing and the ground war, plunges into civil war.

One Iraqi walking along the road was so cold and wet he could scarcely speak. He pleaded: 'We beg the world to keep allied forces here until we have a new king or someone to replace Saddam. You should tell the world about us. You must tell the world what it is like here.'

SADDAM'S CHAMBER OF HORRORS
Harvey Morris
Independent, March 4, 1991

Across a pleasant lawn shaded by conifer trees lies the recreation area for the officers of the *Amn* State Internal Security and their families. An alley of mushroom-shaped lights leads into the restaurant area and on to an inner courtyard. It is conveniently situated for Saddam Hussein's little chamber of horrors which lies 10 yards behind.

Much of the complex was gutted by fire on March 11 when Kurdish guerrillas and the towns-people of Arbil attacked. But the windowless cells – four feet square and into which three or four blindfolded prisoners would be crammed – are still intact; so are the torture rooms with niches in the wall for whips, steel cables and equipment for administering electric shocks.

In each ceiling there are heavy iron hooks. During torture sessions, according to our *peshmerga* guide who was once held there, prisoners would be stripped naked, suspended by their feet, doused with water and then beaten for several hours by up to six interrogators; then the electricity would be applied. The routine was always the same but there were added sophistications: sometimes the torturers would tie a sack around their victim's loins, then torment a cat and put the cat inside the sack. If a new prisoner was unwise enough to plead for water, the guards would urinate into his mouth.

Down the hall is a room, 40 feet long and 15 wide, with a metal bar set nine inches from the floor and running its full length. Naked prisoners would be manacled to the bar and beaten. Two sets of handcuffs hung from metal grilles set into the far wall. Beyond the room lay a charred corpse and outside was another half-burnt body, the left leg lying some yards off, its femur cleanly broken.

Behind the cell block, in what was once a school, is a large auditorium facing a proscenium stage. In the ceiling above the stage are rows of iron hooks, a dozen in all. There is no floor to the stage, but instead a row of steel girders running from back to front. The pit beneath is entered by a side door from a sheltered courtyard. Prisoners would be brought through the side door, stood on the girders with ropes around their necks and then kicked away until they hanged. Senior officials of the Ba'ath Party and invited guests would sit in the auditorium to watch the spectacle.

A few blocks away is the headquarters of the *Estikhbarat*, Iraq's military intelligence service, in charge of repressing organised opposition to the regime. This was where suspected *peshmerga* from throughout the northern region were brought for interrogation. Again, there are the tiny cells, their high windows crudely bricked up, one fetid lavatory for an entire wing. In one corner lay a broken charred bucket filled with indistinguishable slime which carried the distinctive sweet stench of rotting human flesh.

I tried to locate some of the former inmates of the *Amn* and *Estikhbarat* cells at Arbil but was told that they had been taken south by their jailers as last month's uprising spread across Kurdistan. They had left behind their signatures, however, scrawled on the cell walls: 'Javad Mahmouri, June 10/89, by the grace of God,' 'Siyamend Zafar' – 'I knew him,' said our guide, Saleh, 'he was from Shaklawa. He was killed.' Someone had scored a crude heart pierced by an arrow. On the opposite wall was a list of prisoners, all from the same village, including a Christian woman, Katerina Abdnadif Hadi.

Above Arbil, at the mountain village of Kalifan, we spent the night at the home of a local *peshmerga* leader. During the course of the evening, 14 guerrilla fighters called in off patrol for glasses of sweet tea.

It turned out that four of them had been held for up to a year at the *Estikhbarat* headquarters at Arbil and, separately, they gave remarkably similar accounts of their treatment. They all survived by obeying the elementary rule of never confessing, even when threatened with castration – to confess is to invite instant death. One man, clearly describing his own experiences but ashamed to relate them in front of his fellow fighters, said the torturers routinely inserted broomsticks and beer bottles into the rectums of their victims. Throughout their detention they were blindfolded in their cells. They were taken out only to be tortured, usually for three sessions a week.

'In the very cold weather,' said Suleiman, 'they would strip us to our underwear, tie us up and put us in the open; then they would pour cold water over us and stub out cigarettes on our body.' Mohamed, released only in January, showed me a deep burn on his wrist he said was caused by an electric shock, a burn on his left shoulder from a cigarette and a scar in his left foot where a nail had been hammered through. 'In front of me, they brought in two brothers and forced them to sodomise each other. Other people were castrated. One prisoner, Ghafour Taimor from Qisinjak, died after they beat him for nine hours with cable wire, taking it in turns two by two.'

The secret police are probably back in now, cleaning up the rubble of files left by the rebels. They will no doubt wreak a terrible revenge. At the *Estikhbarat* headquarters they tried to hide in the air conditioning ducts. The guerillas smashed the walls and dragged them out. One wall in the courtyard is smeared with blood and scarred by bullet holes where 28 torturers were executed. 'The *peshmerga* didn't want to do it,' said Saleh, 'but the people insisted. They stood outside in their thousands, shouting, 'Kill them, kill them, kill them.'

THE AFTERMATH

IS NEWSNIGHT WORTH MORE THAN THE 7TH ARMOURED BRIGADE?

John Keegan

Spectator and *Daily Telegraph*, March 1, 1991

I told you so is not a charitable phrase. In fairness to myself, let me say that I have never before uttered it in print. If I cannot choke it off this week, it is for a simple reason. It is that what I have thought from the outset of Operation Desert Shield would be the certain outcome of Operation Desert Storm now stares us in the face.

I can say 'I told you so' because, in an article I wrote on Christmas Eve last year, I forecast that the Iraqi Air Force would be eliminated from the war without any significant loss to the allied side and that once the ground war began, with the Iraqi Air Force absent, the Iraqi Army would run away. I take no satisfaction in saying 'I told you so'. I write the words nevertheless with considerable emotion. I did not begin life as a journalist. For most of my years I have been an academic military historian. For the last five years, however, journalism has been my profession. For my fellow print journalists, I early conceived and retain a warm affection and regard. But in the case of some of those who practise the profession in the television medium their coverage of the war has filled me with burning contempt.

It is the television opinion-makers who have aroused my ire. The Dimbleby brothers and Jeremy Paxman, in particular, seem to me to have betrayed their responsibilities to a contemptible degree. I have watched them in action in the past. Then, however, it was politics or economics that was their subject and politicians or economists who were their victims. They are fair game.

Politics and economics – economics even more than politics – are subjects where opinion is king. It is perfectly acceptable, indeed desirable, that practitioners of those subjects should be coaxed into taking an exposed position, at which the interviewer then chips away by intelligent questioning.

When it is well done, television interviewing of that sort renders a public service. The television grandees who have won their reputations by that technique deserve their high standing, at least as long as they confine themselves to areas of opinion only.

Strategy is not, however, a matter of opinion – not at least in the circumstances of the Kuwait war. There is a Soviet concept, 'the correlation of forces', which deserves to be rescued from the wreckage of Marxism. What it lays down is that, when two sides become locked in conflict, there is an objective means of determining which is likely to prove the victor.

It requires close and careful analysis of all the resources available to the two sides – quantity and quality of equipment, match of types, stocks of ammunitions, size, nature and output of the defence industries, numbers of trained personnel – an evaluation of the operating conditions on the front of engagement and how they favour one side or the other, an assessment of the morale of the forces engaged and so on. When two contestants are evenly or closely matched, 'the correlation of forces' is not an easy exercise. Had the television opinion-makers been faced with a situation such as prevailed between Iran and Iraq in 1980, they should have been forgiven for confessing bafflement. It baffled all who attempted it. When, however, one side is as overwhelmingly outmatched as the Iraqis have been by the coalition ever since President Bush announced on November 2 that he was doubling the number of American forces in the Gulf, 'the correlation of forces' is an open and shut case.

On one side stood a country of 18 million Third World people, without a defence industry and with an armoury of second-hand Soviet equipment which could not be replaced if lost in combat. On the other stood three of the strongest states in the First World, with a combined population of 350 million, which are respectively the first, third and fourth international suppliers of advanced military equipment.

Their armed forces are at the peak of world military efficiency and, by the time the United Nations deadline ran out on January 15, the army they had assembled in the Gulf equalled in numbers that which Saddam had deployed in Kuwait, while their air forces outnumbered his by four times. The facts were so stark that the layman could conclude that once battle was joined the Iraqis would be overwhelmed in a few days of fighting. Have the television grandees told us any such thing? They have not.

On the contrary: for day after day they have strung us along, turning an open-and-shut case into a cliffhanger. Sober, responsible military experts, many of them retired officers of high rank, have been brought to the studio to state facts and opinions similar to those I have outlined above, only to hear, in the familiar way, their considered advice being

290

chipped away in the condescending, imperious, incredulous tone which is now the received style wherever the television grandees hold sway. In an earlier article I called the refusal of the grandees to listen 'the higher ignorance'. But now I think it is worse than that. It is a petulant determination not to learn, lest learning interfere with the right they have established for themselves over the years to know better than anyone they interview.

If what they were offering were 'just television', as most transmissions are, that would not matter. But a whole nation has necessarily had to hang on the narcissistic grandees' words for the last months. Worse, tens of thousands of viewers who are relatives and friends of our servicemen in the Gulf have had their anxieties stretched day after day by the relentless expression of professional doubt that the grandees have turned on anyone who dared to utter the simple truth that the allies were bound to win and to win without serious loss among the ranks of the soldiers, sailors and airmen who had gone to the Gulf to do their duty.

I do not know Jeremy Paxman, either of the Dimblebys or any of the other television grandees. I do know many of the soldiers. Some I taught as cadets at Sandhurst, many were my colleagues there or at the Staff college. I know their wives and families. I know the lives they have lived during the 20 years when the Cold War reached its climax. I know that they have scraped, on salaries which would not cover a television grandee's lunches, to keep up appearances, pay their debts and educate their children. I know they have spent months of each year living on cold rations in bleak training areas on the North German plain to wear down the will of the Soviet Union in its confrontation with democracy.

I know that they have lived under a code of behaviour that the television world would regard as an intolerable restriction of individual liberty. I know that their professional lives have been governed by standards of efficiency so rigorous that a single uncomplimentary report can blight a whole career. I know, in short, that they are people of a quality scarcely to be found anywhere in the kingdom today. What is more, I know that the kingdom values them for what they are.

We may well recognise with hindsight that the most successful national institution of the post-1945 years is the British Army – a title that the BBC perhaps deserved when it was the most respected broadcasting institution in the world, but which it has now lost. The army has stoically kept order in Northern Ireland for 20 years without suffering the least taint of political involvement. It has efficiently performed any essential service – fire-fighting, ambulance driving, rubbish collection – left undone by public employees on strike. It won the Falklands war with a despatch that the American Army has clearly been at pains to emulate ever since. With the American Army, it garrisoned the Iron Curtain until the Soviet Union dismantled it in despair.

This wonderful national institution lies under the threat of returning from a historic, just and necessary victory, which will benefit the whole world for decades to come, to face heavy demobilisations under the programme of budgetary reductions known as Options for Change. The British Army, 150,000 strong, probably costs some £4.5 billion a year to maintain. The BBC, which employs 23,000 people, costs £1.5 billion a year. Each BBC employee, in short, costs about twice as much as a soldier.

If, from our pockets, we have to choose between paying taxes for the army or licences for the BBC, which do we think better deserves the outlay? Is *Newsnight* worth more than the 7th Armoured Brigade? Do the smooth men of our screens better deserve their livelihoods than the quiet and unassuming friends of my youth who have led their soldiers to victory on the Euphrates?

THE CULT OF THE BRUTAL SOLDIER

Edward Pearce

Guardian, March 6, 1991

The rage of victors is never pretty but sometimes instructive. The war press has been full of a soul-curdling exultancy at what their boys have done. The cult of the brutal soldier is extensive among brutal journalists.

But the other part of the exercise has been the bad-mouthing of the opponents of war. According to Norman Stone, a good man fallen among adjectives, we at the *Guardian* have been Saddam Hussein's hot-water bottle for the past month, we have been an adjunct to the little pink cloud of drug-induced euphoria which has sustained him. In fairness, Norman Stone goes on to say what a useful paper this is, apart from our tepid-souled response to a great occasion which he celebrates as a four-day turkey shoot.

The burden of our critics is that the opponents failed to see that it would all be easy. John Keegan in the *Spectator* sums up the initial military balance: 'On one side stood a country of 18 million Third World people without a defence industry and with an armoury of second hand Soviet equipment . . . on the other stood three of the strongest states in the First World . . . the first third and fourth international suppliers of advanced military equipment . . .Their armed forces are at the peak of world military efficiency . . . their air forces out-numbered (Saddam's) by four times. The facts were so stark that the simplest layman could conclude that once battle was joined, the Iraqis would be overwhelmed in a few days of fighting.'

I don't expect to see a more spectacular own goal from a strategist. Keegan has conceded that this was a victory of the strong against the weak, of the armed against the naked, of the killer against a standing target. Given his premises, no part, not a single rifle shot, never mind the ignited clouds of petrol vapour, was necessary. The bombing of the M25 which after he wrote would mark the last few days, was thus undistinguishable from terrorism. If your enemy is doomed anyway according to military logic, if he is then running away, burning him to death from above is a purely recreational activity, fulfilling no needs except psychological ones better not discussed.

We contemptible subversives should be grateful to John Keegan. He has made the strongest case yet against the moral foundations of this soiled and degrading war.

That however isn't all he does. The purpose of his piece (reproduced in the *Daily Telegraph*) is to denounce Jeremy Paxman (and David Dimbleby forsooth) who 'seem to me to have betrayed their responsibilities to a contemptible degree'. These people, described with a telling little whine as 'the narcissistic television grandees', have caused all sorts of relatives of our troops to worry unnecessarily by dragging on all sorts of retired military types and nagging them about possible difficulties.

In other words, the vile Paxman (who incidentally *didn't* interview any military men) has rotted fibre by raising the possibility of the turkey shoot proving dangerous. Keegan, inside the military compound, takes a trade union view of his peer group, rages at the BBC for bothering military wives and for not seeing that his crisp, cost-effective, proficient killers could do the job without incomoding a single bridge rubber in Camberley.

(He has an envious whinge, of which Clive Jenkins would be proud, about the superior conditions of the hated television grandees compared to officers 'living on cold rations on the North German plains to wear down the will of the Soviet Union in its confrontation with democracy'. Cue crepuscular violins as chorus of officers weep into their gin.)

He proceeds though to something much more scary. The military 'returning from a historic, just and necessary victory which will benefit the world for decades to come' are in danger of being cut back if the peace dividend is drawn. The BBC which engages in despicable debate about the war, though it costs only a third of the bill for the army, is more inefficient by the unit.

What follows is out of Wonderland: 'If we have to choose between the Royal Scots now crossing the desert to cut off the retreat of the Republican Guard and Panorama no doubt already working itself up to point out all the difficulties that peace in the Gulf will bring, to which do we think we should commit future revenue? Is *Newsnight* worth more than the 7th Armoured Brigade?'

The fribble in me would like to suggest that the British Army should be available, like the BBC, by means of a licence fee. Those of us who find life pleasanter and more conducive to intelligent conversation without it, being able to forego stroppy men with short hair.

But things are more serious than that. Mr Keegan, whom I had thought to be a thoughtful soldier (author of *The Face Of Battle*), I would have expected to have been one of those decent ex-officers who would react to the war by wincing and saying like Cromwell, 'Cruel necessity'. Here he is talking like the most lamentable barker for his caste, one of Sassoon's 'Scarlet Majors at the base'. There has been a dreadful coarsening.

Worse than that, he offers the image of a thin-lipped man in gloves requiring national discipline and swivelling a tank-turret to that end in a city square. One tries to avoid using that beaten-panel of a word, fascism, but it is an effort.

But the real burden of his desolating piece is that military brass fears the loss of status and trade which the Soviet diminuendo ought to bring. Like Arthur Scargill without the charm, Keegan speaks for a close knit community whose way of life is threatened with the scrapheap because some heartless accountant mentality declares it uneconomic. He is arguing for Cortonwood, Cortonwood with kill-power.

The sadness of such talk is that the opponents of the war, though we may mock the soldiery, are *not* against them. The forces are professional, highly skilled and brave and I would pay a decent licence fee for them. Rather we are against a war not historic nor just nor necessary. We think soldiers have been asked to do things, like the slaughter of the retreat, which offend against the name of soldiering and against the human spirit.

There was another soldier in a tank turret. The *Observer* depicted him, an Iraqi, his flesh turned to mud which had been ignited; he smiled with the rictus of third degree burns and he had been burned until the jagged edges of his dead face made him look like Jack Frost. *That* is what we have been against.

BUSH EXORCISES THE GHOST OF VIETNAM

Xan Smiley

Sunday Telegraph, March 3, 1991

And so George Bush has exorcised the ghost of Vietnam. Two decades of American self-doubt and self-flagellation have been laid to rest among the smouldering tanks and corpses and debris of Kuwait.

For this, Americans know they owe a huge debt of gratitude to their president.

Many Americans thought Ronald Reagan made America 'walk tall' again. True, up to a point. But many never quite believed it.

As Mr Bush rests this weekend at Camp David, his Maryland woodland retreat in the Catoctin Mountains, he knows he has pulled off a stunning personal and national triumph that sets the seal on the joyous collapse over the past two years of the Soviet empire and the end of the Cold War. For the first time, an American president stands astride what is now fashionably called a 'unipolar globe'.

The past week has been a watershed for Bush and for America. One commentator hailed this week's victory over Iraq as 'the beginning of the second American century . . . We are the most influential nation in the world. We've beaten the totalitarians of the right, then of the left and now the bandits, all in a half-century's work.'

Even Bush's worst enemies cannot get away from the fact that unless the economy stumbles terribly before the next presidential elections in 1992, Mr Bush is set to hold the greatest office in the world until 1997.

'Good night, Vietnam,' ran the opening line of the *Wall Street Journal* on Friday. 'Those who doubted George Bush's nerve and geopolitical acumen owe him something of an apology,' wrote the *New Republic*, Washington's leading political weekly. 'That includes us,' the editors humbly added, though they strongly supported his actions.

Other powerful voices must eat far larger slices of humble pie. The *New York Times* has sniped, complained, counselled greater patience and generally tried to drag the president back at every single crucial turn of events in the past seven months. A front-page headline on Wednesday referred to 'Bush's luck in war'. But by Friday, the newspaper admitted for the first time: 'The world that overestimated Saddam Hussein also underestimated George Bush.'

The skill far outweighed the luck. From the moment Kuwait was invaded, Mr Bush had to make one hard decision after another, often against the grain of public opinion, invariably against the counsels of the liberal media, and frequently against the advice of Congress. In sharp contrast to many previous presidents, notably Lyndon Johnson and Jimmy Carter, the only body of opinion to which he tended to defer was the military. At every important juncture, he has been proved right.

Of course there have been blemishes. The diplomacy before August was clearly inept. And the Secretary of State, James Baker, so skilful elsewhere, has been cavalier in flicking off responsibility. The Administration's worst failure was its tardiness and inconsistency in fixing on a coherent set of reasons for opposing Iraq so fiercely.

Some diplomatic glitches could have been avoided, among them the irritating juggling over dates of the last-ditch meeting before January 15, when Saddam took advantage of American carelessness.

The idea that he has seen the venture as a personal duel, yet another attempt to expunge the overblown 'wimp factor', holds little water. Mr Bush was never a wimp. That sense of weakness in character, still seen by many critics, is projected by an undue reliance on opinion polls, an innate time-worn politician's desire to cut deals and compromise, a lack of driving ideology or vision of radical change. The feeling also persists that Mr Bush's patrician background makes him overcompensate, to show himself as a macho man of the people to fit American presidential mythology.

But this time he has proved beyond doubt that if he feels strongly, the polls and the deal cutters can go to hell. For seven months he has taken risk after risk when failure might very well have destroyed his presidency.

The first risk was sending the vast army at all. Five days after the invasion, an early poll showed most Americans to be against the deployment.

The next big risk was on November 8, when he decided to double the size of the desert army – amid charges that he had changed his aims without telling anybody. True, the early emphasis had been on defending Saudi Arabia. But it was obvious from the outset that 'this aggression will not stand' meant force might have to be used to free Kuwait.

Next was the daring decision, which would have been unthinkably rash three years ago, to seek backing in the United Nations Security Council. It was here that the skills of Mr Baker were triumphantly displayed. But once again it was Mr Bush's background in the UN, in Peking, in the CIA, even in the Texas oil business, that was invaluable in corralling so disparate a group into virtual unison.

The next risk was the setting of a deadline – 'an artificial deadline' as detractors put it – an upping of the ante to show Saddam that the threat of counter-attack was real. This, of course, accompanied Bush's judgement that economic sanctions, though effective in hemming in the Iraqis, would not alone force Saddam to leave Kuwait. Many knowledgeable soldiers and diplomats disagreed. The argument cannot be proved either way. But the seepage of goods across the Jordanian and Iranian borders and the do-or-die psychology that the Iraqi president increasingly displayed once war began put the weight of judgement heavily in Mr Bush's favour.

The following big gamble was taking on a shilly-shallying Congress – and winning by a bee's whisker. That, in retrospect, was one of the toughest tasks of all.

Later, American success in persuading Israel not to retaliate against Iraq for the Scud missile attacks must be chalked up as one of the Bush-Baker diplomacy's biggest triumphs, enabling the Arab front to hold against Saddam.

But perhaps Mr Bush's finest hour was when, in the face of much of world opinion, he ignored the Soviet Union's last-minute meddling while managing to retain cordiality with President Gorbachev, in the hope that military victory would be quick and comprehensive enough to prevent Saddam slipping off the hook.

Indeed, events proved that the timing of the ground war, when polls a few days before had shown that three-quarters of Americans wanted the aerial bombardment to continue on its own, was masterly. Thanks to Generals Norman Schwarzkopf and Colin Powell for that, but thanks too to Bush for having the nerve to heed them.

In the moment of victory, the tone set by Mr Bush and echoed across America has been remarkably unjingoistic. 'To be very honest with you, I haven't yet felt this wonderfully euphoric feeling that many of the American people feel,' the president said on Friday, adding with typical cautious understatement: 'I still have a little bit of an unfinished agenda.'

While Mr Bush is set to follow military victory with another diplomatic assault on the underlying issues of the Middle East – a task that will prove a good deal harder – many Americans still gravely doubt their ability to lead the world.

But Mr Bush is eminently comfortable as a global leader. In an old-fashioned sort of way perhaps reminiscent of upper-class Victorian Britons, he assumes that the United States must do good, and should risk making bad mistakes, by projecting power from time to time far beyond its borders. Winston Churchill's line that 'the hope of the world lies in the strength and will of the United States' has recently been approvingly quoted by friends of the president. Mr Bush, it is clear, believes it. Perhaps more Americans will too.

True, in a year's time people may be grumbling about the economy and Bush may be struggling to keep it afloat, though most economists are fairly bullish. There is still a chance that the removal of the Vietnam syndrome may give way to a recurrence of the Churchill syndrome – a conqueror in war ignominiously ditched by his own people in peace. But the chances of that must be slender indeed.

Doubtless Bush will soon show that his touch on domestic matters is less sure. For a man who has tried to call himself 'the education President', there was the fascinatingly fitting revelation last week that he finally decided to launch the air war when his mind began to wander during a White House meeting with leading educationalists. As their voices 'droned on', in the words of a Bush confidant, his thoughts focused elsewhere. At the end of the meeting he strode into the operations room in the basement and gave the generals the go-ahead.

Orator he is not, nor ever will be. Mr Bush the speaker is at his best when betraying rare but genuine emotion, when grappling with hard questions, when 'shooting the breeze' with world leaders at the end of the telephone – using his tactical and diplomatic skills, however inelegantly, and digging into his immense reservoir of worldly-wise experience.

His is still a hard personality to pin down. But the events of the past seven months have enhanced his image as a man who is tough, has extraordinarily good judgement and timing, and is fundamentally decent. Perhaps the word that describes him best is canny. And since August 2 he has shown exceptional courage. The old charge that he cannot lead is forever dead.

Above all most Americans will still feel that, whatever his shortcomings at home, their president is a safe pair of hands when it comes to keeping their country secure and influential in the world.

Can one imagine the worthy Mr Michael Dukakis, whose most notable foreign policy pitch was to promise to relocate the American embassy in Israel to Jerusalem, handling the past seven months with the same cool deftness?

This week even the most dyed-in-the-wool American Democrat, who may find good reason to vote against him in 1992, could have found himself muttering: 'Thank God for George Bush.'

A QUIET DEFEAT FOR THE DOGS OF PEACE

Robert Harris

Sunday Times, March 3, 1991

Whatever happened to the peace movement during the Gulf war? Rather like the Iraqi Air Force, it was expected to play an important role in the conflict. The allied leaders were braced for it. Instead, it largely disappeared in the early days of fighting and never gave the military much cause for concern thereafter. It is something of a mystery. Why did the dogs of peace so conspicuously fail to bark?

The most obvious reason is that Operation Desert Storm was vastly popular. Many in the anti-war movement put this down to what Paul Foot, writing in the *London Review of Books*, called 'the chauvinist mass' of the press. And it is true that, with a handful of exceptions, the British media – especially its leader-writers and columnists – supported the war.

But the attitude of the commentators was a symptom of that popular support rather than a cause of it. I supported military action myself, but I can assure Mr Foot that I did not receive a sealed envelope from Mr Rupert Murdoch outlining my operational duties in the event of hostilities. I simply came to the same conclusion as eight-tenths of my fellow citizens.

Were we, then, all the victims of some vast disinformation effort, tricked into making up our minds on the basis of false evidence? Most of us received our information from television and radio. Far from pandering to the militarists, the influential programmes – *Newsnight, Panorama, Today, Channel 4 News* – bent over backwards (some would say, touched the floor with their elbows) in their efforts to spell out the appalling risks, the destruction wrought, the media management.

Very well. Were we all just misguided, then? Mr Foot thinks so. This was was not about the United Nations, about good versus evil, about standing up to dictators, or any of that pious claptrap. It was, in his words, about 'commercial interest – which in the Middle East can be reduced to a single word: oil'.

I could not agree more. Yes. Absolutely. No state in history has ever based its foreign policy upon altruism. It was not a desire to do good that led the United States and 32 other nations to join a coalition against Iraq – many, such as the US and Britain, risking severe economic problems, others such as Syria and Egypt risking civil war. It was, indeed, about oil. And what is wrong with that? It was long-term strategic and commercial interests, rather than any sudden, tender concern about the Poles, which led Britain and France to fight Germany in 1939. Does that make it any less right to have opposed Hitler?

Saddam Hussein would have used captured oil wealth as Hitler planned to use captured mineral and industrial wealth: to re-arm and expand. Sanctions would not have stopped him. His regime insulates him from the anger of his suffering people. He could have sat it out in Kuwait for years. The coalition would have collapsed: anyone who doubts that need only look at the changes in Moscow in the past few months.

The Gulf war was widely supported, and the peace campaigners marginalised, because this was one of those rare occasions (like the Second World War) when self-interest and standing up for the rights of a small country went hand in hand. It was sanctioned by the United Nations. It was democratically debated and approved by, among others, the British Parliament and the American Congress. It was undertaken only after Iraq had been given more than six months to comply with international law.

But, if it was legally just, was it also morally just? If you are a pacifist, placing the sanctity of life above all things, of course not. 'Pacifism,' in the words of Vera Brittain, who was a pacifist during the last world war, 'is nothing other than a belief in the ultimate transcendence of love over power. This belief comes from an inward assurance. It is untouched by logic and beyond arguments.' It was this faith in 'love over power' which led *Peace News*, the pacifist journal, in April 1944 to call upon the allies 'to lay down our arms and let the enemy do his will'.

That is pacifism without equivocation, honestly and frankly stated. Unfortunately, in this war, the peace movement – or, at least, its leaders – has not been prepared to be so frank. Instead, it has evaded the central question – which is, are you prepared to let wickedness triumph rather than shed innocent blood? – and has gone after soft targets, most notably 'American imperialism'.

I have been reading with care the journalism of Mr John Pilger in the *New Statesman*. He relies, week after week, like Beachcomber in the old *Daily Express*, on an unchanging cast of characters: a crippled Vietnam veteran (' "Wake up America!" he said and wheeled himself away'), a hapless conscript, 'an Iraqi doctor amputating the limb of a child without anaesthetic', and – inevitably, in contrast – some militaristic American Aunt Sally ('Colonel Richard "Snake" White') straight out of *Dr Strangelove*.

He proceeds to manipulate these cardboard figures in a fashion which imparts to the phrase 'holier than thou' a whole new meaning. He creates a kind of atrocity propaganda in reverse, in which all the evils of the world are Western. Scan a piece on the so-called deliberate terror bombing of civilians and the one word you will not find is 'Scud' – yet indiscriminate terror bombing of civilian areas using Scuds was Iraq's main strategy.

Wade through the descriptions of severed limbs and blasted bodies, and never, either, will you find the word 'Kuwaitis'. No mention here of the way in which the Iraqi secret police went into Kuwait City a few hours after the army and dragged away 'dissidents' to oblivion in Baghdad; no allusion to the thousands of doctors, teachers, lawyers – almost an entire civilian class – who have been removed to camps; the children shot; the women raped; the gouged-out eyes; the electric shocks. But then, why should he mention them? They're just the poor bloody Kuwaitis.

And this is why the peace movement has done so badly: because it has, both overtly and more subtly, painted the Kuwaitis as a non-nation – as a lot of rich, spoilt Arabs, whose country is merely a false creation of Western 'imperialists'. It has largely ignored their sufferings and concentrated its concern on the agonies of Iraq.

It has been, for Pilger especially, a trip back down the Vietnam memory lane, an opportunity for a bout of Americaphobia. It has accused the 'West' of arming Iraq and ignored the fact that most of Saddam's arms and expertise came from the Soviet Union. It has been as one-sided and manipulative as anything coming out of the Pentagon. It has not won popular support, and, frankly, it has not deserved to.

THE PACIFIST COTERIE ON THE PINK CLOUD

Norman Stone

Sunday Times, March 3, 1991

I have lately been contemplating what sort of penitence we should impose upon the various people who, directly or indirectly, offered aid and comfort to Saddam Hussein. According to Moscow rumour, he has spent the past seven months in a drug-induced haze. He has not been, as it were, himself. He has ruined his country. He has let 100,000 of his people be killed or maimed in pursuit of an utterly pointless war for somebody else's territory. His capital is in a mess. Nothing works. That the West, given time, would assemble the machinery that would shoot him to bits at almost no cost was predictable. Who, in these circumstances, will have kept Saddam going?

Out of Saddam's pink cloud, there will have emerged: Auberon Waugh; Enoch Powell; Jean-Marie Le Pen; Kurt Waldheim; Yasser Arafat; Emma Thompson, acting the part of Vanessa Redgrave; the Rt Hon Anthony Wedgwood Benn; Edward Heath; Denis Healey. All were very wrong. The people who deserve the greatest punishment – each other – are the supposed statesmen who should have understood something about the modern world. The rest deserve to be immured in a version of Sartre's *Huis Clos,* in which hell is the allies with whom you are perpetually cooped up.

There might, hovering around Saddam, be a curious presence: editorials from the *Guardian.* I think that he will have been told about these editorials and pondered: a paper that speaks for all that is most reflective and most learned in Britain is really in favour of letting me get away with my little lot, pink cloud and all?

The *Guardian* speaks for a great part of the British enlightenment, and its fingernails on this subject are very raw. It did not see that the war would be over in hours. It foresaw nothing like the tiny figures for allied casualties. It expected that sanctions against Iraq would work, whereas we now see from Kuwait that the Iraqi troops, killing and looting, were supplied with everything possible while they shovelled tortured victims into alleys. In my opinion, the *Guardian,* in this respect, has let itself down. It is itself a fine flower of Western liberalism: it should remember how far, since the days of Attila the Hun, that has needed to be defended.

Now I have great, great compunction in saying this. The *Guardian* is a very good newspaper indeed. I write for its books pages – always of a seriousness and intelligence which put the modishness of most other such pages to shame – and am glad to contribute on and off to the main paper. Its reporting on the Gulf has been of a high order. As far as the overall philosophy of the *Guardian* is concerned, I quite agree with the ends, if not the means, and altogether endorse the seriousness with which, say, matters of education or health are handled. It is also, rather often, fun to read. But, over the Gulf, it has been Saddam Hussein's mental tepid hot-water bottle, with some editorials that ought to have known better. The *Guardian* guarded; it was sanctimonious over sanctions; it went in for the quarter-truth.

The quarter-truths on this occasion were: war costs; it creates problems; there is always room for reasonable discussion; things might go wrong; there are motes in the eyes of Western civilisation; there are motes – maybe more than motes – in the sensible autocracy of Kuwait and the Gulf states; the United Nations represents a Good Thing; the West has been very silly and sometimes sinister in its dealings with Iraq. These things are not the less true for being 25 per cent of the truth.

But the *Guardian* has a serious responsibility. It speaks for a great part of the educated elements in this country – the teachers, the workers in local government, the health service. It represents an alliance that reaches from the lower ranks of public service, and the people who depend in various ways upon them, to academe: all those dons who apply adjectives such as 'ill-considered' to this war, and 'view with concern' the spending of a great deal more money on Patriot missiles than on dons. The alliance includes a great many people, by no means all of them on the left, who respect the newspaper. However, it has been wrong about the Iraqi war. We won, very easily, and this was a war that needed to be won. Does the *Guardian* want to figure in the history books as having got things wrong where the *Sun* got them right?

Looking back through the files of *Guardian* editorials is an odd experience. On the key occasions *Guardian* editorials have been there with the tepid hot-water bottle for the enemies of civilisation. They started off quite well. On August 3, there is condemnation of Saddam – though there is also an equation of his misdeeds with Suez, which does not, I think, work in terms of international law. On August 8, the sins of the West are recalled rightly: we made no stir about poor Farzad Bazoft, no doubt an unstable character, but not a bad egg. On August 21, Bush is ticked off for taking a holiday, and we note that he does not wish to appear to be a goof like Carter, who (a wonderful American expression which I retain from William Safire) did the Mother of Bug-Outs over the hostages. On August 27, tired of waving fingers at foreigners, the editorial fires at our own Norman Macrae, for thinking that immediate action in the Gulf by the allies would be 'a three-day turkey shoot'. And right he was: a turkey shoot it has been; Norman Macrae's only inaccuracy was to say three days rather than four. His sentiments were ticked off: 'That was not realism: it is brutalism masquerading as realism.' Sanctions, it said, must be given time to work. The alternative consisted of 'the blithe and bloody fantasies of the turkey-shooters'.

And so it goes on. The Americans (September 3) must be 'patient'. They are being dreadfully 'imperial' (September 7). They really have no business to be 'piling troops and armaments into the Gulf as if there were no tomorrow'. The United States can't afford it – awful mortgages back home, debts and what not. The Western emissaries have a 'chance . . . worth taking' on November 6. Brandt goes in to the *Guardian*'s cheers. By November 9, word is that two silly congressmen and Benn will be wafted in down sunbeams from the West to have a photo opportunity. A good thing, opines the *Guardian*. By November 16, not having much applause, it bemoans the lack of 'debate' as to the Gulf war. Now I happen to think that the British have a rather serious moral sense: they do not 'debate' such matters.

On it goes. At any stage where the West buckled and sent its lick-spittles to a man who the world now knows to have been a combination of Hitler and Stalin, the *Guardian* was there – not to offer support, but at least to appear as Fairy Godmother in the pink cocaine-induced dream of a dictator of the nastiest possible kind, whom the West should have seen off long ago. British liberalism ought by now to know that this civilisation has something to say – and not something about finger-chewing.

BACK TO REAL LIFE WITH A BUMP

Michael Ignatieff

Observer, March 3, 1991

It was the image of the war that will be imprinted on many minds for ever; the Iraqi conscript, starved, barefoot and battle-shocked climbing out of his trench, kneeling just beneath the barrel of the M16 and kissing the hand of the United States Marine.

In Paris or London, Des Moines or San Francisco, this was an image of triumph and also of pity. Here was Everyman kissing his enemy in gratitude for deliverance from hell. That, to say the least, is not how they would have seen it in Amman, Algiers, Baghdad and Gaza. For decades to come, that fatal kiss will be there to be brooded upon and to be avenged.

At home, too, for everyone who saw those pictures as an image of triumph, there are those who saw that Marine as the unmasked truth of Western war aims. We were there to make all Arabs bow. These perceptions have the force of fact. They cannot be changed by argument. War touches such deep chords of conviction and revulsion that persuasion is hopeless.

As the war ends, everyone is exactly where they were when it started. The languages of moral concern scarcely connect. Some people's radar of outrage is only picking up the criminal carnage on the Kuwait to Basra road; others are only picking up the atrocities in Kuwait. Inevitably, we have taken sides and the dead on the other side don't count. The editorial columns of the *Independent* invite us to rejoice 'in the miraculously small number of casualties', while the front page of the same paper observes that 40,000 people may have died in the conflict.

Those who supported sanctions can now point to the Iraqi dead and say: we told you so. Those who supported the war, as I have done, will reply: the cost would have been higher had we delayed 18 months to wait for sanctions to fail. Neither side has the slightest hope of convincing the other. To quote Edgar Morin in *Le Monde*, we are dealing here with an encounter between 'blind moralities', 'one-way indignations' and 'unilateral forms of pity'.

If the war's actual result — astonishing victory — changes nothing in the tribal exchange of moral certainties here at home, the distribution of these certainties is surely significant in itself. The war received the overwhelming support of the British people. The percentage was higher than in most other European states, and was significantly higher than in America, where Democratic doubts about the war brought the Congress to within a handful of votes from withholding support for the president's action.

So why is it that the British have belligerency in their bones? War is at the core of most national mythologies in Europe, but only in Britain do we have a memory of war untinged with defeat. Even the Americans had a Vietnam to give their warriors pause. Their imperialist tradition is brief and the competing tradition – isolationism – is just as strong. In Britain we may have lost our empire but not our imperial reflexes. If we were America's poodle, we were certainly straining at the leash.

War offers all societies the fantasy of the brotherhood of arms. The British are uniquely susceptible because we are uniquely divided. We happy band of brothers! Officers from Winchester and Eton, squaddies from Shepherd's Bush comprehensive, all working together as a team. Yet when the television allowed us to eavesdrop on the battlefield pep talks, the language of moral appeal coming from the officer class was straight from the public school chapel and church parade.

The contrast with the Americans was instructive. Their military head was a Jamaican shipping clerk's son, and their generals and their soldiers all spoke the same democratic English of the television age. The British war, by contrast, expressed our deepest social divisions, while at the time offering us the fantasy of overcoming them, in the camaraderie of a fighting regiment. The troops may have been operating late 20th-century laser-guided weaponry, but the mind-set was late imperial class communion.

It is easy to be knowing about the deep entanglement of class, nation and warfare in the British psyche, much less easy truly to disentangle oneself, to remain dry-eyed for example when a regimental band plays a last post, when the language of nationhood taps into the ancient moral appeal of sacrifice and the nation invokes the ancient vision of brotherhood that societies and regiments alike long for but only regiments ever attain.

The fact that war taps into these fantasies and emotions does not necessarily mean that support for it was unreflecting and instinctive. British patriotism's curious resilience may have a lot to do with its moral realism. What kept the home front together was something more thoughtful than jingoism: there was what Max Weber calls an 'ethic of responsibility' at work, a gut feeling that there was a dirty job to be done and that our people were the ones to do it. This ethic may be hateful to its enemies, but they would be mistaken if they thought it was blind. Every squaddie and their loved ones knew what the fine words about sacrifice actually meant.

Now that victory has been won, the dissenting minority that has always refused the blood call of British patriotism is easily dismissed as a pacifist fringe. But it is truly another Britain, forged from two alternative traditions of religious Nonconformity and socialist internationalism. This tradition is just as authentic, just as British, just as patriotic as the majority tradition, and just as incorrigible. It has lost a battle for opinion, but it will surely regroup for another struggle.

Its weakness for me is that it faces the ethic of responsibility – of doing the dirty job – with the ethic of authenticity, of keeping hands clean. It is an ethic whose strength is its scrupulous conscience, its serious scrutiny of intentions; its weakness is its ineffectuality, its unwillingness to use bad means to stop evil men. Those who believe in the ethic of responsibility have won in this war, but it is obvious that the persuasiveness of the ethic of authenticity will endure. To judge from my mail-bag, its call on conscience is as strong as ever.

Whatever our moralities, we are all back to ordinary life with a bump. War gave us all a holiday, a month's excursion into that great world of high political and moral drama where none of us actually live our lives. Now we are back in Britain, no longer a happy band of brothers, liberators in a great cause, just tired and hungry, ready for home and bed. The shoeless starving figures are no longer out there in the desert: they are close to home, where they always were, sleeping rough under the arches, wearing black garbage bags for warmth, just like the Iraqis.

A ONE-SIDED BLOODFEST
John Pilger
New Statesman, March 8, 1991

What ought to have been the main news event of the past week was that as many as 150,000 Iraqis may have been killed in the war in the Gulf, compared with an estimated 2,000 killed in Kuwait and 131 allied dead. The war was a one-sided bloodfest, won at a distance with the power of money and superior technology pitted against a small Third World nation. And no amount of craven silence will alter that truth.

Moreover, it now appears that a large number of the Iraqi dead were slaughtered – and the word is precisely meant – during the brief land war launched by Washington after Iraq had agreed in Moscow to an unconditional withdrawal from Kuwait. And most of these were in retreat, ordered to withdraw, trying to get home. They were, as Colin Hughes wrote in the *Independent*, 'shot in the back'.

So 'ring your churchbells' and 'rejoice' in such a 'great victory': a military operation of 'almost aesthetic beauty' . . . and so on, and on, *ad nauseam*.

'The glee,' wrote Colin Hughes, 'with which American pilots returning to their carriers spoke of the "duck shoot" presented by columns of Iraqis retreating from Kuwait City (has) troubled many humanitarians who otherwise supported the allied objectives. Naturally, it is sickening to witness a routed army being shot in the back.' This 'duck shoot', suggested Hughes, 'risked staining the allied clean-fighting war record'. But no; it seems the Iraqis were to blame for being shot in the back; an Oxford don told the paper, indeed, that the allies 'were well within the rules of international conduct'. The *Independent* reported the deaths of tens of thousands of Iraqis on its front page, while inside a leading article referred to 'miraculously light casualties'.

Yet the *Independent* was the only British newspaper to give consistent, substantial coverage to this slaughter. 'The retreating forces huddling on the Basra beachhead,' reported Karl Waldron, 'were under permanent attack yesterday from the air. Iranian pilots, patrolling their border 10 miles away, described the route as a "rat shoot", with roaming allied jets strafing both banks.' Waldron described the scene as 'Iraq's Dunkirk'; and when I read this, I wondered if that evocative word would stir those deeply uneasy about this war, if not opposed outright to it, and alert the 'many humanitarians' to what had been done in their name.

The Iraqi casualty figures are critical to the 'great victory'. Leave them out and the Murdoch comic version applies: Western technology, and Western heroism, has triumphed. Put them in and the picture bleeds and darkens; and questions are raised, or ought to be raised, about the 'civilised values' for which 'we' fought. Last Friday, the *Guardian* announced the death of 150,000 Iraqis in the body of a piece on page three. *The Times* and *Telegraph* performed a similar burial. The next day, the *Telegraph* referred to a 'massacre' on the road to Basra. American pilots were said to have likened their attack on the convoy to 'shooting fish in a barrel'. Ducks, rats and now fish were massacred. No blame was apportioned.

On the contrary, most newspapers carried prominently a photograph of a US Army medic attending a wounded Iraqi soldier. Here was the supreme image of tenderness and magnanimity, a 'lifeline' as the *Mirror* called it: the antithesis of what had actually happened and a classic piece of propaganda. The American pilots had used Rockeye cluster bombs in the attack. Each Rockeye bomb disperses 247 bomblets containing needle-sharp shrapnel designed for 'soft' targets, in other words people. The technology has ensured that X-rays often fail to detect shrapnel. No US Army medic, however tender, could begin to treat such wounds.

To my knowledge, the silence was interrupted only once. During a discussion about the rehabilitation of wounded soldiers, the BBC's Radio Four delivered a remarkable live report from Stephen Sackur on the road to Basra. Clearly moved and perhaps angered by what he had seen, this one reporter did as few have done or been allowed to do. He dropped the 'we' and 'them'. He separated ordinary Iraqis from the tyrant oppressing them. He converted the duck, rats and fish into human beings. The incinerated figures had been trying to get home, he said. Among them were civilians, including contract workers from the Indian sub-continent; he saw the labels on their suitcases.

However, for the evening television news bulletins – the nation's principal source of information – there was no 'Dunkirk' and no Stephen Sackur. Kate Adie described the 'evidence of the horrible confusion' that was both 'devastating' and 'pathetic'. The camera panned across the 'loot' – toys, bottles of perfume, hair curlers: pathetic indeed – strewn among the blackened dead. There had first been a 'battle', we were told. Battle? A US Marine lieutenant looked distressed. They had no air cover, he said: nothing with which to defend themselves. 'It was not very professional at all,' he said, ambiguously; and he was not asked to clarify that.

Apart from his words, I could find none, written or spoken, that expressed clearly the nature of this crime, this mass murder that was there for all eyes to see, and without the Iraqi ministry of information to 'supervise' those eyes. One recalls the interrogation by satellite that the BBC's man in Baghdad, Jeremy Bowen, had to endure following his harrowing and personally courageous report of the bombing of the air-raid bunker in which hundreds of women and children died.

'Are you absolutely *certain* it wasn't a military bunker,' he was asked: or words to that effect. No such interrogation inconvenienced his colleagues on the road to Basra. 'Are you *absolutely certain* that allied planes did this *deliberately to people running away*?' was never put.

Thus, self-censorship remains the most virulent form. But there is another element. It is almost as if compassion itself has been suspended for the duration of this war and its 'celebrations'. At the time of writing, the message of war with 'miraculously light casualties' drones on and on. There is a radio report of the trauma suffered by British troops in having to bury the victims of the atrocity on the Basra road. In the commentary, there is no recognition of the victims' human rights even in death; and no acknowledgement of the trauma awaiting tens of thousands of Iraqi families for whom there will be no proper process of grief, not even a dog-tag.

Thought control in liberal societies used to be a subtle process: not in recent weeks, and not in the weeks to come. Like the bulldozers that cleared the evidence on the Basra road, the propagandists here now attempt to clear away the debris of our memories. They hope that those subversive glimpses we had of the human consequences of the greatest aerial bombardment in history (a record announced with such pride) will not form the basis for a retrospective of the criminal nature of the relentless assault on populated areas as part of the application of criminal solutions to political problems. These must be struck from the record, in the manner of modern Stalinism, or blurred in our consciences, or immersed in celebration and justification.

Celebration, of course, is a relatively simple affair. For those of us lacking churchbells, David Dimbleby will have to do. However, justification is quite another matter, especially for those who seem incessantly to describe themselves as 'liberals', as if they are well aware that their uncertainty, selectivity and hypocrisy on humanitarian matters is showing. Bereft of reasoned argument, they transmute humanitarianism to the 'far left', just as Senator Joe McCarthy did.

According to Simon Hoggart of the *Observer*, one of the myths of this 'far left' is that 'the allies were unnecessarily brutal to the Iraqi forces. Of course the death of thousands of innocent conscripts is unspeakable. But you cannot fight half a war.' The basis for Hoggart's approval of the 'unspeakable' is apparently that his sisters are married to soldiers who went to the Gulf, where they would have been killed had not retreating Iraqi soldiers been shot in the back and Iraqi women and children obliterated by carpet bombing.

Robert Harris, the *Sunday Times* man, is even more defensive. He writes that Rupert Murdoch didn't tell him to support the war: a familiar refrain. Murdoch, of course, didn't have to. But Harris adds another dimension. Disgracefully, he insults Bobby Muller, a former decorated US Marine who lost the use of his legs in Vietnam, as a 'cripple' and a 'cardboard figure' whom I 'manipulate'.

Even Muller, who is strong, was shocked by this; and at a large meeting in central London last Monday night invoked Harris's name in the appropriate manner. Like so many Vietnam veterans, Bobby Muller has devoted himself to warning his countrymen about 'other Vietnams' and their atrocious nature. Unlike Harris, he has fought and suffered both in war and for his convictions. Harris's main complaint, it seems, is that those against the war have neglected to mention Saddam Hussein's atrocities in Kuwait – which apparently justify slaughtering tens of thousands of Iraqi conscripts and civilians.

The intellectual and moral bankruptcy of this is clear. First, as children we are told that two wrongs do not make a right. Second, those actively opposed to the war are the same people who have tried to alert the world to Saddam Hussein's crimes. In 1988, 30 MPs signed Ann Clwyd's motion condemning Saddam Hussein's gassing of 5,000 Iraqi Kurds. All but one of these MPs have been steadfastly against the war.

In striking contrast, those who have prosecuted and promoted the war include those who *supported* Saddam Hussein, who armed and sustained him and sought to cover up the gravity of his crimes. I recommend the current newspaper advertisement for Amnesty International, which describes the moving plea of an Iraqi Kurdish leader to Thatcher following Saddam Hussein's gassing of the Kurds.

'One of our few remaining hopes,' he wrote, 'is that democrats and those who cherish values of justice, peace and freedom will voice their concern for the plight of the Kurds. That is why I am making this direct appeal to you . . .' The letter was dated September 16, 1988. On October 5, the Thatcher government gave Iraq more than £340 million in export credits, and the trade minister, Tony Newton, flew to Baghdad to shake the hand of the New Hitler – just as Douglas Hurd had done previously.

Equally, the media that now plays a game described by David Beresford as 'hunt the atrocity' in Kuwait – and no one doubts that there were many atrocities committed in Kuwait – is the same media that had little if anything to say about Saddam Hussein's crimes when the tyrant was 'our man'. Robert Harris will recall the attempts by

MI5 to discredit the memory of *Observer* journalist Farzad Bazoft by putting it about that he was a spy: a monstrous smear propagated by those sections of the media whose support for the war Harris undoubtedly shares.

When he resigned at the end of January, the head of Italian naval forces in the Gulf, said, 'I wondered if, in a certain sense, we hadn't all been made fools of . . . if they (the US) hadn't drawn us into a much larger game.' Indeed, many were made fools of, especially those to whom their first allegiance ought to have been to inform the British people as truthfully as possible. And they, in turn, have made fools of their readers, viewers and listeners.

In the beginning, the Americans and the British were in the Middle East to 'defend Saudi Arabia'. This was false. Then 'all diplomacy was exhausted.' This, too, was false. Numerous, potentially successful, attempts to get Saddam Hussein out of Kuwait were blocked by Washington. Then, with the bombing under way, the war became a nightly visit to Norman Schwarzkopf's video-game emporium, where it was demonstrated that missiles distinguished between good things and bad things and of course shed no blood. This was the 'clean fighting record' now 'stained' by the massacre on the Basra road.

No one – at least, no one I can recall – asked to see the videos Schwarzkopf did not show. They represented the majority of his collection. So the censorship worked brilliantly. The video-games were not only entertaining, they also allowed for the atrocious nature of the war simply to be left out. Those who questioned this apparently did so when the camera was turned off – as I observed on more than one occasion.

And, of course, it was fun to report that RAF planes carried the slogan 'landscape gardeners', as long as you did not ask precisely what they were doing and the murderous nature of the new bombs. No doubt Robert Harris would describe the former Nato chief and US Secretary of State, General Haig, as an 'Aunt Sally'; it was Haig who said that the B52s would 'turn Iraq into a talcum-powder bowl'. He was right, of course. But none of us saw what the B52s did. And how many of us – those of us meant to keep the record straight – wondered aloud about the use of B52s by generals said to be devoted to 'pinpoint' bombing and other humanitarian concerns? B52s lay mile upon mile of carpets of death – a fact easily confirmed by published, authoritative, material.

And how many of us declared the obvious: that the ordinary men, women and children who were the victims of 'our' bombs were being punished to death for the misdeeds of a man who could count them as *his* victims, along with the Kuwaitis and the Kurds? It is surely a matter of logic that to kill and torture these people, in whatever form, is no different in principle from the tyrant doing it.

Or perhaps the difference is that, in your air-conditioned video-game 'command and control centre', or high up in the sky, you never suffer the inconvenience of having to look your victim in the face. And if the terrified face of a man about to die violently should appear on the video screen, you conceal it and 'classify' it, as Schwarzkopf did. But then Stormin' Norman did no more than those who constantly appear on our TV screens dressed in Arab scarves and mufti and who were not, as far as we could tell, in anyone's army.

SANITISING THE NEWS
Phillip Knightley
Guardian, March 4, 1991

In Cairo in 1967 to cover the crisis caused by President Nasser, who had kicked the UN peace-keeping force out of the Sinai, I filed my first story to the *Sunday Times* on Saturday, June 3. I had tried to drive to the Sinai and had been arrested by the Egyptian security police. I had interviewed the general commanding the UN forces, attended two public meetings addressed by Nasser, been to a briefing at the British embassy, consulted the Indian ambassador and sought the views of an eminent Egyptian editor, Mohammed Heikel. On the basis of what I had learned, my story said categorically that there was not going to be a war.

It convinced the *Sunday Times* and on the Sunday it recalled me from Cairo and the entire team it had sent to Israel. On the Monday, the Six-Day War started. The atmosphere when I went into the office can best be described as frosty.

The point of this story is that making predictions in time of crisis is high-risk journalism. The Gulf war has turned out to be no exception. As the *Independent* said in a leader last week, the doomsayers have been routed. Those who wrote that the value of air power had been exaggerated and that the war would drag on Vietnam style (I was one) have been proved wrong.

Iraq did not use chemical or biological weapons. Israel was not

314

dragged into the war. The coalition did not fracture. There were no Iraqi terrorist attacks in London as the CIA had warned (*Guardian*, January 7). There were not tens of thousands of allied casualties. The price of oil has not soared ('£4 a gallon is on the way', *Daily Mirror*, January 12). The Americans' overwhelming firepower did not fail ('War flaws', *New Statesman and Society*, February 6).

But some correspondents got it spectacularly right. John Keegan, defence editor of the *Telegraph*, wrote in the *Sunday Telegraph* on January 27 that a quick allied victory was not in doubt and that he expected the Iraqis to run away in the face of attacks from the US Marines, who 'took Guadalcanal, Tarawa and Iwo Jima from the most fanatical defenders who literally fought to the death'.

He was spot on, and in the current *Spectator* understandably attacks those who doubted his assessment, targeting the Dimbleby brothers, Jeremy Paxman and the 'grandees' of the BBC for their 'contemptible coverage of the war'. Going further, he suggests that the army gives Britain better value for money than the BBC.

The inquest into the coverage of the Gulf war is more likely to produce a clash between various sections of the media rather than between the media and the Ministry of Defence, as was the case after the Falklands campaign. The speed of the victory and the fact that it was relatively painless – for the allies – look like burying the fact that the management of the news was not only as effective as in the Falklands but also introduced a new element.

Ever since the British invented military censorship in 1856 (to crush criticism of the way it was running the Crimean war) wartime news management has had two main purposes: to deny information and comfort to the enemy and to create and maintain public support. In the Gulf war the new element has been an effort to change public perception of the nature of war itself, to convince us that new technology has removed a lot of war's horrors.

From early on, the emphasis has been on the 'surgical' nature of air strikes on military targets: the cancer would be removed but the living flesh around it would be left untouched. 'Smart' bombs dropped with 'pinpoint accuracy' would 'take out' only military installations: there would be little or no 'collateral damage' (dead civilians). Iraq's military machine would be destroyed from the air so that there would be no need of a ground war of attrition.

The picture that this painted is of a war almost without death, a sanitised version of what has gone before. It was weeks after the bombing started before any bodies were shown on television and then British TV chiefs voluntarily cut the more horrific scenes.

Scud missiles being intercepted by Patriot missiles over Saudi Arabia and Israel brought an air of video games or fireworks display to the screen. A new language was brought into being to soften the reality. Bombing military targets in the heart of cities was 'denying the enemy an infrastructure'. People were 'soft targets'. Saturation bombing was 'laying down a carpet'.

The idea was to suggest that hardly any people were involved in modern warfare, only machines. This explains the emphasis at press briefings on the damage 'our' machines had caused to 'their' machines and the reluctance of briefing officers to discuss casualties – on either side. Convinced that viewers and readers were interested, the media was happy to go along with this emphasis on technology.

Behind this new aim of news management, as yet unproved, is the rationale that today's public has no stomach for a war in which large numbers of civilians are going to be killed, especially by Western hi-tech armaments. The general reaction to the alliance's bombing of an air-raid shelter in Iraq seemed to justify this belief. But now the war has been quick, successful and with allied casualties remarkably low – in short, the picture the news managers wanted to project has turned out to be partly true – when the full extent of Iraqi casualties do emerge they will be swallowed and lost in the euphoria of victory.

How did the military pull it off? The pool system was an enormous help. It tends to produce the lowest common denominator reporter, one acceptable to every client of the pool. This rules out the independent-minded, maverick correspondent in favour of the reliable, anodyne one. The old 'sense of identification with the subject' worked as it always does. At first TV chiefs were determined to rotate their reporters so that they would not have time to become too involved with the troops, but when the time came to do this the British military commanders begged that the original reporters be allowed to stay on and they were.

Some began to wear military clothing, contrary to MoD guidelines to correspondents: 'We do not recommend that you dress in desert battledress uniform items'. This could have proved dangerous: one report from Iraq said that Bob Simon and the CBS crew, still missing at the time of writing, had been arrested by Iraqi troops who refused to believe they were journalists because they were in uniform. (Anthony Terry, a veteran war correspondent, covered the war in Biafra wearing a three-piece suit, a bowler hat and carrying a tightly rolled umbrella, lest anyone should mistake him for something other than an English gentleman.)

And the military was careful to keep out the better breed of stills photographer because, unlike TV cameramen, they do not always need action and can linger on some of the horrors of warfare. So once again, the best war photographer of them all, Donald McCullin, was kept hanging around London waiting for a Saudi visa until it was too late. It is difficult to believe that if the MoD had really wanted McCullin in the Gulf he would have had this trouble.

Lest, despite all this, too much realism crept into the British media, the MoD was meticulous in writing to any editor whose paper published anything which met with the military's disapproval. One editor told me: 'The letter we got was very polite, of the more-in-sorrow-than-in-anger variety, but left no doubt that we had better not do it again.'

Where do the bouquets go? The biggest to the *Independent*'s Robert Fisk, whose analysis, depth of focus, knowledge of the history of the area, scepticism of the news management process and sympathy for the people who were dying, civilian and military, were outstanding examples of how war can be reported in spite of all the obstacles the news managers construct.

Other bouquets go to all the correspondents who were prepared to risk their lives in Baghdad so that they could be abused as traitors, tools of Saddam and enemies of 'our boys' by most of the tabloid press.

A particular mention for Peter Arnett, the New Zealander who surfaced as a war correspondent in Vietnam in 1962 and in his 13 years there spent more time in the field than anyone. Broadcasting from Baghdad for CNN, Arnett, pushing 60, showed that war reporting is not necessarily a young man's game. He even gets a herogram from John Keegan.

ON THE EVE OF THE IRAQI-SOVIET PEACE TALKS

Edward Said

London Review of Books, March 7, 1991

The United States is at an extraordinarily bloody moment in its history as the last superpower. Perhaps because I come from the Arab world, I have often thought during the past few months, and more anxiously during the past few days, that such a war as we Americans are now engaged in, with such aims, rhetoric, and all-encompassing violence and destruction, could now have been waged only against an Arab-Islamic-Third World country. It does no one in it any credit, and it will not produce any of the great results which have been predicted, however ostensibly victorious either side may prove to be, and whatever the results may prove to be for the other. It will not solve the problems of the Middle East, or those of America, now in a deep recession, plagued by poverty, joblessness, and an urban, education and health crisis of gigantic proportions.

A war like this could only have occurred in a part of the world beset with huge inequities of endowment and rule, bearing within itself a history of promises postponed and endlessly betrayed for justice and fairness at the hands of the West, and now exploding in an agony of hatred, anti-Americanism and tremendous, largely unforeseen upheaval. I do not excuse and have not excused the aggression of Iraq against Kuwait. I have condemned it from the beginning, just as I have long condemned the abuses of Saddam Hussein's government, and those of the other governments of the region, whether Arab or Israeli. Democracy in any real sense of the word is nowhere to be found in the Middle East: there are either privileged oligarchies or privileged ethnic groups. The large mass of the people is crushed beneath dictatorship or unyielding, unresponsive unpopular government. But I dispute the notion that the US is a virtuous innocent in this awful conflict, just as I dispute the notion that this is not a war between George Bush and Saddam Hussein – it most certainly is – and that the US is acting solely or principally in the interests of the United Nations. The United Nations resolutions have already been exceeded, and the bombing campaign against Iraq's population is now murderous. Yet at bottom this is a personalised struggle between, on the one hand, a Third World dictator of a kind the US has long dealt with, whose rule it has encouraged, whose favours it has long enjoyed, and, on the other, the president of a country which has taken on the mantle of empire inherited from Britain and France and is determined to remain in the Middle East for reasons of oil and of geo-strategic and political advantage.

There has been a great deal of talk about linkage, a word I find ugly and a concept I find slippery. 'Analogy', 'relationship', 'association' are three possible alternatives, which suggest to me that the US has no record of consistent opposition to aggression – the instances of Namibia, South Africa, Cyprus, Panama, Nicaragua and the Israeli-occupied territories come quickly to mind – and that Iraq and Kuwait do not exist only in some unhistorical region of the mind or on a map in Dick Cheney's office. For two generations the US has sided in the Middle East mostly with tyranny and injustice. I defy anyone to tell me of a single struggle for democracy, or women's rights, or secularism, or the rights of minorities, that the US has supported. Instead we have propped up compliant and unpopular clients, and turned our backs on the efforts of small peoples to liberate themselves from military occupation, while subsidising their enemies. We have prompted unlimited militarism and engaged in vast arms sales everywhere in the region, mostly to governments which have now been driven to ever more desperate actions as a result of the US's obsession with, and exaggeration of, the power of Saddam Hussein. To conceive of a post-war Arab world dominated by the rulers of Egypt, Saudi Arabia and Syria, all of them working in a new Pax Americana, is neither intellectually nor morally credible.

Two things have occurred, quickly and completely, over the past few months. One is that, in the information blitz which has been going on since the summer, the media and its personnel have, with a few exceptions, internalised norms which prevent dispassionate analysis and induce self-censorship, as well as a very shallow sort of news presentation. The other is that we have not yet developed a discourse that does anything more than identify with power, despite the dangers of that power in a world which has shrunk so small and become so impressively interconnected. The US cannot belligerently declare its right, as six per cent of the world's population, to consume 30 per cent of the world's energy; nor for that matter can it unilaterally declare a new world order because it exercises the military power to destroy a few complaining countries along the way. There was no evidence that Iraqi expansion would continue after Kuwait. Indeed, there is now ample evidence that an arrangement between Iraq, Saudi Arabia, Jordan and Egypt had been worked out in early August: this would have involved Iraqi withdrawal and an adjudication of the dispute with Kuwait. Like every other regional compromise, this was rejected out of hand by the US. There was considerable evidence that, if further provoked by an exterminist gesture on the part of the US, Iraq would settle for universal destruction, rather than back down. Even the anti-Saddam Iraqi opposition outside Iraq has now closed ranks and sides against the US.

There are many Arabs who believe, as I do, that Iraq's invasion and occupation must be reversed, but few would agree with the strategy of immediately sending troops because George Bush and Margaret Thatcher assumed that wogs could be told to behave by the white man: there is a pattern of such contemptuous attitudes towards the Arab world, from the days of the British expeditionary force sent to Egypt in 1882 to put down the Orabi rebellion to the 1956 attack on Egypt undertaken by Anthony Eden in collusion with Israel and France – Eden's attitude, delivered in the accents of a petty and vengeful stubbornness, strangely prefigures Bush's personalised hatred of Saddam Hussein. The question that none of the media has asked is what right does the US have to send a massive military force around the world in order to attack Iraq in this tough, relentless, preachy way? This is very different from opposing aggression, which many Arabs would have been anxious to do. What the American move has done is effectively to turn a regional issue into an imperial one, especially since the US has shown no concern over other aggressions – its own or those, like Israel's, which it supported and paid for. Bush has treated Saddam as his personal Moby Dick, to be punished and destroyed – the war plan was designed for that – as if bombing and frightening the natives would be sure to lead to a crumbling of their will.

I have written elsewhere of the dreadful situation inside the Arab world: in countries that are now allied with the US and in those that are not, there is a lot to be disturbed about, all of it attributable, not to the Arab character or to Islam, but to specific political and social distortions, all of them remediable by strenuous policies of reform. What concerns me here is the United States itself.

For decades in America there has been a cultural war against the

Arabs and Islam: the most appalling racist caricatures of Arabs and Muslims have conveyed that they are all either terrorists or sheikhs, and that the region is a large arid slum, fit only for profit or war. The very notion that there might be a history, a culture, a society – indeed many societies – to be thought of as interlocutor or as partner has never held the stage for more than a moment or two. A flow of trivial books by journalists has flooded the market, and has gained currency for a handful of dehumanising stereotypes. Nearly every recent movie about American commandos pits a hulking Rambo or a whizz-like Delta Force against Arab/Muslim terrorist-desperados. Now it is as if an almost metaphysical need to defeat Iraq has come into being, not because Iraq's offence, though great, is cataclysmic, but because a small non-white country has rankled a suddenly energised super-nation imbued with a fervour that can only be satisfied with subservience from sheikhs, dictators, terrorists and camel-jockeys. The truly acceptable Arabs are those like Sadat who can be made to seem almost completely purified of their national selfhood – folksy talk-show guests.

Arabs may only be an attenuated example of those others who in the past have incurred the wrath of the stern white man, a kind of Puritan super-ego whose errand into the wilderness knows few boundaries and who will go to very great lengths to make his points. One of the ingredients conspicuously missing from today's discussions about the Gulf is the word 'imperialism'. But it is difficult not to catch in the moralistic accents of American leaders, and in their obedient media echoes, repetitions of the grandiose self-endowment of previous imperialisms (muffled though they may be by the pious formula that Saddam's wrong against Kuwait is to be righted by the US). And as the Iraqi infraction seems to grow before our eyes, Saddam has become Hitler, the butcher of Baghdad, the madman who has to be brought low.

'All roads lead to the bazaar,' 'Arabs only understand force,' 'brutality and violence are central to Arab civilisation,' 'Islam is an intolerant, segregationalist, medieval, fanatical, cruel religion.' No other major cultural group could be spoken of in this way, yet the context, framework, setting of any discussion has been limited, indeed frozen, by these ideas. There has seemed to be a kind of pleasure in the prospect of the Arabs as represented by Saddam at last getting their comeuppance. Scores would be settled with Palestinians, Arab nationalism, Islamic civilisation. Most of these old enemies of the 'West', it should be noted, had the further cheek to be anti-Israeli.

The worst offenders in all this have been the academic experts on the Arab mind, the usual suspects who can always be rounded up and counted on for egregious displays of phoney expertise. The public mood has been such as to decontextualise and isolate Iraq, to exaggerate its power fantastically, to subsume its entire population in the two routinely mispronounced words 'Saddam Hussein' – as if all 'we' were doing was fighting the one dreadful spectre of evil. This enables us to bomb Iraq without a twinge of compunction, and to do it, indeed, with a horrific sense of righteous exhilaration. This is something the media has encouraged, even promoted, as if Iraq could most appropriately be seen through the sights of an F-15 or a smart missile. Note also that with the sudden disappearance of April Glaspie and John Kelly, the present war-making Administration has been run without a single professional who has any real knowledge or experience of the Middle East, its languages or its peoples. Such as it was, Iraq's case against Kuwait – a case to some degree encouraged and bolstered by the US, as the transcript of April Glaspie's conversations with Saddam in late July testifies – was given no hearing, thereby ensuring the need for war. It is my supposition that Iraq is being destroyed today, not because of its aggression against Kuwait, which could have been reversed patiently, regionally, economically and politically, but because the US wants a physical presence in the Gulf, wants to have direct leverage on oil to affect Europe and Japan, because it wishes to set the world agenda, because Iraq was perceived as a threat to Israel.

I know that loyalty and patriotism come into all this: but these should be based on a critical sense of what the facts are, what our interests are, and what as residents of this shrinking and depleted planet we owe our neighbours and the rest of mankind. Uncritical solidarity with the policy of the moment, especially when it is so unimaginably costly, cannot be allowed to rule. America's survival is not at stake in the Persian Gulf, and never has been. Why have we no criticism of such ridiculous statements as 'we have to stop him now, otherwise it will be harder later'? Why have we not heard anyone say that the UN resolutions were bullied out of the Security Council, and that these resolutions say nothing whatever about destroying a country in order to liberate Kuwait and to restore to its throne a dynasty which, along with other Gulf monarchies, has put two and a half trillion dollars on deposit outside the Arab world. These are monarchies which respect neither human rights nor the priorities of their own people.

Desert Storm is ultimately a war against the Iraqi people, an effort to break and kill them as part of an effort to break and kill Saddam. Yet this is largely kept from the American television audience, as a way of maintaining the image of the war as a painless Nintendo exercise, and the image of the American as a virtuous, clean warrior. On January 27, in the lead *New York Times* article by R.W. Apple, Bush was described as 'a strict Marquess of Queensberry rules man', as if what the US has been doing is not, in effect, carpet-bombing the cities and towns of Iraq, violating the Geneva and Hague conventions by destroying water and fuel supplies for civilians, and doing only very unascertainable damage to the armed forces in the process. It might make a difference even to Americans who are not interested in history to know that the last time Baghdad was destroyed was in 1258, by the Mongols: to know what precedents there are for what we are doing.

What else in the many pictures we are getting is deliberately manipulative? I would say that the lingering over scenes in Israeli cities where a few missiles have hit is part of the same distortion. Not that such scenes shouldn't be shown, or that I condone Scud attacks against civilians: they should be shown and I am against these attacks. But why is it granted that only Israeli and Western affliction should be to this extent available – if not to maintain the fiction that Arabs are not equal with 'our' side, that their lives and sorrows are not worth listening to?

The claim that Iraq gassed its own citizens has often been repeated. At best, this is uncertain. There is as least one War College report, done while Iraq was a US ally, which claims that the gassings of the Kurds in Halabja was done by Iran. Few people mention such reports in the media today, although references to them turn up occasionally in the alternative press. Now 'gassing his own citizens' has become a fact about Saddam, elevated into one of the proofs that the US should destroy him, as if by doing so it wouldn't also destroy Iraq, kill thousands of people, sacrifice thousands of American lives (mostly the poor and disadvantaged) and create a host of new problems.

The whole premise of the way the war was prepared and is being fought is colonial: the assumption is that a small Third World country doesn't have the right to resist America, which is white and superior. I submit that such notions are amoral, anachronistic, and supremely mischevious, since they not only make wars possible, but also prevent diplomacy and politics from playing the role they should. When the historical record is fully revealed, we shall know what we

323

already partly know now: that the United States steadily resisted and subverted every attempt at mediation, compromise or adjudication, and pressed for war almost from the very beginning. Thus one can have only the slightest hope that Bush will react positively to an Iraqi-Soviet proposal for withdrawal.

It would therefore seem that the point of this war is not to permit lesser nations and subject peoples to enjoy the same privileges that 'we' do. Had the US from the beginning earned moral authority by getting behind Arab and UN action, expanding the rule of UN resolutions to include the whole region and not just one demonised and demeaned country, there would have been no war, and we would be able to speak about dialogue and reconciliation. How absurd and morally repugnant George Bush's phrase that to resolve the Palestinian question now would be 'to reward aggression', as if a peace settlement on an issue that antedates not only Saddam but George Bush himself could be spoken of in so coarse and schoolmasterish a way.

There has been scarcely any serious thought about the aftermath of the war: the tremendous economic, ecological and human waste; the strengthening of powerful religious sentiment and the defeat of secularism, dialogue and moderation; the destruction of Iraq, its possible dismemberment, the long and awful period of depredations for its citizens; the rise of extremism, of calls for vengeance and more killing and destruction; the instability of many governments, especially those of unpopular US allies like Egypt, Syria and Saudi Arabia; the endless prolongation of an American presence, with occupation, killing and collaboration as our legacy; the growth of intransigence in Israel, which will use its US lobby to extract more concessions; the destruction of the environment, of the economy. The list is very long.

An article in last winter's issue of the journal *Foreign Affairs* is entitled 'The Summer of Arab Discontent', and contains the following passage:

> No sooner had the Arab/Muslim world said farewell to the wrath and passion of the Ayatollah Khomeini's crusade than another contender rose in Baghdad. The new claimant was made of material different from the turbaned saviour from Qum: Saddam Hussein was not a writer of treatises on Islamic government nor a product of high learning in religious seminaries. Not for him were the drawn-out ideological struggles for the hearts and minds of the faithful. He came from a brittle land, a frontier country between Persia and Arabia, with little claim to culture and books and grand ideas. The new contender was a despot, a ruthless and skilled warden who had tamed his domain and turned it into a large prison.

The merest Arab schoolchild knows that Baghdad was not only the seat of the Abbasid civilisation, the highest flowering of Arab culture, between the 9th and 12th centuries, which produced works of literature still read today as Shakespeare, Dante and Dickens are still read, but as a city is also one of the great monuments of Islamic art. In addition, Baghdad is the city in which, along with Cairo and Damascus, the 19th and 20th-century revival of art and literature took place. Baghdad produced at least five of the greatest 20th-century Arab poets, and without any question all of the top artists and sculptors. To say of Iraq that it has no relation to books and ideas is to be amnesiac about Sumer, and Babylon, and Nineveh, and Hammurabi, and Assyria, and all the great monuments of ancient Mesopotamian (and world) civilisation. To say that Iraq is a 'brittle' land, with the suggestion of aridity and emptiness, is also to show ignorance which an elementary school child would be embarrassed to reveal. What happened to the Tigris and the Euphrates? What happened to the fact that of all the countries in the Middle East Iraq is by far the most fertile?

This author sings the praises of contemporary Saudi Arabia, more brittle and out of touch with books, ideas and culture than Iraq ever was. The point is not to belittle Saudi Arabia, which is an important country and has much to contribute. I do, however, want to say that such writing as this, appearing as the US was poised on the edge of war in the pages of the country's most influential foreign affairs quarterly, is neither informative, nor illuminating, nor valuable. Even more important, it is symptomatic of the intellectual will to please power, to tell it what it wants to hear, to say to it that it can go ahead and kill and bomb and destroy, since what is being attacked is really negligible, brittle, with no relationship to books, ideas, cultures, and no relation either, it gently suggests, to real people. There is only the Iraqi dictator and, like a monstrous disease, he must be extirpated.

With such information then, what forgiveness, what humanity, what chance for humane argument? Very little, alas. Yet there are signs that all over the country, beneath the misleading euphoria and the manufactured consent put together by the media, people are angry, consciences disturbed, spirits anguished. Our duty as intellectuals is to the truth, as Benda said, and not to the encouragement of collective passions in the interests of mass slaughter. When one hears philosophers like Michael Walzer or columnists like Anthony Lewis proclaim this as a 'just war', one realises once more that words are the first casualty in any conflict.

THE NEW BRITISH ARMY

Philip Jacobson

The Times, March 23, 1991

On the eve of the start of the land battle in the Gulf, I came across Brigadier Patrick Cordingley, commander of Britain's 7th Armoured Brigade, playing chess with one of his bright young staff officers. Crouched over the board beneath the camouflage netting of his tent, floppy brown beret stuffed under the epaulette of a desert sweater, he was clearly heading for ignominious defeat.

A few minutes later, the distinctive Cordingley laugh signified that it was all over and he stalked off to another of the briefing sessions at which plans for leading the Desert Rats into action were rehearsed and refined for the umpteenth time. I looked on from the back of an armoured vehicle as each of the brigade's specialised arms – from the Challenger tank regiments and the infantry to artillery, engineers and signals – submitted their reports, and it dawned upon me that this was no longer a bloodless exercise in strategy, with pieces being shuffled around the maps and umpires allocating the casualties.

Here were professional soldiers consciously preparing for the climactic moment of their career: going to war. At that stage, of course, nobody really knew what this might entail; few of the 25,000 British soldiers assembled in the Saudi desert had ever been in combat, none had experience of the sort of fighting to be expected of them in a frontal assault on the Iraqi defensive lines.

There were journalists attached to the brigade who had seen more conflict, covering foreign wars, and we would occasionally be asked what it felt like to come under fire (I always told them that it was frightening), or how troops could be expected to hold up in the face of the unbelievable intensity of modern battle.

There was a curious ambivalence about such questions, a product of the natural curiosity of volunteer soldiers contemplating the ultimate test of the profession of arms and an equally natural fear of what might lie ahead.

It was rare to hear anybody who expected to be in the front line ('going sharp' was the usual phrase) brag of itching to get at the enemy. One rear echelon corporal who talked about getting stuck into the Iraqis with a bayonet was derided by most of his comrades as a headcase.

Far more typical was Sergeant Andy Mason, a wiry paratrooper who had seen action in the Falklands and was now doubling up as an escort for our small pool of journalists and official war photographer. Between filthy jokes and anecdotes illustrating the absurdity of army life, he would talk quietly about the difficult conquest of fear, of how no soldier, however tough, could ever be sure that he would not crack next time the shooting began.

For me, only half-spectator, there was a rich seam of recollection to be mined while the Desert Rats trained and waited and wondered in a succession of bleak encampments. Back in the mid-Fifties, before a great many of the soldiers around us were born, 23404264 Trooper Jacobson P had been a (perfectly willing) conscript in a rather smart cavalry regiment. Two years in the ranks had left me with no great admiration for the army of the day as an institution, and precious little respect for the quality of the average career soldier then serving in it.

The contrast with the British Army of the Nineties, bracing itself for what we all feared might turn into a prolonged and bloody conflict, was sharp and, to this privileged outsider's eye, instructive. You could expect professional soldiers today to be masters of their trades; after all, they had been training long enough in Germany and Northern Ireland before coming to the Gulf, where every skill from tank gunnery to trench warfare, advanced communications to field catering, was honed to perfection during the prolonged build-up to war.

What struck me more was the transformation of relations between officers, non-commissioned officers and what we must still call, for want of a better word, other ranks. In place of the rigid military caste system of my day, where the stripes on a sleeve or pips on a shoulder counted for much more than the qualities of the men wearing them, there was now an unforced atmosphere of mutual respect among fellow professionals. When Cordingley and his staff came into the cookhouse, they stood in the food line like everybody else, sat wherever there was space on a bench and disposed of their plastic plates before leaving. Officers had no priority over privates when the showers were working, and used the same canvas-sided field latrines, remembering to remove the black bin-liners when the metal drums below had filled up. If a vehicle bogged down in the sand, or a shell scrape was needed in a hurry, rank took second place to digging.

Perhaps no less should be expected from an all-volunteer force that must compete for its manpower. How many potential recruits today would tolerate the ranting sergeants and bullying corporals, the supercilious junior officers and their remote superiors of the conscription era?

The young soldiers, with whom I shared some gruelling night moves as the brigade manoeuvred into battle positions, found my accounts of polishing coal, cutting grass with nail scissors and buffing up broomsticks barely credible. 'Breaking the civilian to make the squaddy,' it used to be called, but for someone like Corporal Alex Jack, driver for the commanding officer of the Queen's Royal Irish Hussars, this was a mystifying doctrine. 'Who needs that sort of bollocks now?' he observed, before letting on, shyly, that he had badgered his colonel for permission to rejoin the regiment from a soft posting in Canada before it went to war.

There were a good many like Jack in the 7th Armoured: officers who were overstaying their time, NCOs who had wangled their way back to front-line units. Cordingley's driver, universally called Corporal Mack, had left the army to take up a university place in Salford before the Gulf war began: somewhere, somehow, strings were pulled and he came back again, studies postponed until the next academic year.

Then there was Captain Arthur Currie, another Irish Hussar, whose career in many ways sums up the changes that have taken place in the British Army of today. A dark, rangy fellow with a bristling moustache and a Coleraine accent you could cut with a knife, he was popularly believed to have joined the regiment to avoid being jailed for some youthful indiscretion (in some versions, the magistrate had him marched straight down to the recruiting booth).

In the fullness of time, and not without certain disciplinary hiccups, Currie rose to become the regimental sergeant major. Once, that would probably have been his ceiling: crack cavalry regiments used to be notoriously hostile to promotion from the ranks. Nevertheless, he had made it, on merit – and, I would wager, sheer force of personality – to become one of the army's great experts on the Challenger tank. Over an illicit Irish whiskey on the night before the Gulf ceasefire came into effect, a beaming Currie pronounced himself the most fortunate of men to have been with his regiment when its Challengers finally proved themselves on the battlefield.

My own war had begun, somewhat disconcertingly, with the news that the column to which I was attached would be first through a breach cut into the Iraqi wall by American engineers. Fortunately, I was placed in the care of Major Jim Tanner, of the Staffordshire Regiment, an unflappable infantryman who never seemed to notice that our rattletrap armoured troop carrier had forged far ahead of the main force on the first day of the British advance.

Sharing the occasional anxious moment with me in the back was an articulate young captain from a tank regiment, seconded to staff duties for the duration of hostilities. Jerome would not, could not, have missed it for a king's ransom, but, like a good many other officers to whom I talked after the ceasefire, he expected to be leaving the army soon. 'I don't want to sound like Rambo, but you have to assume this is the last time the British Army will ever go to war in such force and, quite honestly, peacetime soldiering will never be the same,' he said.

Let us finish, as we began, with a glimpse of Cordingley, whose professional delight at being asked to lead the 7th Armoured Brigade into action at the head of the British contingent never outweighed his desire to avoid needless bloodshed on both sides. Soon after it became clear that the enemy was beaten, as Iraqi prisoners streamed in from every direction gratefully accepting a pack of field rations and a dry pair of socks, I discovered him in the back of a command vehicle, devouring a hefty slice of fruitcake donated by his aide-de-camp.

It all seemed to be going very well, Cordingley observed, sounding faintly surprised that meticulous planning and immaculate execution had paid off on the day. 'But, look here, don't go giving me the credit for that,' he said. 'Anybody who knew the British Army well could have told you that it was up to this job.'

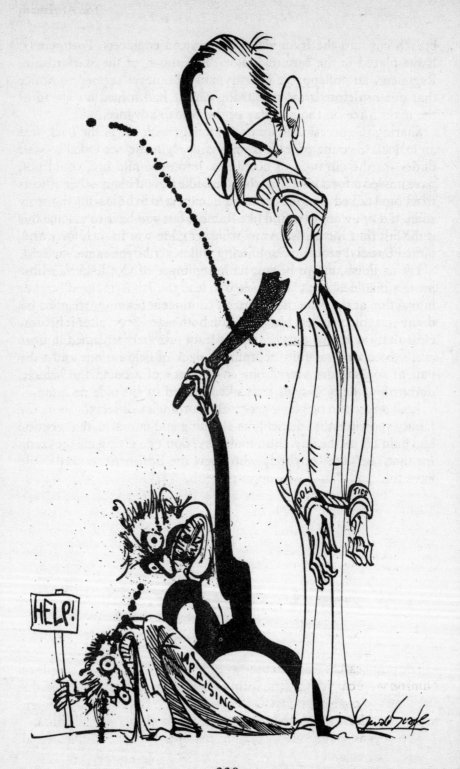

FOR THE FALLEN

Eric Bailey

Daily Telegraph, March 9, 1991

In a simple ceremony officially described as the Reception Of Those Who Gave Their Lives For Their Country in the Gulf, 17 British soldiers who fell in the Gulf war were honoured when they arrived at RAF Brize Norton in Oxfordshire yesterday.

The Duke of Kent's standard rippled in the wind above Brize Norton's terminal, where at 11.50am precisely the C-130 Hercules bearing the dead was due.

The Duke wore the uniform of Colonel-in-Chief of the Royal Regiment of Fusiliers, six of whose young men were killed when an American A-10 opened fire on their Warrior armoured vehicle. Armed Forces Minister Archie Hamilton, General Sir David Ramsbotham and Air Marshal Sir John Kemball joined him in the VIP enclosure.

A few yards away, the next of kin clung to each other, and waited.

But the men who had marched on to the apron were largely the comrades of the dead: the St George's Band of the Royal Regiment of Fusiliers; hatless pall-bearers from each bereaved regiment and corps.

The Hercules came on time, first a faint roar somewhere at the edge of the airfield, then a dark behemoth inching up the runway, its looming bulk driven by two of its four propellors. The great noise died and left a silence troubled only by the rushing wind. Senior chaplains of all three services, wearing medals and carrying prayer books, walked forward.

But there were no words, bar the bawl of commands and the uniform slap of boots on concrete. Then the guards of honour from the three Services stood perfectly still, the tails of their jackets flapping.

The pall-bearers boarded the aircraft, and as the swelling chords of Nimrod were carried into the spring air, the first coffin emerged on the shoulders of comrades; David Denbury, of the Corps of Royal Engineers, is understood to have been killed behind the enemy's lines.

The coffins came out in regimental order. Those of the Royal

331

Scots and the Queen's Own Highlanders were accompanied by the mournful lament Flowers of the Forest, played by Pipe Major David McKinsey. The band moved through Beethoven's Funeral March, to The Last Honours. Boots and buttons glittered in the brief sunlight: honour had been done with brush and polish.

It took 35 minutes. They were aged from 17 to 34; they came from many corners of the kingdom. Each was borne at the pace of the drum by young men whose scrubbed faces looked old.

A succession of Granadas and Princesses came from behind the building, engines ticking quietly; the relatives held each other tighter, and there were tears. The hearses rolled slowly away, followed by the pall-bearers in strict order.

Somewhere on the airbase, a coroner opened and adjourned inquests, so that evidence of identification could be given and the bodies released for burial. Afterwards Mr Hamilton made a brief statement, expressing sympathy for the next-of-kin, acknowledging the nation's debt.

General Ramsbotham added on behalf of the Army Board: 'The theme of what we have been watching is simple dignity. We have come to pay our respects not only to those who have given the sacrifice, but also to their relatives, acknowledging what they must be going through at this moment.'

Words, however, were not needed. It had been beautifully done, a ritual that belonged in the blustery air – under an English heaven. But the brass, the spectacle, the music, could only be faint embellishments to the real substance of the occasion: something incalculable, something noble.

The dead soldiers, in regimental order, were:

Corps of Royal Engineers: Cpl David Denbury, 26, from Ponthir, near Newport, Gwent, understood to be attached to the SAS and killed in action behind enemy lines.

The Royal Scots: Pte Thomas Haggerty, 20, from Glasgow, killed in Kuwait by a landmine after the ceasefire.

Queen's Own Highlanders: Pte John Lang, 19, from Munster, Germany; Pte Neil Donald, 18, from Forres, Grampian; Martin Ferguson, 21, from Fort William, Highland; all killed in a 'friendly fire' attack by a US A-10 Thunderbolt 'tank-killer' aircraft.

Royal Regiment of Fusiliers: Fusiliers Conrad Cole, 17, from Rochdale, Lancs; Stephen Satchell, 18, from Rye, East Sussex; Paul Atkinson, 19, from Co Durham; Richard Gillespie, 19, from Tynemouth; Kevin Leech, 20, from Prudhoe, Northumberland; Lee Thompson, 19, from Coventry; all killed in the A-10 attack.

The Staffordshire Regiment: Pte Shaun Taylor, 20, from Stourbridge, W Midlands; Pte Carl Moult, 22, from Burton-on-Trent.

Royal Corps of Transport: Driver Jason McFadden, 19, from Coventry; L/Cpl Terence Hill, 26, from Middlesex.

Corps of Royal Electrical and Mechanical Engineers: Sgt Michael Dowling, 34, from Dorset; L/Cpl Francis Evans, 25, from Flint, Clwyd.

SADDAM ROUTS THE KURDS

Harvey Morris

Independent, April 2, 1991

The beginning of the end came on Thursday morning. Groups of Kurdish guerrillas in beaten-up Datsun pick-ups and mud-covered cars formed an orderly if noisy queue at the last petrol station out of Arbil before heading for the front line, 25 miles south towards Kirkuk.

A man at the nearby tea stall – there is only smuggled red Iranian tea now and the Kurds hate it – was making an all too familiar appeal to the West: 'You must tell Bush, you must tell John Major, they must help the Kurds by attacking. We need help.'

Down near the front, however, it was clear that the Kurds, as so often in the past, were having to rely on their own devices. Washington's threat to the Iraqis that 'if you fly, you die' clearly did not extend to the two helicopter gunships that hovered lazily over the battle line, out of range of the guerrillas' captured Dushka anti-aircraft guns, occasionally firing a rocket into guerrilla positions at the small town of Alton Kopry. The town straddles the Arbil-Kirkuk highway and the government column had moved up in the night to seize the road and cut off Kirkuk from the rest of rebel-held Kurdistan and prevent reinforcements reaching it.

The government advance came right on cue, just a few hours after the US State Department spokeswoman, Margaret Tutweiler, had announced that Iraqi forces were massing to retake the oil city. If the Kurds had had the right weapons it is unlikely that the remnants of Saddam Hussein's demoralised army would have stood a chance. As it was, the *peshmerga* guerrillas, armed – apart from the odd artillery piece – with nothing bigger than shoulder-held RPG rocket-launchers and the occasional machine gun, succeeded in seeing off the first strike and opening up the road.

But in the end they had no defences against the gunships. They have a loathing of the helicopters and a constantly expressed unease that they might be carrying poison gas. Also, the *peshmerga* do not like fighting in open country; they prefer the more familiar mountains and the cover they provide.

Up at the hill resort of Salahuddin, above Arbil, where the Kurdish commander, Masoud Barzani, had set up his headquarters in one of Saddam's innumerable residences, a senior aide said that the government had assembled a mixed force of some 10,000 to retake Kirkuk. 'We estimate that at the end of the Gulf war, Saddam had maybe 400 tanks left,' said Fadhil Mirani. 'Of those, he sent 250 against us. What can we do against 250 tanks? We aren't used to fighting in the town. It is the first time.'

In many ways, the seven-party alliance of the Kurdistan National Front, of which General Barzani is military commander, was a victim of its own success. 'It was imposed on us to take these towns,' Mr Mirani acknowledged. The chief cities of Kurdistan – Kirkuk, Arbil, Dihok, Zakho – lie on the plains and foothills facing south towards Baghdad. They are practically indefensible against a superior force, particularly one which is not concerned about civilian casualties.

From early March, however, every city, town and village in Kurdistan rose up *en masse* against President Saddam's rule, and within 10 days the whole region was in rebel hands, north-east of a line running from Khaneqin, near the Iranian border, through Kirkuk and Arbil, skirting the predominantly Arab town of Mosul, and on to Dihok and Zakho, near the borders with Turkey and Syria. The Iraqi Army collapsed in as spectacular a fashion as it had in the south, and this time not in the face of a well-equipped Western army but in the face of a popular uprising. The troops simply refused to fight and the previously pro-government Kurdish units of the Popular Army joined the rebellion almost to a man. The Kurds captured up to 50,000 prisoners in little more than a week. The city of Arbil fell in three hours, between 7.00 and 10.00 on the morning of March 11.

Siza Jambaz, a young woman who returned last year after 10 years in London and was trapped by the war, described the scene. 'Suddenly, in the morning, there was lots of shooting and young boys running about with guns. When the *peshmerga* moved down from the mountains the Popular Army all joined the people. The *peshmerga* were much fewer than the ordinary people. After Arbil was captured the guerrillas moved on to Kirkuk. Everyone was so happy. The army just gave up.'

'We destroyed the First Army, the Fifth Army and half the Second Army,' Barzani told me at Salahuddin. 'Some 70,000 or 80,000 men. Some, of course, ran away, but 40–50,000 were captured. We gave them the choice: join the rebellion or go where you like. We asked the Red Cross to come and help us, but they didn't.'

The four million Kurds of the north had precious little food to feed themselves, let alone 50,000 captives. But there were no reprisals against the army; many soldiers stayed in the north, wandering around the Kurdish towns rather than return south and face punishment or death for their failure to resist. Some headed for Syria or Turkey; others found refuge in Kurdish homes; in Arbil, a young Arab conscript had been adopted into the family of a Kurdish friend, a *peshmerga* wounded in the attack on police HQ.

The army may have disintegrated, but its officers had time to wreck much of its equipment, including trucks and artillery pieces, depriving the Kurds of much-needed weaponry. Where there was ammunition there were no weapons, and where there were weapons there was no ammunition. In the mountain village of Kalifan the *peshmerga* proudly displayed a captured 175mm cannon, but there is no earthly chance they will ever be able to use it.

The inadequacy of the *peshmerga* army was all too obvious by Friday morning. Despite recapturing Alton Kopry, guerrilla forces were facing heavy land and air bombardment in Kirkuk. Hundreds if not thousands of civilians were being killed. And then the army launched a new offensive at Kalak, where a bridge spanned the Greater Zab river on the road to Mosul. Once more the *peshmerga* dashed enthusiastically to the front, fanning out across the fields above Kalak, apparently unconcerned about the incoming shell fire. In the opposite direction, trucks, tractors and cars carrying refugees and their belongings streamed eastwards towards Arbil and on into the mountains.

The *peshmerga* put anti-aircraft guns on the steel Bailey bridge at Kalak and managed to hold on to the eastern side of the town, where a eucalyptus grove around the abandoned army barracks provides some cover. But it was clear that the main road to the north was now effectively cut. The only way out now was through the mountains.

Up at Salahuddin, General Barzani was giving a final interview before leaving for a war council with his guerrilla commanders. The *peshmerga* presence was less than before. There was a sense that everyone was ready to pack up and leave. At 4.15 on Friday afternoon, General Barzani posed for a photograph against the background of the Arbil plain then climbed into his white Toyota saloon and was driven away.

THE VALLEYS OF DEATH

Martin Woollacott

Guardian, April 3, 1991

A monstrous crime is being perpetrated in Kurdistan. As the Kurdish people's brief springtime of freedom ends, they are, and will be, subject not only to the effects of a war waged in their own cities and towns without restraint or morality, but to the reimposition of Saddam Hussein's brutal rule and his revenge on those who have challenged him.

'Let nobody say the Kurdish people is dead,' was spray-painted in English on the end of an oil tanker, its flanks crammed with people, ahead of us in Sunday's chaotic refugee queue out of Salahuddin, the Kurdish headquarters. But the fear must be that Iraqi Kurds are about to suffer blows which could indeed be mortal. Certainly it will be the worst reprisal in 100 years of struggle.

Yesterday Turkey's National Security Council said that more than 200,000 people fleeing Iraq, mostly women and children, were in danger of death near the Turkish border. 'Where is Bush?' was a question we must have heard a thousand times as we toiled on Monday up the slopes of the 8,000-foot mountain passes that separate Iraq from Turkey. 'Why did he start if he was not going to finish?' or 'Why has he not finished Saddam?'

Sometimes all the bitterness and despair are compressed into the single word Bush, pronounced with a terrible resignation. The name of a man who was a hero to the Kurds only a few days ago has become almost a curse.

Up the rock-strewn hills, through gorges bristling with dwarf oaks, and over rushing grey streams, a miserable procession of people claws and staggers its way out of Iraqi Kurdistan. There is no road, only a horse track that winds endlessly upward, normally used only by smugglers.

Babies cry, old people stand panting by the side of the pass, one pointing wordlessly at his two bottles of pills. The walk, a stiff five-hour hike for fit adults, can be literally killing for the elderly and the sick. Two people died on the path the day before our crossing, the Turks on the other side told us.

But it is one of the few places where people can still escape from the tightening vice of the government forces. Some other crossing points are under artillery fire; Iran is letting in only women and children; sheer chaos on the roads prevents access to other routes. And it will not be too long, the Turks reckon, before Iraqi helicopters poke their guns and rockets into these gorges and valleys.

Turkish villagers whip sure-footedly up and down the steep inclines with their wiry horses and donkeys. For a fee they will carry some of the goods which these pathetic people have brought with them.

This is the middle class of stricken towns like Kirkuk and Tuz Kurmatu, joined by families from Irbil as that city came under bombardment. They are the people who have the vehicles and can afford the black market prices for petrol. 'I've left 100,000 dinars behind, three houses and two cars,' is a typical cry.

They are ill-equipped for the trip. High-heeled shoes buckle, badly secured possessions are swept away in the first stream, one woman in a leopardskin dress walks along with a box containing shampoo, conditioner, and hair tint.

A businessman in a grey pin-striped suit and a fur hat, trouser legs caked with mud, says tearfully: 'They killed all the Turkish people in Tuz Kurmatu . . . when they came they started to kill all the Kurdish and Turkish people. Just shoot, shoot, shoot by the government. The United States caused all this, why, why, why?'

He is a Turcoman like many on this crossing, confident that because of their Turkish origins the authorities on the other side will extend some kind of welcome. His family trudges along the path as he speaks, two small children in red and white rompers wailing. His wife gestures angrily with a briefcase: 'Bush is Saddam's friend. Why did he stop?'

These are just a fraction of the hundreds of thousands of people on the move in Iraqi Kurdistan. Many have made it over the borders into Turkey, Iran, and Syria. But many more, reeling from threatened town to threatened town, will not get out.

The Iraqis, at the speed they are advancing, will soon control all the crossings and no one has any doubt that if necessary they will bomb the refugee columns to stop the exodus. They already have bombed refugees on the road from Irbil to Salahuddin. As we left the town the dull thud of helicopter bombing on the other side sent shivers of panic through the refugee traffic snarled on the western side – the way out to Iran and Turkey.

A Kurdish officer, his hands covered in the blood of his children, hit earlier in the day, was frantically trying to open up the blocked road so that they could get to hospital in the next town. An hour afterwards, we were told by refugees who caught up with us later, the helicopters came over to the eastern side of the hill and bombed and rocketed the cars, and Salahuddin itself was shelled.

Although there were a few military vehicles in the traffic – we saw one jeep piled with military maps and others with staff files – the column could not conceivably be described as a military target.

The fate of those who escape the helicopters, with few possessions and facing months, perhaps longer, in refugee camps, is hard enough, but it is the fate of those who stay which is most tragic to contemplate.

There is no doubt that after he has re-established control, President Saddam will take a terrible revenge on those who rose against him and effaced his image from every corner of their land. This is the man who gassed a whole town and who took hostage thousands of Kurds who disappeared, almost certainly dead, in 1983.

You have only to visit one of the torture palaces which exist in every city and town in Kurdistan to realise how brutal his rule has been. And not just brutal; the tactics of his intelligence services go beyond brutality to the most ingenious refinements of cruelty. There is the raping room, for instance – a sort of hut off the main interrogation room, with a bloodied mattress inside and a pile of discarded women's clothes outside. And there are persistent tales of naked men being thrown to dogs trained to bite their private parts. In other countries you might discount such tales: in Iraq, the chances are that they are true.

The Kurdish response to the revolution was so wholehearted and so widespread that it could be said that virtually everybody has committed offences that would have warranted imprisonment, torture, and execution in the old Iraq. When the security services get back into their burned and blasted headquarters, the list-making will begin and the arrests will soon follow. Their revenge will be the more ferocious because of the evidence that in some towns Iraqi security men were done to death after the fighting was over. In the

Sulaymaniyah security centre, the severed forearm of one was still stuck on a hook on the wall.

There were not many such deaths, because on the whole the Kurdish revolution tried to be magnanimous even towards its worst enemies. One middle-class Kurd, who tried to stop the killing of a security man, was shouted at by a woman: 'Have you had a sister who was raped and tortured? If you have, then you can speak. If you haven't, you have nothing to say.'

Another man pushed him away from the scene, telling the story of losing three sons, of whose fate at the hands of the security services he learned only when curt demands for 70 dinars 'burial charges' came through the post. Everybody involved in the revolution, even in a minor way, is potentially on the death list.

In Sulaymaniyah, at a dinner party given by middle-class supporters of the revolution for visiting journalists, the best Kurdish dishes were on the table and the last beer in the town was brought out.

Local intellectuals spoke grandly of the problems facing a new reformed Iraqi administration: how to revive agriculture, changes in education, how to instil democratic habits in a people long unused to them.

The news that Kirkuk was in trouble cast a sudden chill on the gathering. The dream castles were already crumbling and the sound of the ambulances and refugee-filled trucks roaring into the town from Kirkuk silenced the happy talk. Everybody in that room – the academics and doctors on the 'Western press reception committee', the young women in their beautiful Kurdish finery, the hostess whose 'pilaff behind a curtain' is famous among the town's gourmets – is marked for death. Even the children.

Later, at the mass grave of the victims of the Halabja gassing, another middle-class man said: 'There are many mass graves in Iraq. If Saddam wins, there will be more, and I will probably be in one of them.'

Kurdistan's brief freedom began three weeks ago when a tentative push at the structure of oppression in a town called Rania was so brilliantly successful that it led to a chain reaction throughout Kurdistan. There was an extraordinary euphoria, a feeling that after many betrayals and disasters the Kurdish people's moment had finally come.

It all turned to dust in two days, from the fall of Kirkuk last Thursday to the collapse of Kurdish defences in the last few days. The problem was that the Kurds had won in the north by guile,

339

not by main force. They had persuaded the government mercenaries to change sides, and organised the surrender of President Saddam's unsteady units in many places. The people had done the rest and only in a few towns did the guerrillas have to fight hard battles.

President Saddam proved to have more resources of men and equipment than was believed, and more political control at the centre than had been expected. Only 10 days ago Massoud Barzani, the leader of the Kurdish Democratic Party, was talking confidently of establishing a temporary government for all Iraq in free Kurdistan.

The Kurdish military leaders were over-confident, inexperienced in conventional war, and disorganised. They believed too readily that a collapse in Baghdad would come soon and that, if things did by some mischance go wrong, the United States would rescue the situation.

These were their faults. But what of ours? The US, which to the Kurds is shorthand for all of the West, failed to make the intervention that the Kurds are convinced might have tipped the balance their way. Its reconnaissance planes circled lazily over Kurdish towns as Iraqi helicopters bombed the civil population with terrible results. If just one or two of those helicopters had been shot down, like the fixed-wing aircraft that were downed earlier by US planes, it just might have made the difference. It would have had a tremendous effect on Kurdish morale, and it might have convinced President Saddam that further military moves in the north would attract serious American military intervention.

Why didn't the US and the allies do it? God knows, we bent international law and the UN Charter whenever we wanted to in the effort to free Kuwait. We spent millions and killed many thousands to punish President Saddam's aggression and, bluntly, to bring him down. Why then this sudden excess of legalism, this prating about internal affairs, these oh-so-wise thoughts about the undesirability of a divided Iraq?

Saddam Hussein has no more right to Kurdistan than he had to Kuwait. He has forfeited any such right by a vicious record of oppression of the Kurds worse even than his treatment of Iraq's Arab population. When he gets back full control he will kill, and kill, and kill.

It is not too late to intervene, taking up the conditions the Kurds have apparently demanded – a UN-brokered autonomy, demilitarisation, a substantial UN presence – on pain of visiting on President Saddam's forces a punishment from the air as swift and complete as that which we administered over Kuwait.

WHEN THE WOLVES
STOPPED HOWLING

John Edwards from the Zakho Mountains
on the Turkey/Iraq border

Daily Mail, April 6, 1991

When the wolves stopped howling, the people began to move again.

Now thousands of them were stumbling in the lead-coloured water of violent little rivers, passing babies across fallen logs.

The valleys were full of snow and lightning and the babies stared cold and hungry through a wrap of wet blankets at the miserable sky.

Sometimes the infants fell and mothers screamed after them with snow squeezing through the toes of their bare feet.

Then the columns of people joined up below the snowline at 6,000 feet. And afterwards it was a human avalanche filling the mountainside. The sound of wailing and crying began as a small noise way up there and became something that covered the slopes with its awful sound.

These were the Kurds of Iraq, desperate in their search for sanctuary from the murderous pursuit of Saddam Hussein.

The Turkish Army waited for them in the village of Isikveren. It is a nothing collection of wood huts and stone hovels which is all any place is up here in the Zakho Mountains dividing East Turkey from Iraq. Soon, though, Isikveren will be part of history.

The great columns of refugees shuffled around the last turn of the lowest valley. They came in a huge mass, a haunting sight of families, children half-blind with exhaustion, old men with their chests pumping, mothers and girls carrying babies, some of them in buckets.

President Bush worries about his 8-iron golf shots pulling up short of the putting greens in Florida. But there is no golf in Isikveren. Just people falling into pits of mud and fighting with vanishing strength to live another day in the hell of the Zakho Mountains.

The soldiers raised their rifles and fired suddenly over the heads of the people. The mountains roared back the echo of the shooting. The sound changed from wailing to the noise of battle.

It wasn't a single shot here and there. Thousands of rounds went over their heads, even a rip of machine-gun fire, and behind that the thud of something heavier. But the people just walked on to face the guns and the soldiers stepped back and fired wildly. They didn't change step. The front rank went right up to the soldiers and almost touched noses. The soldiers raised their guns higher and more long volleys shook the ground.

Bullets ricocheted from the boulder-strewn hillsides and whined everywhere. The people kept walking.

A woman in a blue coat was killed when a shot came off a rock. She fell down dead, and her friends, or people walking with her anyway, got around her body and carried it with them.

'An accident, a terrible accident,' an army lieutenant came over and said. He was distressed. They had not meant to hurt anybody, he said.

Why are you shooting? 'We can't have all of them scattering into the countryside,' he explained his orders.

'We have to keep them together. We are building a camp with good facilities.'

When the mountains petered out into level ground the area was Uludere province. The provincial governor went to Isikveren in a dark blue suit and a white shirt and a black tie. He looked like he had an appointment with a bank manager. He slapped his forehead when he heard the woman was shot and babbled something into a hand radio.

Nothing stopped the Kurds. All they did was walk on in this huge crowd, 20,000 maybe.

'We are told there are hundreds of thousands more up there,' the lieutenant said, pointing behind him.

Another fury of shooting cut him short.

'Try to tell them we are not going to send them back to Iraq,' he pleaded, 'try, please try.'

A refugee who spoke English was brought through the crowd. 'This officer says you are not being sent back to Iraq but you must stay together here,' he was told.

The man screamed with anger. 'Many children have died in the mountains there, why can't we be let into Turkey?'

The officer had gone before he could answer.

'Saddam, Saddam, die, die,' one group shouted. They all drew flat hands across their throats.

'In hospital in Zakho (*a Kurdish city in North Iraq*) Saddam's soldiers killed 30 people, children and women,' another man said. 'We will all be killed if we go back.'

How were they killed? 'Stab,' he said, 'stab all over and shoot-ing.'

Children sat exhausted on bed-rolls and old coats under the storm of bullets which went in sheets over their heads. The sound of shooting meant nothing. 'We've been shot at by Saddam for days,' somebody said.

Mothers fed babies in a rainstorm holding bits of carpets over their little heads. Dark-faced boys, six or seven years old, hunted for their families in the mass where it stopped next to the vil-lage.

When you talked to them, smoothed their mud-stiff hair, they smiled.

A tiny boy, perhaps seven, wore the jacket of a man. His little hands were 12 inches up the sleeves. He struggled to get his hand out to shake yours. The jacket was nearly an overcoat for him.

Where did he get it? 'From somebody who died in the snow,' the man with good English said.

The child saluted with the end of the sleeve hanging over his hand.

When did he last eat? 'Two days ago at least,' the man said. He told the story.

'We are all Kurds. Saddam wants us killed. The army shelled us in Zakho. All the people tried to cross the mountains to escape.'

Some of them were in the bucket of a bulldozer.

'When we cross first river we begin to climb. People couldn't carry all their goods so they left them. In a short time they had very little and no food. We ate grass and things on the ground.

'When we were in the forest we could light fires from the wood. Beyond the forest and the snow there is no wood and no trees. People began to freeze to death. They died everywhere. Look, look how few old women? Babies die because mothers got no milk inside them.'

But they tramped all the way over the top of the mountains, 20,000 at a time, and they came through rain and storms when the wind chopped off slices of ice and threw them around like circular saws.

It was the same as crossing the Alps and must be one of the greatest mass escapes and feats of endurance ever known.

If Mr Bush could get out here and see it he would pick up the phone on his golf trolley and tell his air force commanders to bomb Saddam's army into metal dust.

The women got into vast groups when the Turkish Army stopped them in the village. They had nothing really. Rags. The rags had kept them warm.

A mountain track from the lowlands was a ribbon of bogged-down trucks from Turkish Kurds trying to get supplies to them. Men tried to push a 10-tonner uphill through a mud hole. The open back was full of fresh bread. Potatoes were in other lorries, spinach and cabbage in the rest.

An old man on a dirty white horse yelled the name of a relative from Iraq at a seethe of faces. No one came to him. He wept.

A place on the grass as big as 10 football pitches was solid with refugees. Children filled their mouths with uncooked noodles. Mothers held out cans to the soldiers and begged for fresh water. There was a laziness that comes from exhaustion.

Now a man with face burns came to a puddle and splashed the blisters. 'Saddam soldier put gasoline on him and set him on fire,' it was said.

The man even managed to grin through the blisters.

A woman they said spoke English was asked, 'Are you glad to be in Turkey?' She wiped her mouth with the end of a black scarf. A sentence began but she was too tired to finish it.

Mud was dry on her dress up to the waist. This was the depth of the last river she waded. Her child, a girl with red hair, tugged at the dress.

More people pressed in and sat on the ground. They had nothing, rags and pieces of blanket.

The mountains were a litter of pots and pans and mattresses thrown down when they could take the strain of carrying them no more.

One of the massive tragedies of the world begins to make pictures in the high mountains of Turkey. And still there are more people sliding through the stunted, leafless trees with fingers numbed from frostbite and bare feet showing a painful blue under long dresses.

Cold rain hosed down, making a swamp out of everything. The Kurds crouched under old plastic sacks and children stared out from the makeshift tents. Their eyes were like those of small animals staring out of holes.

THE VICTIMS OF THE PEACE

Hugo Young

Guardian, April 2, 1991

As the Iraqi Kurds are massacred, we stand idly by. Idleness in this case is proposed as a virtue. Since the Western part in the Gulf war finished, a palsy has descended. For seven months there was a policy for Iraq, which was the clearest, most concerted policy the powers of the world have ever directed at a single country. But now there is no policy. It is, as much as anything, this precipitate contrast that most bewilders the Kurds: and not the Kurds alone.

The switch from calculated aggression to calculated inertia enjoys bipartisan support from the parties who disputed the original policy. Through this curtain of pragmatic indifference few voices escape to argue that what is now happening is an outrage that will substantially efface the triumph so recently achieved in Kuwait.

The chief proponents of inertia are governments, led by Washington and backed by London. The foreign office wrings its hands over the resurrection of Saddam Hussein, but it favours doing nothing. Like Washington it suggests that any further interventions could be interpreted as a desire to extend the American imperium, which is the last thing anyone could want. Like Washington, it rests with relief on a minimalist interpretation of UN resolutions that it so recently found convenient to broaden at will. Let the Kurds go hang, literally.

At the back of this may or may not be a deeper cynicism. Some say the powers find it convenient to retain Saddam in place, his army routed from Kuwait but still big enough to resist encroaching Iranian domination. The evidence for this is more negative than positive, but it is in any case not essential to the story. What we have witnessed, at quite astonishing speed, is a reversion from the brutalities of a crusade to the different but equal brutalities of compromise. War has been succeeded not by peace but by another kind of war. A global mission is fulfilled, only to make way for the renewal of vicious civil conflict. Far from beckoning in a new order, this reaffirms the old order in which tyrants survive, realpolitik triumphs and the powerless bite

345

the bullet. Having been summoned to insurrection in support of the war, the Kurds now play their allotted role in this old order: of being summarily returned to domestic captivity once the global war is won.

Governments, however, supply only half the picture. Their case for doing nothing is reinforced by the people who opposed war in the first place. The wretched Kurds will find no comfort there, even though it is in such quarters that the appeal of the underdog usually resounds to most effect.

For do these events not exemplify the very case made by the anti-war school, which said that one certain consequence of war would be upheaval in the Middle East, with the peoples of the region thrown into chaos? Doesn't the torture of Kurdish children only reinforce George Bush's error in going to war, and remove from him every entitlement to be called a victor? One sometimes feels that the masterly inaction of Washington, as it watches the routing of the Kurds, meets the grim relish of anti-war opinion, as it sees its prophetic warnings vindicated.

This symbiotic endorsement, it must be admitted, enjoys a certain strength. Doing nothing is by far the easiest strategy. Permitting the Iraqi wasteland to continue untamed, whether as economy or democracy, may be the least expensive form of realism. The resurgence of the Republican Guard may well keep Teheran in its place. Above all, President Bush's unwillingness to engage the American military in further action probably stands the best chance of sustaining his support at home and the illusion, on which it depends, that he presided over a mighty peacekeeping triumph for America.

This illusion, however, must now be reckoned increasingly fragile. The more we see what is happening to the Kurds, the more difficult it is to believe that peace, still less justice, has been brought to the region. Some might say the same when they look at the scandalous behaviour of the Kuwaitis towards the Palestinians, but that is another matter. With regard to what is happening inside Iraq we have a choice between accepting the status quo with a weary shrug or reassembling the energy to act.

This does not mean marching on Baghdad and taking over an impossible task of government. But there is something logically repellent, after 40 days and nights of bombing the daylight out of every Iraqi city, about resting policy on the basis that the powers should not intervene in the internal affairs of another country. As a minimum, the destruction of Iraqi helicopters unleashed against the Kurds could easily have been construed as falling within the temporary ceasefire agreement. It should still be undertaken – if, Saddam resurgent, it is not too late.

The most blatant failure lies at the United Nations. How swiftly it has reverted to discreditable impotence! That it was the focus of the world's reaction to the predicament of Kuwait seemed to herald an enduring recovery. Mr Bush unveiled an entire vision of foreign policy in which the UN was the centrepiece of a wholly new diplomacy. Without a series of UN resolutions eliciting, especially from the Americans and the British, diplomatic activity of a high order, Kuwait would still be occupied by Iraq.

But since the war, the UN has appeared comatose. The terms of a permanent ceasefire have yet to be agreed. The impositions the Security Council is prepared to make on Saddam Hussein in pursuit of earlier resolutions affirming the need for permanent peace and security in the Middle East are far from clear. Easter, which was supposed to be the deadline by which the future of Iraq would be determined by the world, instead appears as the moment when Saddam Hussein reassumed control of the greater part of Iraq on his own brutal terms. In place of an acceptable formula providing for a humanitarian end to food and medical sanctions, along with the rigid maintenance of an arms embargo, famine and epidemic threaten even as the arms-dealers regroup.

Before the war began, there was a general apprehension that, so long as it ended in a swift victory for the coalition forces, it would have a constructive effect. The moral righteousness of the crusade was directed in particular to the liberation of Kuwait, but also extended to an improvement in the quality of life in Iraq. While disavowing the war aim of despatching Saddam, Mr Bush indicated that democratic forces in Iraq would be supported and encouraged.

After the war what is most conspicuous is the absence of any policy, save bringing the boys home as soon as possible. It was as if war exhausted not only the munitions factories but the think tanks of the state department and the foreign office. Yet it is already striking how distant the war seems, and how small its domestic dividends may be. How much more futile if Saddam Hussein is taught nothing.

FORCES FOR THE FUTURE

Max Hastings

Daily Telegraph, March 6, 1991

Now they talk mostly about going home; oh yes, and they ask what people have made of it all in England. We tell them that in England, everybody thinks they were wonderful, except maybe Ted Heath and John Pilger. The men of 1st Armoured Division, washing their socks and cleaning up their vehicles beneath their careful canopy of camouflage netting and forest of wireless aerials a few miles outside Kuwait City, are learning to live with peace again.

But what kind of peace will it be for the British armed forces? On Sunday morning, in a fly-blown little Operations room at Muharraq air base in Bahrain, the defence secretary Tom King talked to a cluster of Tornado and Buccaneer pilots. It was a moving occasion, because these tanned men in flying suits and suede shoes looked so tired, and were still so deeply concerned about their missing comrades.

When Mr King had told them how warmly their country appreciates what they have done for it, he asked for questions. There was only one: 'Can you tell us, sir, whether "Options" is still on?' Having lived for weeks in an unreal world of triple A, airfield denial and bridge-busting with laser-guided bombs, these men are now returning to real life, of impending defence cuts and the ministry of defence proposal 'Options For Change'.

The defence secretary gave the aircrew the obvious answer – that everything will have to be looked at again, in the light of the Gulf experience. And indeed, it is extraordinary how a picture which seemed so clear has become clouded and ill-focused, after seven months of crisis and war in the Middle East.

In the summer of 1990, the British Goverment was looking at a world in which the Warsaw Pact had collapsed, while Britain was still spending a higher proportion of her Gross National Product on defence than any of her European partners or commercial rivals. Other national spending priorities beckoned, education prominent among them. The slogan of the hour was 'lean and mean'. The thrust of defence thinking was that the days of according primacy to British heavy armour were over, and that the future lay in light, flexible, fast-moving intervention forces.

Today, we see a British armoured division resting upon the laurels of a quick and brilliant desert victory, in which the decisive instruments were the overwhelming application of air power, and the deployment of massed heavy tanks and artillery. It will be many weeks, if not months, before the lessons of the Gulf war can be digested and applied to reshaping Britain's defence policy. But, talking to the men in the desert, it is already possible to identify some of the issues being most intensely debated.

When 1st Armoured Division left Germany for the Gulf, some of us expressed doubts whether its tank regiments (or those of the Americans) would ever return there. The combination of the Warsaw Pact collapse and the increasingly intolerable constraints upon military training in Germany seemed to raise real doubts about the Rhine Army's future deployment.

In the short term, it appears almost certain that the British units in the Gulf will go back to Germany, not least because there is nowhere else for them – or at least, nowhere in Britain immediately available with barracks, married quarters, and training facilities. In the longer term, however, it must still be highly doubtful whether there is a strategic or economic case for keeping more than a single division in Germany.

Nobody wants to see a long-term British ground commitment in the Middle East. But the ministry of defence is thinking seriously about the possibilities of Saudi Arabia and the other Gulf states as a training area, for both land and air forces. The war has focused attention upon the simple fact that the vast desert emptinesses offer ideal opportunities for both tank units and aircraft to practise their skills in a fashion that is impossible anywhere in Europe. Some training agreement with the Gulf rulers might prove an ideal political compromise between avoiding a new east of Suez commitment, and making plain the West's continued interest in the stability of the region.

The Gulf war has conspicuously narrowed the options for one of Tom King's most sensitive procurement decisions. For more than three years, Britain has been wavering between buying the American Abrams tank, or the Vickers-built Challenger II. Yet now, after the Challenger's extraordinarily impressive display of reliability in the desert, it seems almost impossible that the Abrams will be preferred.

349

Chobham armour passed its only battlefield test when a Warrior vehicle was hit by a shell and lost only one armour plate. Seven Brigade's commander, Brigadier Patrick Cordingley, told me on Monday that after years of practising in Germany to engage enemy tanks at a range of 1,500 metres, in the desert they repeatedly knocked out T-55s at 3,000 metres, which is partially a tribute to the new long round with which 1st Armoured's tank guns were supplied at the last moment.

The war has opened a further debate, about whether the great success of American A-10 aircraft and Apache helicopters in the 'tank-busting' role argues that Britain should be thinking of buying these, rather than a lot of new tanks. Much will have to await statistical analysis of each weapons system's impact upon Iraqi targets. Some soldiers also argue that this war was not a proper test of tank-busting aircraft, because the Iraqis did not put up significant anti-aircraft fire on the battlefield. A 'proper' enemy could have made the going far tougher for tactical air units.

The war was dominated by America's most advanced high technology. A fundamental issue for every major power is whether any nation save the United States can afford to keep pace with such equipment. Britain could not conceivably buy the Stealth fighter, at a billion dollars a copy. But the Royal Air Force is thinking very hard indeed about whether, in any future conflict, it can sensibly expose very expensive aircraft to drop unguided 'iron' bombs.

The foremost lesson of allied bomber operations seems to be that the precision-guided munitions performed superbly. But the free-fall bombing, including 'carpet-bombing' by the B-52s, was of far more doubtful value. It was only when the air forces began to concentrate their laser-guided and other 'smart' bombs on the Iraqi Army that the heaviest scale of damage on emplaced equipment was achieved.

British soldiers give high praise to their inertial navigation systems, which enabled them to move long distances at night with absolute certainty about their own positions. The artillery, and perhaps above all the MLRS rocket batteries, were devastatingly effective. Almost all the equipment achieved far higher serviceability rates in the desert than in Europe, partly because of the drier climate, partly because intensive use suited it far better than the rare outings which training restrictions permit in the Rhine Army.

Every man in 1st Armoured Division recognises that the Iraqi resistance was very poor, and thus it would be foolish to assume that an equally crushing victory could be achieved against any enemy. But nothing can detract from the fact that it was the ruthless efficiency of the allied offensive, by air and land, which reduced the enemy's huge resources to mere broken toys.

There is great satisfaction about the effectiveness of allied command and control, and the harmony with which the British worked with the Americans. High tributes are paid to Lieutenant-General Sir Peter de la Billière for his diplomatic skills. The British are very conscious that, in order to equip a small armoured division, it proved necessary to strip the whole Rhine Army of equipment and spares. A third brigade would have been sorely missed if the Iraqis had put up serious resistance.

This operation has exposed how absurdly thinly Britain's armed forces have been spread in recent years, to maintain the façade of a much larger army than its real resources permit. What is most needed now is a hard look at how Britain's forces can be reshaped, to ensure that our army is properly manned and resourced for its future commitments. It must never be allowed, as it so nearly was in the past, to become a film-set army, with an imposing frontage unsupported by the real means to do its job.

But perhaps the greatest achievement of Desert Storm is that it has given a new generation of soldiers, sailors and airmen a surge of confidence in themselves and the forces to which they belong, to carry forward into the 21st century. They have shown themselves, as well as the world, that the commanders, the men, the equipment can perform as splendidly as their predecessors. Man for man, this is probably as fine a fighting force as Britain has ever put into the field.

NOT THIS WAY TO THE NEW WORLD
Peter Jenkins
Independent, April 9, 1991

Distressing scenes of wretched, starving Kurds fleeing from the vengeance of Saddam Hussein make mockery of the continuing celebration of Kuwait's liberation. Is there, or ought not there to be, some connection between the two events? Most people think so. How else to make sense of the world?

There are two ways of morally squaring this circle of inconsistency. One is to argue, as do President Bush's critics, that having encouraged the Iraqi peoples to rise up against Saddam, Mr Bush should have finished the dictator off militarily or, at very least, denied him the use of his helicopter gunships – although that may not have made a crucial difference. The other is to argue, as I do and did, that it was wilfully and cruelly misleading to present the war against Saddam as a moral crusade from whose carnage would rise a 'new world order' like a new Jerusalem.

It was this promotion of a brutal but tin-pot dictator into a devil worse than Hitler, this dressing up of interest as principle, and the moralistic hyperbole which accompanied the necessary enterprise of recovering Kuwait and containing Saddam, which made one dubious not of the feasibility of waging war but its wisdom. What good would come of it in the end? What good ever came of war?

Perhaps, as so few other gains were in prospect for the peoples of the region (not even Kuwaiti democracy), it would have been better to have gone the final mile to Baghdad and, at least, been rid of the monster Saddam. But let no one suppose that Iran and Syria would not have fought over the bones of Iraq, or that the Kurds would have lived happily ever after, or that democracy and peace would have flowered in the deserts of Arabia. How could anyone have supposed that honey would flow from the carcass of a Middle Eastern war? Only, perhaps, Americans in their bruised moral innocence.

What if there had been such a 'hidden agenda', as the critics of the war were the quickest to allege? Were the Syrians and the Saudis there in Desert Shield in order to make the region safe for democracy and human rights? Was self-determination for the Kurds ever on the Turkish, Soviet or Iranian agendas?

The war was fought for much more limited and realistic goals – for oil, yes, but also to punish and undo a blatant territorial aggression and, in the process, contain the malignant ambitions of Iraq. Those goals were achieved and the scale of Saddam's defeat should not be underrated simply because he retains the power to oppress his own peoples. The terms of the ceasefire laid down by the Security Council last week and accepted by Iraq are humiliating and punitive. Iraq's capacity to wage further war against her neighbours is effectively destroyed. Sanctions are to continue until Saddam has complied in full, and provide a strong incentive for his eventual removal. His barbaric treatment of the Kurdish people is good cause for twisting the tourniquet tighter, in which process the European Community can take the lead as it sought to do in Luxembourg last night. Sanctions should be further linked to his compliance with the amnesty he has

352

declared for the Kurdish and Shia rebels. The UN should be called upon to supervise and monitor their safe return to their villages. A peace-keeping force could be installed in the north as well as on the Kuwaiti border to provide a haven for refugees. If the Security Council will not take these steps, the EC and the United States can use their own considerable economic leverage in the cause of justice and humanity.

It was the apparent nonchalance of the joggin', fishin' and golfin' president which stuck in people's gullets as they witnessed the immediate consequences of his crusade. But this is how wars usually end – in reprisal, misery, anarchy and massive displacement. Arguments of moral equivalence are of small help in deciding what to do, or what should have been done. Old-fashioned territorial aggressions like Saddam's are rare in the post-war world but there have been scores of civil wars or internal aggressions, some verging upon genocide, and the world has done precious little about them. The Middle East, in particular, is thick with dictators and their prisons and their torture chambers, some of whom were among our best allies in the liberation of Kuwait. If Saddam deserves overthrow by military might why not Haffiz Assad in Syria or the Islamic fundamentalists in Iraq?

The answer does not lie in any principle of non-intervention but, rather, in the practical problems of extending international policing to the internal affairs of sovereign states. It might have been convenient to have disposed finally of Saddam under the cover of implementing the various UN resolutions concerning Kuwait, but to have done so might have embroiled the western powers in endless conflicts of peoples – Shias, Sunnis, Kurds, Palestinians, Jews – overspilling the disputed borders of predominantly undemocratic regimes. The world, sadly, is a long way from a rule of law which transcends frontiers and it is idle to pretend that disposing of one particularly nasty dictator would have brought that any nearer.

After the First World War, Wilsonian idealism soon gave way to a squalid territorial carve-up, and Mr Bush's Wilsonian rhetoric is already giving way to crude balance-of-power politics. If we do not like what we now see, a first modest step would be to start calling things by their names and not pretend that playing one nasty regime against another or the championing of reactionary feudal rulers is the way to build a new order of democracy and peace.

HOW TO KEEP THE PEACE

Anthony Parsons

London Review of Books, March 21, 1991

In the months following the Iraqi invasion of Kuwait, accusations of appeasement were directed at those who doubted the wisdom of adopting an uncompromisingly hard line towards Saddam Hussein. In practice, the history of appeasement of the Ba'athist regime in Iraq goes back many years and only came to an end on August 2, 1991, before these charges were made. It has been well-known in the Middle East for over 20 years that Saddam Hussein is a brutal and ambitious dictator with aspirations to dominate the oil-rich Arabian peninsula, indeed to succeed President Nasser as a regional Arab leader. In 1979, I visited almost all the states in the peninsula in the wake of the Iranian revolution. I discovered that the principal source of anxiety was not the spread of the Iranian revolutionary message but Iraqi attempts to dominate the smaller Gulf states. This was clear to Western governments and also, presumably, to Moscow, which had concluded a Treaty of Friendship with Iraq seven years earlier. However, such was the fear in the industrialised world of the destabilising influence of Khomeinism, as well as the odium attaching to Iran for the seizure of the staff of the American embassy in Teheran, that no government sought to take pre-emptive action against the obvious Iraqi preparations to 'teach Khomeini a lesson'.

When Iraqi forces invaded Iran in September 1980, the UN Security Council, at Iraqi urging, delayed meeting for a few days. When it met, it adopted a resolution which, while calling for a ceasefire, did not condemn the Iraqi action or call for Iraqi withdrawal from Iranian territory. Indeed, throughout the eight-year conflict, the Council only called for withdrawal when it was a question of Iranian forces withdrawing from Iraqi territory.

This was not the only example of pro-Iraqi bias shown by the Security Council between 1980 and 1988. When there was Council criticism of the actions of the belligerents, it was almost always scrupulously even-handed in spite of the fact that Iraq was more often than not the prime mover: for example, over initiation of the 'tanker war' in the Gulf, the bombardment of open cities and the use of poison gas. When the foreign naval armada, led by the United States, assembled in the Gulf in 1987, its task was to escort shipping off the Arab shore, thus freeing the Iraqi Air Force (equipped with the latest Soviet and French aircraft) to attack shipping plying to and from Iranian ports and oil terminals. Furthermore, while a stringent international arms embargo, Operation Staunch, was applied to Iran throughout the conflict at America's insistence, the saturation of Iraq with modern weaponry and the transfer of military technology from East and West continued unabated.

After the ceasefire in 1988, no serious attempt was made by the Great Powers to coerce Iraq into reinstating the 1975 Agreement with Iran on the land frontier and the division of the Shatt-el-Arab waterway, which Saddam had publicly torn up before invading Iran. Nor was there any move to establish the impartial body to enquire into responsibility for the conflict which was the nearest the Security Council came in Resolution 598 (1987) to meeting the Iranian demand for the 'identification and punishment of the aggressor'. Virtually no progress had been made towards the implementation of this resolution by the time Saddam invaded Kuwait and presented the Iranians with all their important war aims, asking nothing in return.

In the past two years, since the Iran/Iraq ceasefire, there has been a general tendency in the West, including the United States and the principal states of Western Europe, to regard Saddam's Iraq with a benevolent eye, as an orderly and businesslike, albeit dictatorial regime with an unlimited commercial potential. Cabinet ministers, industrialists and businessmen beat a path to Baghdad in a steady stream. Against this overall background, it is scarcely surprising that Saddam judged that his friends in Moscow, Washington, London, Paris, Bonn and elsewhere would not be too upset if he 'taught the Kuwaitis a lesson' for refusing to cede him control over two uninhabited islands and part of an oilfield, for overproducing oil and thus lowering the market price, and for their reluctance to cancel the huge debt which Kuwait had accumulated against Iraq thanks to its financial support during the war.

His political confidence in his immunity from serious reaction was matched by his military might, the product of the unprecedented Middle Eastern arms sales spree over the previous 20 years. In the Fifties and Sixties all Middle Eastern states were relatively lightly armed, especially those far distant from the Arab/Israeli conflict. From the Seventies the combination of East-West competition, commercial advantage and oil wealth, all working in a conflict-ridden environment, led to massive transfers of heavy weapons to all states in the region. The Middle East became the most lucrative arms market in the world. Countries, like Iraq, which had measured their tank and aircraft inventories in tens now possessed thousands and hundreds respectively. Their armed forces swelled in numbers to absorb the new weaponry. By the Eighties, any one of four or five Middle Eastern states, most of them with small populations, possessed far larger and more lavishly equipped armed forces than any Nato or Warsaw Pact country except for the two superpowers. Virtually all the hardware was imported, all the technology transferred. In a nutshell, Saddam was a military monster created by the industrialised world, with his political ambitions encouraged by what he took to be the support of major powers.

He miscalculated grossly. He failed to see that, with the Cold War over, the United States and the Soviet Union would co-operate, not compete, in the United Nations. He failed to see that he had endangered the two cardinal American interests in the Middle East – namely, the security of Israel and the status quo in Saudi Arabia. He failed to anticipate that the whole international community would reject his forcible annexation of a UN member state – especially as this was something that had never happened before. He failed to appreciate that his regime was so hated and feared in the Arabian peninsula and elsewhere in the Arab world that many governments, including Egypt and Syria as well as Saudi Arabia and the Gulf States, would have the political courage to invoke the direct military aid of 'Western imperialism'.

Even so, was it necessary to fight a major war to expel Saddam's forces from Kuwait? The UN Security Council moved with unprecedented speed and decisiveness to condemn his action, demand its reversal and impose mandatory economic sanctions backed by a naval blockade. This was the first time in the history of both the League of Nations and the United Nations that sanctions had been imposed on a sovereign state with no important defectors (as South Africa was in the case of Southern Rhodesia, as the United States, Germany and Japan were in the case of Mussolini's invasion of Abyssinia). On paper, Iraq was vulnerable to sanctions, dependent for foreign-exchange earnings on oil exports and dependent on imports for virtually all manufactured goods including military supplies.

I personally was in favour of giving sanctions longer to work before deciding on the resort to armed force. But, with hindsight, the acceleration of the programme was probably justified and the use of force inevitable. The total militarisation of the Iraqi state had created a situation in which Saddam could have held out against the pressure of sanctions for a year or more. Would public opinion among the Arab members of the coalition, or indeed in the Western world, have held firm for that long? I doubt it. Would it have been possible to have maintained hundreds of thousands of troops in a state of high readiness in north-east Saudi Arabia until 1992? I doubt it. Most important, we have now learnt that the ransacking and rape of Kuwait was proceeding at such a pace and on such a scale that, in a year's time, there would have been only a phantom state to liberate.

With the astonishing speed and comprehensiveness of the military victory, the argument about sanctions has become largely academic. However, with future such crises in mind, it is important that the United States and other leading governments in the coalition should dispel the mounting atmosphere of cynicism, the view that sanctions are not serious measures, only a formal preliminary to the use of armed force. This is not, in my judgement, necessarily the case. All crises are different, and I can envisage many situations in the climate of international co-operation in which sanctions alone would be effective. For example, had the Argentine invasion of the Falkland Islands taken place in the aftermath of the Cold War, when it would have been possible to adopt mandatory sanctions plus a naval/air blockade to force Argentina to withdraw, it is difficult to see how their garrison could have avoided compliance.

There is another important conclusion to be drawn about the capabilities of the UN Security Council. When the United States, the Soviet Union and Britain met at Dumbarton Oaks in 1944 to begin the drafting of what became the UN Charter, the heart of the matter was what eventually emerged as Chapter Seven – action with respect to threats to the peace, breaches of the peace and acts of aggression. This chapter provides for mandatory sanctions (Article 41) and, if they fail, armed force (Articles 42–47). These so-called 'military articles' were to provide the 'teeth' which the League of Nations had lacked. The three principal wartime allies envisaged a post-war world in which they would be the only heavily armed states: they would dominate the Security Council, and the like-mindedness which characterised the wartime alliance would persist. The Cold War broke out within months of the cessation of hostilities, however, and with decolonisation, the UN has expanded from a reasonably like-minded (or responsive to great powers) membership of 51 states to a decidedly un-like-minded and diverse membership of 160 states, many of them heavily armed. The military articles have consequently remained as dead letters and the Security Council has, with one or two exceptions, had to operate by means of persuasion under Chapter Six of the Charter (the pacific settlement of disputes) rather than Chapter Seven – coercion. The Gulf crisis has provided the first test of this unused machinery and in the event it proved irrelevant to the world of the Nineties.

The military articles envisage the Security Council (15 members including the five permanent veto-holding members – US, UK, USSR, France, China) and its Military Staff Committee (the permanent members) taking charge of planning the application of armed force (Article 46), and the Military Staff Committee assuming responsibility for strategic direction (Article 47). We have seen the vast scale and meticulousness of the planning which has gone into the Gulf war on the coalition side. It is inconceivable that the formidable logistic task which it presented at the outset, or the strategic and tactical formulation and execution of the plan, could have been achieved by so heterogenous a body as the Security Council. To start with, there would have been no military security in a body, at present containing the Yemen and Cuba, in which opinions were always to some extent divided. Secondly, five new non-permanent members came onto the Council on January 1 in place of the five whose membership term of two years had expired. This would not have helped the continuity of military planning and co-ordination. Thirdly I cannot imagine the five-member Military Staff Committee, including the Chinese and the Soviet Union, being able to replicate the unity, mutual confidence and speed of decision which must have been so intrinsic to the operations of General Colin Powell and his allied colleagues. In a nutshell, the Security Council can proceed only by adopting resolutions, painstakingly worked out and involving compromise. War cannot be fought like that.

It seems to me that what will come to be known as the Kuwait precedent will now be the only option if the Council feels the need to go beyond economic sanctions. This precedent is enshrined in Resolution 678, which, in effect, delegated authority to 'member states' to use force if necessary. It is very likely that the future pattern will be on these lines and that the action will be taken, as in the Gulf crisis, by a major power (not necessarily always the United States) in alliance with regional powers. Having said that, one caveat must be entered. It cannot have been easy for the

Soviet Union and China to acquiesce in giving the United States and its Western allies carte blanche to use force against a Third World country, particularly one that was a long-standing ally of the Soviet Union. Indeed I was surprised that neither government vetoed the resolution. Having now seen the consequences – the massive aerial campaign lasting for many weeks, the widespread destruction of Iraq's national infrastructure and the culminating rout of the Iraqi armed forces which the Soviet Union had helped to build up over more than 20 years – will the permanent members agree to similar action in a future case of aggression, or will the Kuwait precedent prove too large a pill to swallow twice? If it proves impracticable to rewrite the military articles in a form compatible with the world of the Nineties, the probability is that the United Nations will have little or no part to play in future military action.

I share neither the euphoria of the advocates of a United States- or UN-managed 'new world order' nor the scepticism of those who see the Americans as nothing more than hypocritical imperialists. I do not foresee major difficulties in re-establishing security in the Persian Gulf once the dust has settled, provided always that there is no recrudescence of an Iraqi threat. No other state, including Iran, has territorial designs over the small, weak sheikhdoms. 'Over the horizon' naval and air support will be provided for a time by the United States with help from Britain and others. But already Saudi Arabia, the Gulf States and Iran are drawing together. It will be up to them in the long run to keep the peace. If the West is concerned about the rise of another Iraqi dictator with ambitions to control 50 per cent of the world's oil reserves, one answer would be to move the military centre of gravity of Nato from Western Europe, where there now appears to be no threat, to Turkey, where it could deter future Saddam Husseins from flexing their muscles. One thing is sure. If the Great Powers go back to the bad old ways – supporting dictators for reasons of short-term expediency, saturating the region with arms and leaving the Palestine problem to fester in a heightened atmosphere of frustration and despair – there will be more Saddams, more wars and more terrorism.

'SADDAM IS STRONGER THAN EVER'

Martin Fletcher and James Bone

The Times, April 20, 1991

President Saddam Hussein now has a stronger grip on power in Iraq than ever before, according to the American Central Intelligence Agency. The latest assessment was made as Baghdad admitted in a confidential letter to the United Nations that it still has significant stocks of nerve gas and chemical warheads.

The CIA's sobering view of the Iraqi leader's position appears to undermine President Bush's belief that he would be overthrown in the aftermath of the Gulf war. One American source who has read the CIA report said: 'The feeling is that Saddam is in a very strong position. He seems to have reasserted his authority and control.'

Iraq says it still has 52 Scud misiles, 30 of which have chemical warheads, and large stockpiles of Sarin and Tabun nerve agents and mustard gas. Baghdad supplied a formal list of its arsenal to the UN to meet the ceasefire resolution. This is the first stage in the supervised destruction of all the country's ballistic missiles and unconventional weapons. The letter to Javier Pérez de Cuéllar, the UN secretary-general, from Ahmad Hussein al-Khodair, Iraq's foreign minister, said however, that Iraq had no nuclear or biological weapons capability.

The United States said yesterday that Baghdad's list of its nuclear, chemical and biological weaponry fell 'far short of reality'. The administration said it would review all its information on Iraq's capabilities and help the UN inspection commission, which is expected to be set up next week, draw up a list of places to be visited and investigated.

The Iraqi inventory says that most of the material is stored at the large Muthanna State Establishment, 45 miles west of Baghdad. The report discloses that Iraq still has almost 7,000 120mm 'missile warheads', presumably referring to artillery shells, armed with Sarin nerve agent. A further 2,500 Saqr-30 missile warheads (shells) and 200 DB-2 aerial bombs, also loaded with Sarin, are buried under debris from a levelled storehouse. Iraq also reported that it had 336 binary-system aerial bombs carrying Sarin at the al-Walid airbase and more than 1,000 mustard gas bombs elsewhere in the country.

The Iraqi foreign minister denied in his letter to the UN, however, that Iraq had ever used such weapons and complained that Israel was not subjected to the same standard.

Baghdad also disclosed that it retains the capacity to attack Israel with chemically armed ballistic missiles. The letter said Iraq had one ordinary Scud and 51 al-Husseins, which could be armed with conventional or chemical warheads. It said the missiles are stored at Taji, while the chemical warheads are at Dujayl.

In Washington, the source who had read the CIA briefing emphasised that it appeared to confirm that Saddam was still ruling a regime of fear. 'He has reinforced that fear quotient on which his regime has survived all along. The Iraqis have seen the ruthlessness with which he crushed the rebellion. There have been summary executions of army commanders. In a regime that lives on fear, he has dished it out in large proportions.'

The intelligence assessment would explain why Mr Bush, who confidently predicted Saddam's demise within a year on April 2, suggested on Tuesday that he would be prepared to let the Iraqi leaders live a 'happy life' in a third country, if that were the only way of restoring stability to Iraq. 'That was a plea to take this problem away,' one American official was quoted as saying.

The CIA report also conflicts with the administration's insistence that the Kurdish refugee camps being set up in northern Iraq will be temporary. The agency believes that while Saddam remains in power it is questionable whether the refugees will leave the mountains for the camps, let alone leave the camps for their homes.

Mr Bush has done his best to remove Saddam, urging the Iraqi people and military to 'take matters into their own hands', maintaining tough economic sanctions against Baghdad, and repeatedly emphasising that Iraq would remain a pariah nation until it changed its leadership.

Washington counted on one of Saddam's military commanders moving against him either immediately after the war or following the suppression of the Kurdish and Shia rebellions. These hopes have, however, been dashed.

There are growing doubts that continued sanctions will achieve the Iraqi leader's departure. 'We destroyed his whole country and that didn't work,' the source said. Congressmen, some of whom have received CIA briefings, share the agency's assessment. By refusing to help the Shia and Kurdish rebels 'we have taken away the impetus for an overthrow', Malcolm Wallop, a Republican senator, said. 'I would guess Saddam Hussein will be in power after George Bush leaves power.'

Doonesbury

BY GARRY TRUDEAU

THE VOICES AGAINST SADDAM

John Simpson

Observer, April 28, 1991

The war and the rebellions have changed everything in Baghdad. There's even information nowadays, instead of the old quarter-truths: the prime minister says fewer than 100,000 soldiers and civilians died in the war with the allies. A senior Ba'ath Party figure says four times as many people have been killed in the uprisings against Saddam Hussein as died in the war. Only 29 buildings were destroyed in Baghdad during the allied bombing, says a man at another ministry.

That at least I checked for myself. There's so little damage that it can take you 15 minutes to drive from one bomb-site to another. If the Iraqi Air Force had destroyed Hammersmith Bridge and Iraqi Television came to the film the wreckage, they could expect to be thrown in the river. On the 15th July Bridge in Baghdad, which stuck out of the river like a broken W, the guard placed his hand politely over his heart. 'A British pilot did this,' he told me and my television colleagues in an admiring sort of way, as though beings from another planet had swooped down and manifested their power.

Iraq couldn't, after all, defeat the West, and few of its citizens thought it could. But its leader certainly knows how to treat Kurds and Shias. He can crush them, he can do deals with them, he can divide and rule them. Now the war is over, Saddam Hussein is back in business.

'There are rumours of talks between representatives of the Kurds and the Iraqi government.' I read through my report and called one of the ministry of information officials over: 'Do you think I'll get away with this?' It was strange, after the months of skirmishing with our censors and minders, to find myself asking one for help.

He listened as I read out the words, then looked around. 'Don't say I said so, but Jalal al-Talabani is here, talking to the government.' I found it as hard to believe that Talabani could do a thing like that as that an Iraqi official would tell me about it. 'You won't be able to name him,' he added. Yet when the engineer put our edited cassette

363

into the playback machine and ran through it before feeding it up to the satellite, the censor nodded mildly. He had no objection to my using the name.

So, many changes: minders passing us information, easy-going censors, Talabani kissing Saddam Hussein on both cheeks. A few weeks earlier, when I was thrown out of Baghdad after five months of reporting, none of these things was conceivable.

But Saddam needs international help for reconstruction, so he has to present himself to the world in a better way. His people know why he's doing it, but they see him differently now. The old terror of speaking frankly seems to have evaporated. Even government officials criticise him now. 'General Schwarzkopf didn't go far enough. He should have come to Baghdad and finished the job,' said one. Four others who were standing round nodded.

In the towns and cities of the south, Shia officials would tip us off about who was responsible for the terrible damage we encountered. 'Tell your country what Saddam has done to us,' one said. But if the old habit of silence is changing, so are the old loyalties. A new situation has brought new accommodations. The Kurdish grouping, with Talabani as its negotiator, made its preliminary contacts with Saddam's officials even before joining a score of other opposition groups for talks in Beirut last month. Few of the others thought the Kurds would do a separate deal with Saddam. Western opinion was caught on the hop as well.

On television, Talabani kissed the man who had once sent a car bomb to blow him up, who had ordered the use of chemical weapons against the Kurdish town of Halabje in 1988, and who had systematically destroyed the places which welcomed Iranian troops in the closing months of the Iran-Iraq war. Suddenly, the Kurds stopped talking about how the allies had betrayed them. 'Sometimes it's necessary to do deals,' said a Kurdish official in London, with an air of mild discomfort.

Yet the Kurdish deal is not necessarily cynical. Talabani's aim appears to be to safeguard the future of Kurdistan by reinforcing the process of democratisation which Saddam Hussein has himself introduced. The agreement commits Saddam to a policy of greater press freedom and a greater opening-up of the political system generally.

But wolves, of course, are rarely good at keeping vows of vegetarianism. At a dinner party recently, a senior member of the Iraqi

Ba'athist Party said he and his colleagues had been assured privately that the move towards democracy was merely a ploy, soon to be forgotten. No great surprise in that. The surprise is that a leading Ba'athist should talk about such things at a dinner party with Westerners present, and that he should be worried that the process of greater democracy might come to nothing.

Back in London a smiling, tolerant, world-weary figure in the Iraqi opposition listened to my account of the changes in Baghdad and shook his head. One of his acquaintances had lost 22 members of his family to Saddam's men. He himself has only recently started using his real name, and he always peers under his car in the morning.

It isn't easy to persuade such people that the debate which is under way in Baghdad is genuine. Indeed, if the Ba'athist at the dinner-table is right, the intention is that it shouldn't be. But the habit of speaking freely is easy to acquire, and hard to break.

Last week the party newspaper, *Ath Thawra*, carried two articles, next to each other, on the question of greater democracy. One was by Abdul Jabar Muhsin, Saddam Hussein's press secretary. His point was that Iraq could be governed only from strength; that if the leader had to worry about public opinion or depend upon the support of other politicians, then the delicate racial and religious balance of the country would be lost. 'For a country like ours, what we need is not democracy, but a powerful, able, faithful leader behind whom we can rally. We have such a leader,' he announced, and began to extol the merits of Saddam; at which point the article ceased to be so interesting.

Next to it was one by a senior editorial figure on the newspaper. He argued the need for a greater opening-up of the system. 'We should listen to the views of others, because no one now can impose his own view. People may agree with that view under pressure, but deep in their hearts they will disagree.' It wasn't difficult to work out whose view he was talking about.

The whole debate may indeed be a simple fraud, as the Iraqi opposition assumes. Yet even if that is Saddam Hussein's intention, there are plenty of people inside Iraq who feel it is worth taking the offer of greater freedom at face value.

It is a political truism that an autocracy is most vulnerable when it begins to liberalise; which makes it all the stranger that autocrats try it so often. No doubt Saddam Hussein, like others before him, regards the process of democracy as a tap which can be turned on and off at will. The Shah of Iran, nagged at by President Jimmy Carter, thought something of the kind in 1978. Yet once people see that speaking their mind doesn't instantly lead to their own and their family's death, it requires more and more force to shut them up again. During 1978 in Iran, talking led to demonstrations, demonstrations led to shooting, and the demonstrations got bigger and angrier until the Shah had to leave. In China in 1989, Deng Xiaoping didn't leave; instead, he summoned up all his energies and cleared Tiananmen Square with rifle fire. But the cost was immense, and not every autocrat can count on total loyalty from his troops.

When I talked to the crew of a Chieftain tank parked outside the shrine of Al Abbas in the Shia holy city of Kerbala last week, it was plain that Saddam had *their* total loyalty, at least. Like him, they were Sunni Muslims. They had even stuck pictures of him inside the tank. Finding them there was like finding the Ulster Defence Regiment outside the Pro-Cathedral in Dublin. They didn't like Shias much: one said they were dirty animals.

A little later, in the deserted centre of Najaf, smashed beyond recognition around the great Shia shrine, I faintly heard the call to prayer. The Shia call includes mention of the doctrine which separates the Shia from Sunni Islam: 'There is no God but God, and Muhammad is His Prophet – and Ali His Deputy.' The muezzins can no longer proclaim the Shias' belief in the religious significance of Ali. There are few enough to do so anyway. Thousands of Shia clerics have simply been rounded up in Najaf and Kerbala and disappeared. Normally the streets would be full of them. Not now.

Sixty per cent of Iraq's population are Shia. Their history and tradition show them to be peaceable people, who may resent their relative lack of political power compared with the Sunnis, but have rarely done anything about it.

Saddam Hussein has usually been careful to balance the various religious groupings of the country with some precision. But the uprising in southern Iraq seems to have impaired his sense of even-handedness.

It wasn't a very successful uprising. It began well enough; officials in several towns and cities agree that anything up to half their populations came out and joined the rebels. There was much talk of creating an Islamic republic along Iranian lines.

But sectarianism was the rebellion's downfall. Many of the soldiers streaming back from Kuwait were Shia, and defeated soldiers are usually good revolutionary material. Yet they instinctively looked

366

to their officers for a lead, and Saddam Hussein had ensured that most of his officer corps were Sunni. The officers saw little advantage in joining a Shia fundamentalist uprising. They drifted off, and the soldiers drifted with them. The rebellion turned into a settling of scores with officials of the regime, and there was a good deal of looting. Law-abiding people withdrew their support fast; many welcomed the arrival of Saddam's forces.

The army, however, acted like conquerors. They pursued the rebels to the holy shrines of Shi'ism, and stormed their last positions there. Being Sunni, they cared little for the buildings or the saints to whose memory the shrines were dedicated.

Thousands were killed in each of the cities they retook. Tens, perhaps hundreds, of thousands, escaped to the marshes or the borders with Kuwait, Saudi Arabia and Iran. Their condition is probably every bit as bad as that of the Kurds in the mountains of the north; but no one sees it on television, so no one feels disturbed by it. Western newspapers have not been printing editorials condemning the allies for abandoning the Shia, and governments see no advantage in helping people whom the Western mind usually associates with fundamentalism and terror.

The other night in Basra, I slipped out of the hotel while our minders were preoccupied and went for a walk. There was no electricity, and in the clammy heat there was a smell of rotting garbage. Crickets sang. We had heard reports that at night-time the resistance still operated in the city, and I wanted to see if it were true.

I skirted round a roadblock: several men in civilian clothes were standing in the middle of the street. They were young men in their early twenties, mostly wearing suits: Saddam's security men. If they were around, there would be no rebels on the streets tonight. A car with four men in it spotted me as I crossed the road, and followed me at walking pace until I cut across some waste ground and gave them the slip.

Away from the buildings there was light from a low moon, and I could see that the ground was littered with bits of metal. A couple of armoured personnel carriers had been attacked and destroyed there during the uprising. There was even a turret with a heavy gun lying on the ground. I walked along the front of the governor's palace. This had been sacked and burned, and the smoke had blackened the white paint over every window. There were soldiers here, with light machine guns set up on tripods. They watched me with curiosity, but didn't stop me.

They had set up a large new portrait of Saddam Hussein on the other side of the road, the icon of the imperial power. The previous picture must have been destroyed by the rebels; there were few undamaged portraits of Saddam in the whole of southern Iraq.

In the darkness I could just make out that he was smiling and wearing a panama hat, dark glasses and a short-sleeved shirt, as though running Iraq was a kind of holiday. At present, he's stronger than he was. But the people who destroyed his earlier portrait and burned the residence of his governor are still around. He has offended the religious sentiments of the greater part of the Iraqi population, while at the same time undertaking to give everybody greater freedom of expression.

He has survived with skill. There hasn't, as I once expected, been a military coup against him, and the Kurds and Shias have failed to overthrow him. I looked up at the smile and the dark glasses and thought, if he really is so strong, why aren't people more afraid of him now?

SWEET JOY AS KURDS FIND A SAFE HAVEN

John Sweeney

Observer, April 28, 1991

The first 250 Kurdish refugees to return to Iraq under the 'safe havens' plan came down from the mountains in military helicopters yesterday. As soon as they got out of the choppers, they seized and smelt blades of grass. Sweet joy, these rolling wheatfields converted to a refugee camp, after nearly a month on a barren mountainside.

Almost immediately, however, tragedy whiplashed to farce as a Special Forces sergeant, Gilbert Shatto, ordered: 'No shitting in the grass.' 'We say no shitting in the grass,' Corporal Conrad Matt, his translator, pointed out, 'but we haven't built the latrines yet.'

A few miles away, Lieutenant-Colonel Jonathan Thomson, commanding officer of 4/5 Commando, Royal Marines, drove a bearded ruffian dressed in Royal Marine camouflage uniform around the town of Zakho in an attempt to persuade *peshmergas* that Saddam Hussein's men were finally gone. Only when the *peshmergas* are convinced and endorse 'Operation Haven' will the hundreds of thousands of civilians on the mountains come down to the plains. The problem then will be that many fled from homes south of the 36th parallel, still Saddamland.

And the cause of that problem is still very much alive – as alive as Arin, aged three, and Chalang, aged one, are dead. For them, the American airlift came too late: Chalang died last Thursday; his sister gave up fighting dehydration and amoebic dysentery yesterday. Their mother, sister and aunts wailed for them, their keening made the more eerie by the blue plastic tent that cast a blue pallor on their faces.

No comfort for them that the refugees are dying less quickly now that Western aid and Uncle Sam's helicopters are saving lives; nor that Saddam's secret police have finally been driven from Zakho and the Kurds can start drifting down from the mountains, their descent accelerated by the Turks, whose behaviour towards the oppressed people makes you homesick for Iran.

Only a few days ago, the Iraqis were still standing on the bridge over a tributary of the Tigris, the river as muddy as British Rail tea, watching.

Most wore bottle-green uniforms, special forces masquerading as village bobbies, brandishing their Kalashnikovs, watching. Not a few were out of uniform. The Mukhabarat – Saddam's secret police – followed us around with their eyes.

There is watching and watching, of course. Some watching is just good-natured nosiness enjoying the spectacle of the world going by. This watching was not like that, but pregnant with menace, a cosh raised before it smashes into your face.

Down a side street in this dusty town, the sky crisscrossed by useless phone cables, a black-clad priest who serves a small minority of Christians scuttled from his church. He saw us and offered 'hallo'. But his eyes were elsewhere, watching two men in jeans and T-shirts watching him. The priest vanished like a spider down a hole. One of the secret policemen smiled at us, the smile of an enemy.

But the Iraqis were being watched themselves. Overhead, American A-10 Warthogs grunted in the sky; on the main road a US 'Humvee' cruised past the police station, the Marines wearing mirror shades. Creepy? Zakho was Creepsville City.

To the east of town, the US Army and Marines had erected 'Tent City', hundreds of Sears Roebuck blue and white tents – still empty then.

In the centre of Zakho, a water filtration station erected by the Americans was deluged by customers on its opening day. On the second day, no one came. The Mukhabarat had passed the word, enforcing a complete boycott.

Outside 'Tent City' the *peshmergas* enjoyed the protection of Uncle Sam. One of their number, snuggling into a bandoleer of bullets, spelt out the problem: 'Our problem is not tents. It is security. People won't come down from the mountain until the police get out. There are too many secret police.'

US Sergeant Frank Jordan had a handle on Zakho too. 'I come from Bangor, Maine, where Stephen King lives. This is like one of his novels. It's like *It*.'

In a tea shop in Zakho, a retired schoolteacher who looked like Harold's dad in *Steptoe and Son* trotted through his old lessons. He talked about Shakespeare and Koo Stark. The mood changed when three truckloads of Iraqis, their rifles pricking the sky like hedgehog quills, pulled out of town. Dangerous topics – the absence of a Saddam poster in his room – could be raised.

Saddam's plainclothes men were still throwing their weight around last Thursday. But then the British and Americans started showing muscle too.

Lieutenant-Colonel Thomson had a brief chat with the skeleton staff of Iraqi policemen manning their station. Now the Iraqi cops were outnumbered, watching us still, but no longer with the eyes of a school bully.

As dusk fell, you could almost hear the power drain from the Iraqis.

Two hours later, at 9.00pm, the Kurds struck, lobbing a hand-grenade into the porch of the police station. They were squealing like piglets, two Iraqi policemen spouting blood on the floor of the impromptu hospital set up in Zakho by French army medics.

One man had been wounded by grenade fragments in the legs, and he was letting the world know about it. The sight of any human being in pain is always distressing, made more so by the lack of electricity or any light in the hospital. Yet, having seen enough dying Kurdish babies in the mountains of Iran, terrified of killers very like this man, it was hard not to think that some form of royal justice had been carried out. The ugliness of this thought kept me awake all night.

Outside the French hospital, the Royal Marines were standing guard, now protecting Iraqi police against Kurdish vengeance. The lads from Sheffield, Barnsley and Rutland were given tea by a Kurdish family. TV footage of Catholics welcoming British troops in Northern Ireland flickered in the mind, a fearful warning of what might happen should the heavily armed *peshmerga* chafe against American and allied rule. In the morning, the Royal Marines patrolled with flowers in their flak jackets – presents from a grateful population.

The police station, shortly after dawn, was an eerie place. Two trails of blood showed where the Iraqis had fled. One going upstairs, another into the cell area, blood on the wall depicting a cut to the hand.

But none of this bloody mess obscures the big truth, that the man in Baghdad is the Villain. His framed picture hung in the commander's office, grinning his ape-like grin.

I took the picture down and let it fall. In the quiet of the early morning it made a satisfying smash.

A NOTE ON THE AUTHOR

Brian MacArthur is an assistant editor of the *Sunday Times* and writes the Paper Round column. He was the founding editor of *Today* and the *Times Higher Education Supplement* and worked for many years on the *The Times*, where he was executive editor.